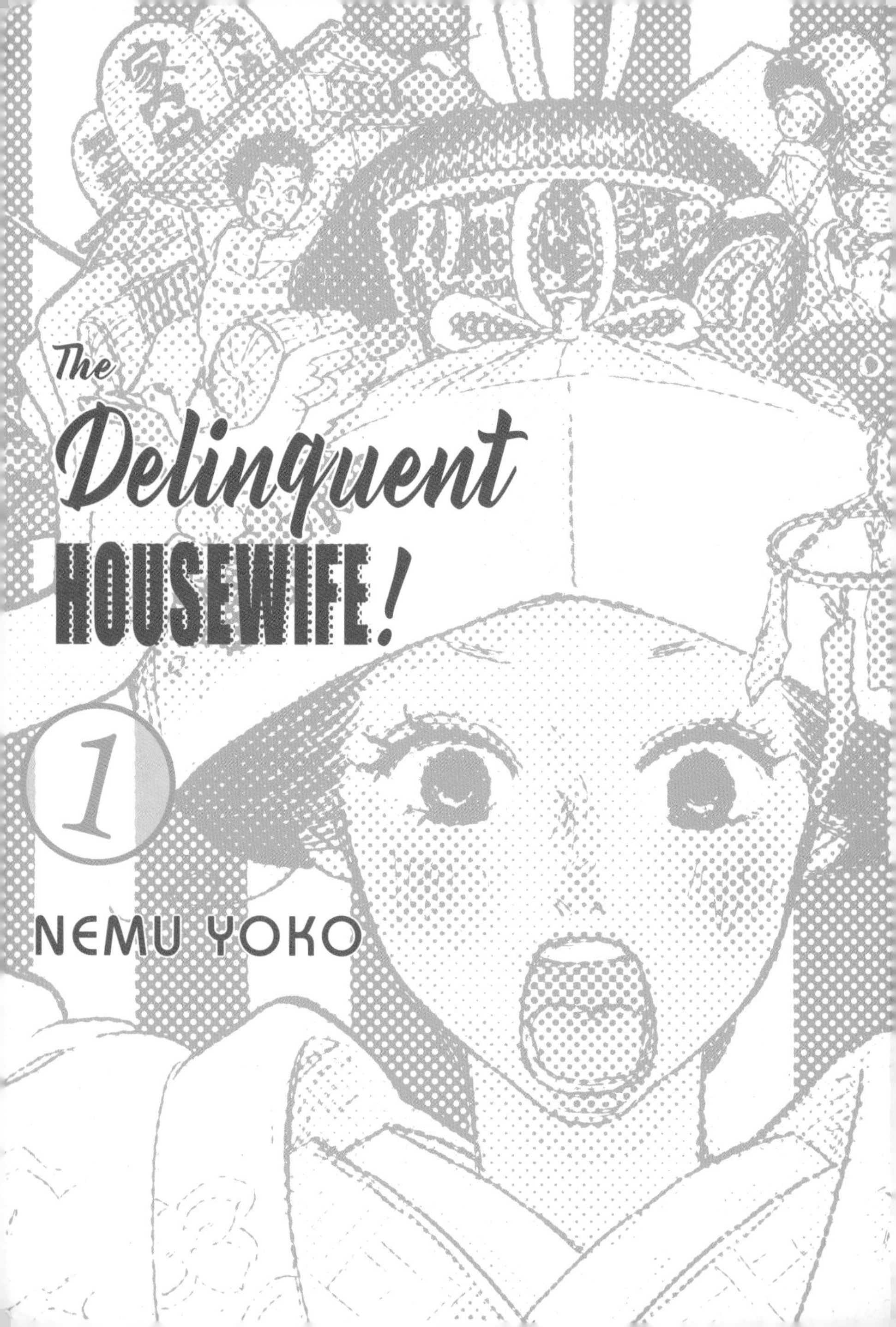
The Delinquent HOUSEWIFE!
1
NEMU YOKO

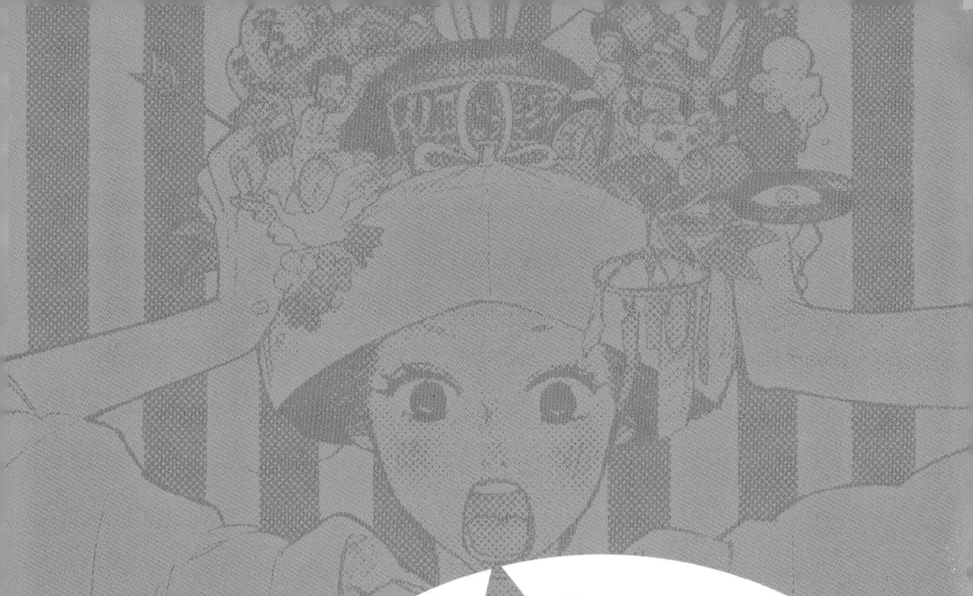

CONTENTS

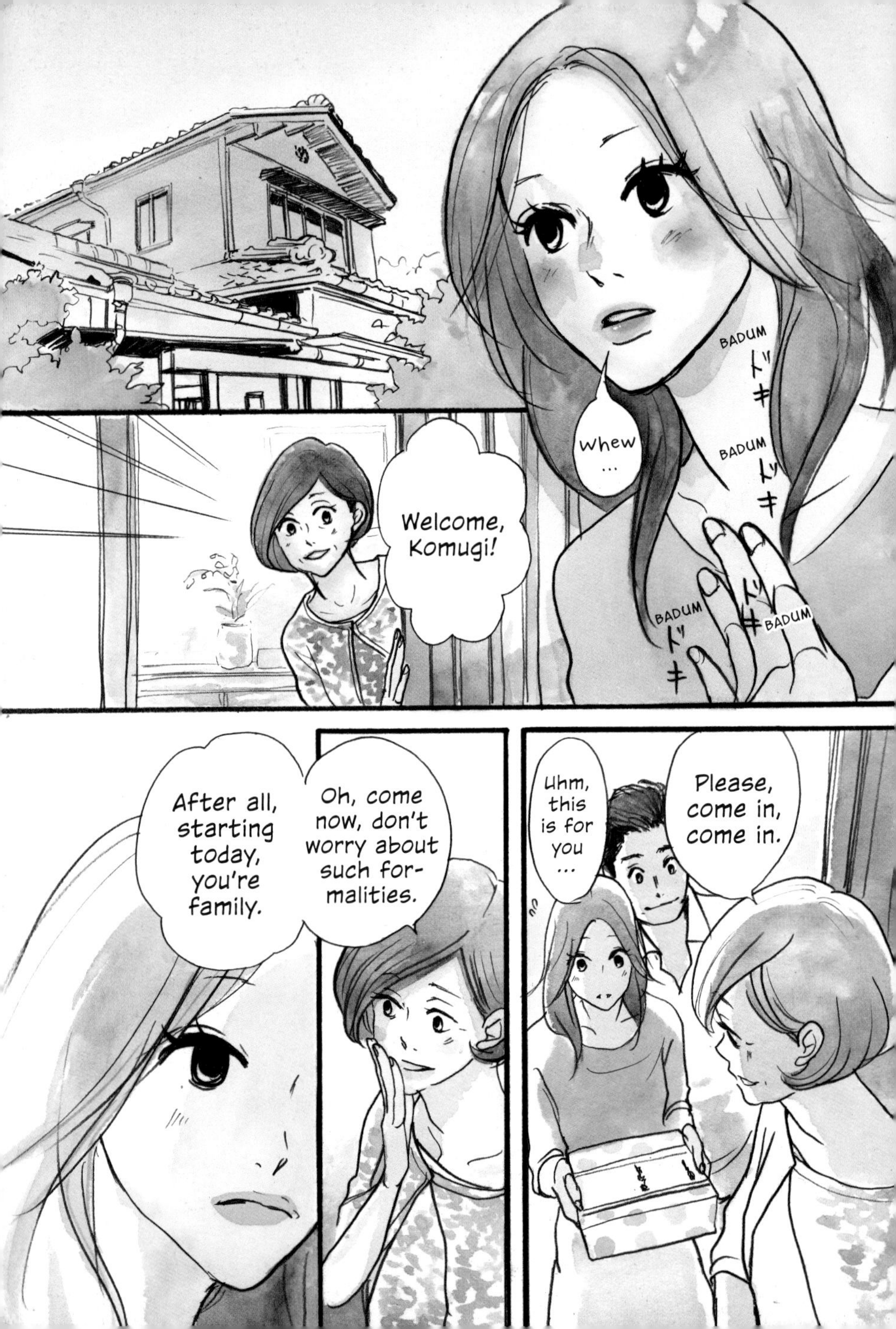
BADUM ドキ
Whew …
BADUM ドキ
BADUM ドキ
BADUM ドキ
Welcome, Komugi!
Please, come in, come in.
Uhm, this is for you …
Oh, come now, don't worry about such formalities.
After all, starting today, you're family.

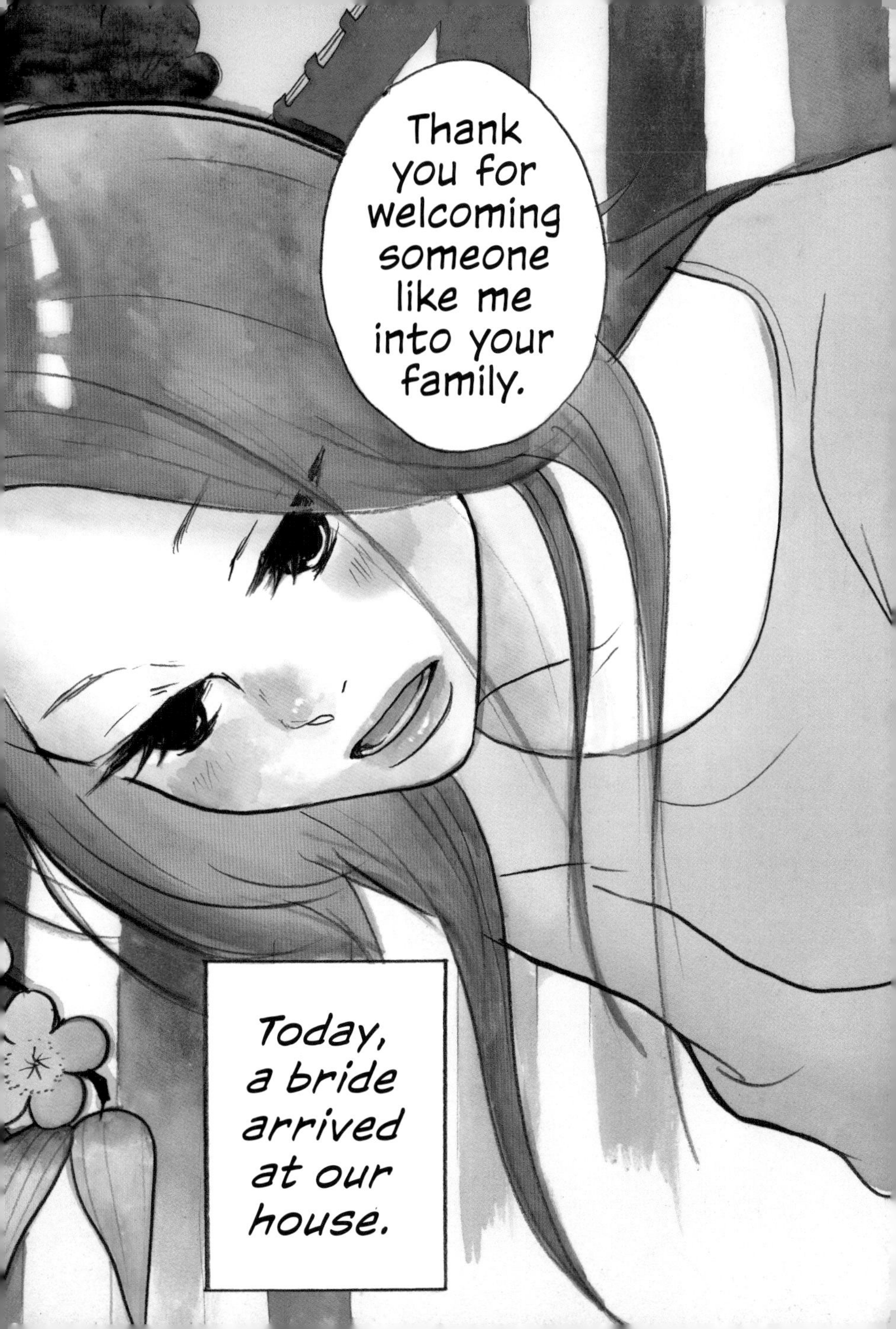
Thank you for welcoming someone like me into your family.
Today, a bride arrived at our house.

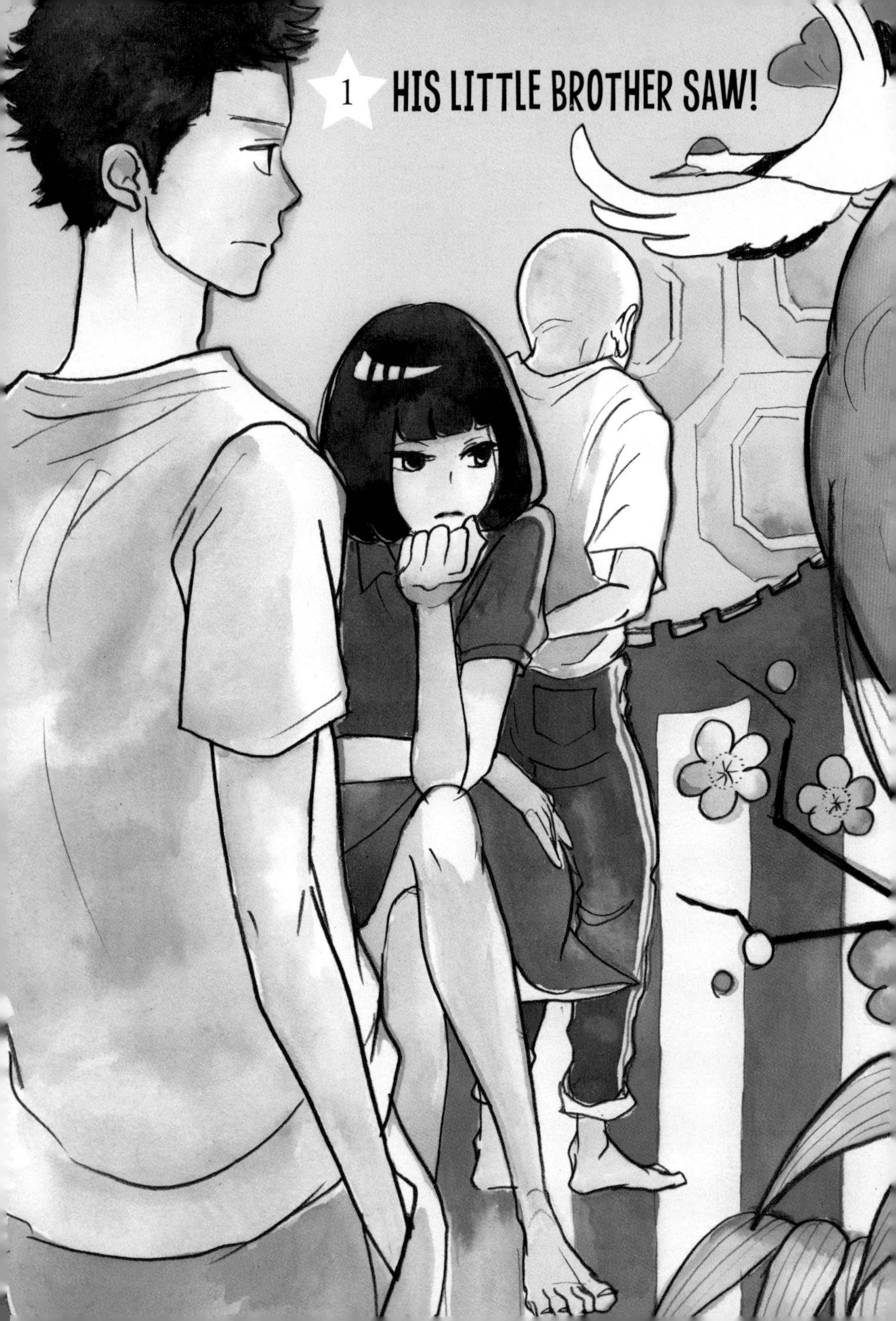
1
HIS LITTLE BROTHER SAW!

The Delinquent HOUSEWIFE!

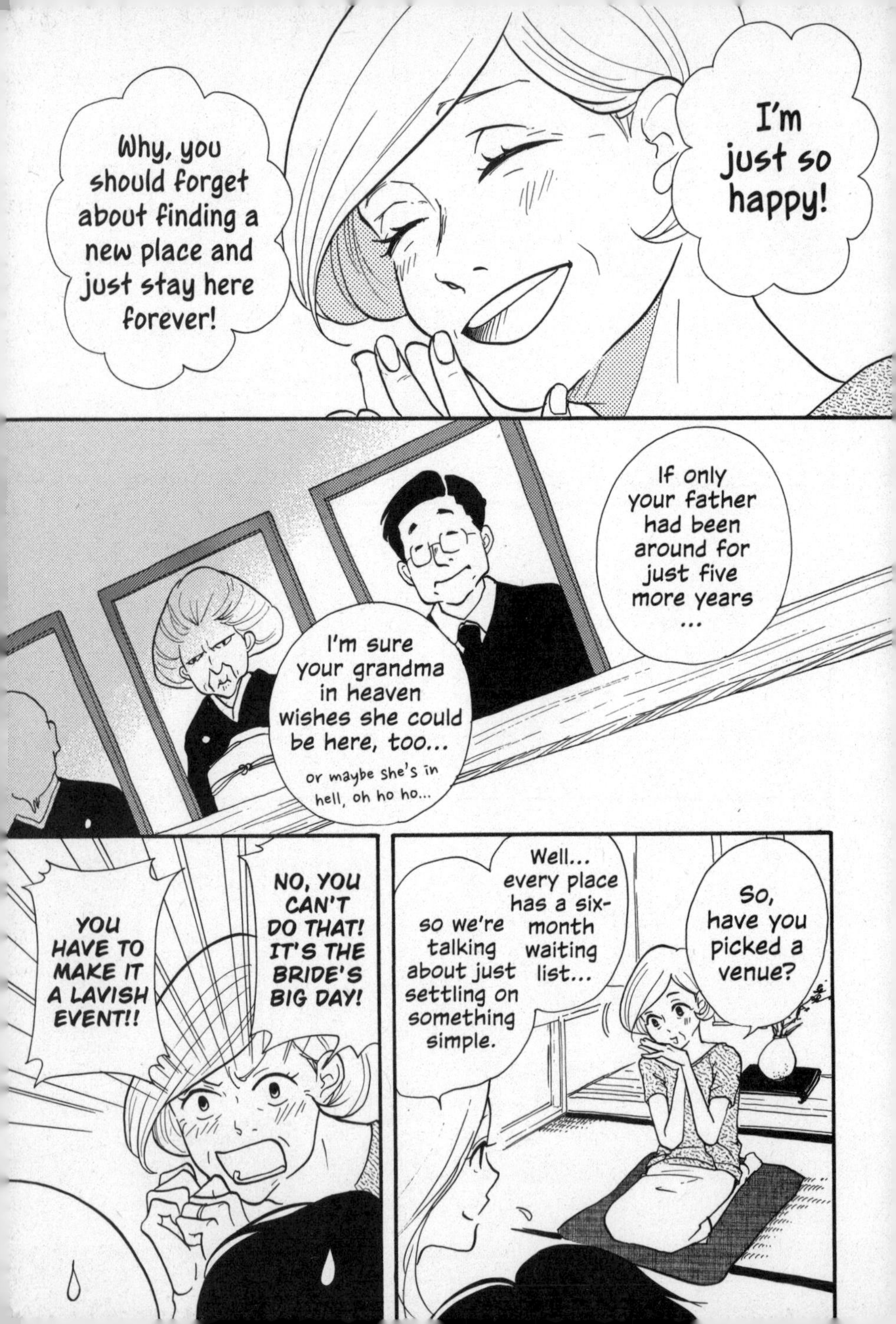
I'm just so happy!
Why, you should forget about finding a new place and just stay here forever!
If only your father had been around for just five more years ...
I'm sure your grandma in heaven wishes she could be here, too...
or maybe she's in hell, oh ho ho...
So, have you picked a venue?
Well... every place has a six-month waiting list...
so we're talking about just settling on something simple.
NO, YOU CAN'T DO THAT! IT'S THE BRIDE'S BIG DAY!
YOU HAVE TO MAKE IT A LAVISH EVENT!!

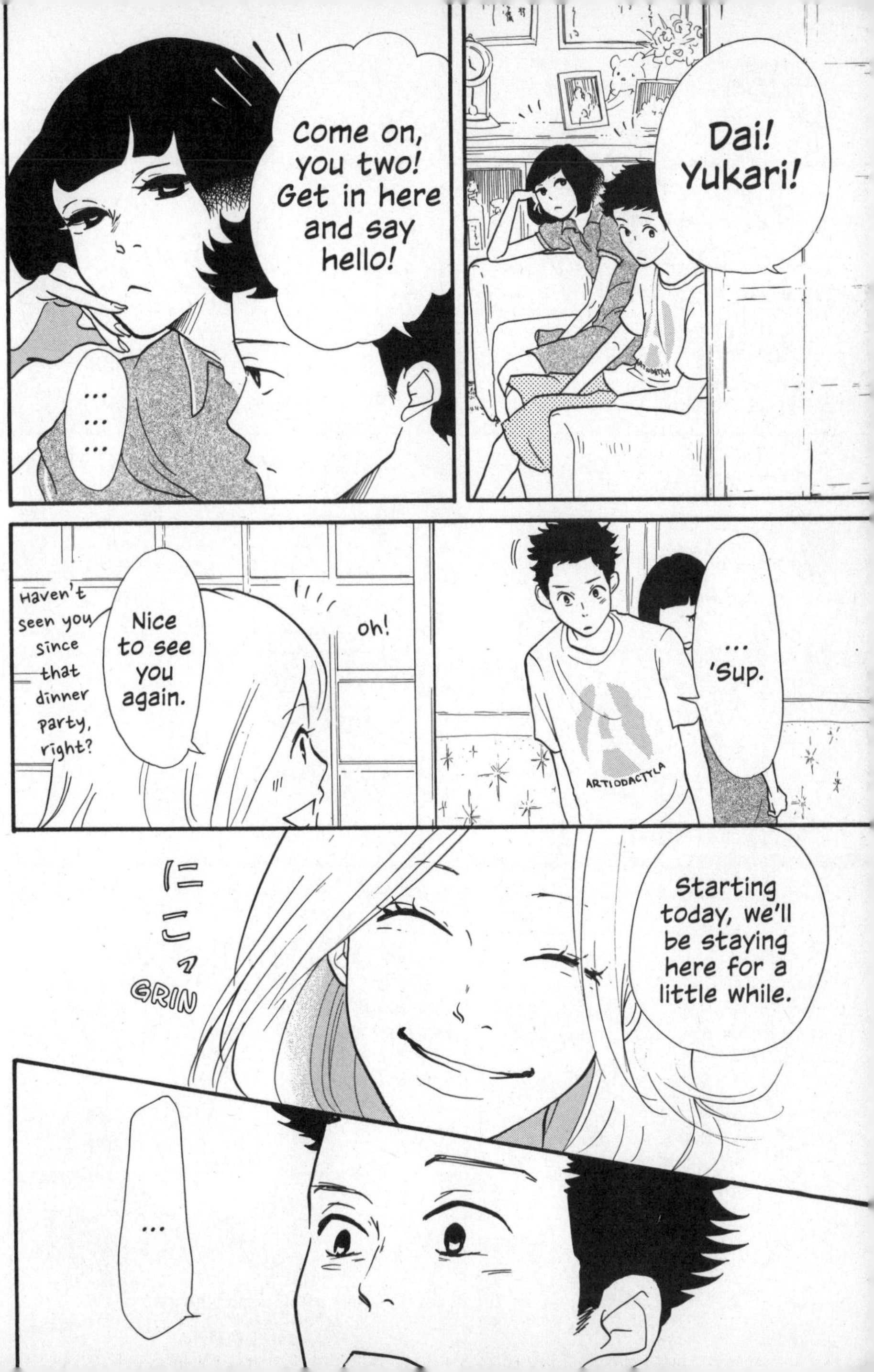
Dai! Yukari!
Come on, you two! Get in here and say hello!
... ...
... 'Sup.
oh!
Nice to see you again.
Haven't seen you since that dinner party, right?
Starting today, we'll be staying here for a little while.
にこっ
GRIN
...

High School

Battle of the Books 2023-2024

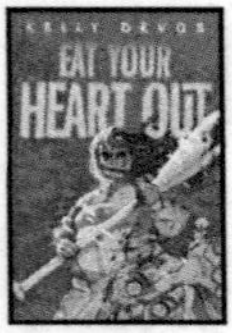
KELLY DEVOS
EAT YOUR HEART OUT

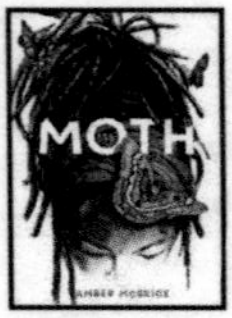
MOTH
AMBER MCBRIDE

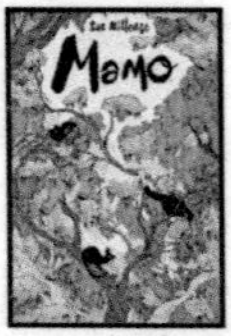
Memo

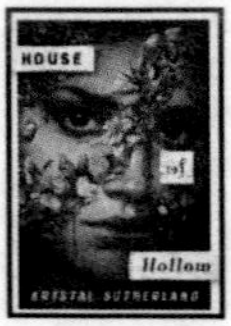
HOUSE
of
Hollow
KRYSTAL SUTHERLAND

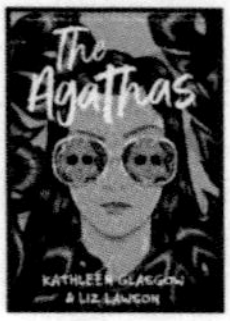
The Agathas
KATHLEEN GLASGOW
& LIZ LAWSON

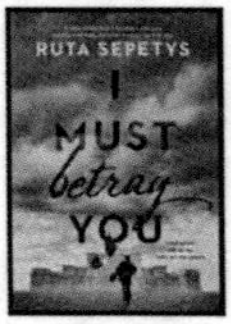
RUTA SEPETYS
I MUST betray YOU

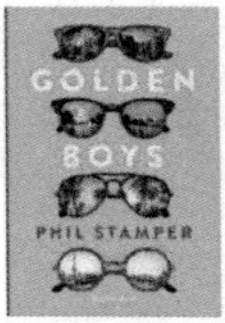
GOLDEN BOYS
PHIL STAMPER

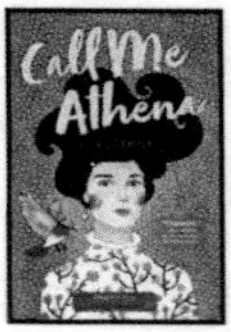
Call Me Athena

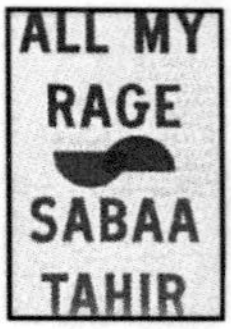
ALL MY RAGE
SABAA TAHIR

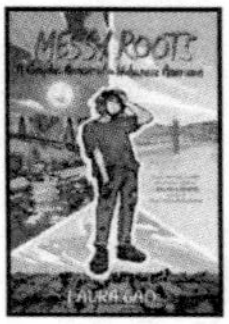
MESSY ROOTS
LAURA GAO

How you play

1. Watch Book Buzz videos and work with your school library media specialist and friends to learn about the 10 books.
2. Read one or more of the books.
3. Select your favorite book.
4. Create a final project—a work of expressive art based on your personal interpretation or reflection of the book.
5. Submit your project by Wednesday, January 31 to be entered into the battles for a chance to win.

Upcoming events

Story Board Collages
Tuesday, October 24 • 6-7 PM • Owings Mills

DIY Zine
Saturday, November 4 • 2-3 PM • North Point

Writing Mania
Monday, November 6 • 6-7 PM • Owings Mills

Zine Machine
Monday, December 18 • 6-7 PM • Owings Mills

Create Your Own Graphic Novel
Wednesday, January 10 • 6:30-8 PM • Cockeysville

Mixed Media Edition
Monday, January 15 • 4:30-5:30 PM • Towson

Interpreting the Narrative
Thursday, January 18 • 6-7 PM • Parkville-Carney

Make Your Own Book Trailer
Saturday, January 27 • 2-3 PM • Owings Mills

Author Visits

Kathleen Glasgow and Liz Lawson
The Agathas
Thursday, October 26 • 11:30 a.m.–12:30 PM • Zoom link provided

Laura Gao
Messy Roots: Graphic Memoir of a Wuhanese American
Thursday, December 14 • 11:30–12:30 PM • Zoom link provided

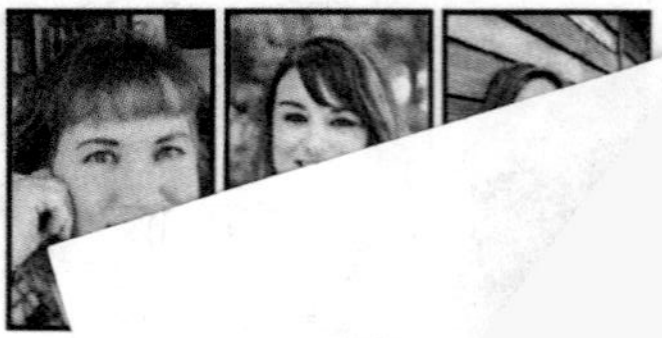

BALTIMORE COUNTY PUBLIC LIBRARY

bcpl.info

More infol

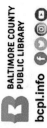

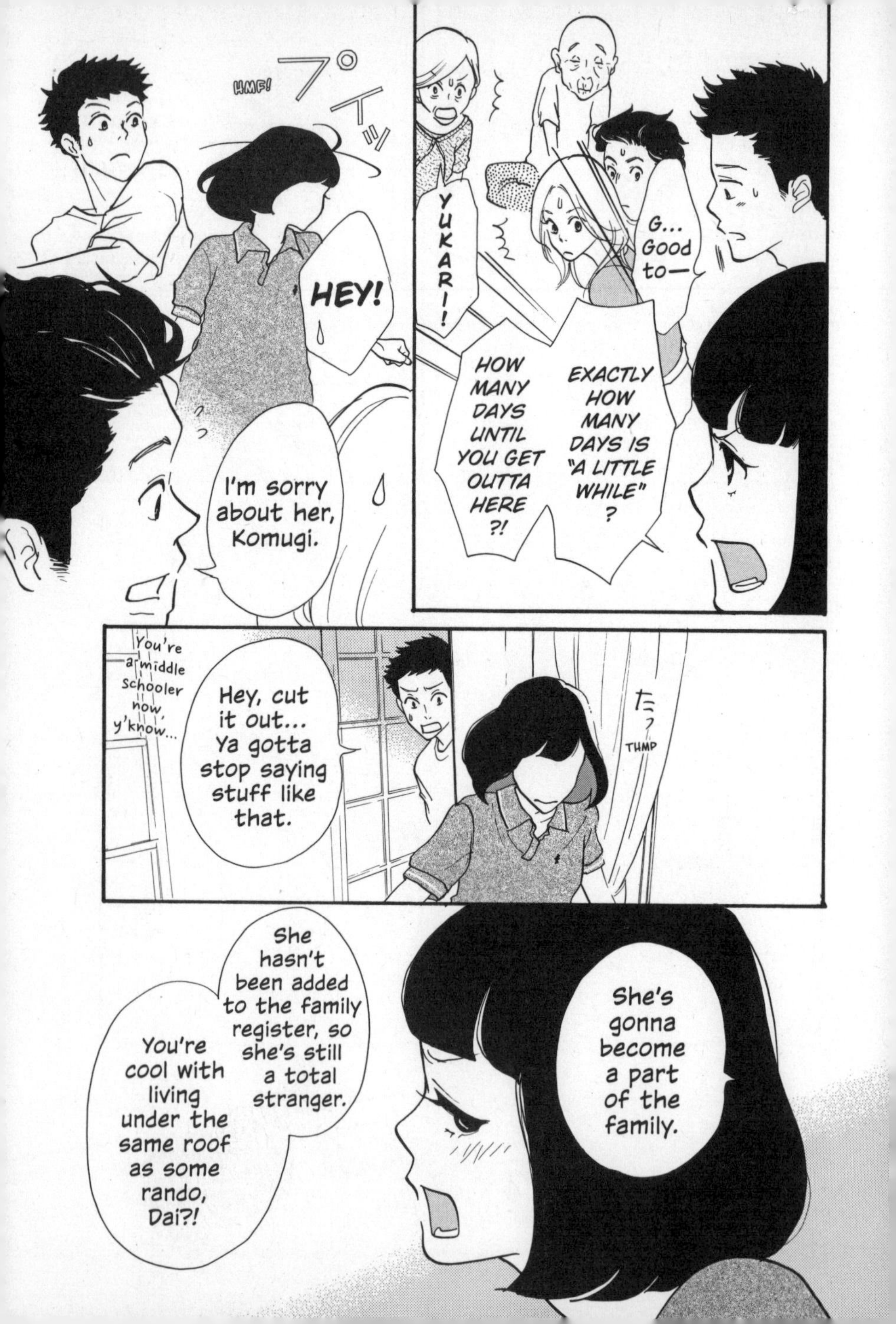

G... Good to—
EXACTLY HOW MANY DAYS IS "A LITTLE WHILE"?
HOW MANY DAYS UNTIL YOU GET OUTTA HERE?!
YUKARI!
HMF!
HEY!
I'm sorry about her, Komugi.
THMP
Hey, cut it out... Ya gotta stop saying stuff like that.
You're a middle schooler now, y'know...
She's gonna become a part of the family.
She hasn't been added to the family register, so she's still a total stranger.
You're cool with living under the same roof as some rando, Dai?!

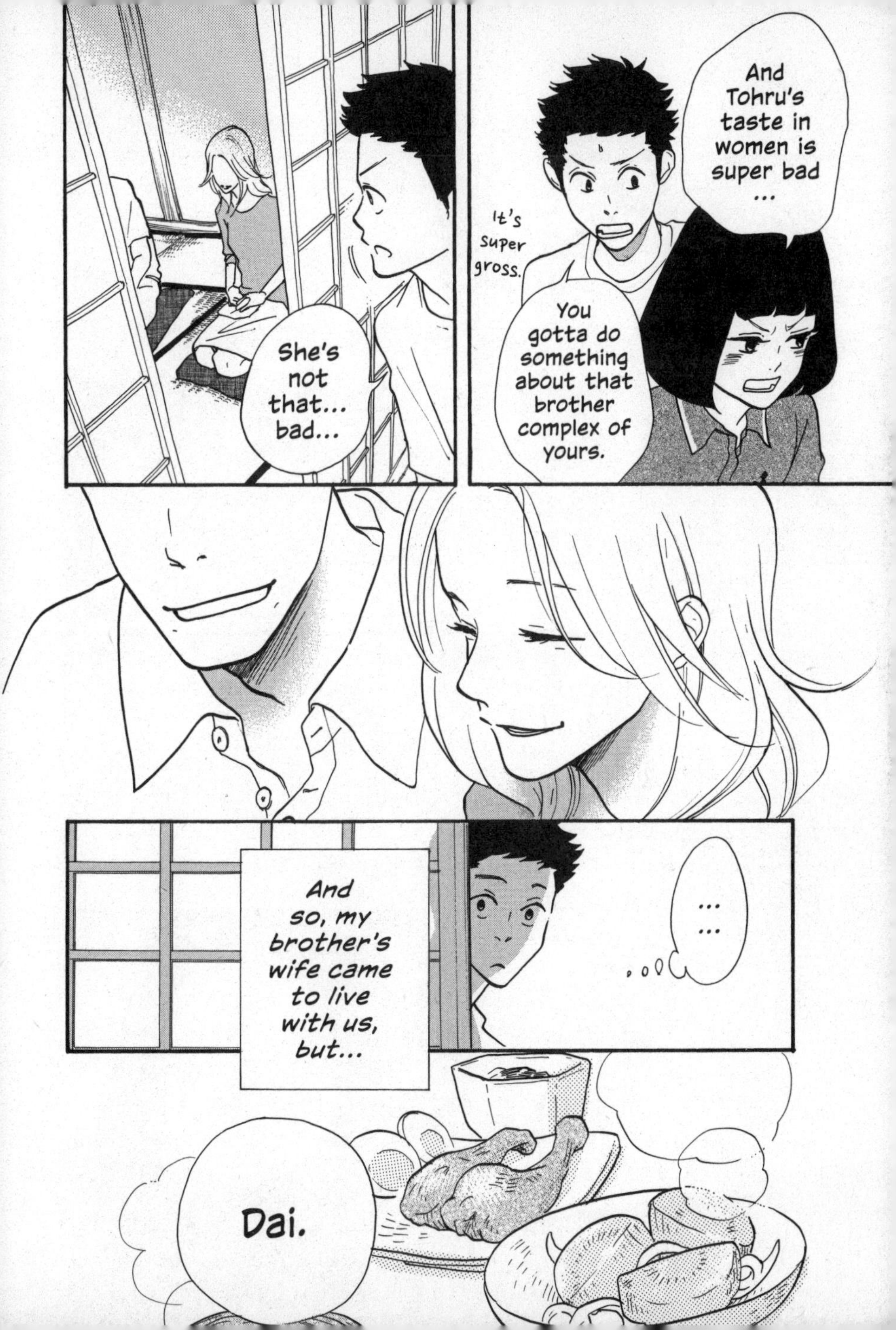
And Tohru's taste in women is super bad ...
It's super gross.
You gotta do something about that brother complex of yours.
She's not that... bad...
......
And so, my brother's wife came to live with us, but...
Dai.

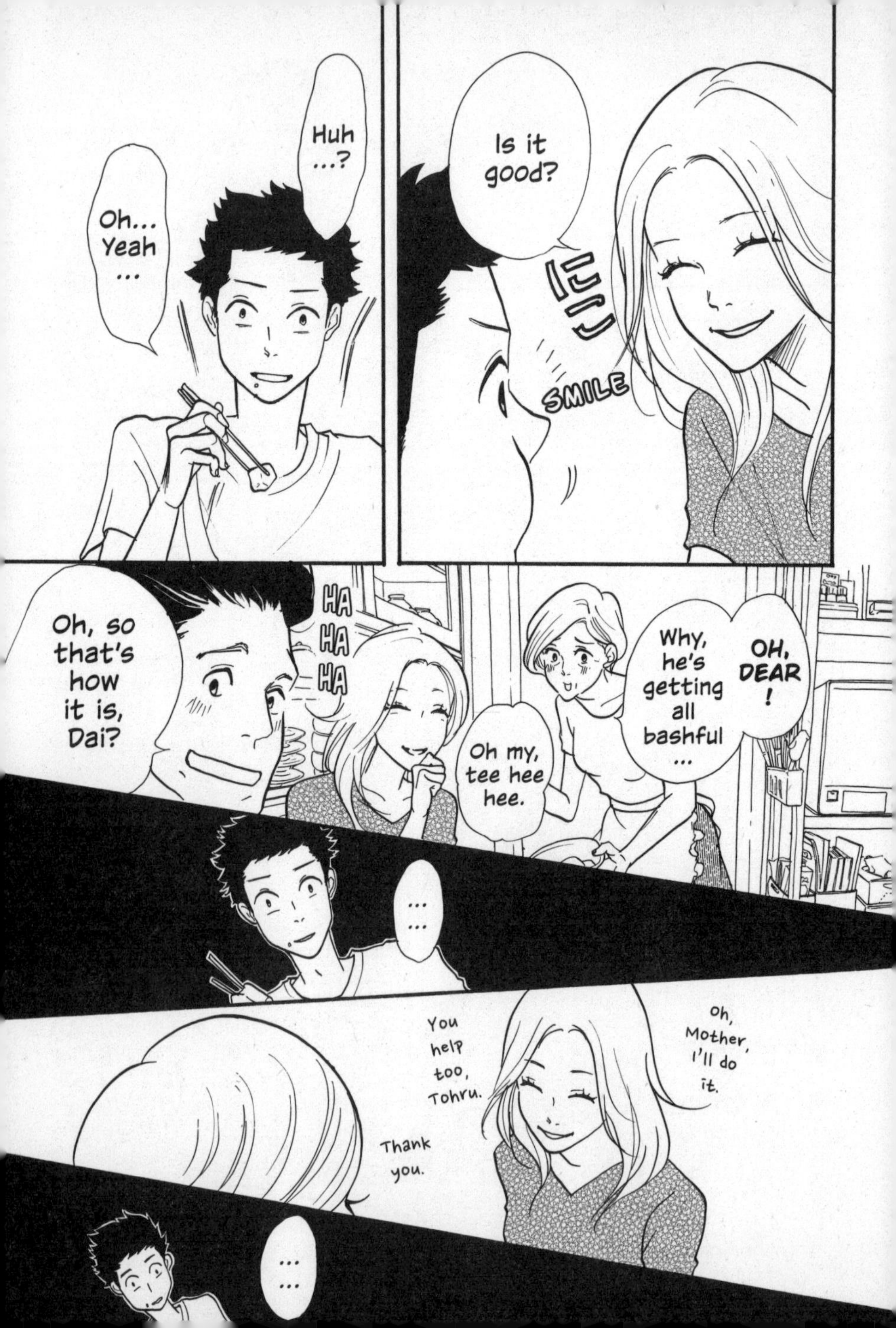
Is it good?
にこ
SMILE
Huh ...?
Oh... Yeah ...
OH, DEAR!
Why, he's getting all bashful ...
Oh my, tee hee hee.
HA HA HA
Oh, so that's how it is, Dai?
....
Oh, Mother, I'll do it.
You help too, Tohru.
Thank you.
....

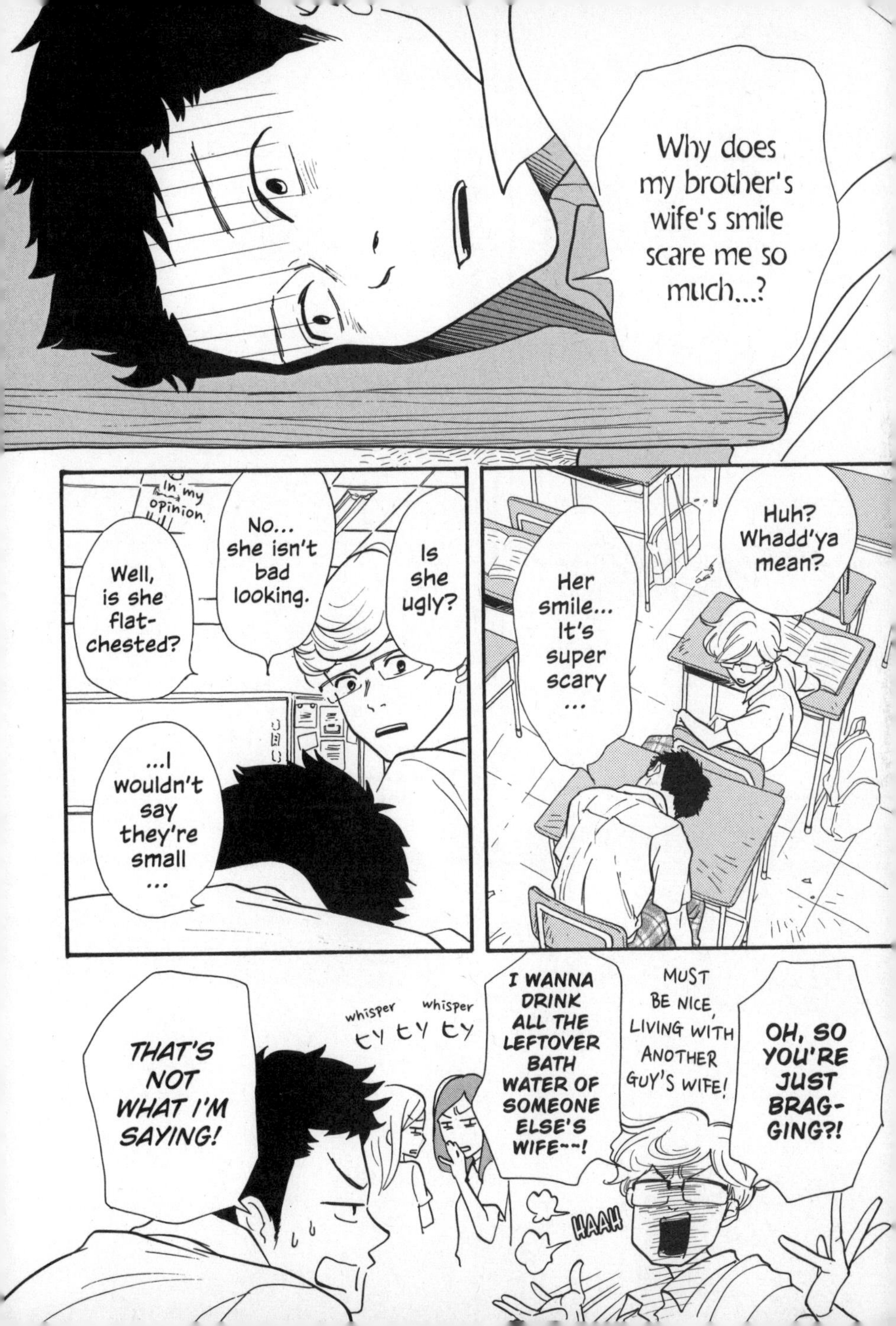
Why does my brother's wife's smile scare me so much...?
Huh? Whadd'ya mean?
Her smile... It's super scary ...
Is she ugly?
No... she isn't bad looking.
In my opinion.
Well, is she flat-chested?
...I wouldn't say they're small ...
OH, SO YOU'RE JUST BRAG-GING?!
MUST BE NICE, LIVING WITH ANOTHER GUY'S WIFE!
I WANNA DRINK ALL THE LEFTOVER BATH WATER OF SOMEONE ELSE'S WIFE~~!
whisper whisper
ヒソ ヒソ ヒソ
HAAH
THAT'S NOT WHAT I'M SAYING!

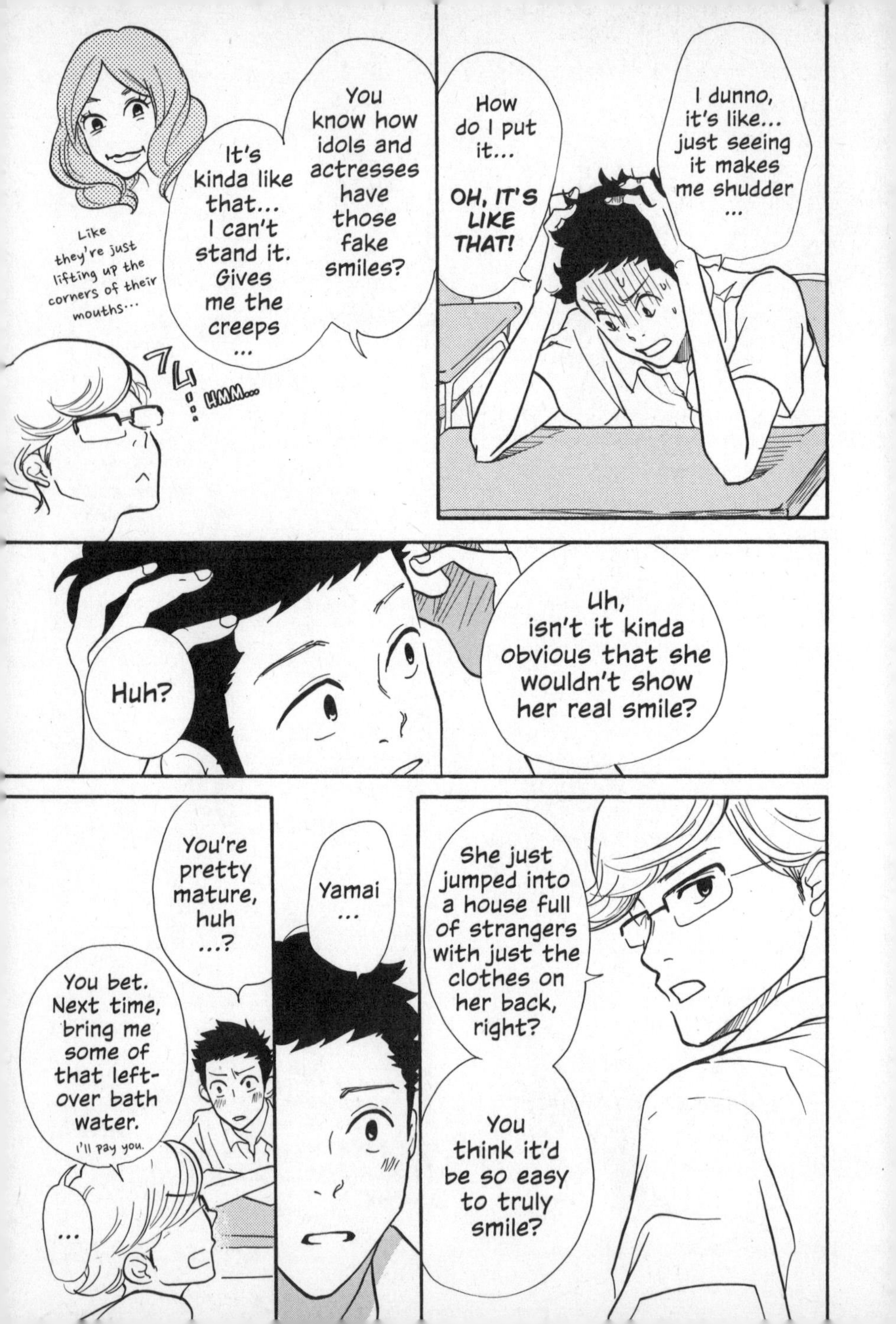
I dunno, it's like... just seeing it makes me shudder ...
How do I put it... OH, IT'S LIKE THAT!
You know how idols and actresses have those fake smiles?
It's kinda like that... I can't stand it. Gives me the creeps ...
Like they're just lifting up the corners of their mouths...
フム HMM...
Uh, isn't it kinda obvious that she wouldn't show her real smile?
Huh?
She just jumped into a house full of strangers with just the clothes on her back, right?
You think it'd be so easy to truly smile?
Yamai ...
You're pretty mature, huh ...?
You bet. Next time, bring me some of that left-over bath water.
I'll pay you.
...

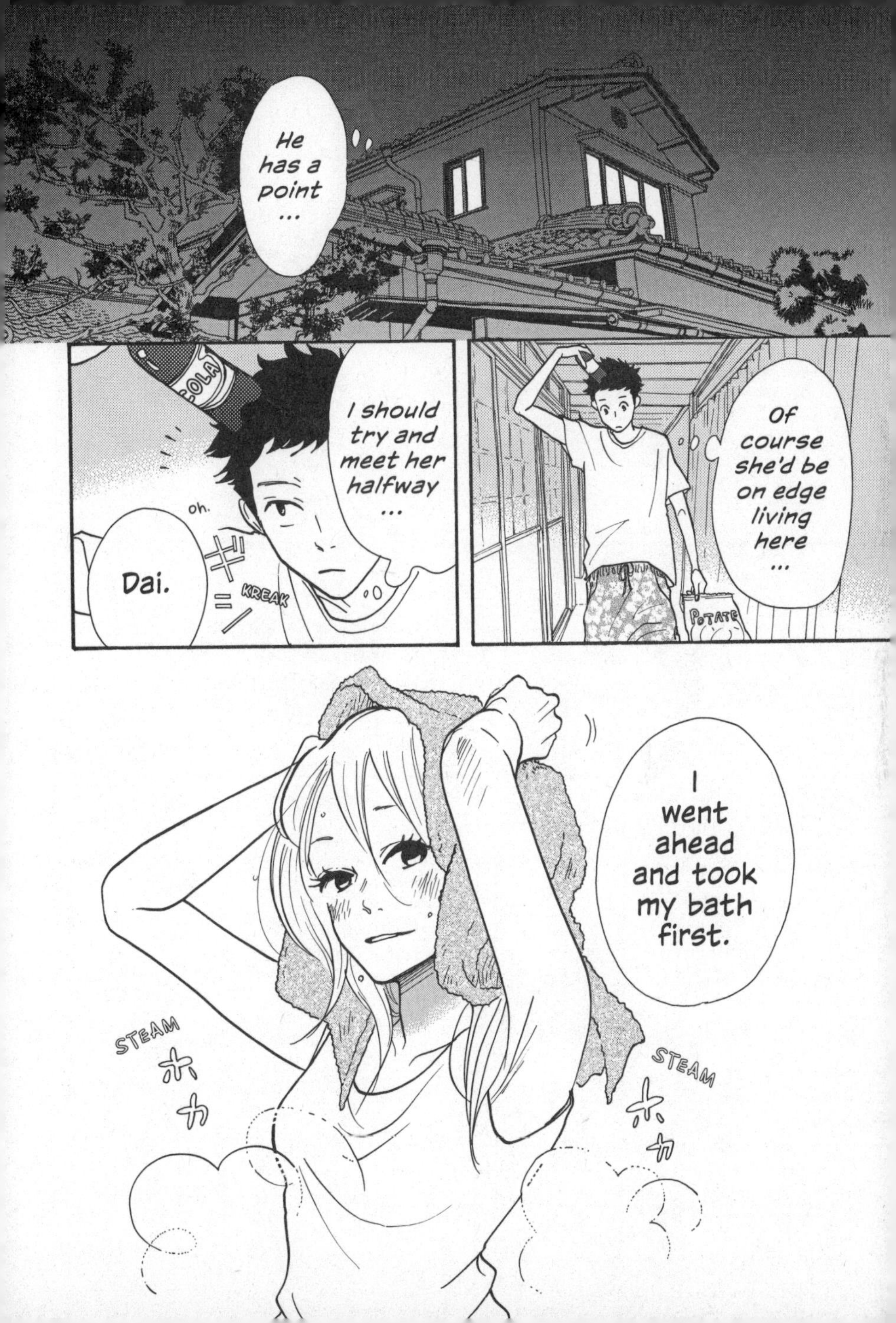
He has a point ...
Of course she'd be on edge living here ...
I should try and meet her halfway ...
oh.
KREAK
Dai.
I went ahead and took my bath first.
STEAM
STEAM

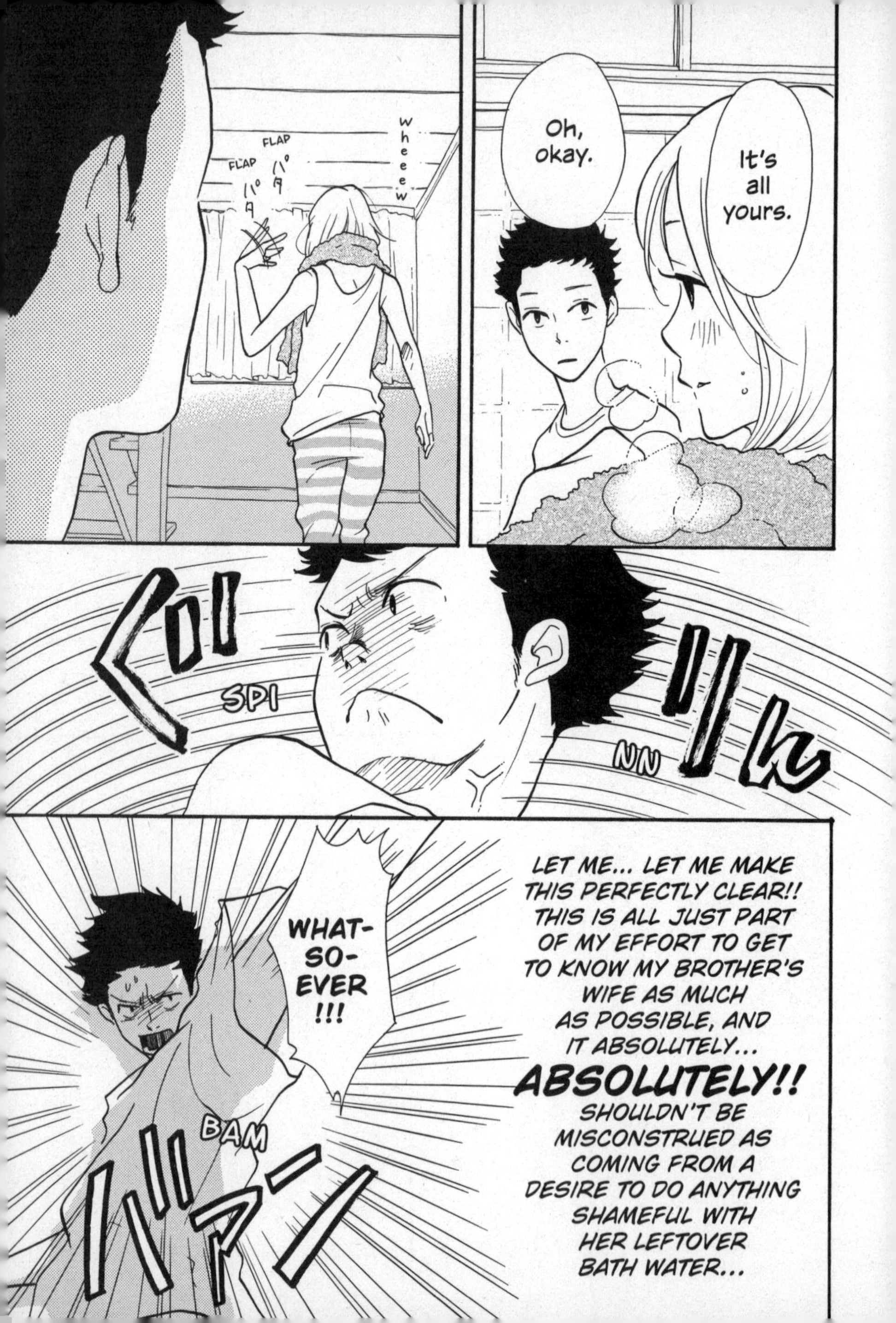
It's all yours.
Oh, okay.
wheeeew
FLAP パタ
FLAP パタ
くい
SPI
ッん
NN
LET ME... LET ME MAKE THIS PERFECTLY CLEAR!! THIS IS ALL JUST PART OF MY EFFORT TO GET TO KNOW MY BROTHER'S WIFE AS MUCH AS POSSIBLE, AND IT ABSOLUTELY... ABSOLUTELY!! SHOULDN'T BE MISCONSTRUED AS COMING FROM A DESIRE TO DO ANYTHING SHAMEFUL WITH HER LEFTOVER BATH WATER...
WHAT-SO-EVER!!!
BAM
バァーン

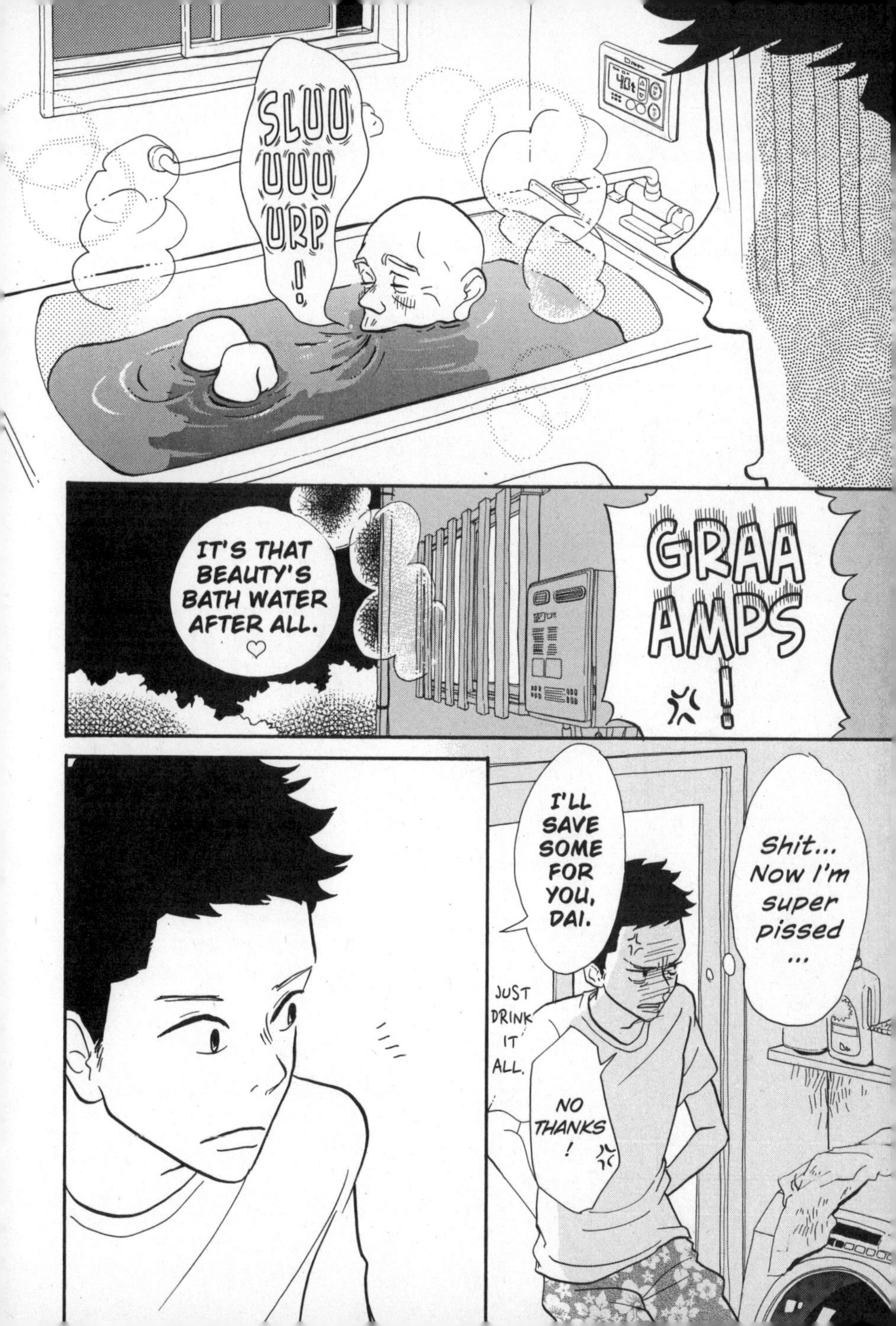
SLUUUUUURP!
GRAAAMPS!
IT'S THAT BEAUTY'S BATH WATER AFTER ALL. ♡
Shit... Now I'm super pissed...
I'LL SAVE SOME FOR YOU, DAI.
JUST DRINK IT ALL.
NO THANKS!

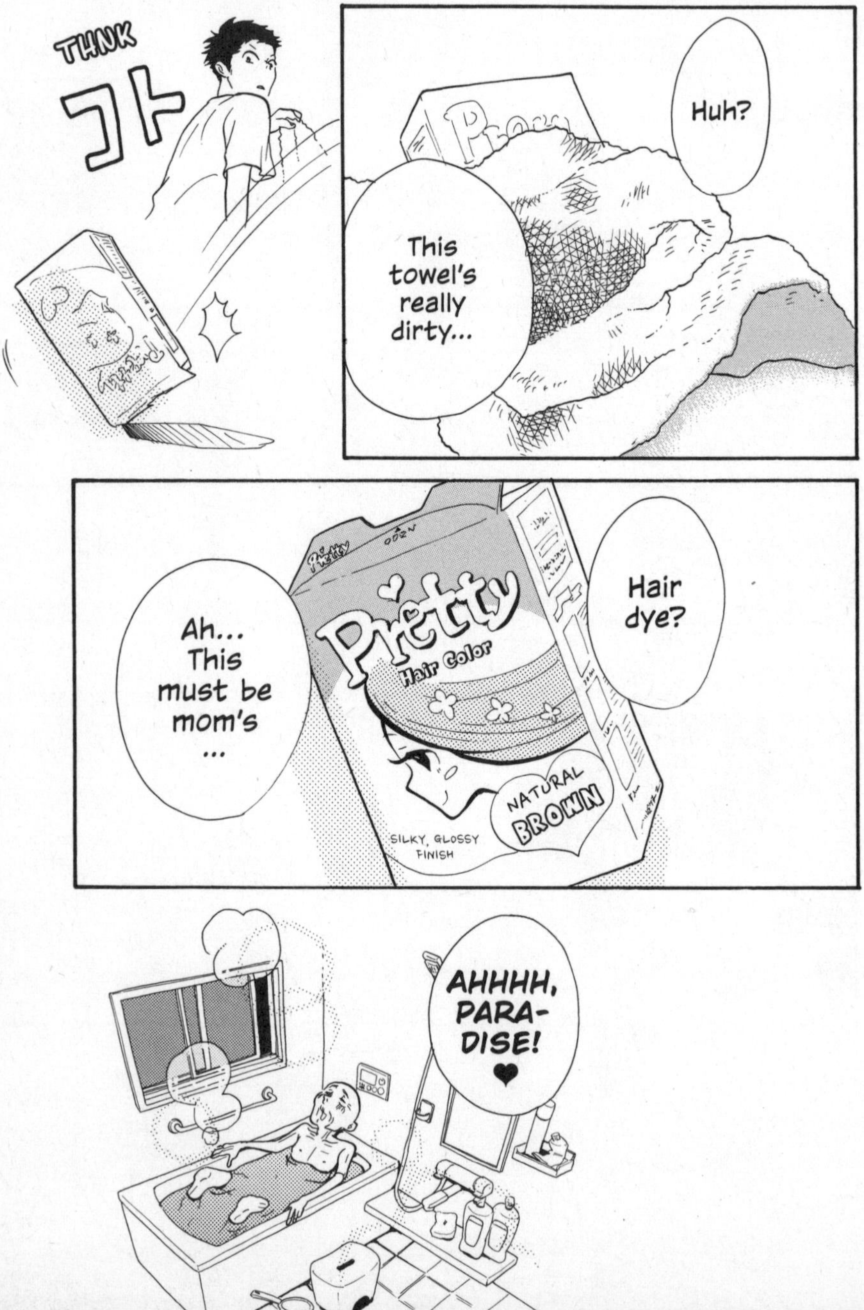
Huh?
This towel's really dirty...
THNK
コト
Hair dye?
Ah... This must be mom's...
Pretty
Hair Color
NATURAL BROWN
SILKY, GLOSSY FINISH
AHHHH, PARA-DISE! ♥

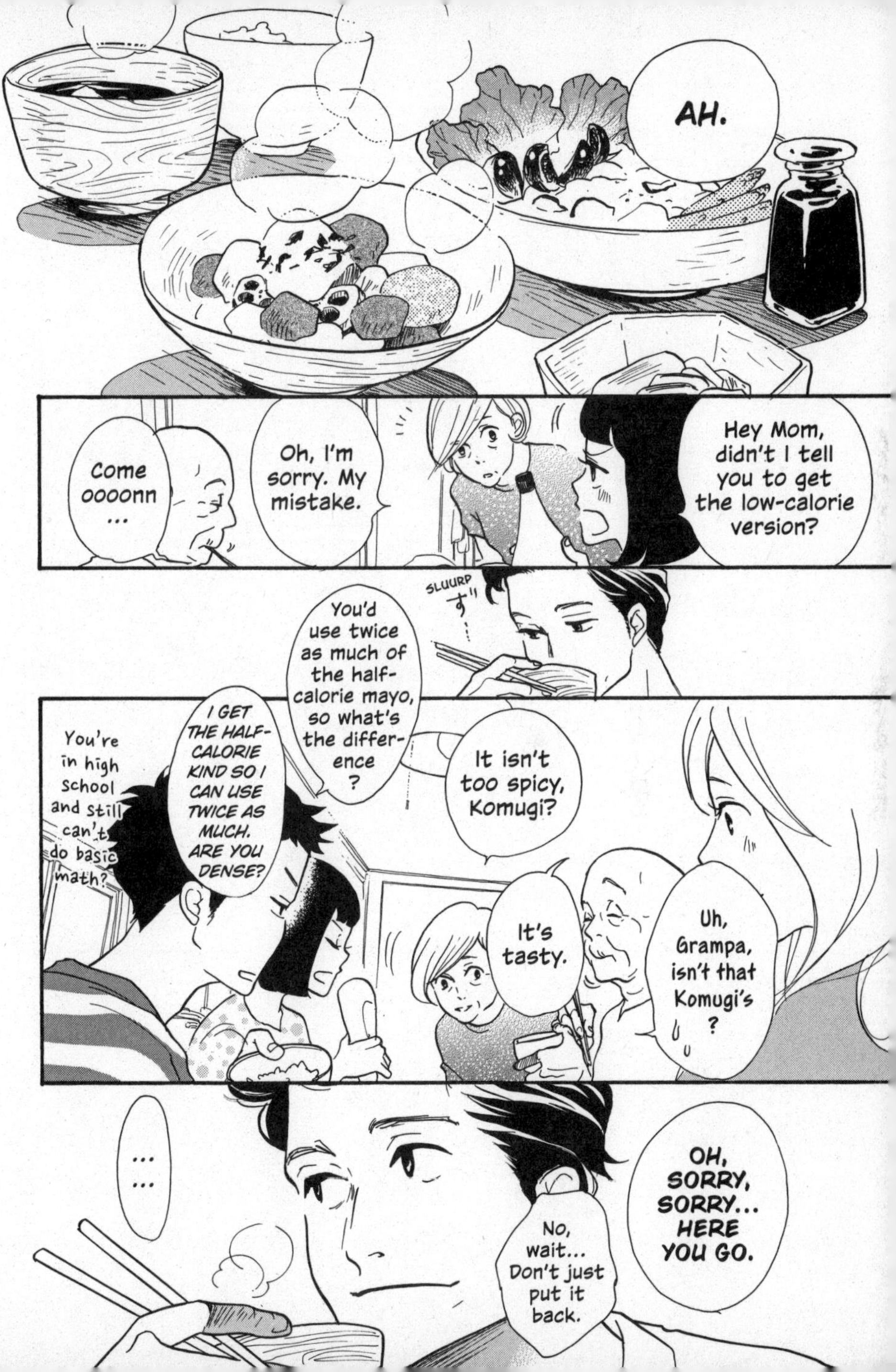
AH.
Hey Mom, didn't I tell you to get the low-calorie version?
Oh, I'm sorry. My mistake.
Come oooonn ...
SLUURP
ず
You'd use twice as much of the half-calorie mayo, so what's the difference?
It isn't too spicy, Komugi?
Uh, Grampa, isn't that Komugi's?
It's tasty.
I GET THE HALF-CALORIE KIND SO I CAN USE TWICE AS MUCH. ARE YOU DENSE?
You're in high school and still can't do basic math?
OH, SORRY, SORRY... HERE YOU GO.
No, wait... Don't just put it back.
... ...

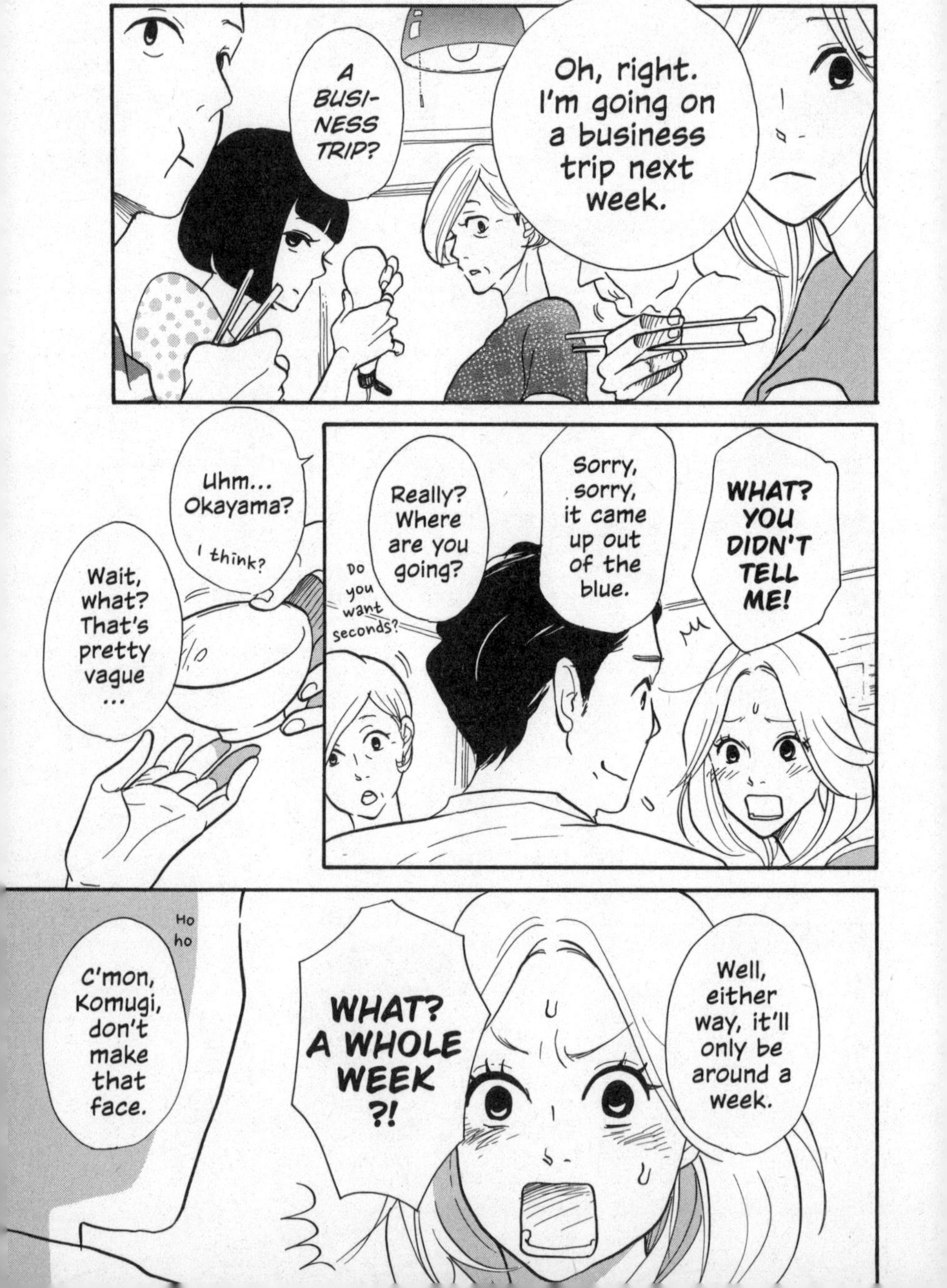
Oh, right. I'm going on a business trip next week.
A BUSI-NESS TRIP?
WHAT? YOU DIDN'T TELL ME!
Sorry, sorry, it came up out of the blue.
Really? Where are you going?
Do you want seconds?
Uhm... Okayama?
I think?
Wait, what? That's pretty vague ...
Well, either way, it'll only be around a week.
WHAT? A WHOLE WEEK ?!
Ho ho
C'mon, Komugi, don't make that face.

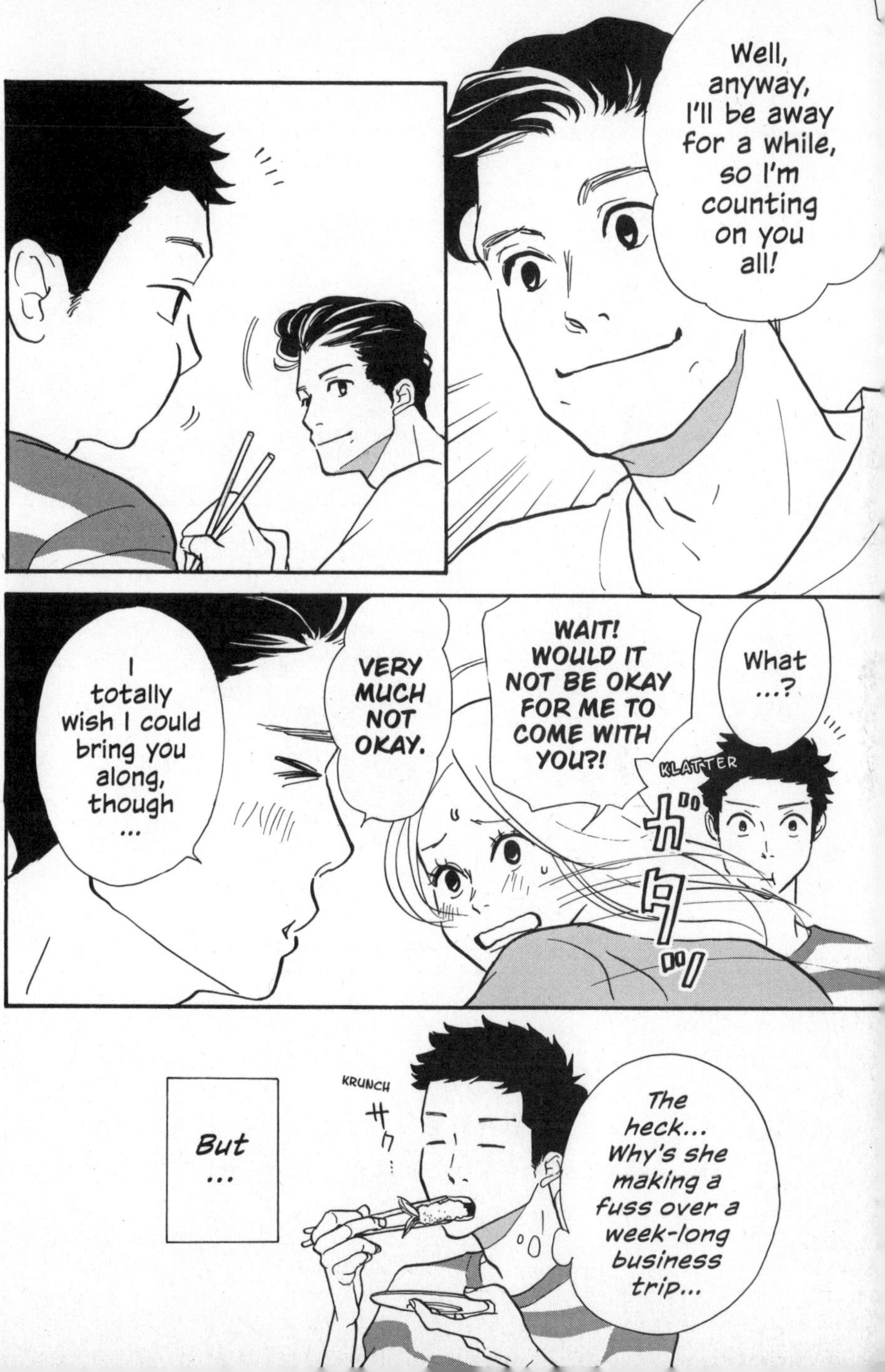
Well, anyway, I'll be away for a while, so I'm counting on you all!
What ...?
KLATTER
WAIT! WOULD IT NOT BE OKAY FOR ME TO COME WITH YOU?!
VERY MUCH NOT OKAY.
I totally wish I could bring you along, though ...
The heck... Why's she making a fuss over a week-long business trip...
KRUNCH
But ...

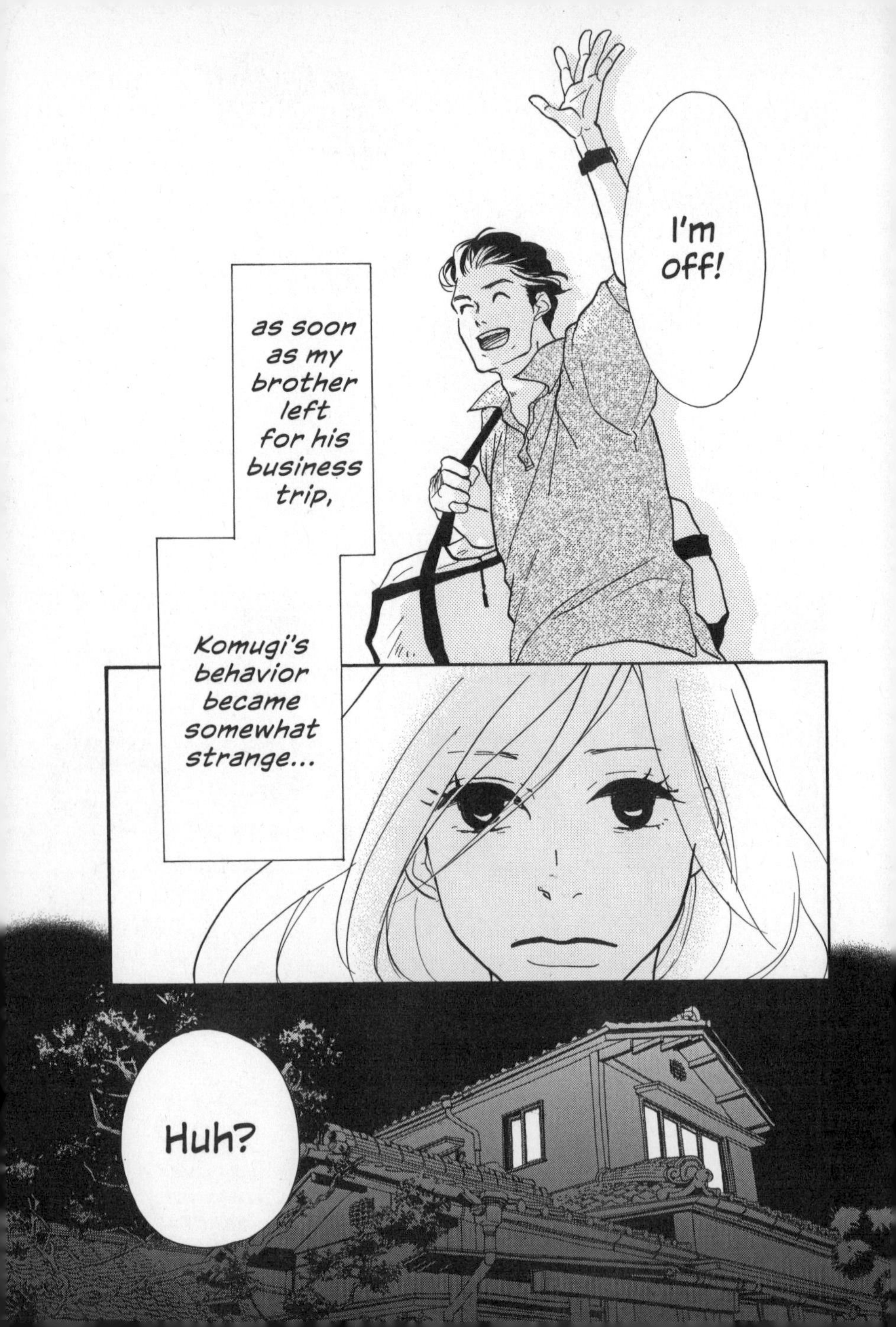
I'm off!
as soon as my brother left for his business trip,
Komugi's behavior became somewhat strange...
Huh?

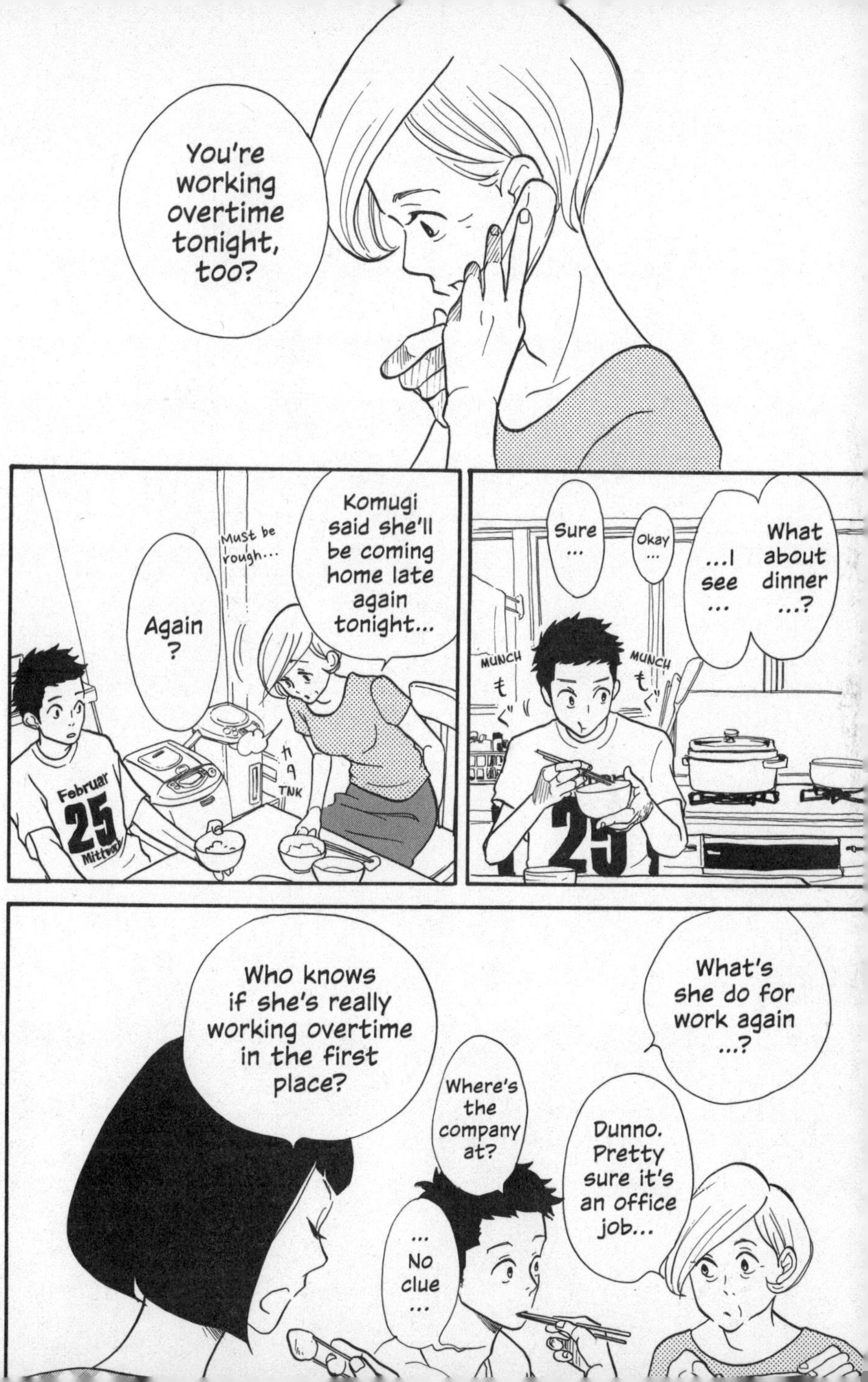
You're working overtime tonight, too?
What about dinner ...?
...I see ...
Okay ...
Sure ...
MUNCH
もぐ
MUNCH
もぐ
Komugi said she'll be coming home late again tonight...
Must be rough...
カタ
TNK
Again ?
What's she do for work again ...?
Dunno. Pretty sure it's an office job...
Where's the company at?
Who knows if she's really working overtime in the first place?
... No clue ...

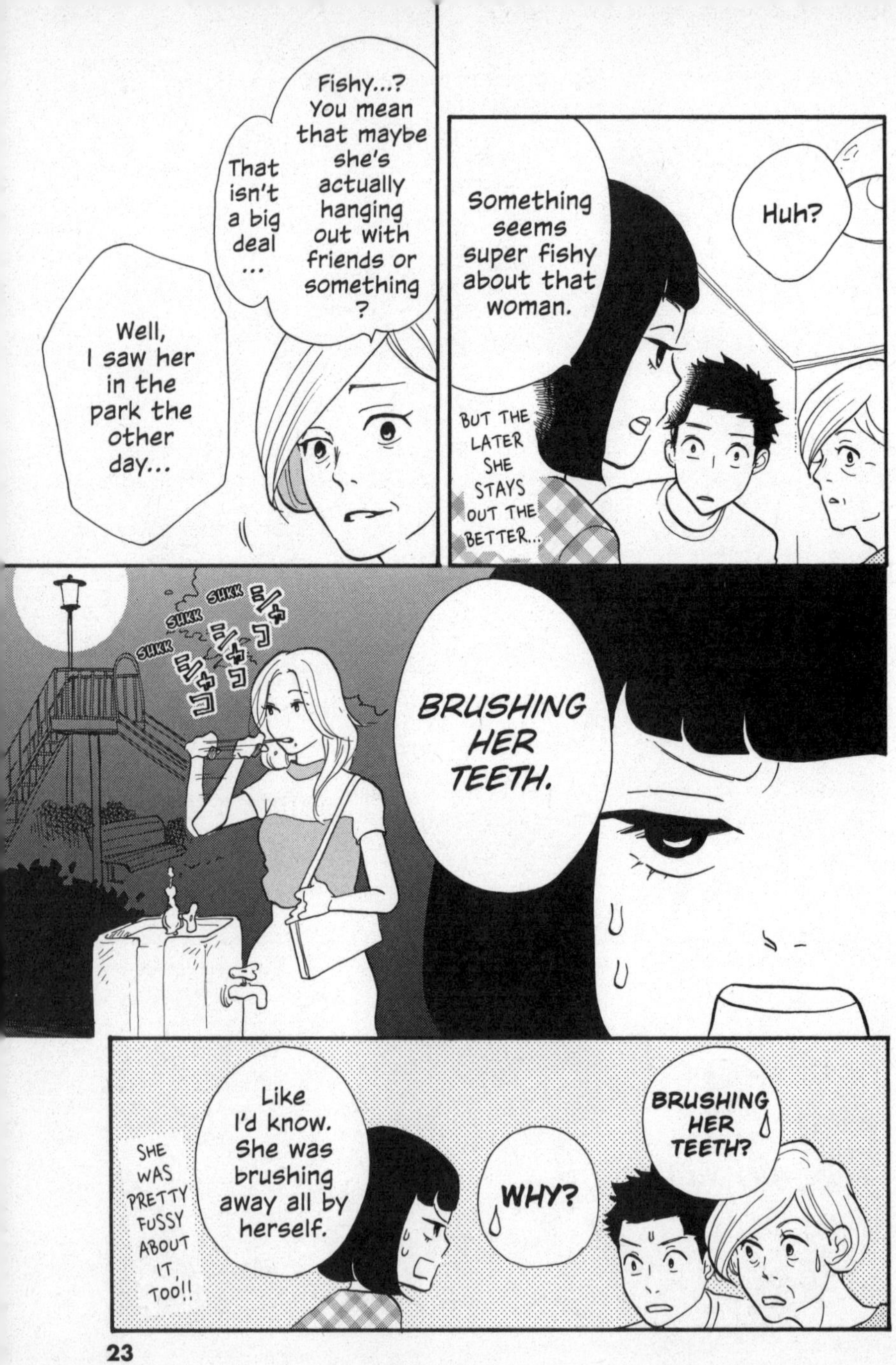
Huh?
Something seems super fishy about that woman.
BUT THE LATER SHE STAYS OUT THE BETTER...
Fishy...? You mean that maybe she's actually hanging out with friends or something?
That isn't a big deal...
Well, I saw her in the park the other day...
BRUSHING HER TEETH.
シャコ
SHKK
シャコ
SHKK
シャコ
SHKK
BRUSHING HER TEETH?
WHY?
Like I'd know. She was brushing away all by herself.
SHE WAS PRETTY FUSSY ABOUT IT, TOO!!

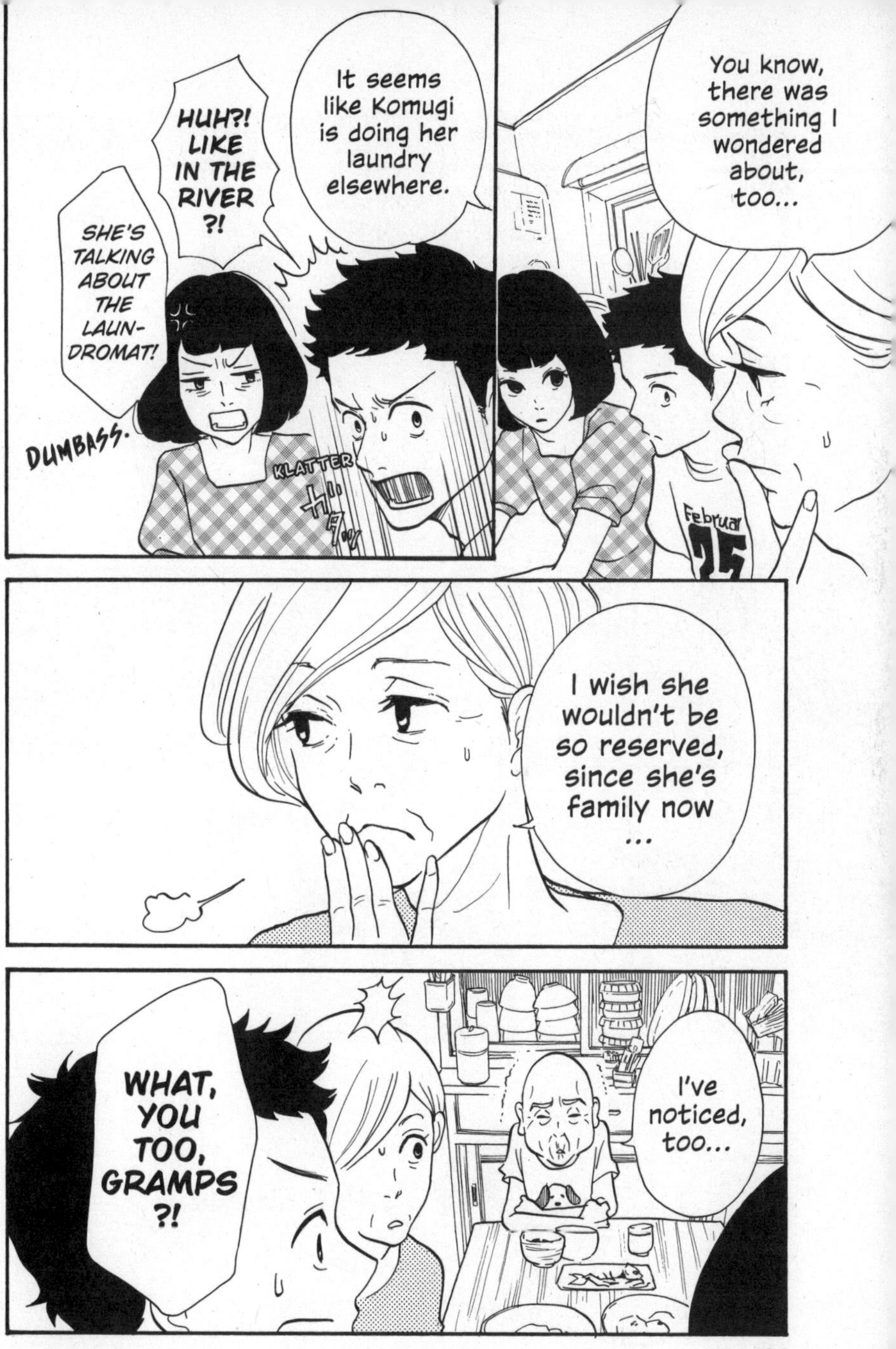
You know, there was something I wondered about, too...
It seems like Komugi is doing her laundry elsewhere.
HUH?! LIKE IN THE RIVER?!
SHE'S TALKING ABOUT THE LAUN-DROMAT!
DUMBASS.
KLATTER
I wish she wouldn't be so reserved, since she's family now...
I've noticed, too...
WHAT, YOU TOO, GRAMPS?!

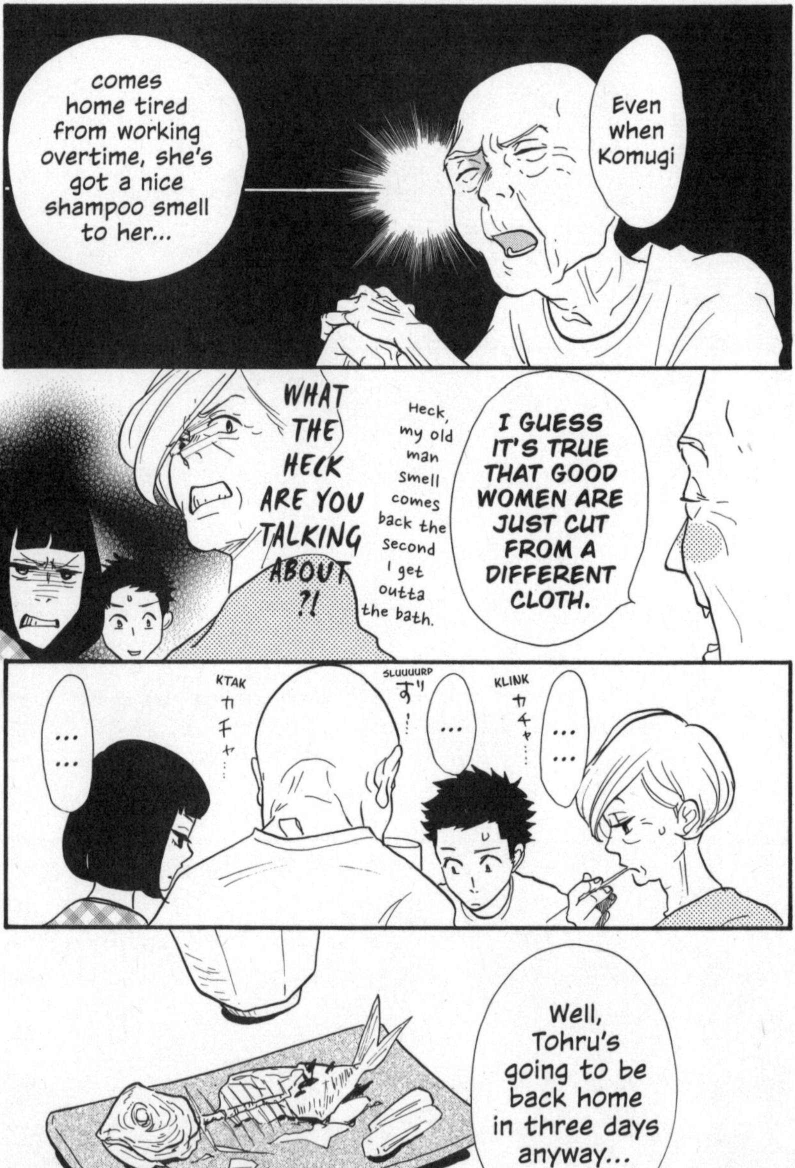

Even when Komugi
comes home tired from working overtime, she's got a nice shampoo smell to her...
I GUESS IT'S TRUE THAT GOOD WOMEN ARE JUST CUT FROM A DIFFERENT CLOTH.
Heck, my old man smell comes back the second I get outta the bath.
WHAT THE HECK ARE YOU TALKING ABOUT?!
... ...
KLINK
カチャ…
...
SLUUUURP
KTAK
カチャ…
... ...
Well, Tohru's going to be back home in three days anyway...

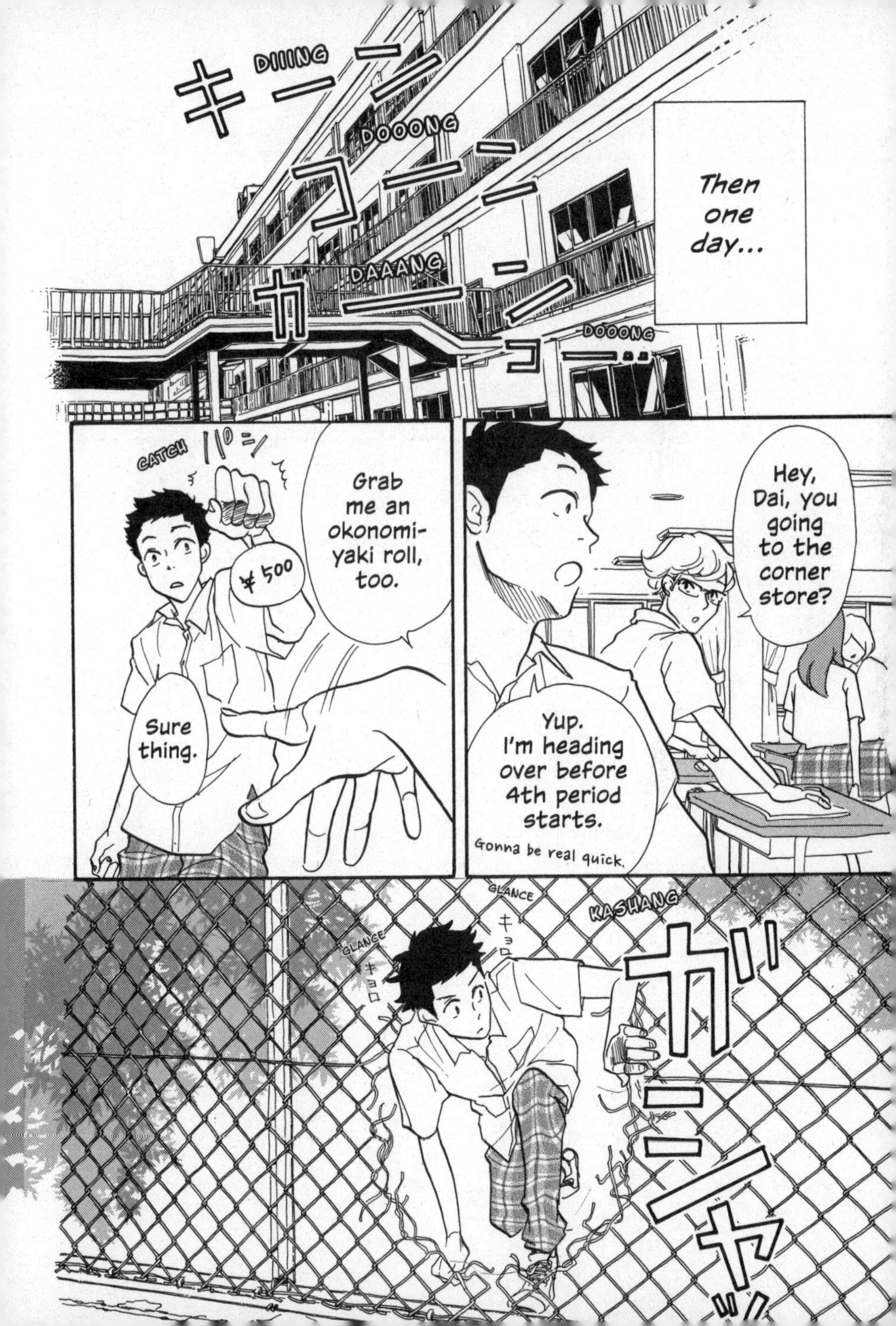

Then one day...
DIIING
DOOONG
DAAANG
DOOONG
Hey, Dai, you going to the corner store?
Yup. I'm heading over before 4th period starts.
Gonna be real quick.
CATCH
Grab me an okonomiyaki roll, too.
¥500
Sure thing.
KASHANG
GLANCE
GLANCE

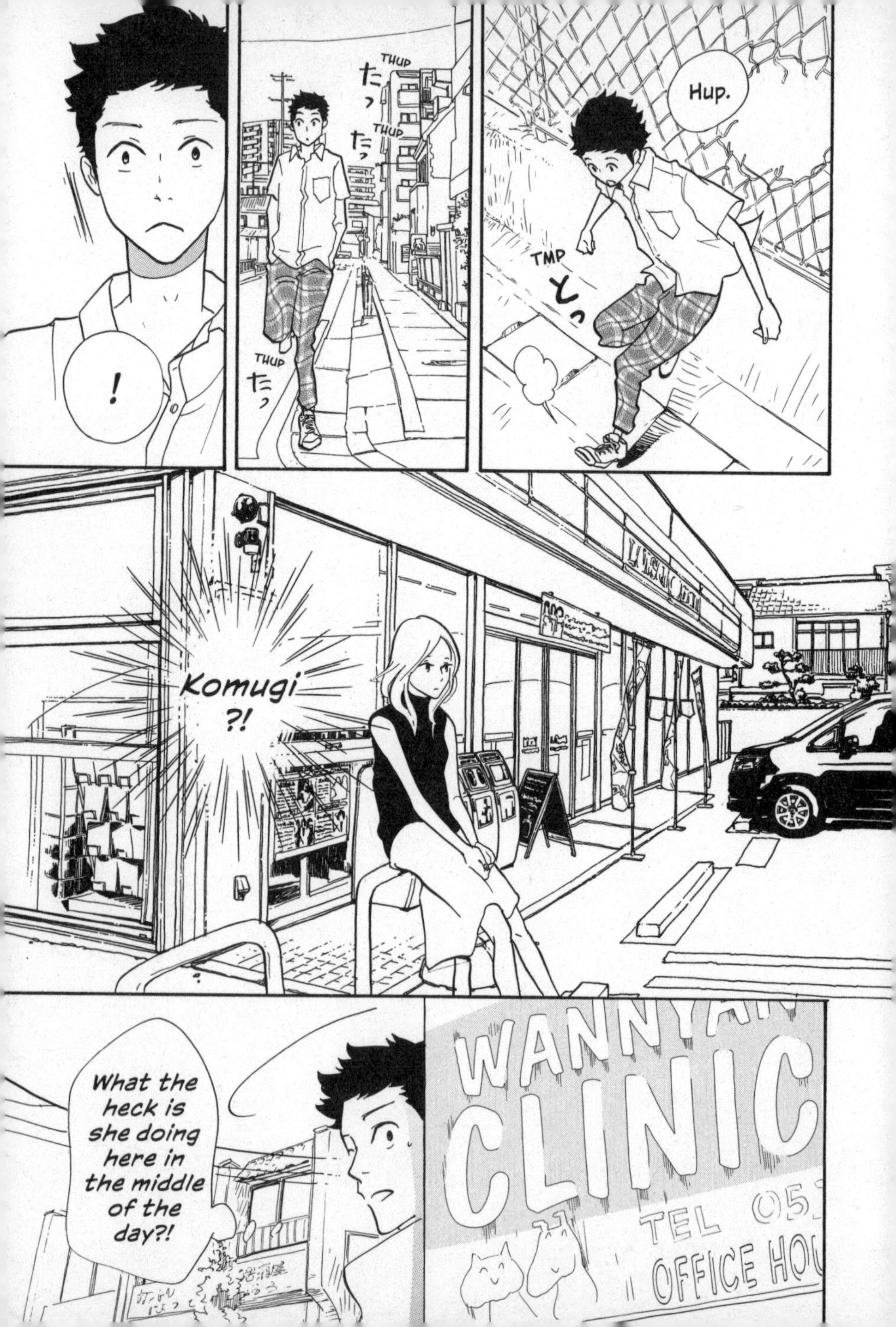
Hup.
TMP
とっ
THUP
たっ
THUP
たっ
THUP
たっ
!
Komugi?!
CLINIC
What the heck is she doing here in the middle of the day?!

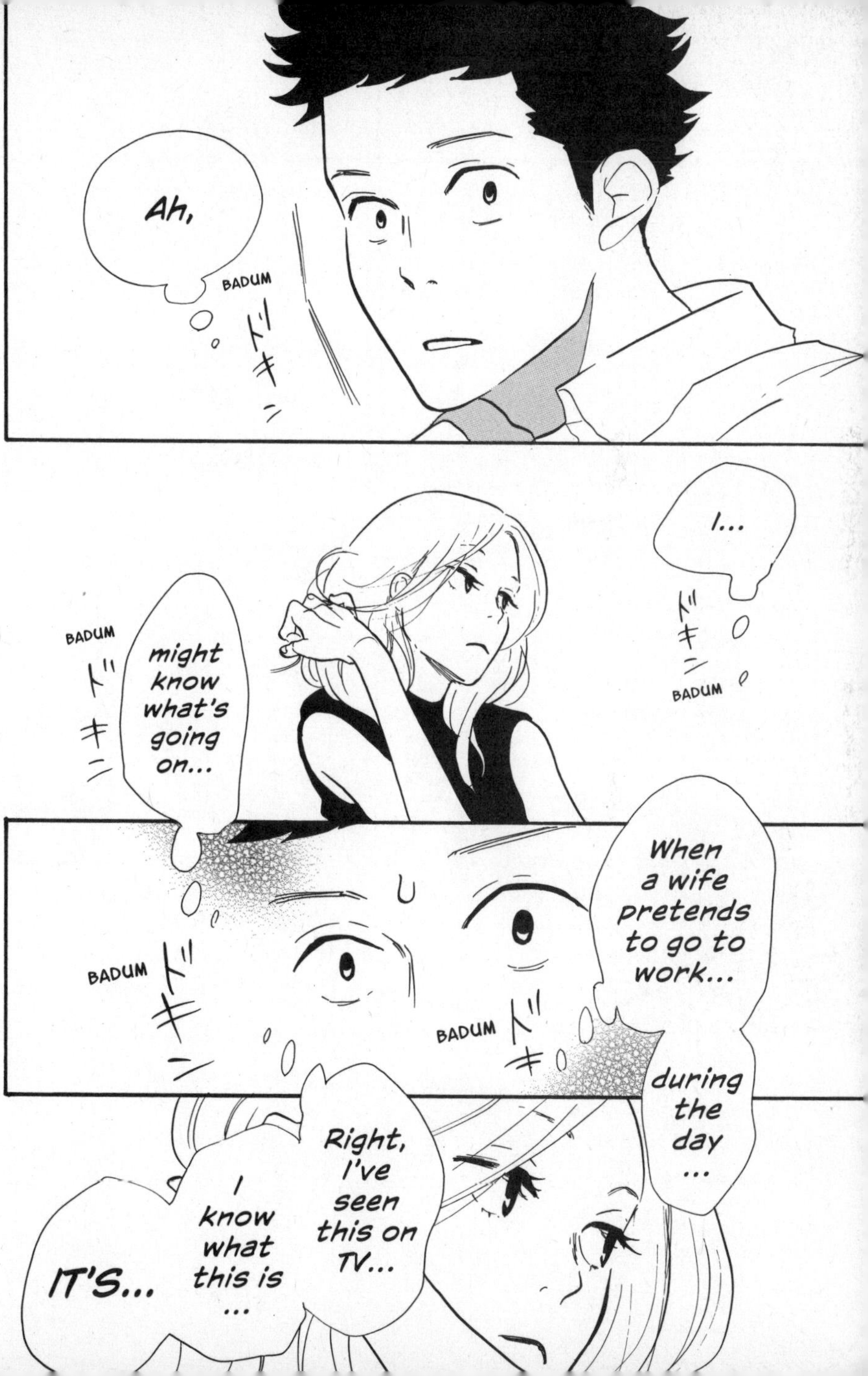
Ah,
BADUM
ドキ
I...
BADUM
ドキ
might know what's going on...
BADUM
ドキ
When a wife pretends to go to work...
BADUM
ドキ
BADUM
ドキ
during the day...
Right, I've seen this on TV...
I know what this is...
IT'S...

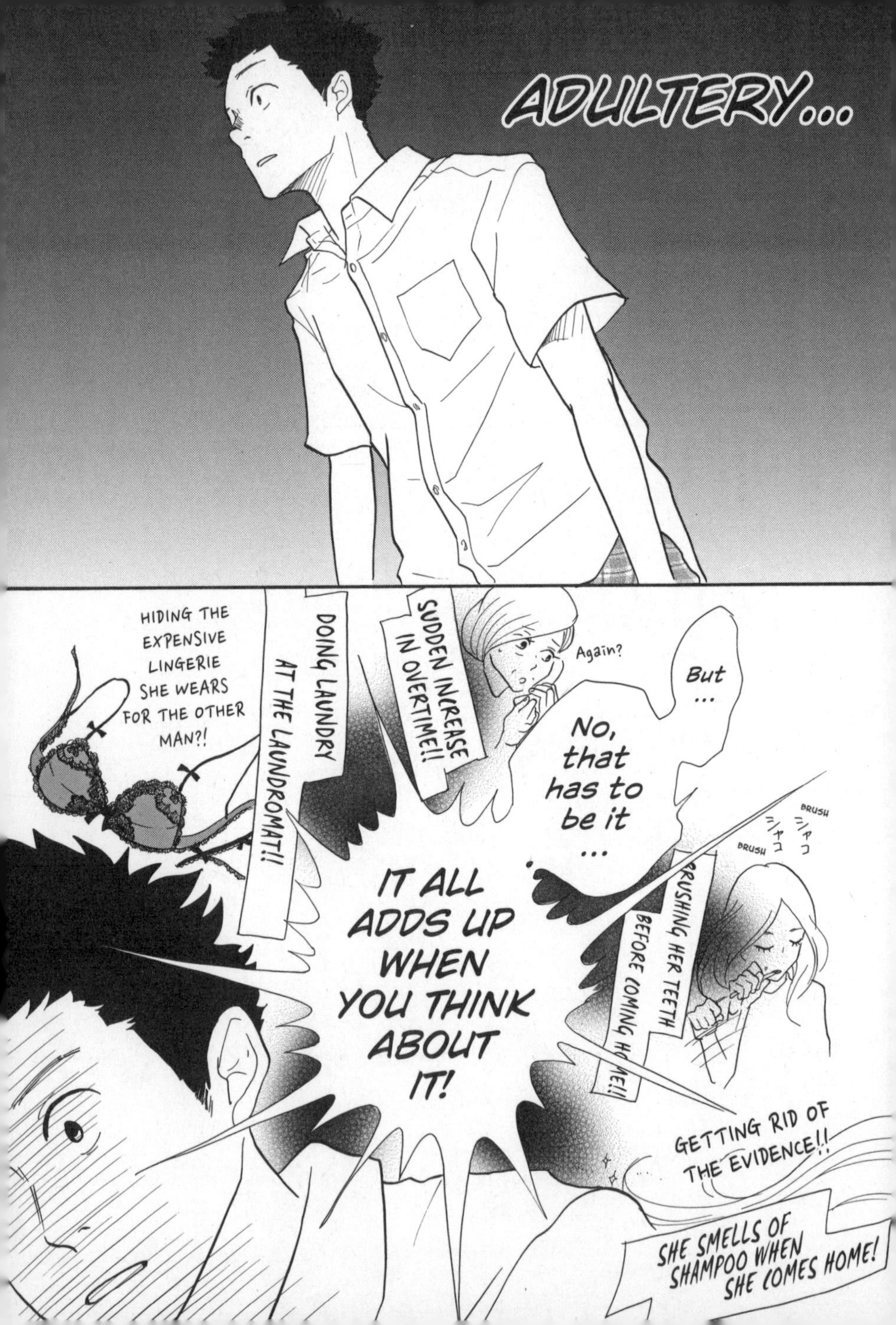
ADULTERY...
But ...
Again?
SUDDEN INCREASE IN OVERTIME!!
DOING LAUNDRY AT THE LAUNDROMAT!!
HIDING THE EXPENSIVE LINGERIE SHE WEARS FOR THE OTHER MAN?!
No, that has to be it ...
BRUSH シャコ
BRUSH シャコ
BRUSHING HER TEETH BEFORE COMING HOME!!
IT ALL ADDS UP WHEN YOU THINK ABOUT IT!
GETTING RID OF THE EVIDENCE!!
SHE SMELLS OF SHAMPOO WHEN SHE COMES HOME!

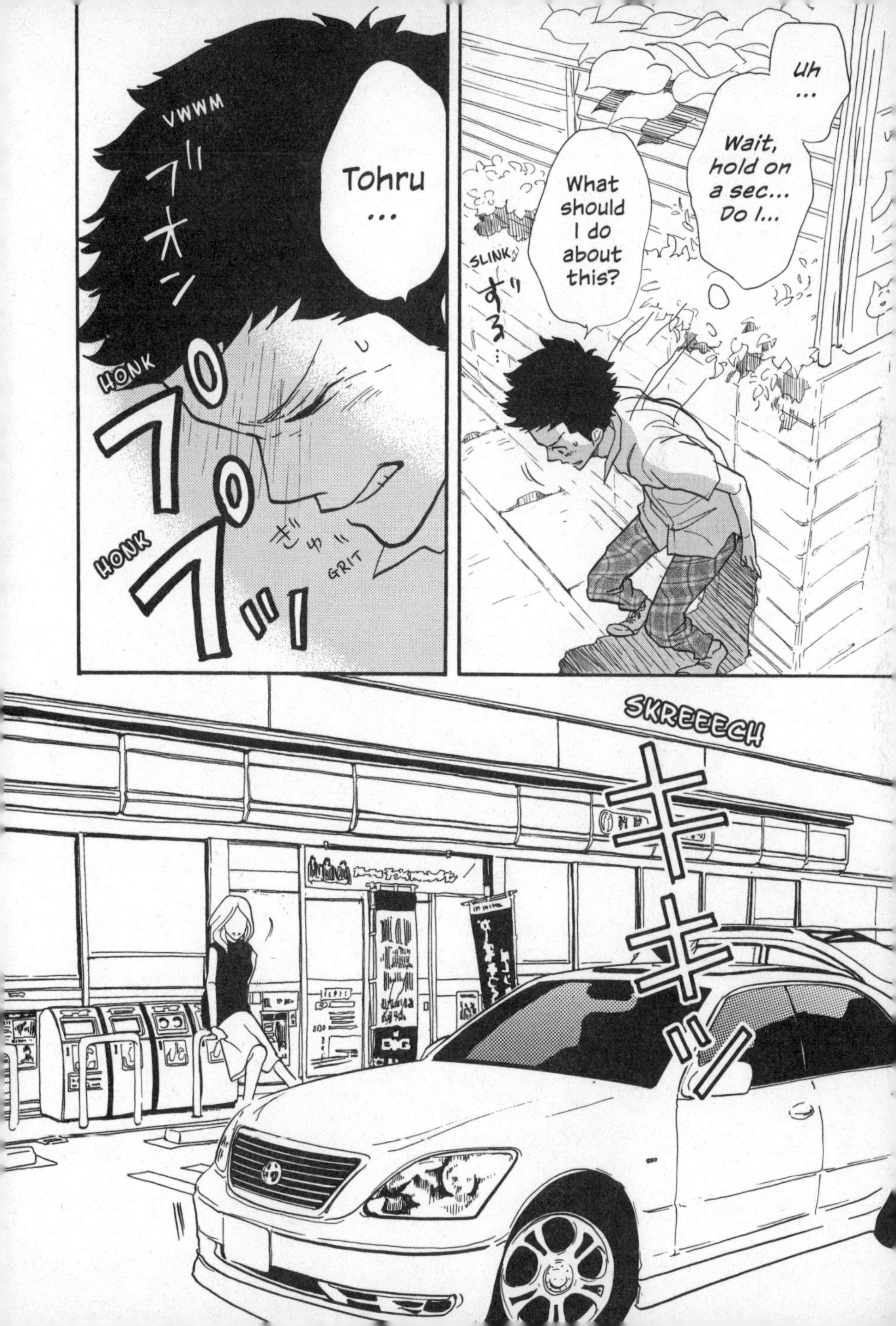
Uh ...
Wait, hold on a sec... Do I...
What should I do about this?
SLINK
VWWM
Tohru ...
HONK
HONK
GRIT
SKREEECH

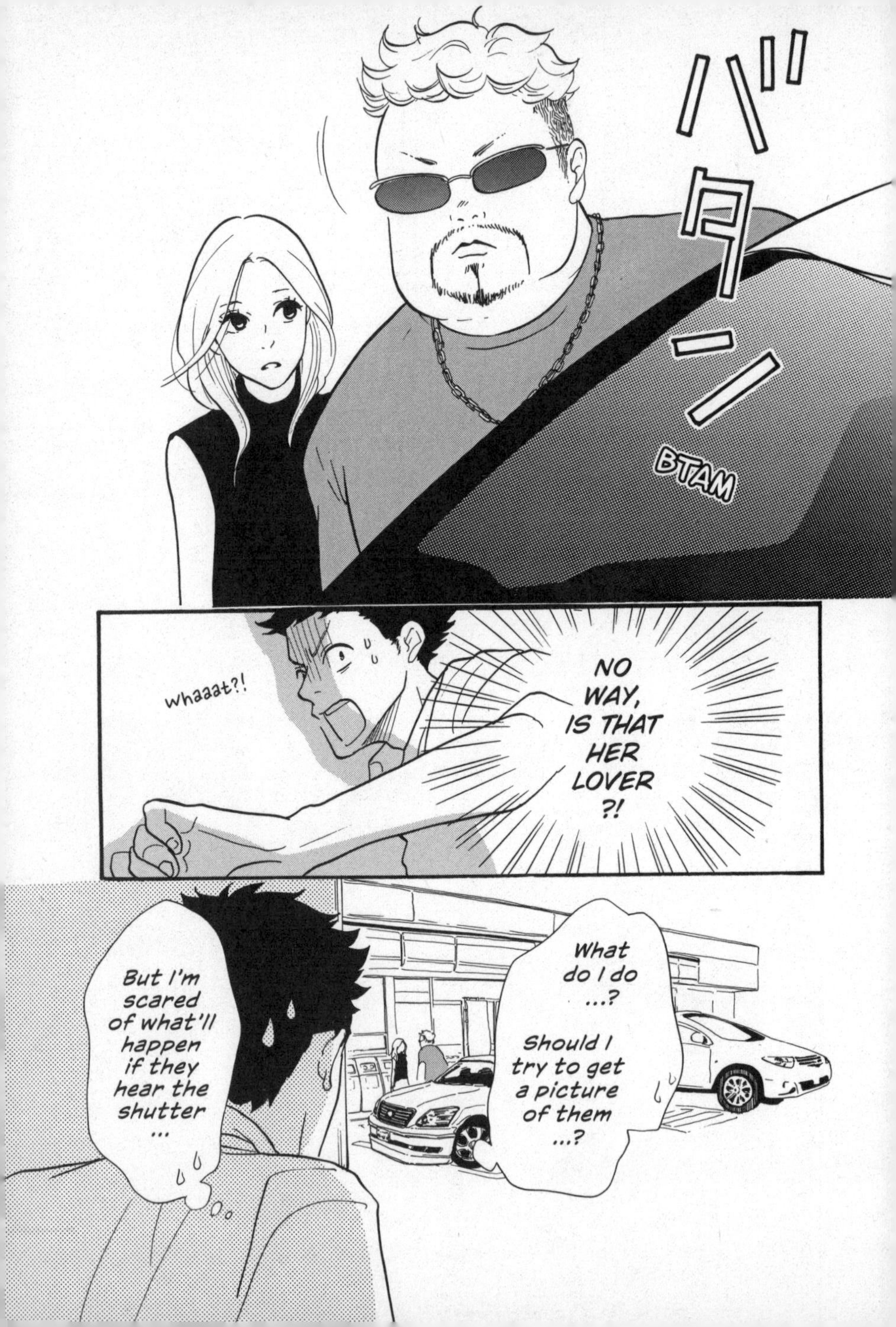
バタン
BTAM
NO WAY, IS THAT HER LOVER ?!
whaaat?!
What do I do ...?
Should I try to get a picture of them ...?
But I'm scared of what'll happen if they hear the shutter ...

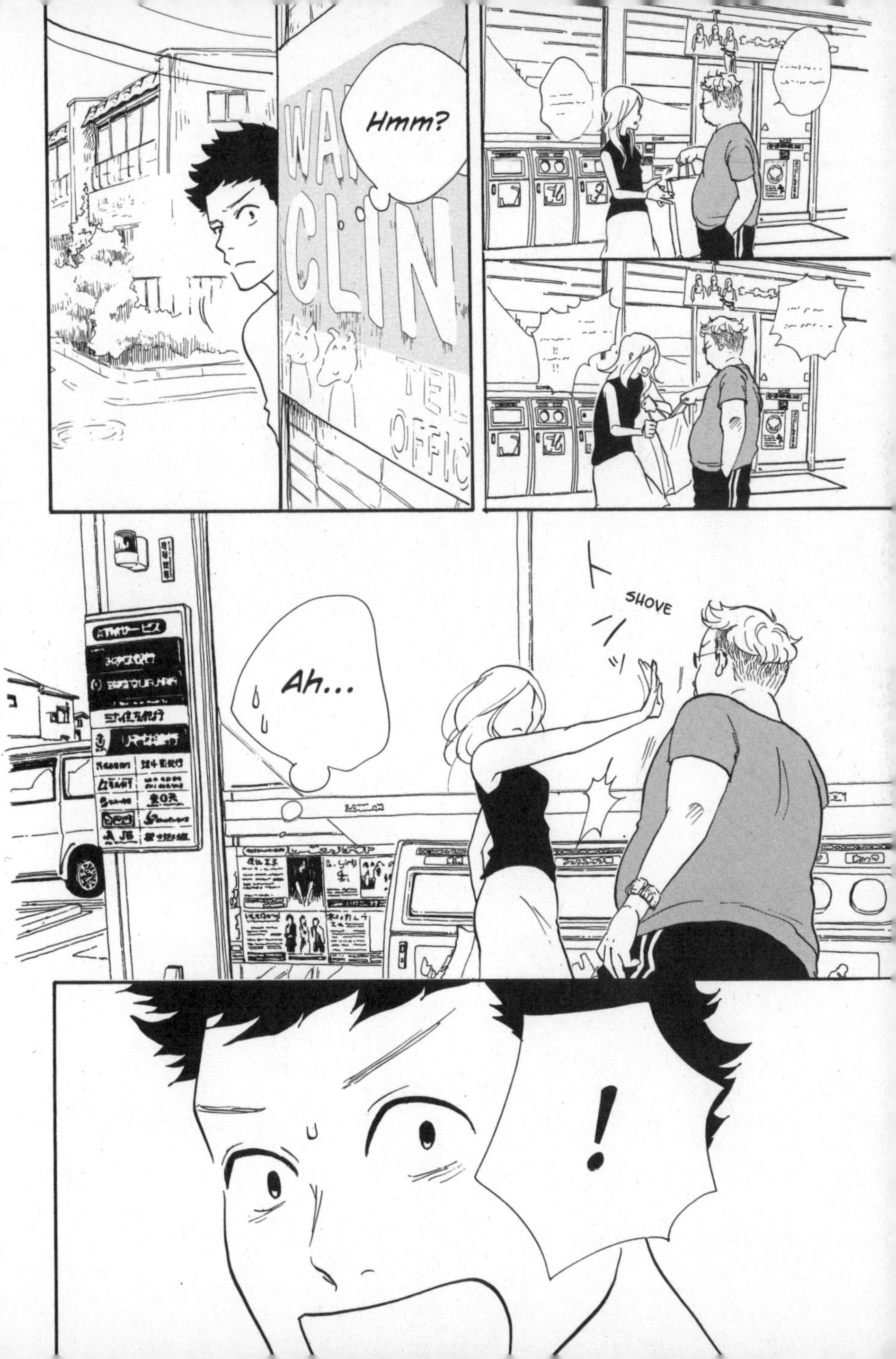
Hmm?
SHOVE
Ah...
!

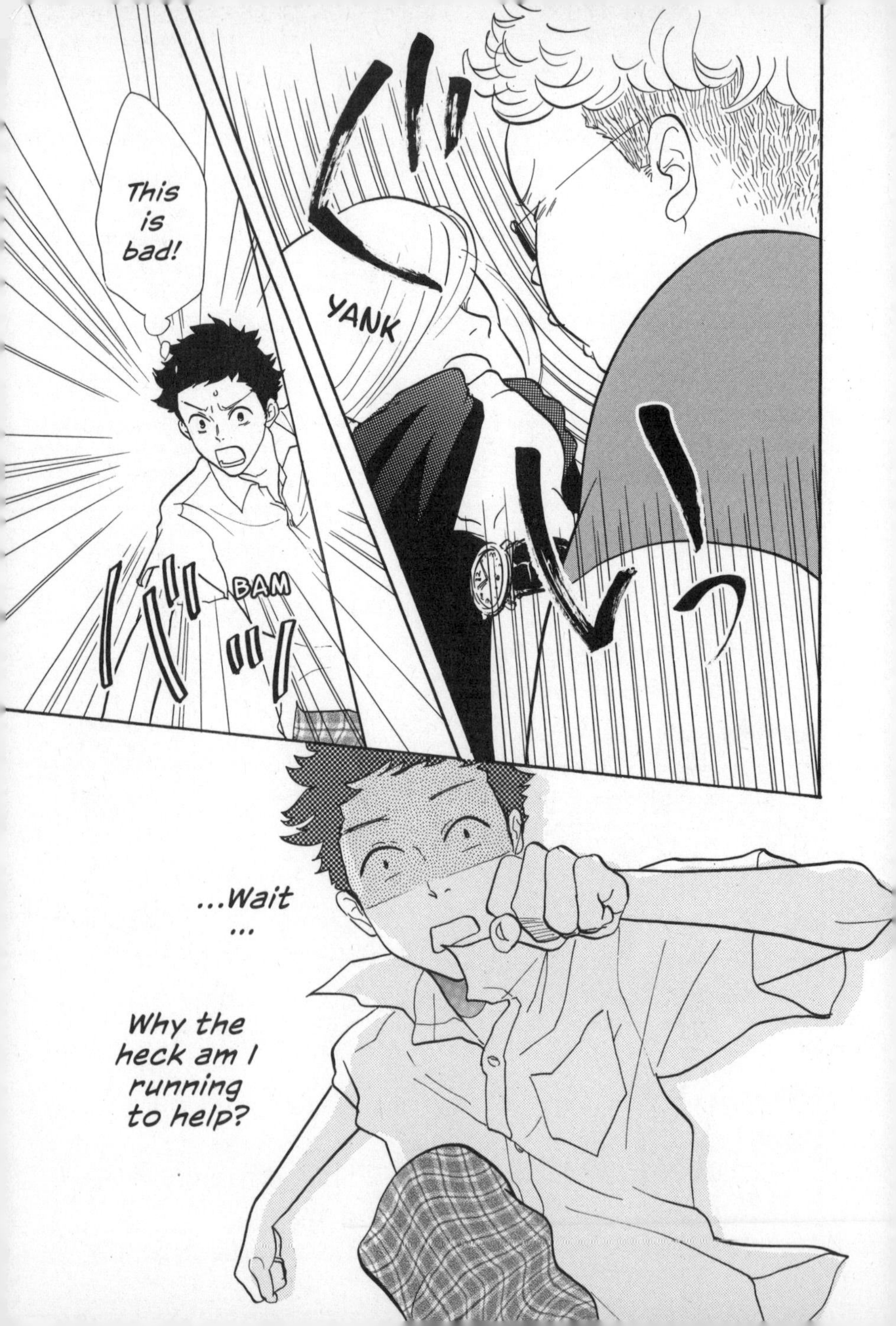
YANK
This is bad!
BAM
...Wait ...
Why the heck am I running to help?

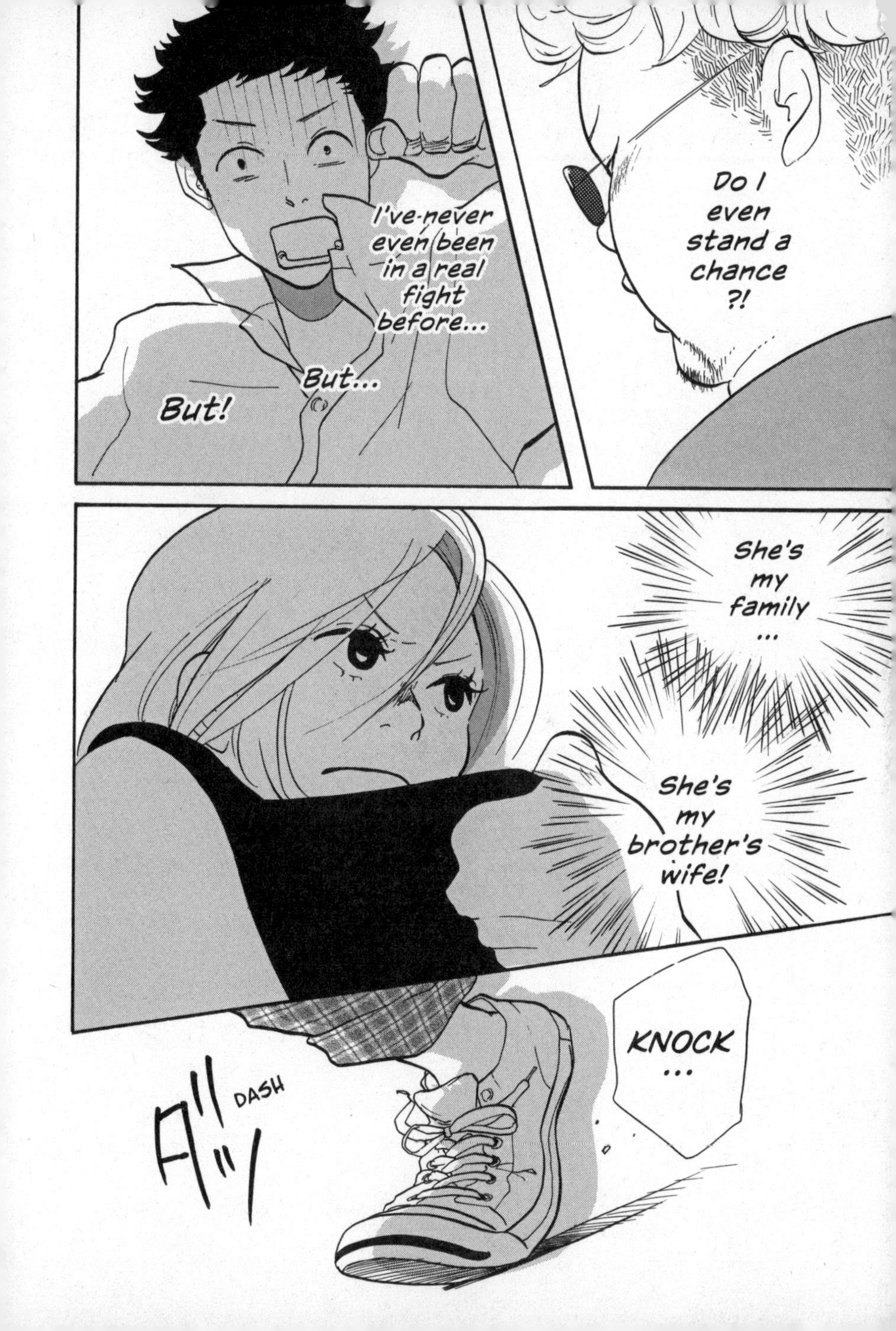
Do I even stand a chance?!
I've never even been in a real fight before...
But...
But!
She's my family...
She's my brother's wife!
KNOCK...
DASH

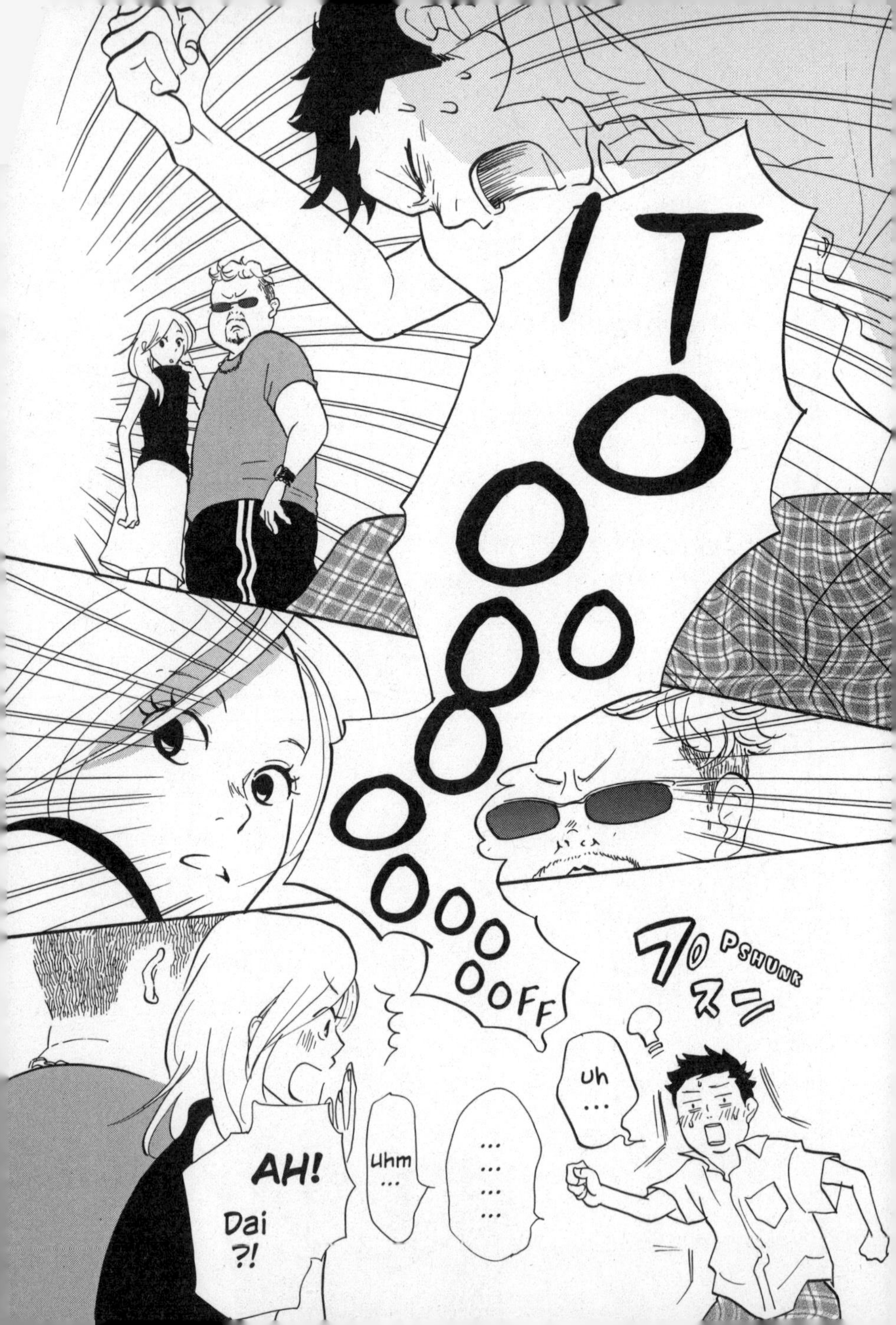
ITOOOOOOOOOOOOOOOFF
プスン PSHUNK
Uh ...
... ...
Uhm ...
AH!
Dai ?!

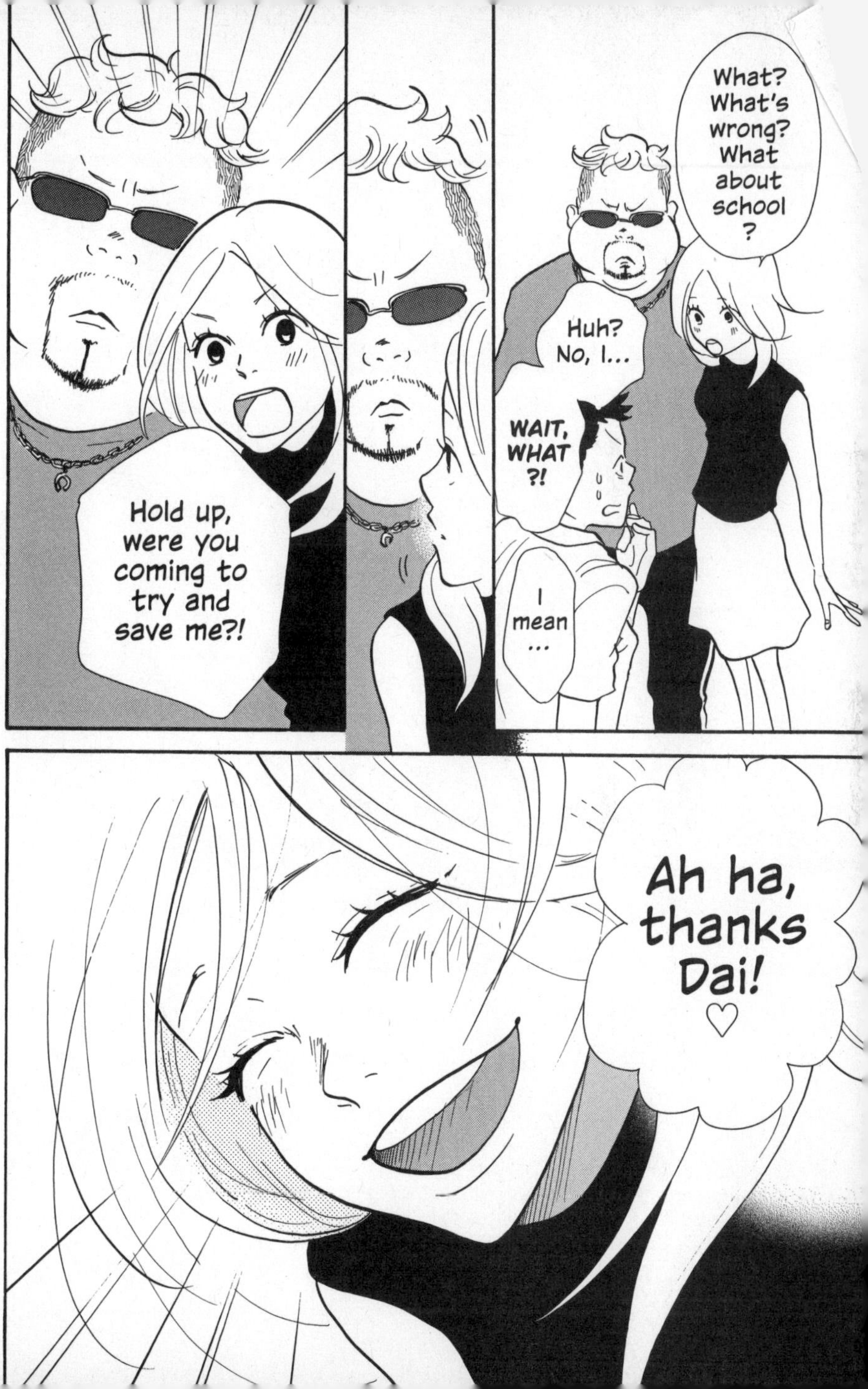
What? What's wrong? What about school?
Huh? No, I...
WAIT, WHAT?!
I mean...
Hold up, were you coming to try and save me?!
Ah ha, thanks Dai! ♡

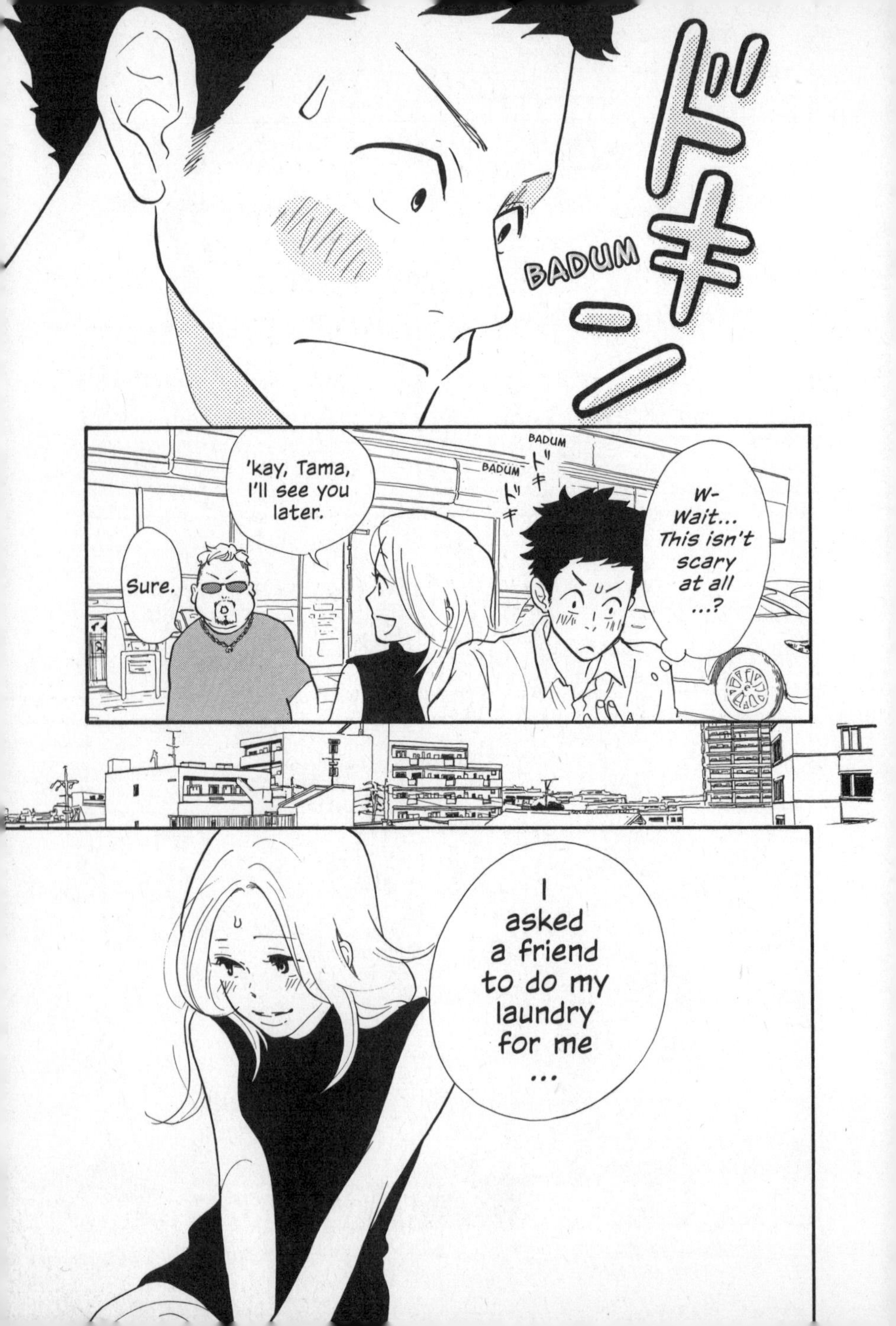
ドキーー
BADUM
BADUM ドキ
BADUM ドキ
W-Wait... This isn't scary at all ...?
'kay, Tama, I'll see you later.
Sure.
I asked a friend to do my laundry for me ...

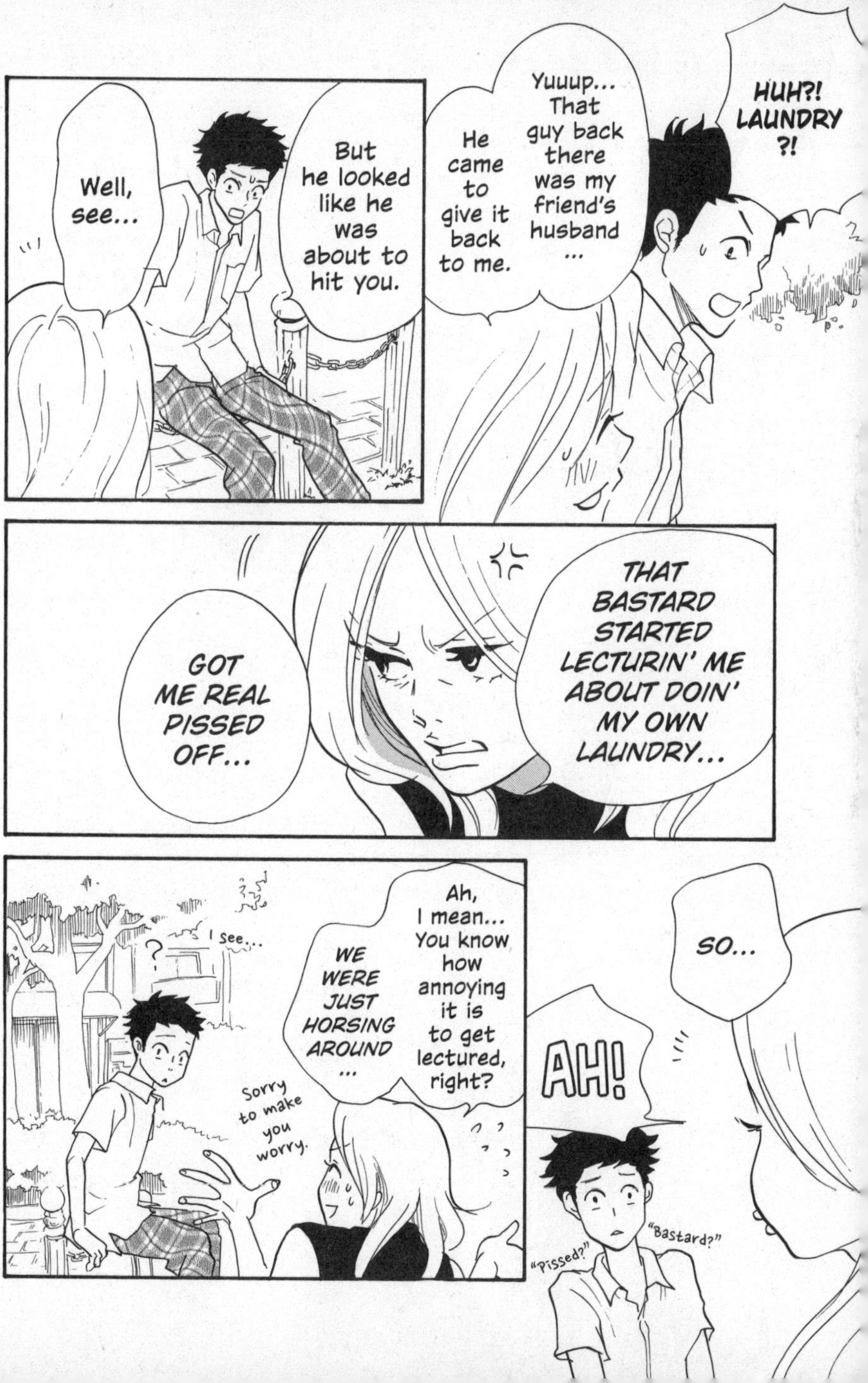

HUH?! LAUNDRY ?!
Yuuup... That guy back there was my friend's husband ...
He came to give it back to me.
But he looked like he was about to hit you.
Well, see...
THAT BASTARD STARTED LECTURIN' ME ABOUT DOIN' MY OWN LAUNDRY...
GOT ME REAL PISSED OFF...
SO...
AH!
"Bastard?"
"Pissed?"
Ah, I mean... You know how annoying it is to get lectured, right?
WE WERE JUST HORSING AROUND ...
Sorry to make you worry.
I see...

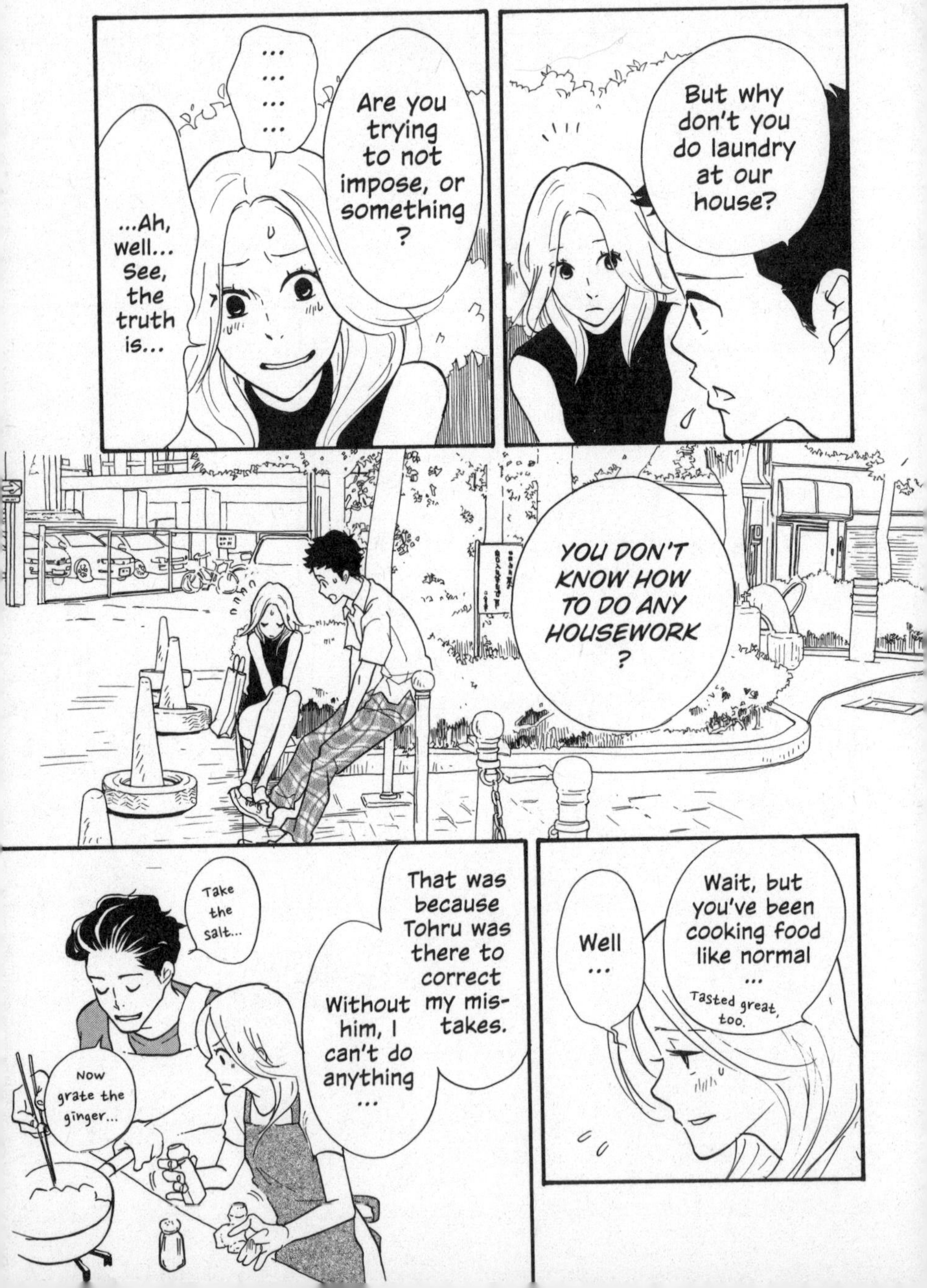
But why don't you do laundry at our house?
Are you trying to not impose, or something?
...
...
...
...
...Ah, well... See, the truth is...
YOU DON'T KNOW HOW TO DO ANY HOUSEWORK?
Wait, but you've been cooking food like normal...
Tasted great, too.
Well...
That was because Tohru was there to correct my mistakes.
Without him, I can't do anything...
Take the salt...
Now grate the ginger...

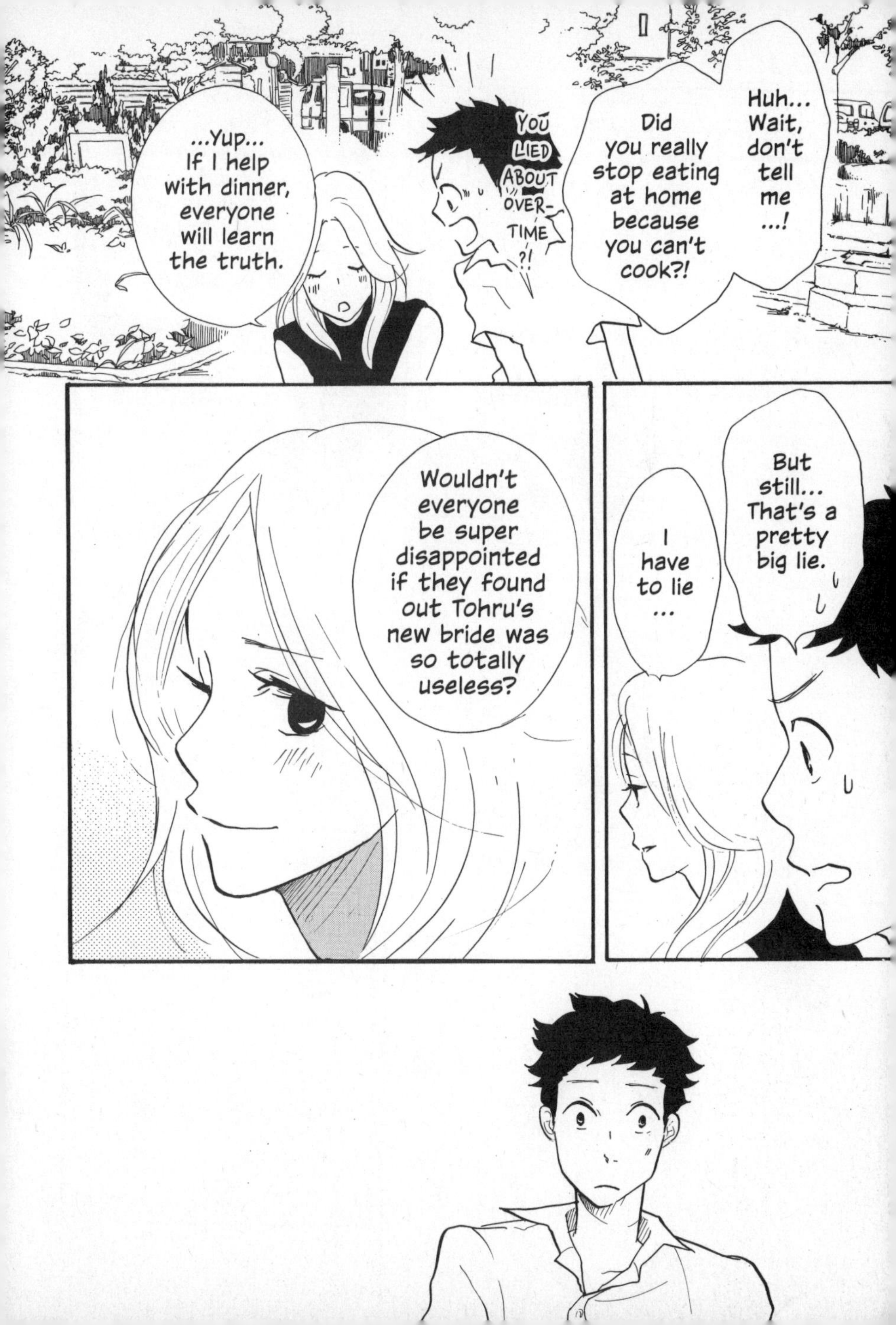
Huh... Wait, don't tell me ...!
Did you really stop eating at home because you can't cook?!
YOU LIED ABOUT OVER-TIME?!
...Yup... If I help with dinner, everyone will learn the truth.
But still... That's a pretty big lie.
I have to lie ...
Wouldn't everyone be super disappointed if they found out Tohru's new bride was so totally useless?

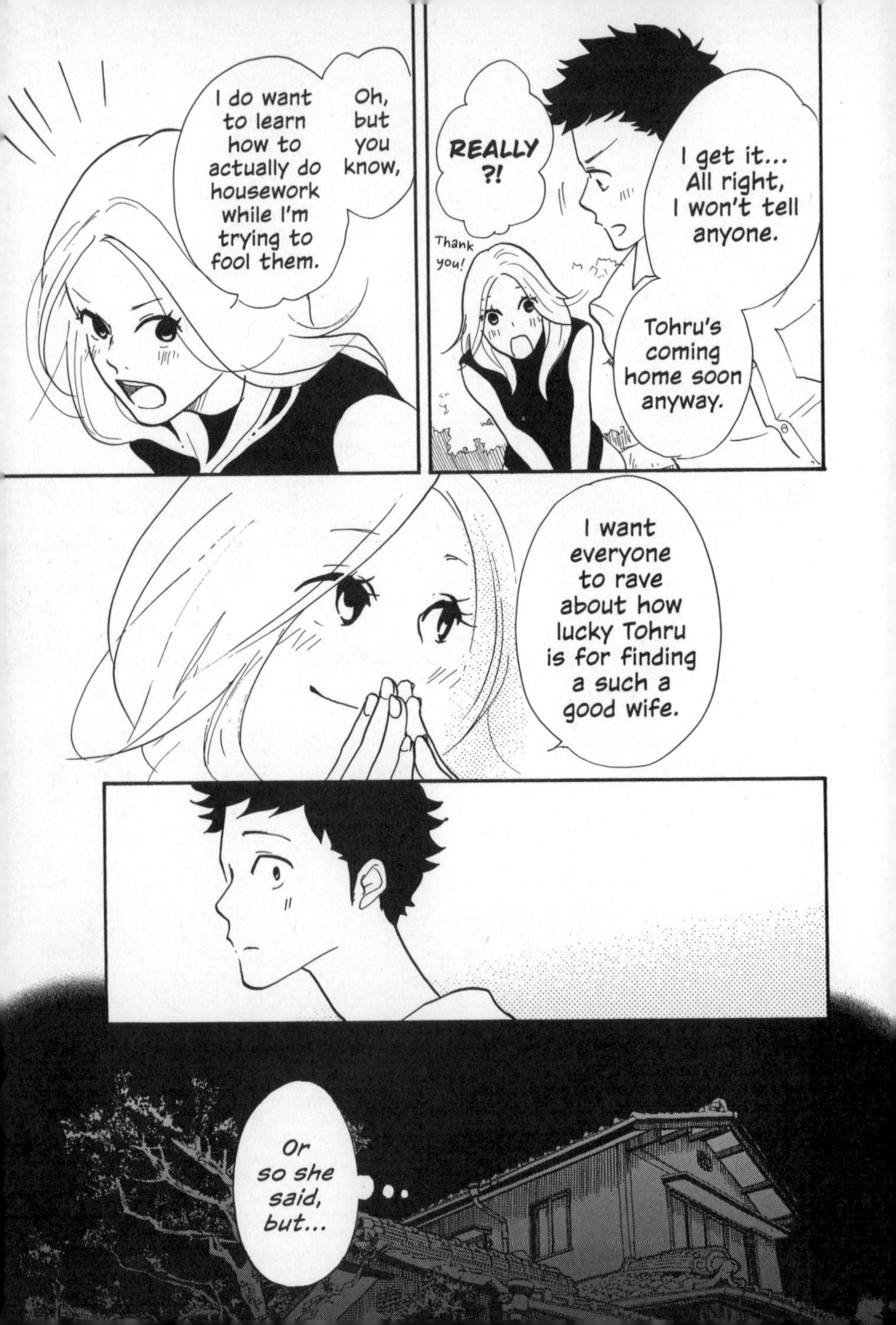
I get it... All right, I won't tell anyone.
REALLY ?!
Thank you!
Tohru's coming home soon anyway.
Oh, but you know,
I do want to learn how to actually do housework while I'm trying to fool them.
I want everyone to rave about how lucky Tohru is for finding a such a good wife.
Or so she said, but...

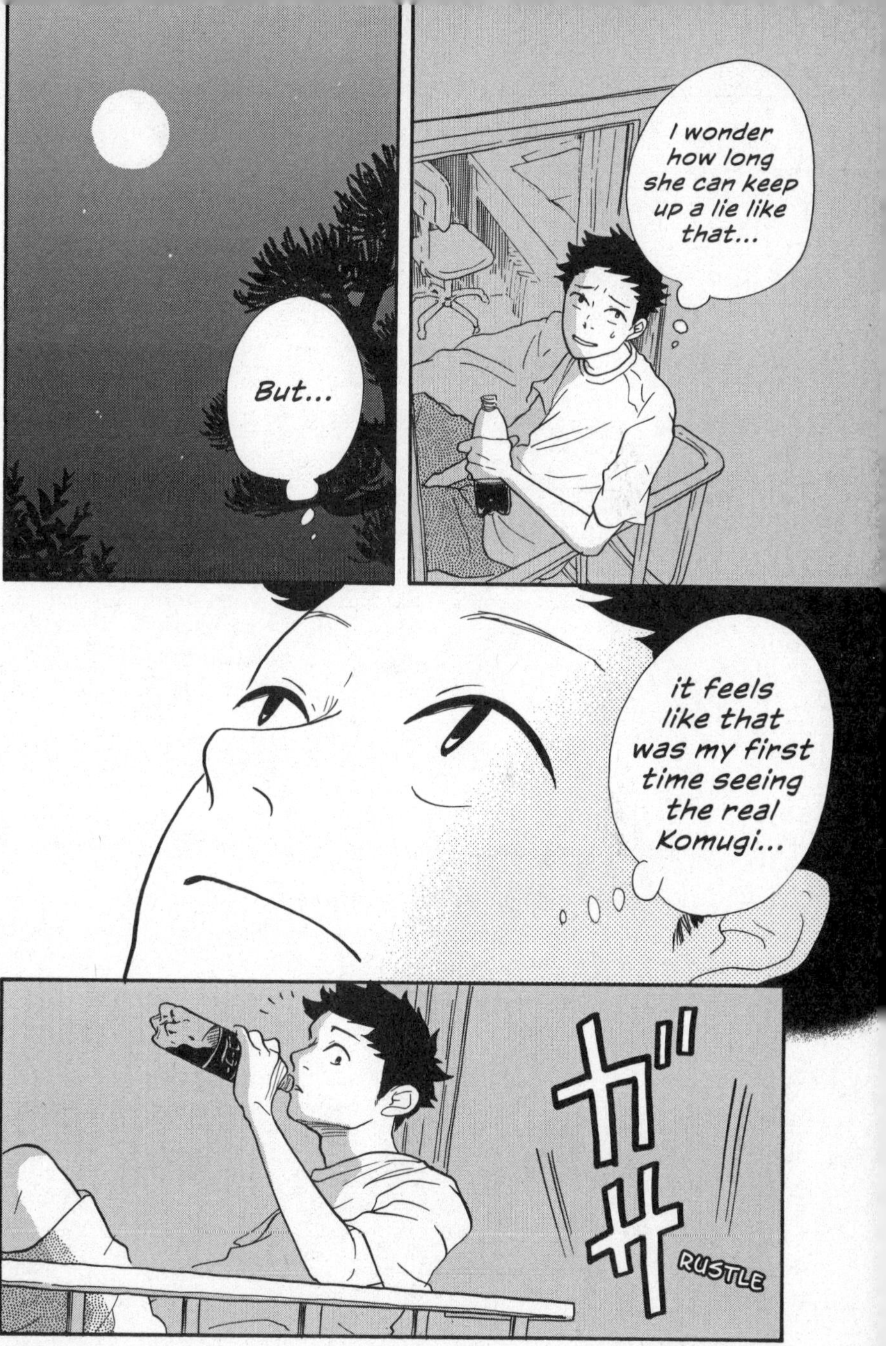
I wonder how long she can keep up a lie like that...
But...
it feels like that was my first time seeing the real Komugi...
ガサ
RUSTLE

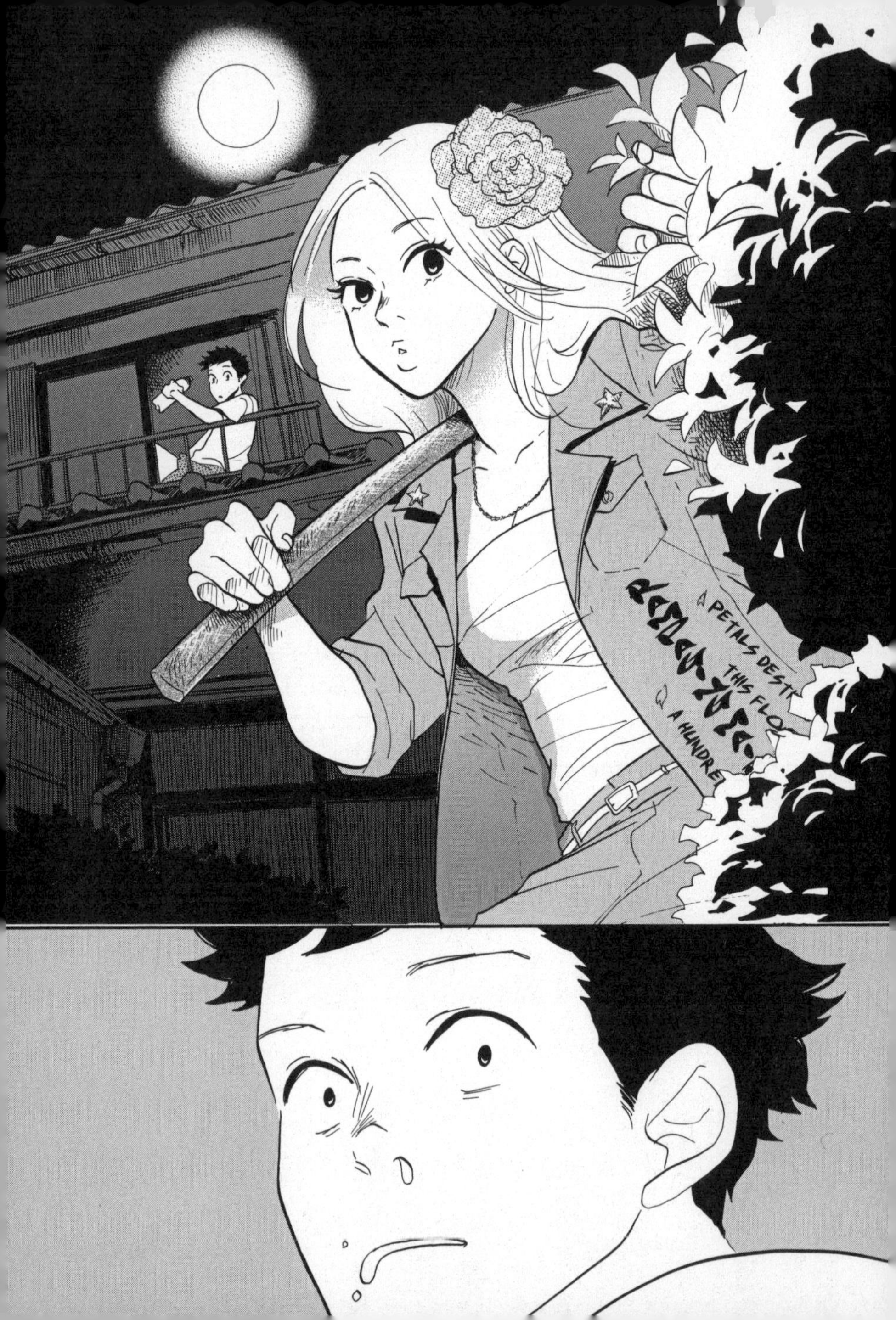
PETALS DEST
THIS FLO
A HUNDRE

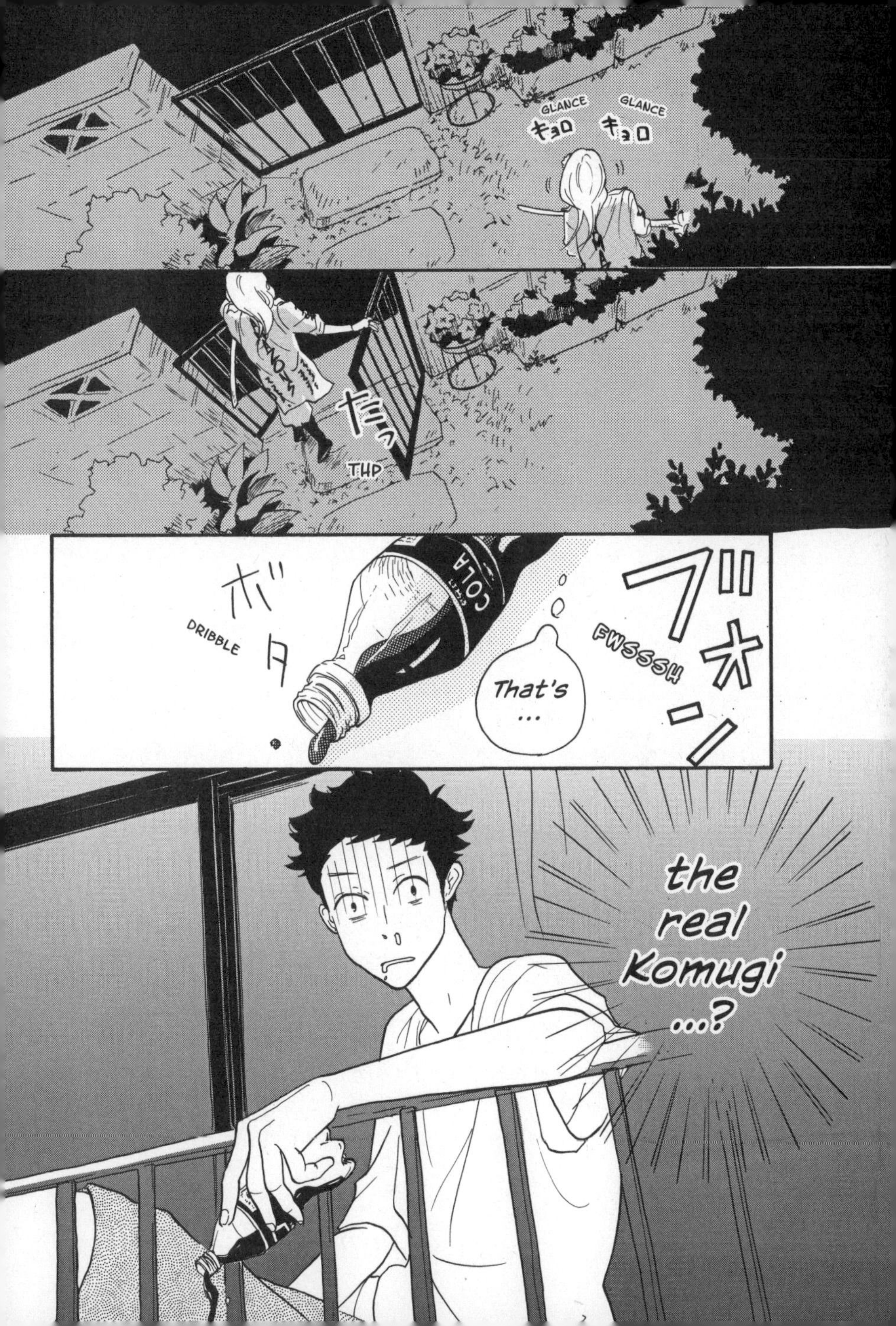
GLANCE
キョロ
GLANCE
キョロ
タッ
THP
ブオーン
FWSSSH
That's ...
ボタ
DRIBBLE
COLA
the real Komugi ...?

2
LATE NIGHT GIRLS' PARTY

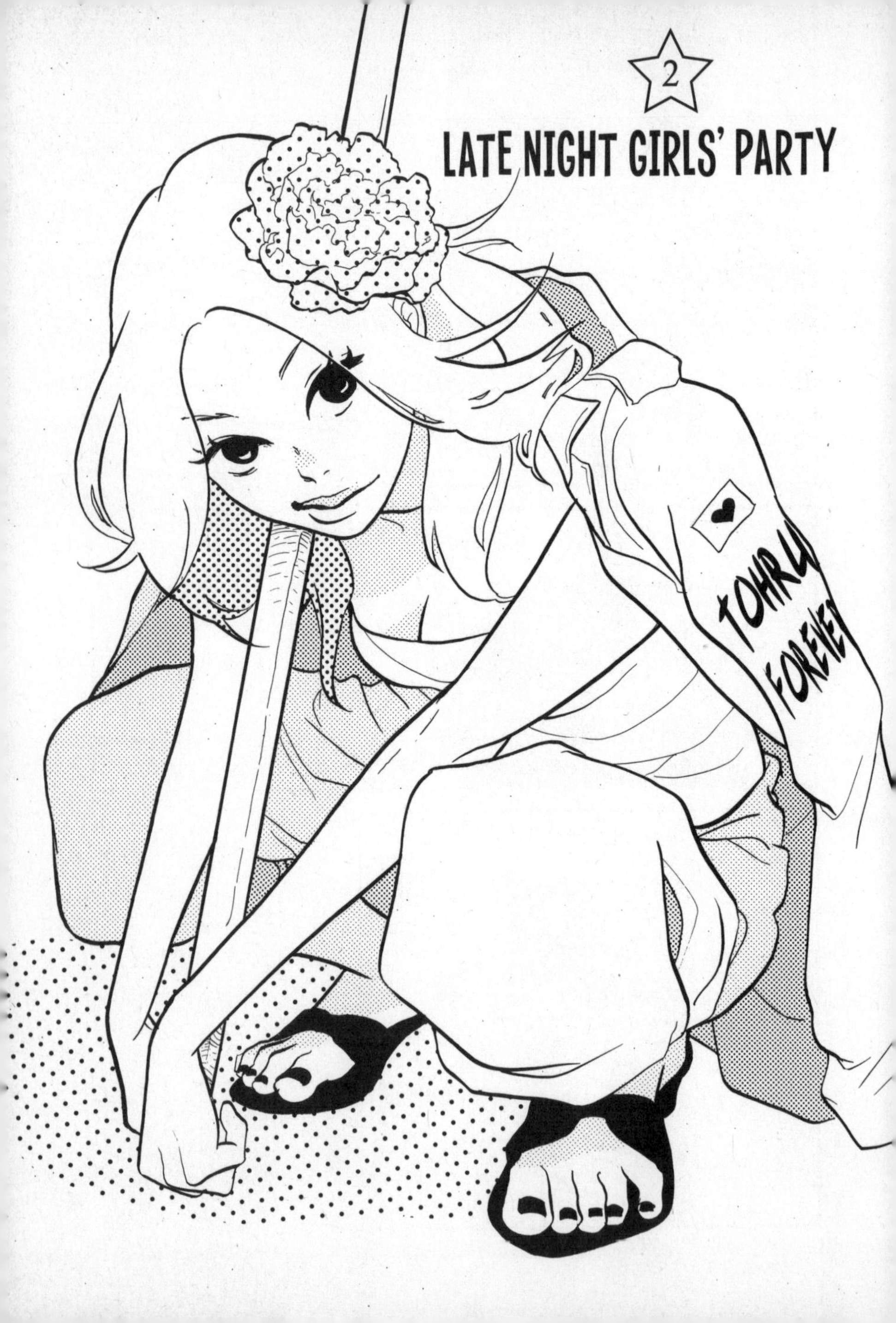

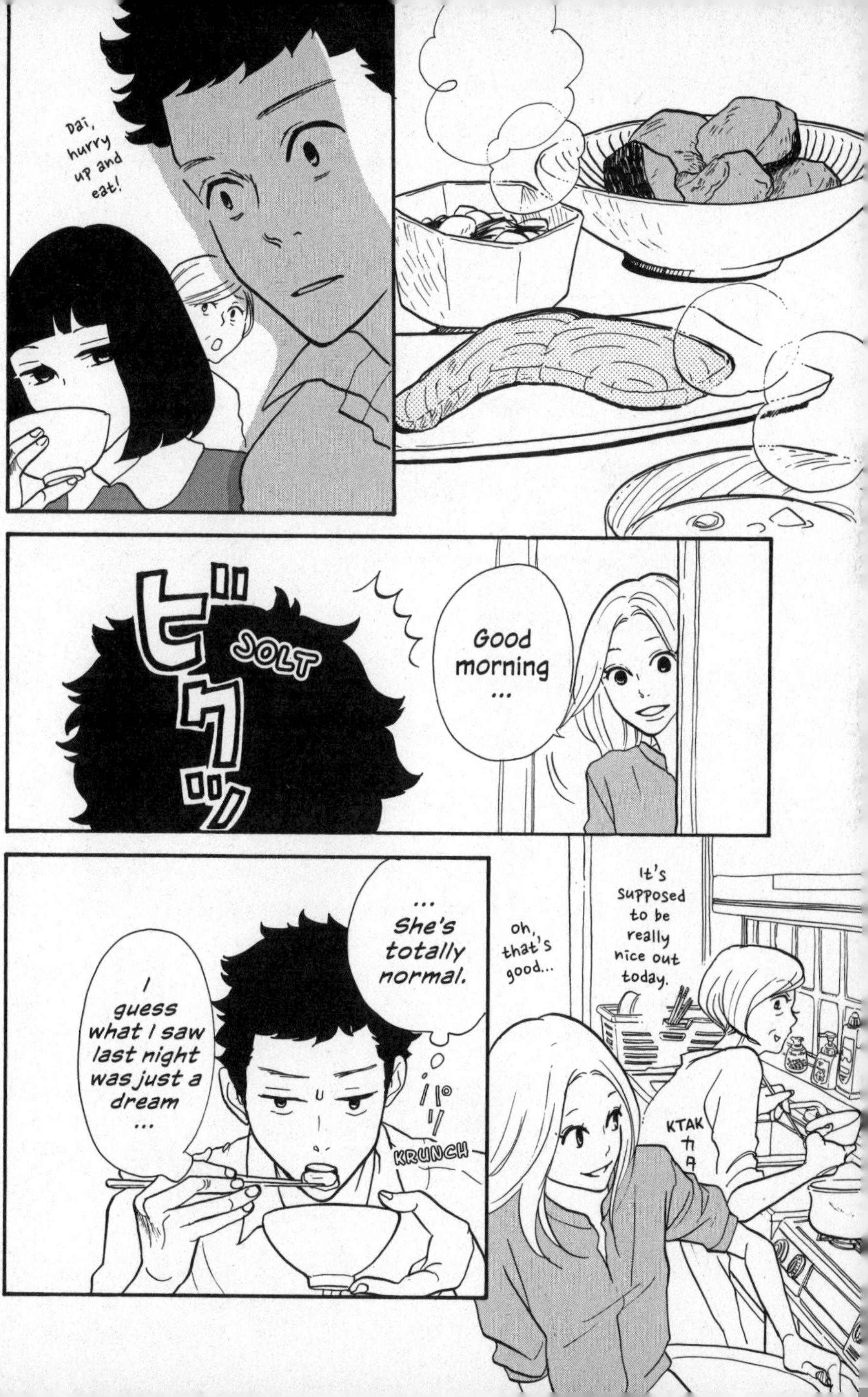
Dai, hurry up and eat!
Good morning ...
ビクッ
JOLT
It's supposed to be really nice out today.
KTAK
カタ
Oh, that's good...
... She's totally normal.
I guess what I saw last night was just a dream ...
パリ
KRUNCH

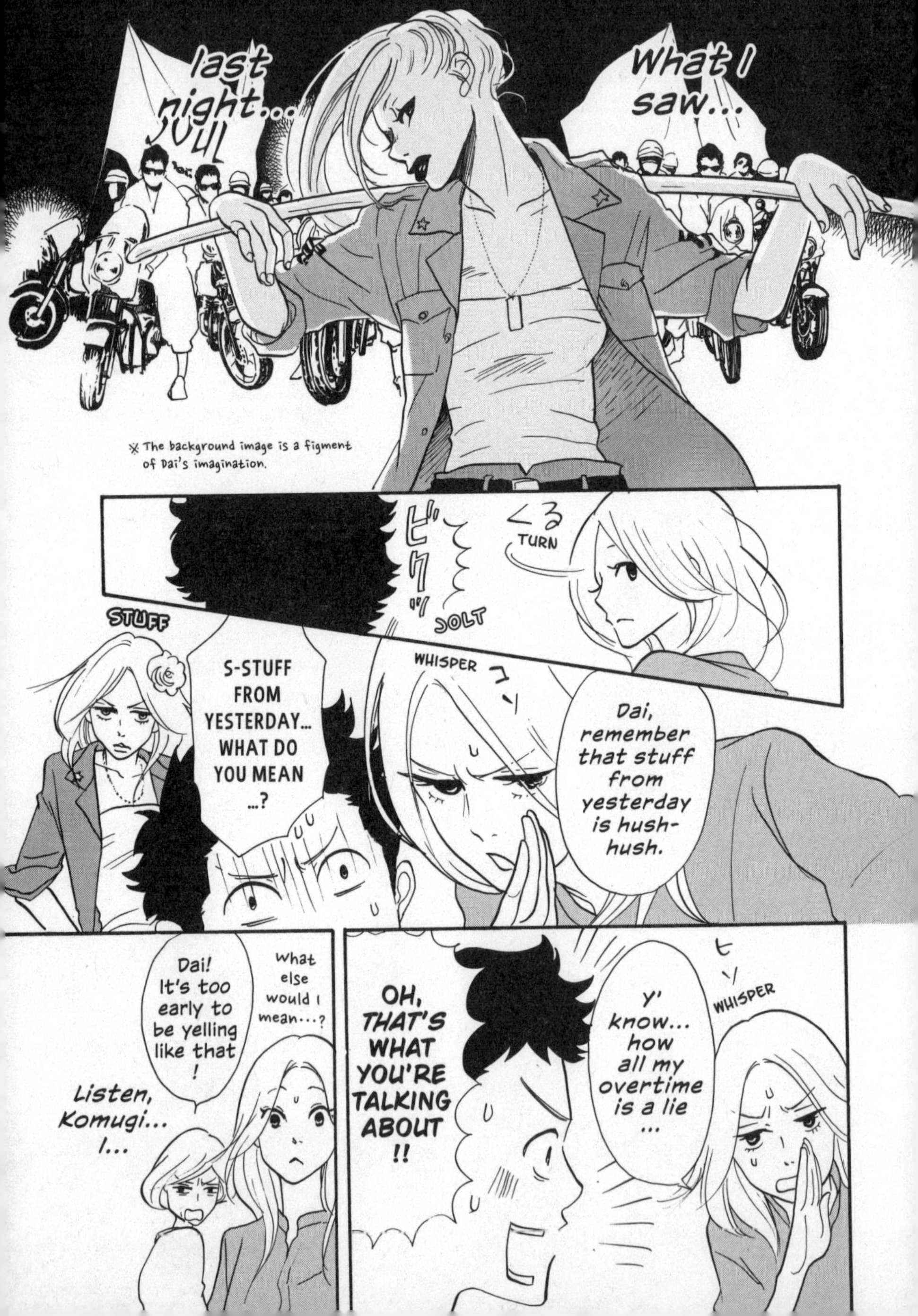
What I saw...
last night...
※ The background image is a figment of Dai's imagination.
くる
TURN
ビクッ
JOLT
WHISPER
コソ
Dai, remember that stuff from yesterday is hush-hush.
S-STUFF FROM YESTERDAY... WHAT DO YOU MEAN ...?
STUFF
ヒソ
WHISPER
y' know... how all my overtime is a lie ...
OH, THAT'S WHAT YOU'RE TALKING ABOUT !!
What else would I mean...?
Dai! It's too early to be yelling like that!
Listen, Komugi... I...

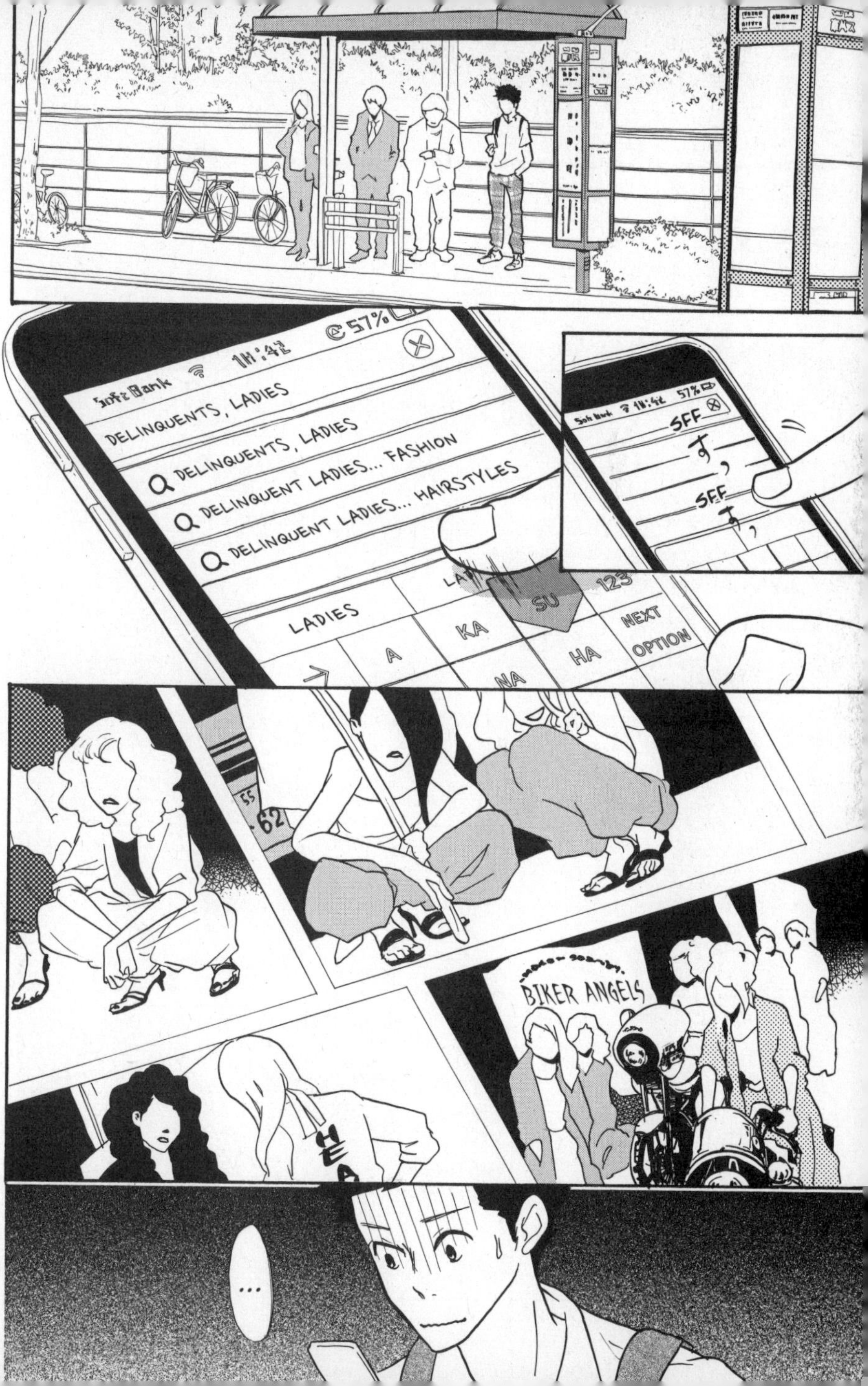

SFF
す,
SFF
す,
DELINQUENTS, LADIES
DELINQUENTS, LADIES
DELINQUENT LADIES... FASHION
DELINQUENT LADIES... HAIRSTYLES
LADIES
SU
123
A
KA
NA
HA
NEXT OPTION
BIKER ANGELS
...

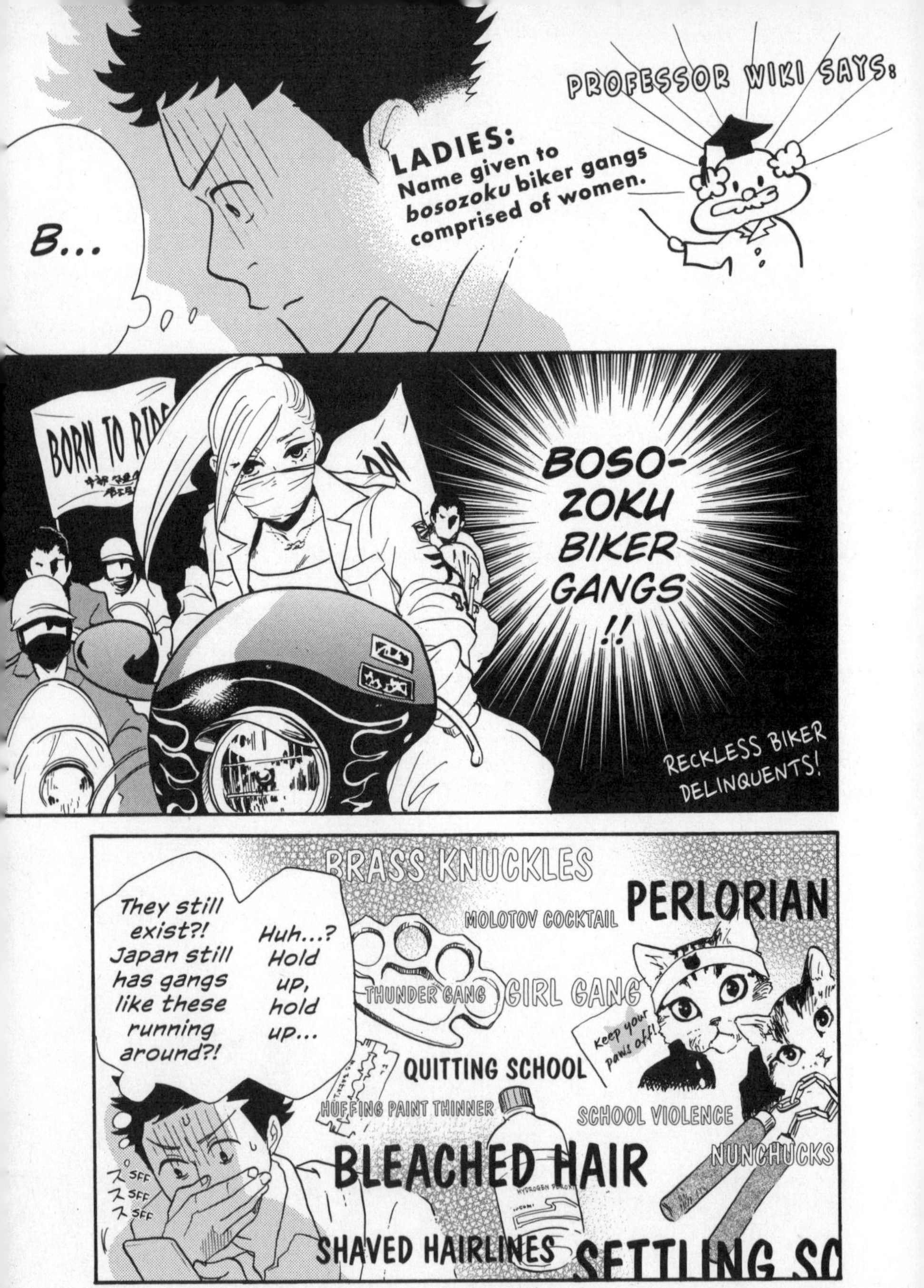
PROFESSOR WIKI SAYS:
LADIES: Name given to bosozoku biker gangs comprised of women.
B...
BOSO-ZOKU BIKER GANGS!!
RECKLESS BIKER DELINQUENTS!
BORN TO RIDE
BRASS KNUCKLES
PERLORIAN
MOLOTOV COCKTAIL
GIRL GANG
THUNDER GANG
Keep your paws off!
QUITTING SCHOOL
SCHOOL VIOLENCE
HUFFING PAINT THINNER
NUNCHUCKS
BLEACHED HAIR
SHAVED HAIRLINES
SETTLING SC
Huh...? Hold up, hold up...
They still exist?! Japan still has gangs like these running around?!
ス SFF
ス SFF
ス SFF

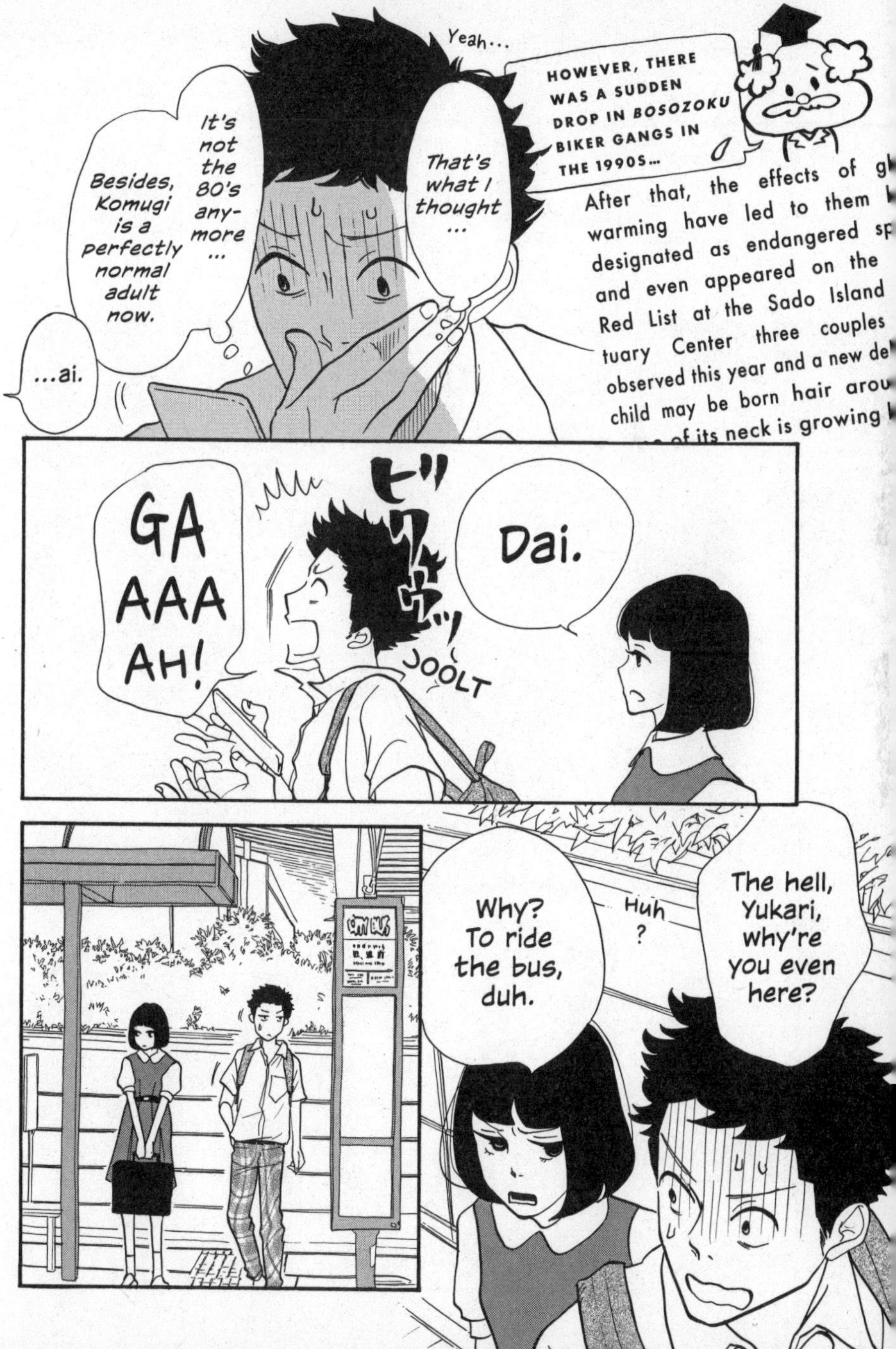
HOWEVER, THERE WAS A SUDDEN DROP IN *BOSOZOKU* BIKER GANGS IN THE 1990S...
After that, the effects of
warming have led to them
designated as endangered
and even appeared on the
Red List at the Sado Island
tuary Center three couples
observed this year and a new
child may be born hair
of its neck is growing
Yeah...
That's what I thought...
It's not the 80's anymore...
Besides, Komugi is a perfectly normal adult now.
...ai.
Dai.
ビリッ
JOOLT
GA AAA AH!
The hell, Yukari, why're you even here?
Huh?
Why? To ride the bus, duh.

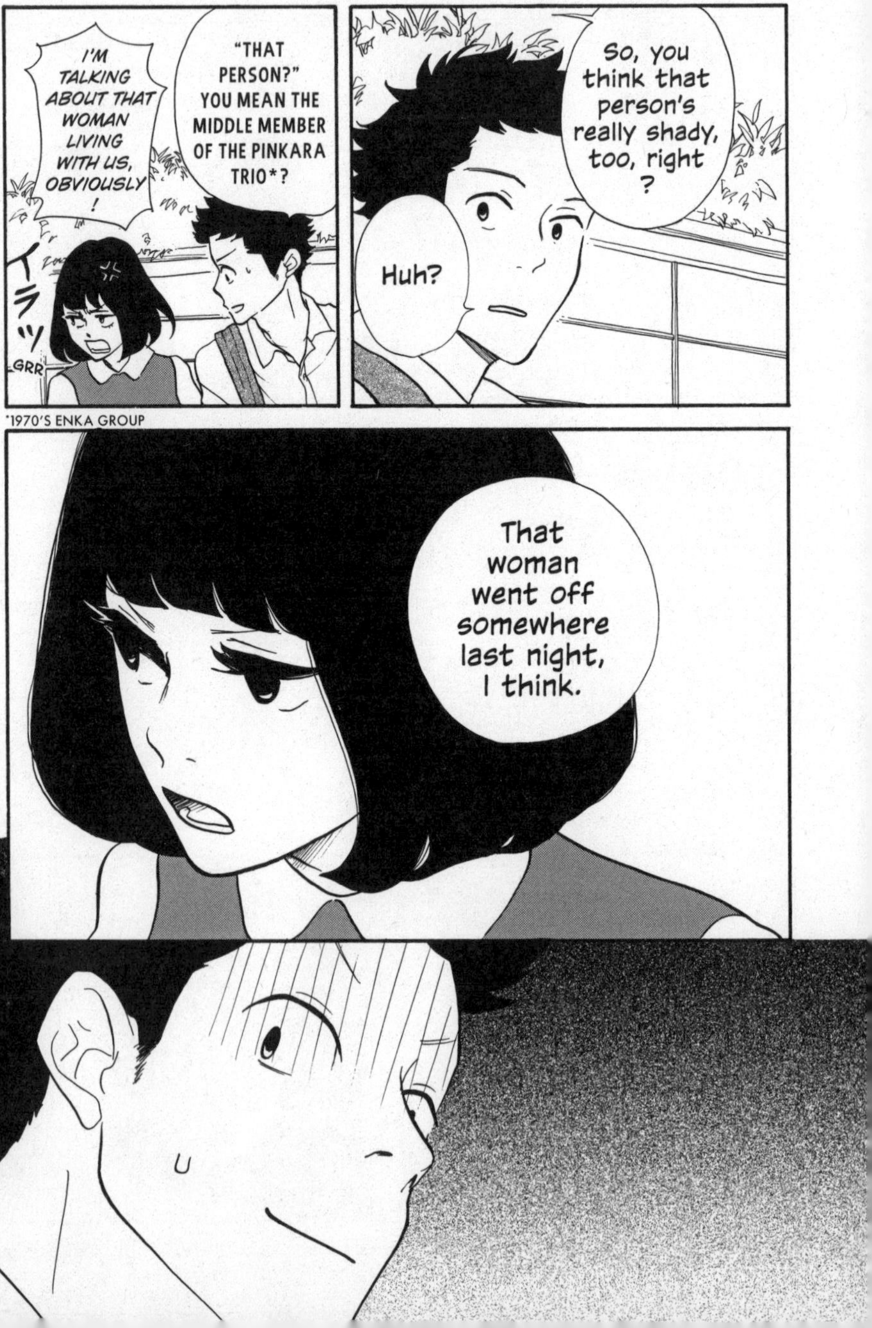
So, you think that person's really shady, too, right?
Huh?
"THAT PERSON?" YOU MEAN THE MIDDLE MEMBER OF THE PINKARA TRIO*?
I'M TALKING ABOUT THAT WOMAN LIVING WITH US, OBVIOUSLY!
イラッ
GRR
That woman went off somewhere last night, I think.
*1970'S ENKA GROUP

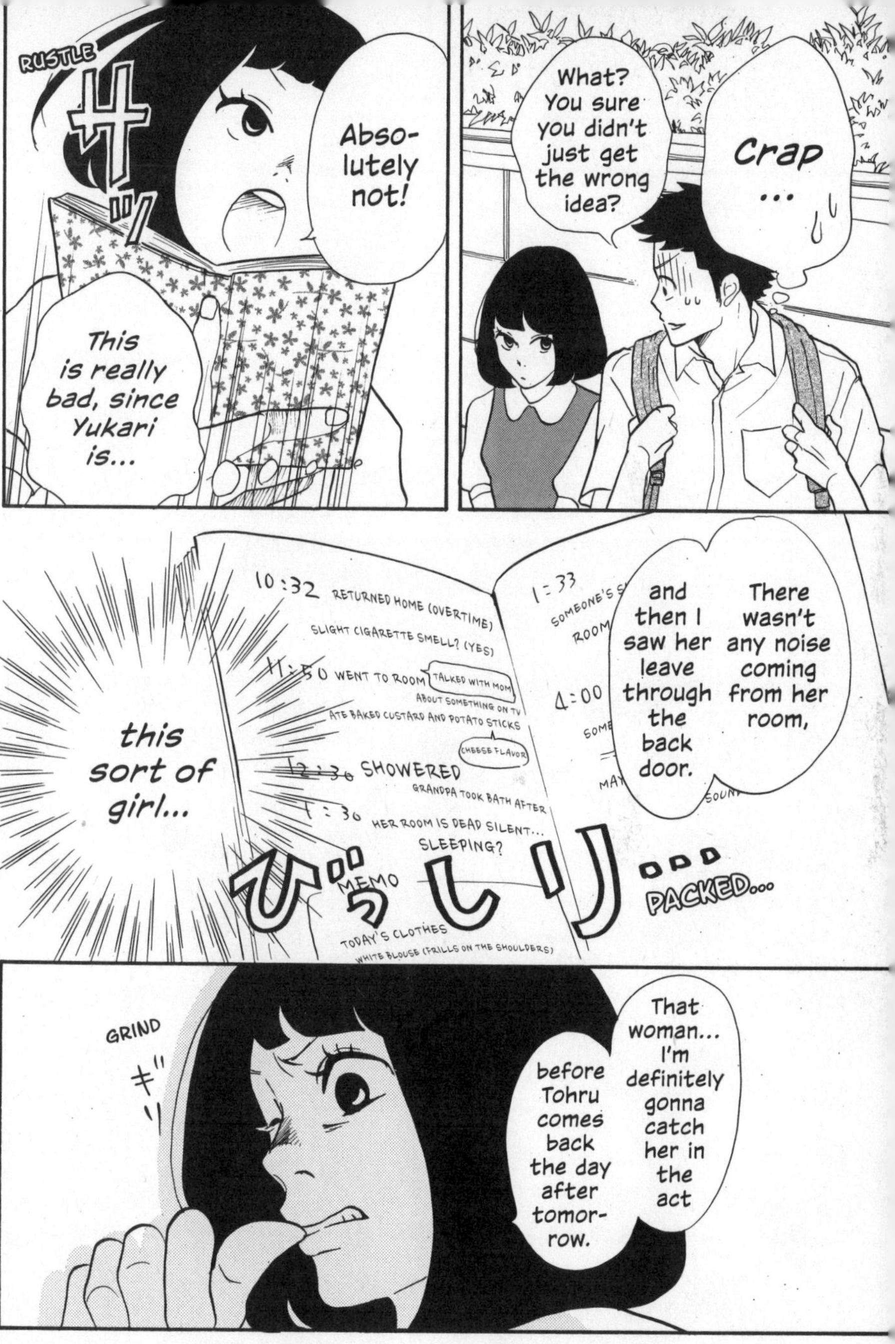

Crap...
What? You sure you didn't just get the wrong idea?
Absolutely not!
RUSTLE
This is really bad, since Yukari is...
There wasn't any noise coming from her room,
and then I saw her leave through the back door.
10:32 RETURNED HOME (OVERTIME)
SLIGHT CIGARETTE SMELL? (YES)
11:50 WENT TO ROOM
TALKED WITH MOM ABOUT SOMETHING ON TV
ATE BAKED CUSTARD AND POTATO STICKS
CHEESE FLAVOR
12:30 SHOWERED
GRANDPA TOOK BATH AFTER
1:30 HER ROOM IS DEAD SILENT... SLEEPING?
MEMO
TODAY'S CLOTHES
WHITE BLOUSE (FRILLS ON THE SHOULDERS)
1:33
4:00
this sort of girl...
PACKED...
That woman... I'm definitely gonna catch her in the act
before Tohru comes back the day after tomorrow.
GRIND

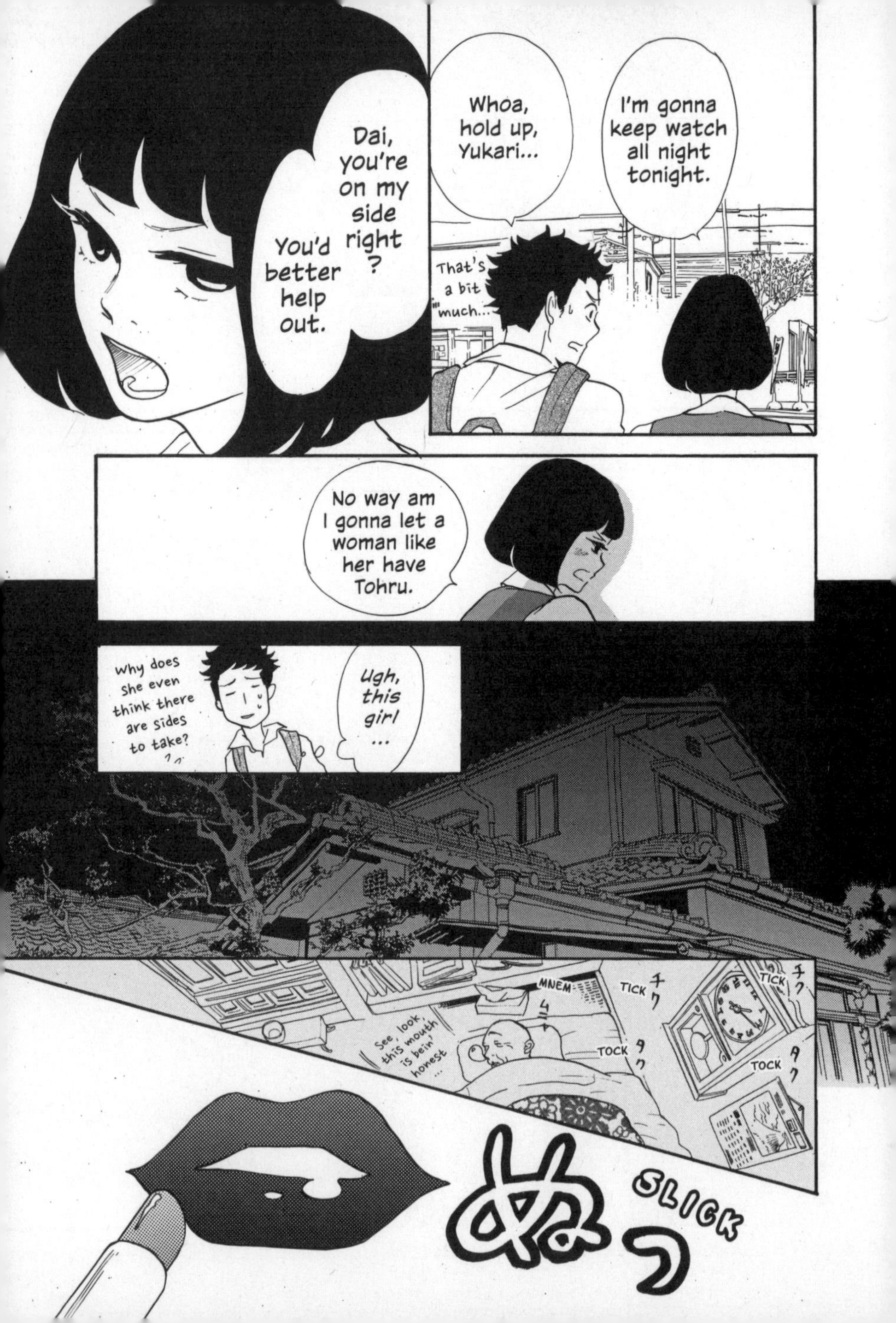

I'm gonna keep watch all night tonight.
Whoa, hold up, Yukari...
That's a bit much...
Dai, you're on my side right?
You'd better help out.
No way am I gonna let a woman like her have Tohru.
Ugh, this girl...
Why does she even think there are sides to take?
TICK
TICK
TOCK
TOCK
MNEM
See, look, this mouth is bein' honest...
ぬっ
SLICK

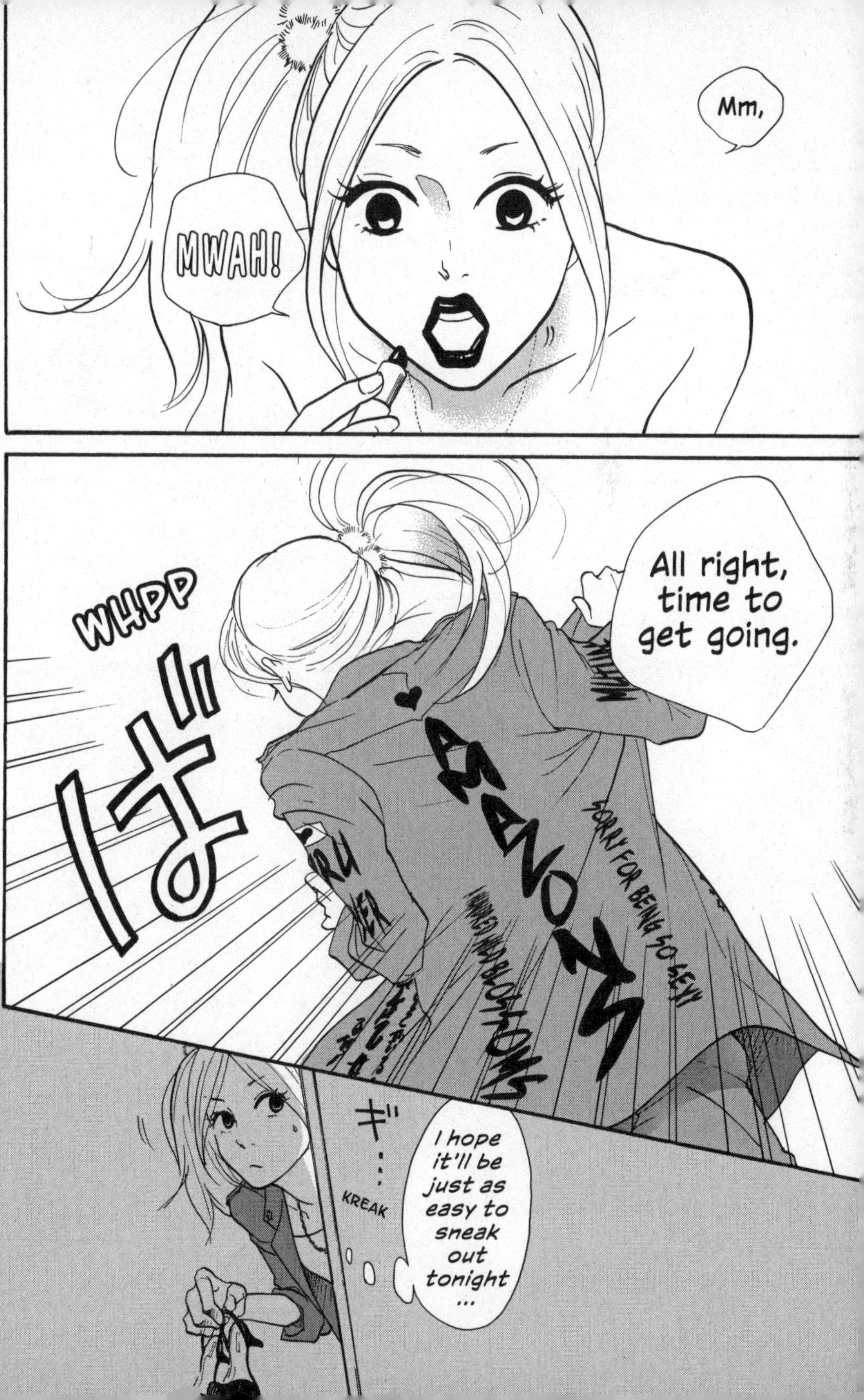
Mm,
MWAH!
All right, time to get going.
WHPP
ば
SORRY FOR BEING SO SEXY
ギ…
KREAK
I hope it'll be just as easy to sneak out tonight ...

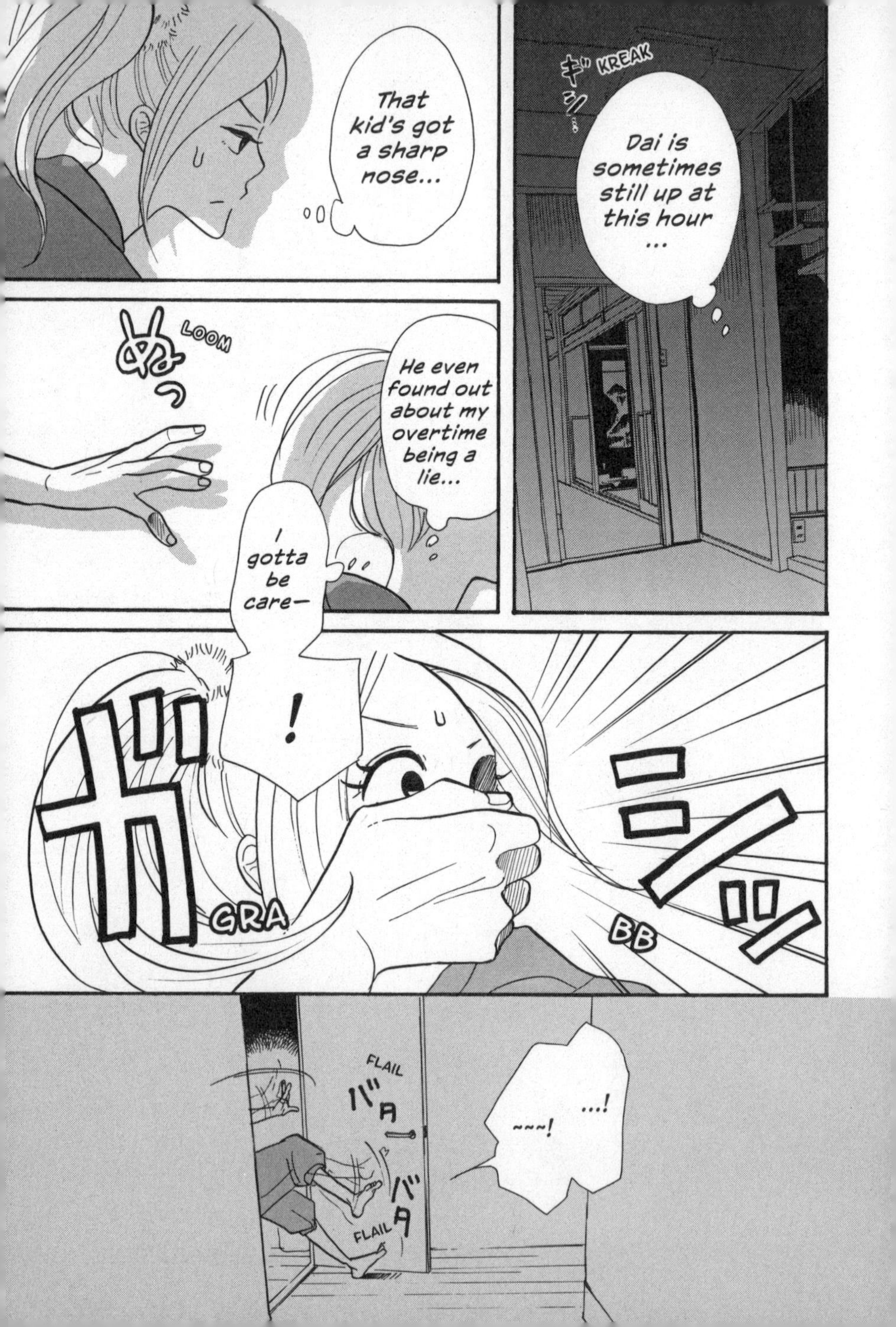
KREAK
Dai is sometimes still up at this hour ...
That kid's got a sharp nose...
LOOM
He even found out about my overtime being a lie...
I gotta be care—
!
GRA
BB
FLAIL
FLAIL
~~~!
...!
~~~

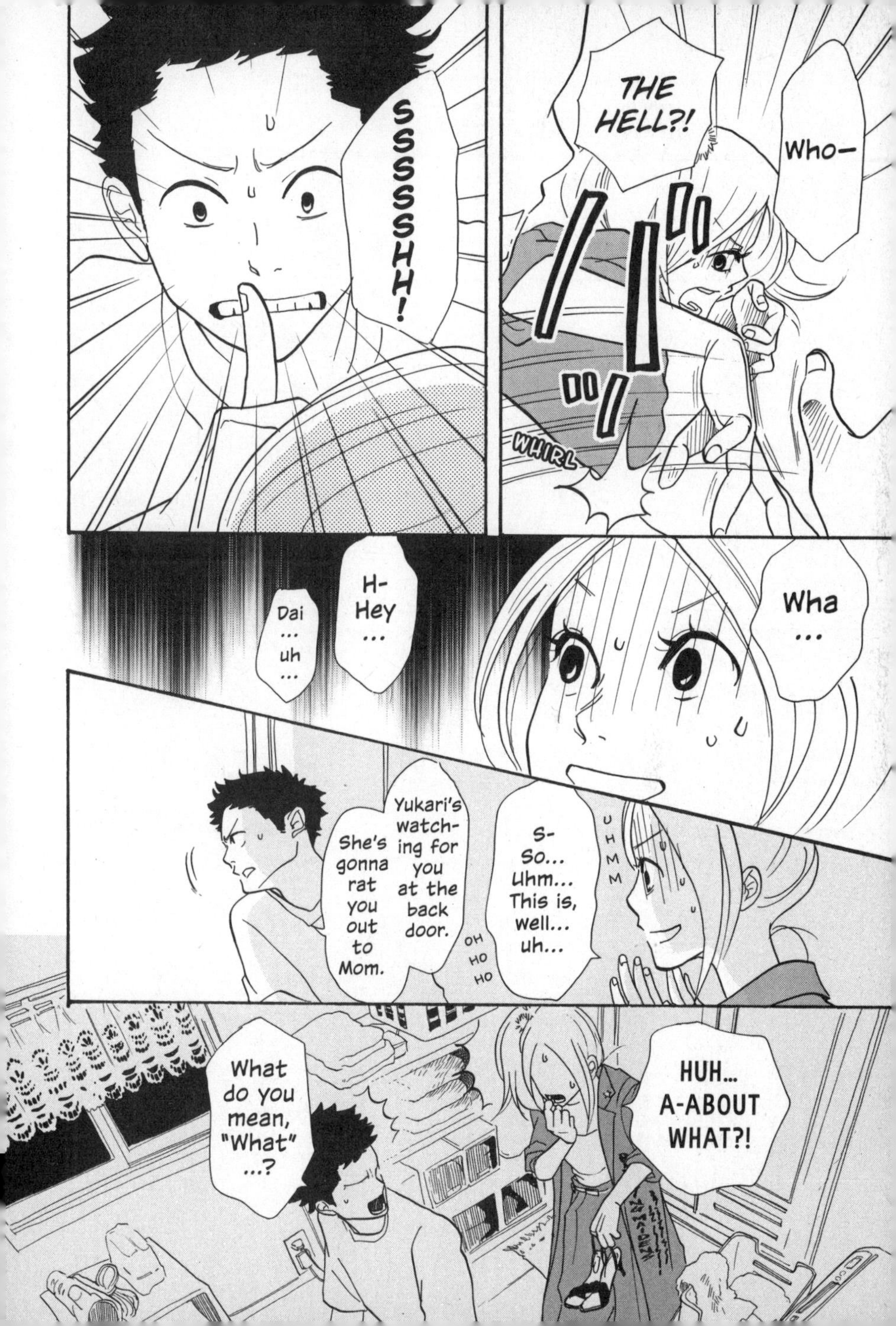
Who–
THE HELL?!
WHIRL
SSSSSHH!
Wha ...
H-Hey ...
Dai ... uh ...
UHMM
S-So... Uhm... This is, well... uh...
OH HO HO
Yukari's watching for you at the back door.
She's gonna rat you out to Mom.
HUH... A-ABOUT WHAT?!
What do you mean, "What" ...?

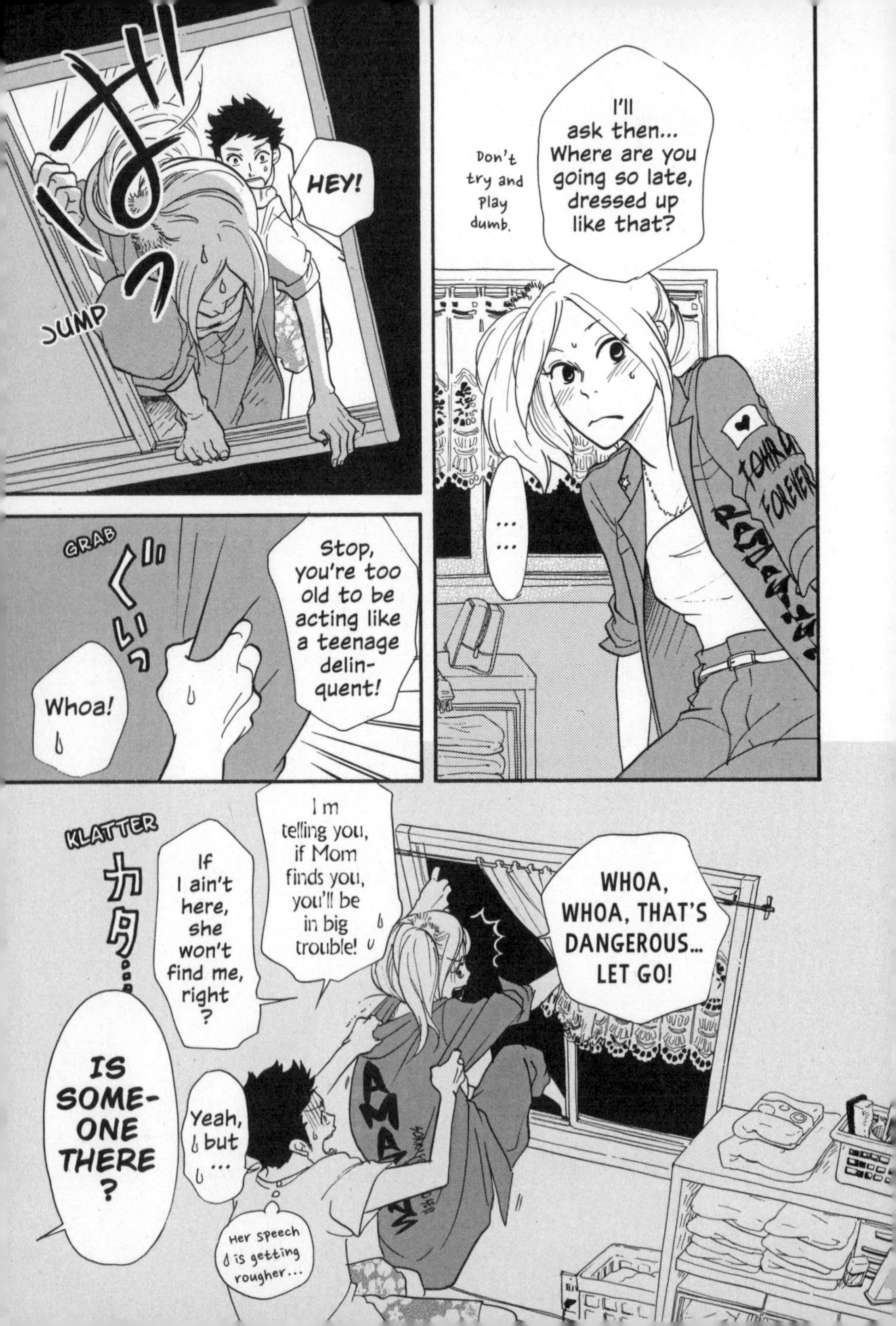
I'll ask then... Where are you going so late, dressed up like that?
Don't try and Play dumb.
... ...
HEY!
JUMP
Stop, you're too old to be acting like a teenage delin-quent!
GRAB
ぐいっ
Whoa!
WHOA, WHOA, THAT'S DANGEROUS... LET GO!
I'm telling you, if Mom finds you, you'll be in big trouble!
If I ain't here, she won't find me, right?
KLATTER
カタ...
IS SOME-ONE THERE?
Yeah, but ...
Her speech is getting rougher...

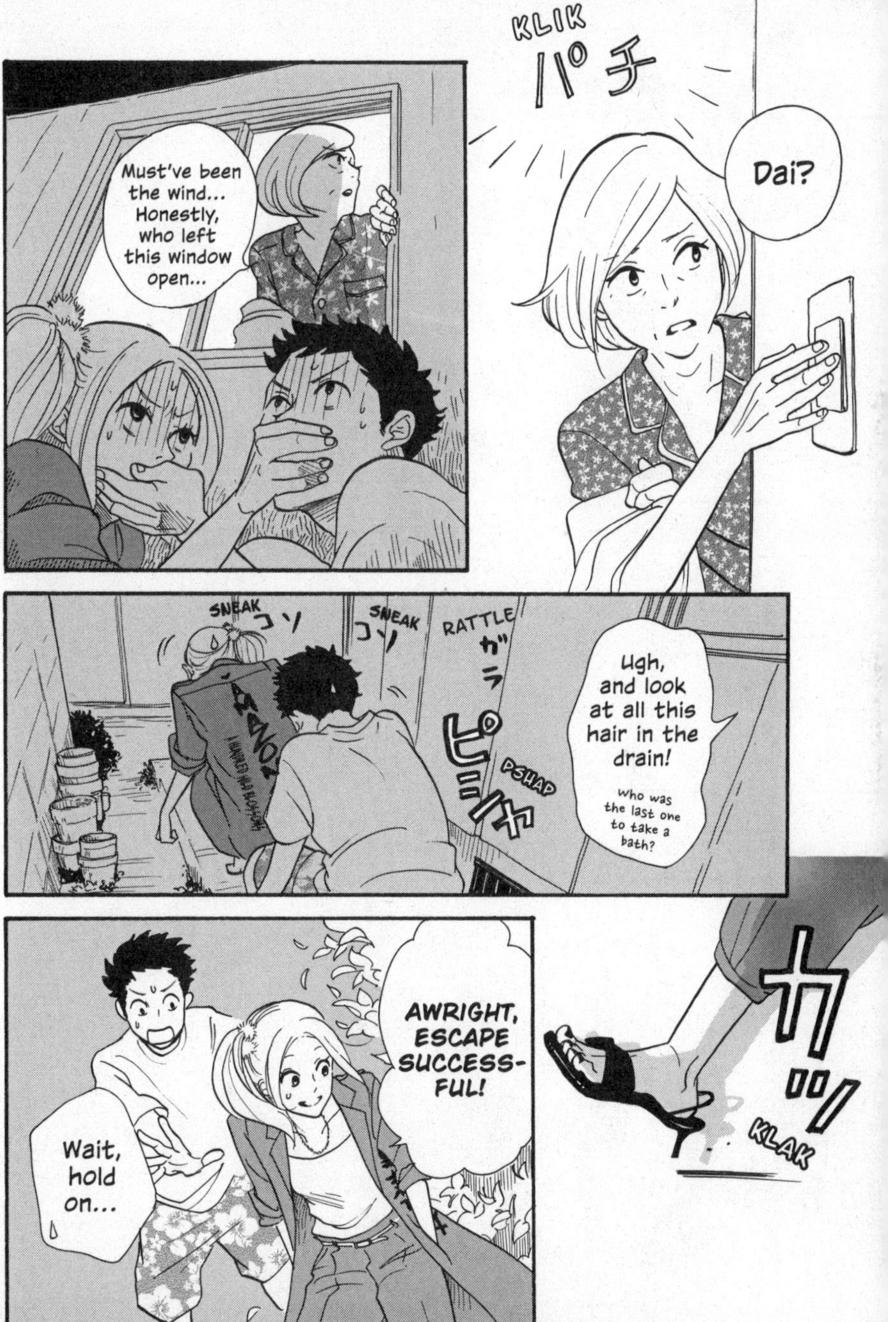
KLIK
パチ
Dai?
Must've been the wind... Honestly, who left this window open...
Ugh, and look at all this hair in the drain!
Who was the last one to take a bath?
RATTLE
ガラ
PSHAP
ピシャ
SNEAK
コソ
SNEAK
コソ
カッ
KLAK
AWRIGHT, ESCAPE SUCCESS-FUL!
Wait, hold on...

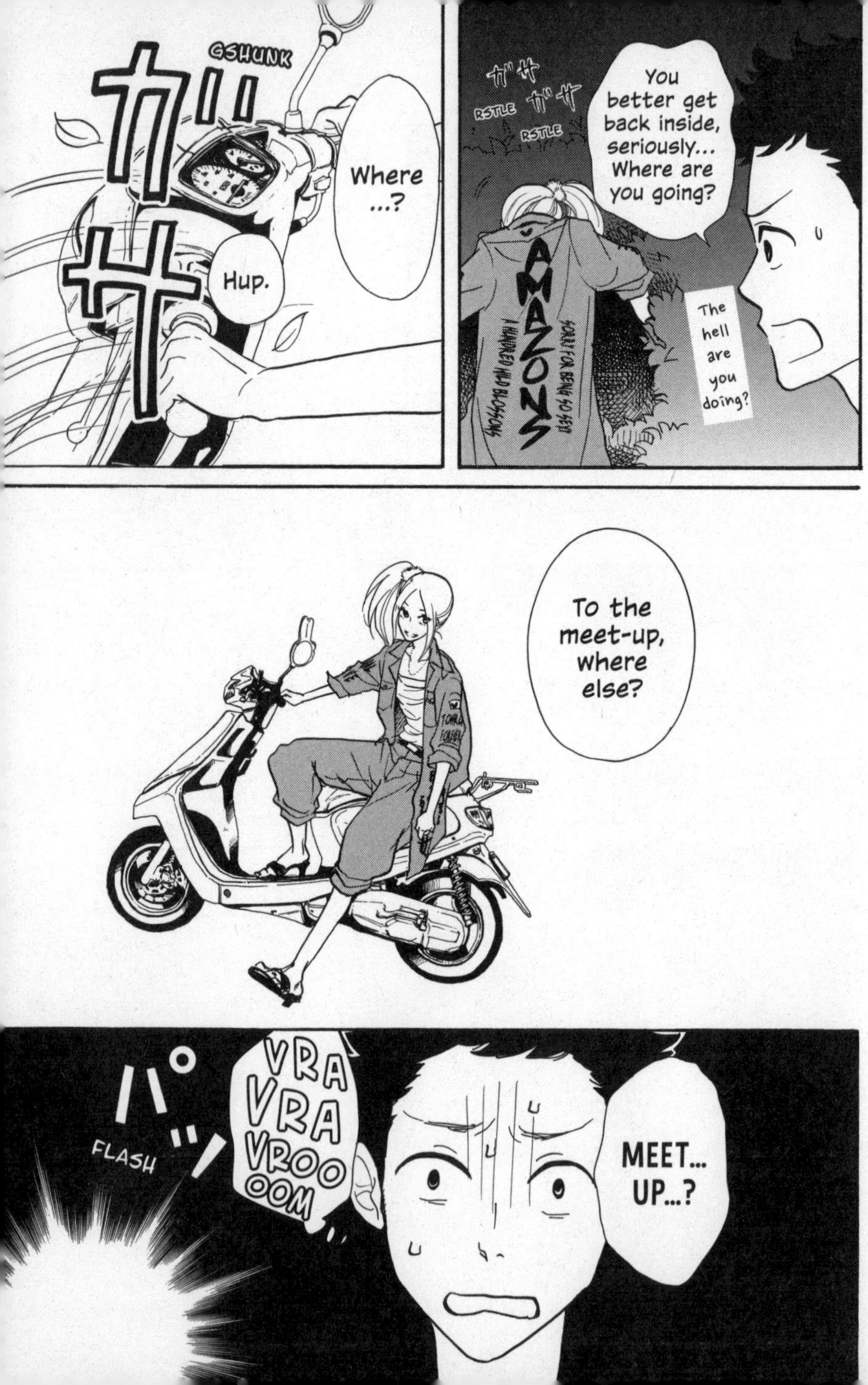
ガサ ガサ
RSTLE
RSTLE
You better get back inside, seriously... Where are you going?
The hell are you doing?
AMAZONS
GSHUNK
Where ...?
Hup.
To the meet-up, where else?
MEET... UP...?
VRA VRA VROOOOM
パッ
FLASH

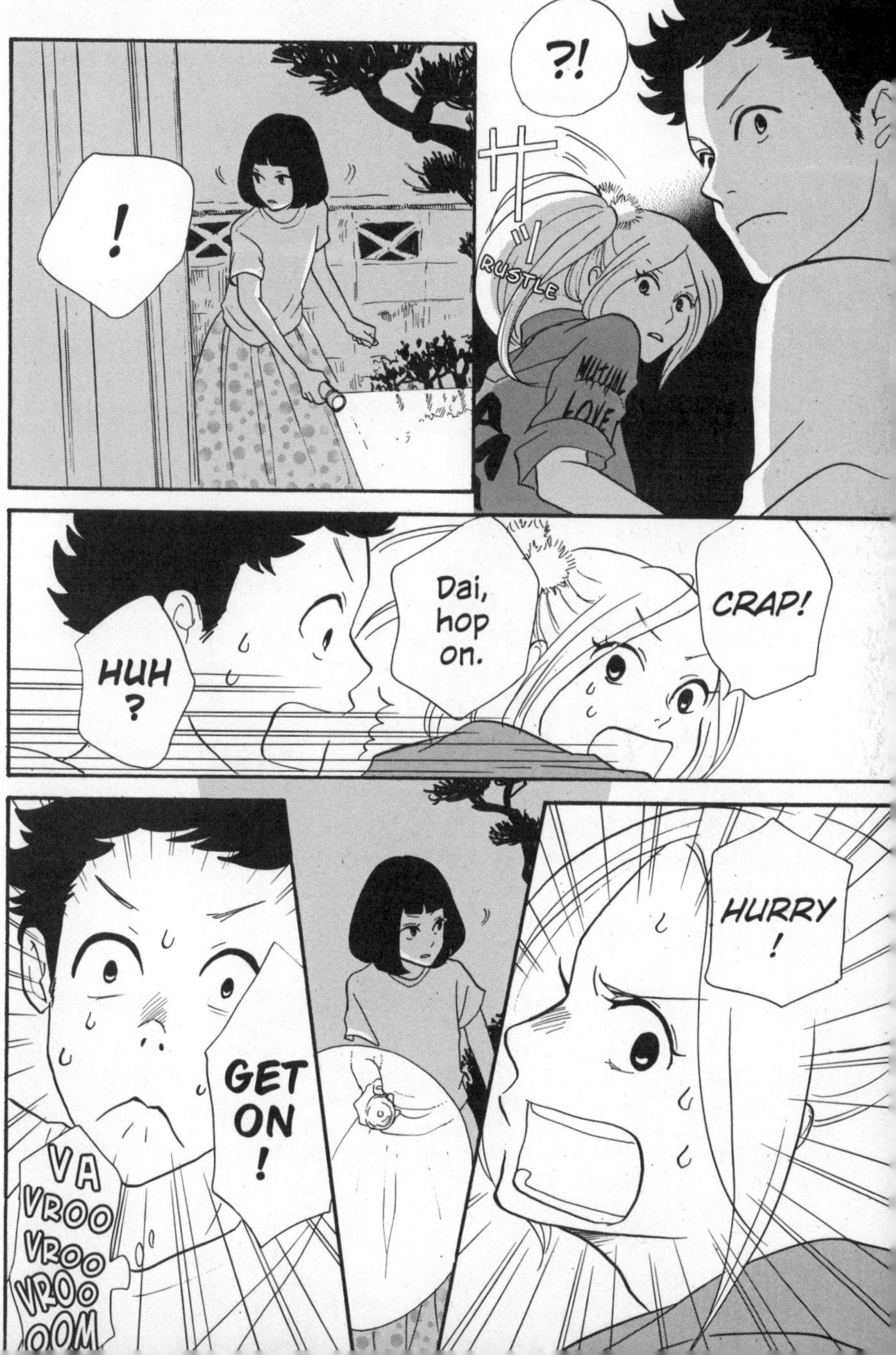
?!
RUSTLE
MUTUAL LOVE
!
CRAP!
Dai, hop on.
HUH ?
HURRY !
GET ON !
VA VROO VROO VROOOOM

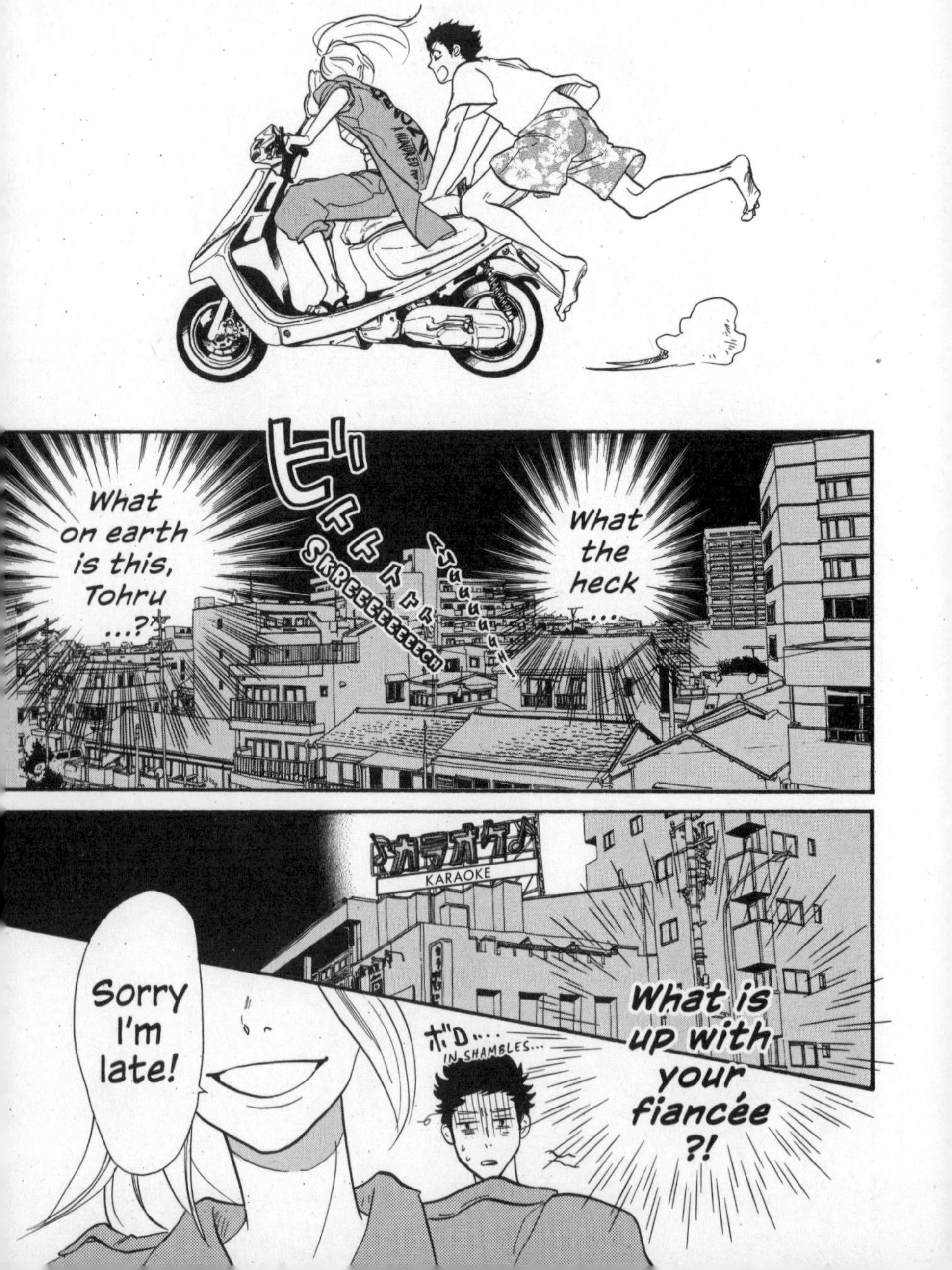

What the heck ...
SKREEEEEEEEEECH
What on earth is this, Tohru ...?
What is up with your fiancée ?!
IN SHAMBLES...
KARAOKE
Sorry I'm late!

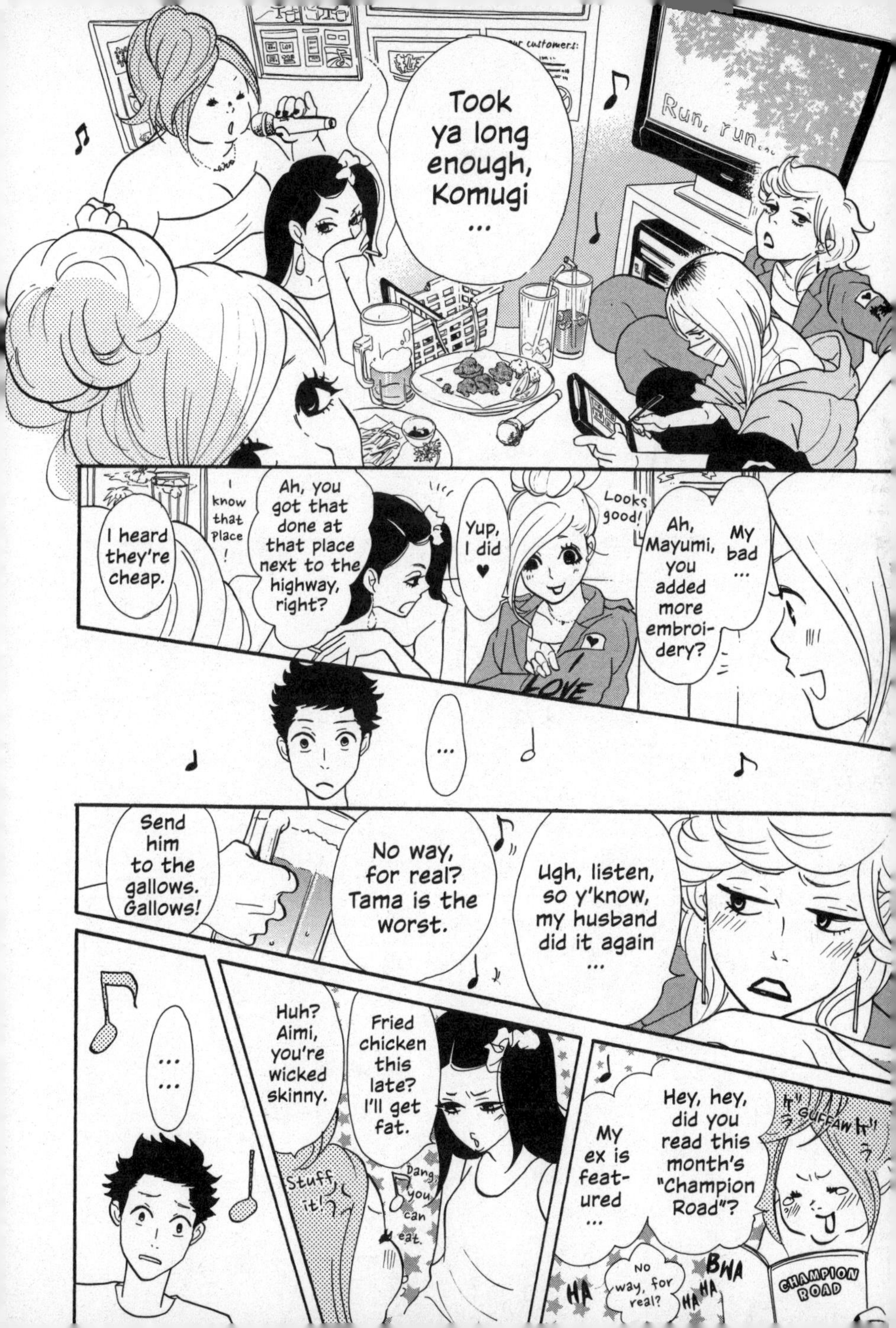
Run, run...
Took ya long enough, Komugi ...
My bad ...
Ah, Mayumi, you added more embroidery?
Looks good!
Yup, I did ♥
Ah, you got that done at that place next to the highway, right?
I know that place!
I heard they're cheap.
LOVE
...
Ugh, listen, so y'know, my husband did it again ...
No way, for real? Tama is the worst.
Send him to the gallows. Gallows!
GUFFAW
Hey, hey, did you read this month's "Champion Road"?
My ex is featured ...
CHAMPION ROAD
BWA HA HA HA HA
No way, for real?
Fried chicken this late? I'll get fat.
Huh? Aimi, you're wicked skinny.
Dang, you can eat.
Stuff it!
... ...

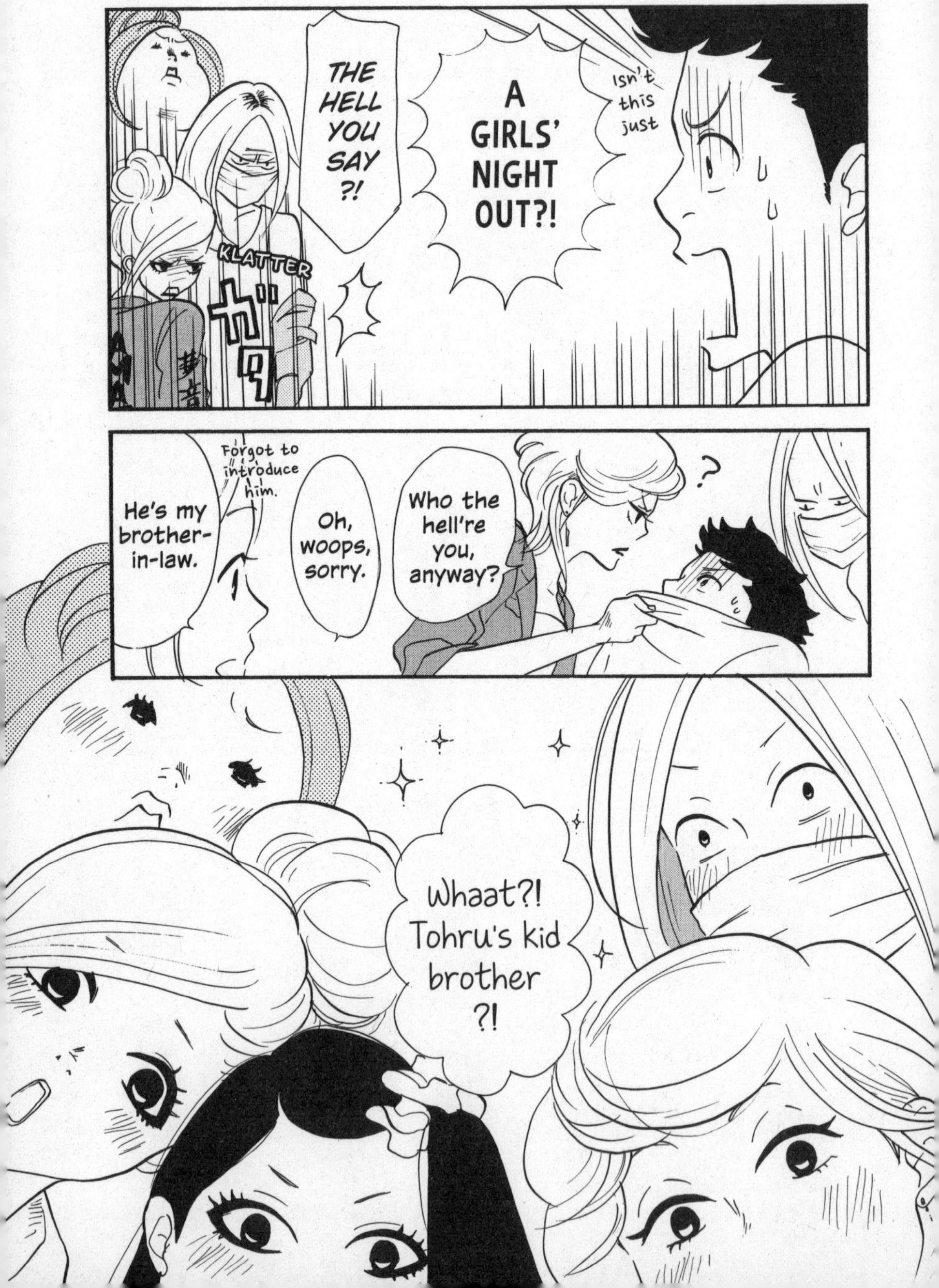
Isn't this just
A GIRLS' NIGHT OUT?!
THE HELL YOU SAY?!
KLATTER
Who the hell're you, anyway?
Oh, woops, sorry.
Forgot to introduce him.
He's my brother-in-law.
Whaat?! Tohru's kid brother ?!

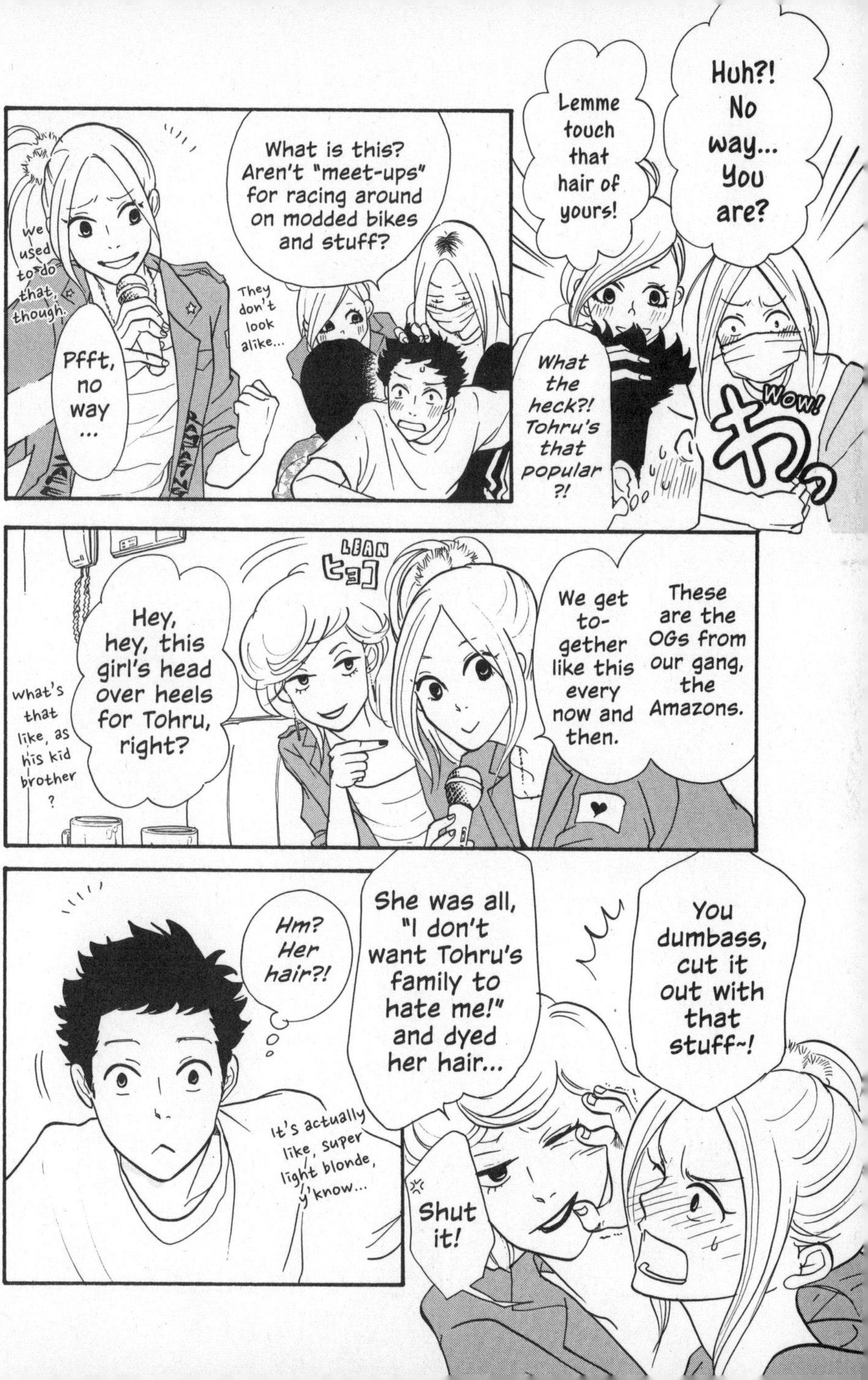
Huh?! No way... You are?
Lemme touch that hair of yours!
What the heck?! Tohru's that popular?!
WOW!
わっ
What is this? Aren't "meet-ups" for racing around on modded bikes and stuff?
They don't look alike...
We used to do that, though.
Pfft, no way...
These are the OGs from our gang, the Amazons.
We get to-gether like this every now and then.
LEAN
ヒョコ
Hey, hey, this girl's head over heels for Tohru, right?
what's that like, as his kid brother?
You dumbass, cut it out with that stuff~!
She was all, "I don't want Tohru's family to hate me!" and dyed her hair...
Hm? Her hair?!
It's actually like, super light blonde, y'know...
Shut it!

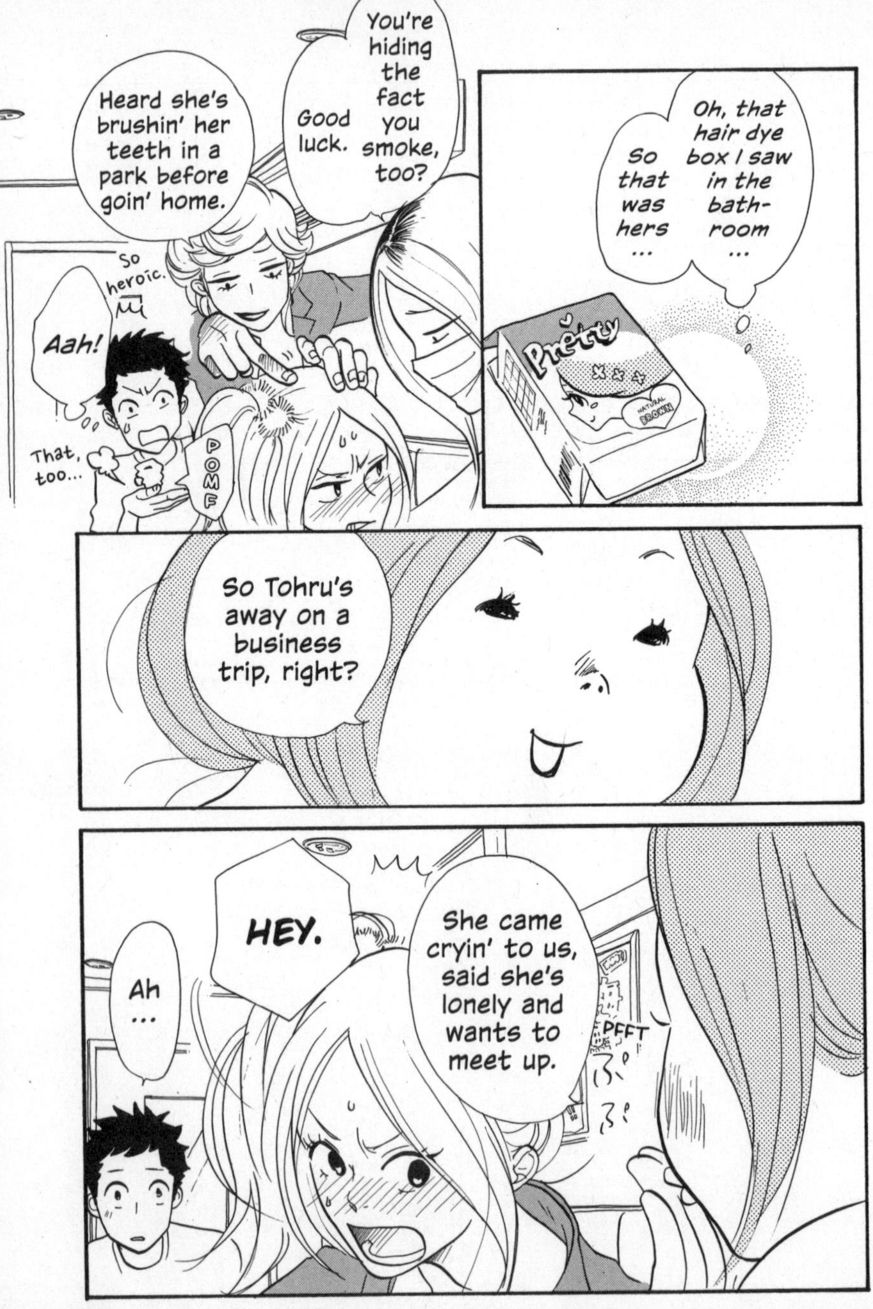

Oh, that hair dye box I saw in the bath-room...
So that was hers...
Pretty
NATURAL BROWN
You're hiding the fact you smoke, too?
Good luck.
Heard she's brushin' her teeth in a park before goin' home.
So heroic.
Aah!
POMF
That, too...
So Tohru's away on a business trip, right?
She came cryin' to us, said she's lonely and wants to meet up.
HEY.
PFFT
Ah...

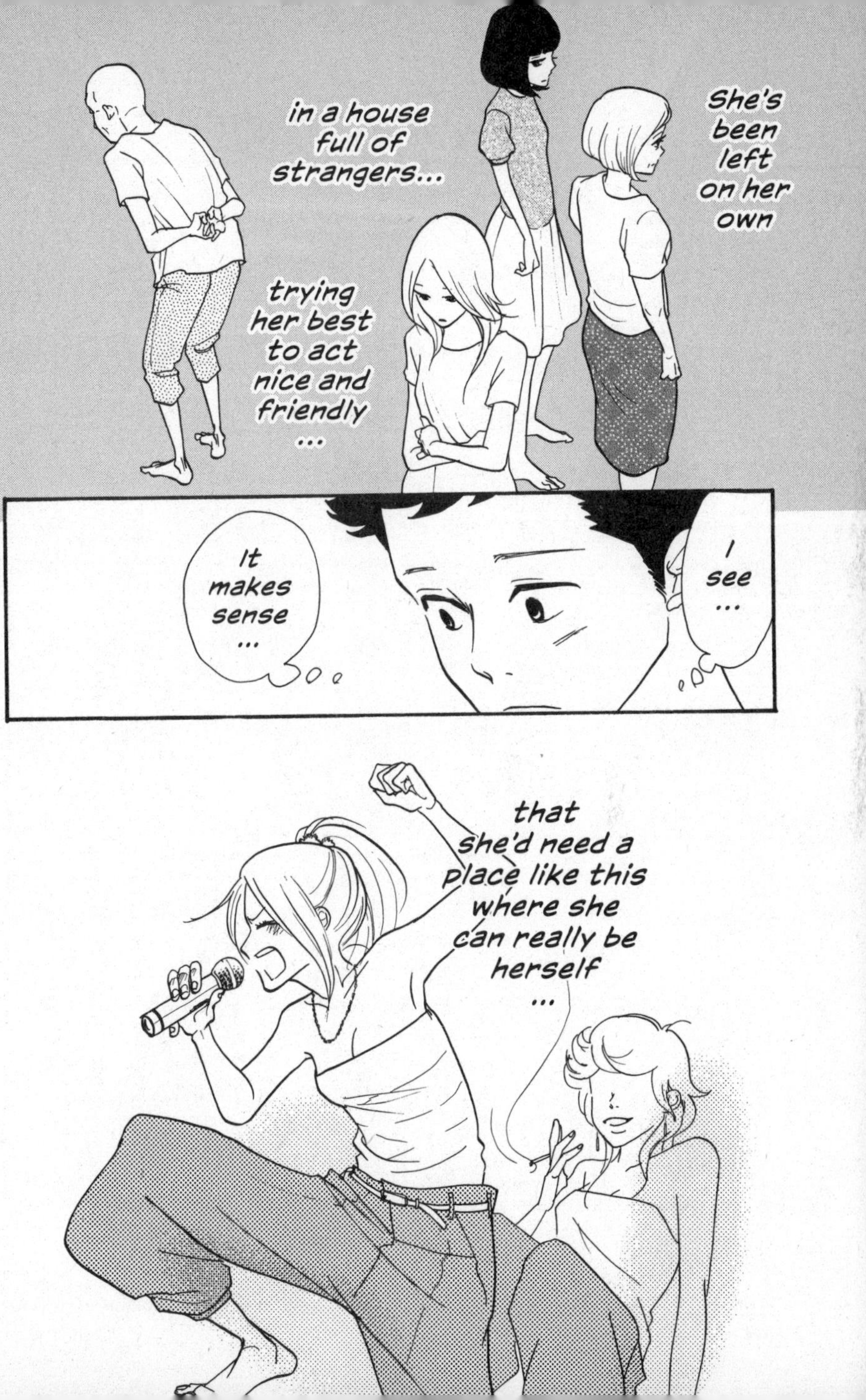
She's been left on her own
in a house full of strangers...
trying her best to act nice and friendly ...
I see ...
It makes sense ...
that she'd need a place like this where she can really be herself ...

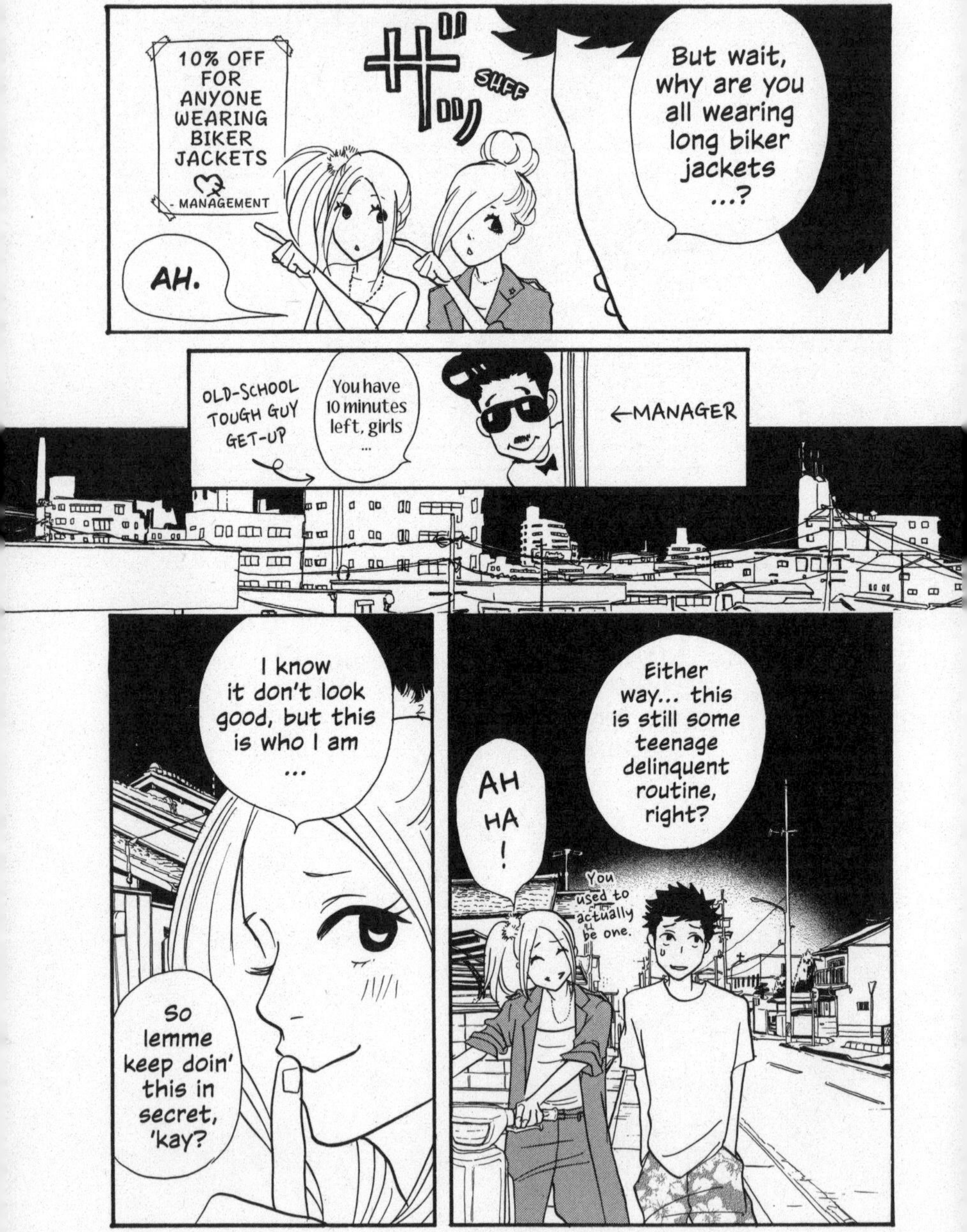
But wait, why are you all wearing long biker jackets ...?
SHFF
10% OFF FOR ANYONE WEARING BIKER JACKETS - MANAGEMENT
AH.
←MANAGER
You have 10 minutes left, girls ...
OLD-SCHOOL TOUGH GUY GET-UP
Either way... this is still some teenage delinquent routine, right?
AH HA !
You used to actually be one.
I know it don't look good, but this is who I am ...
So lemme keep doin' this in secret, 'kay?

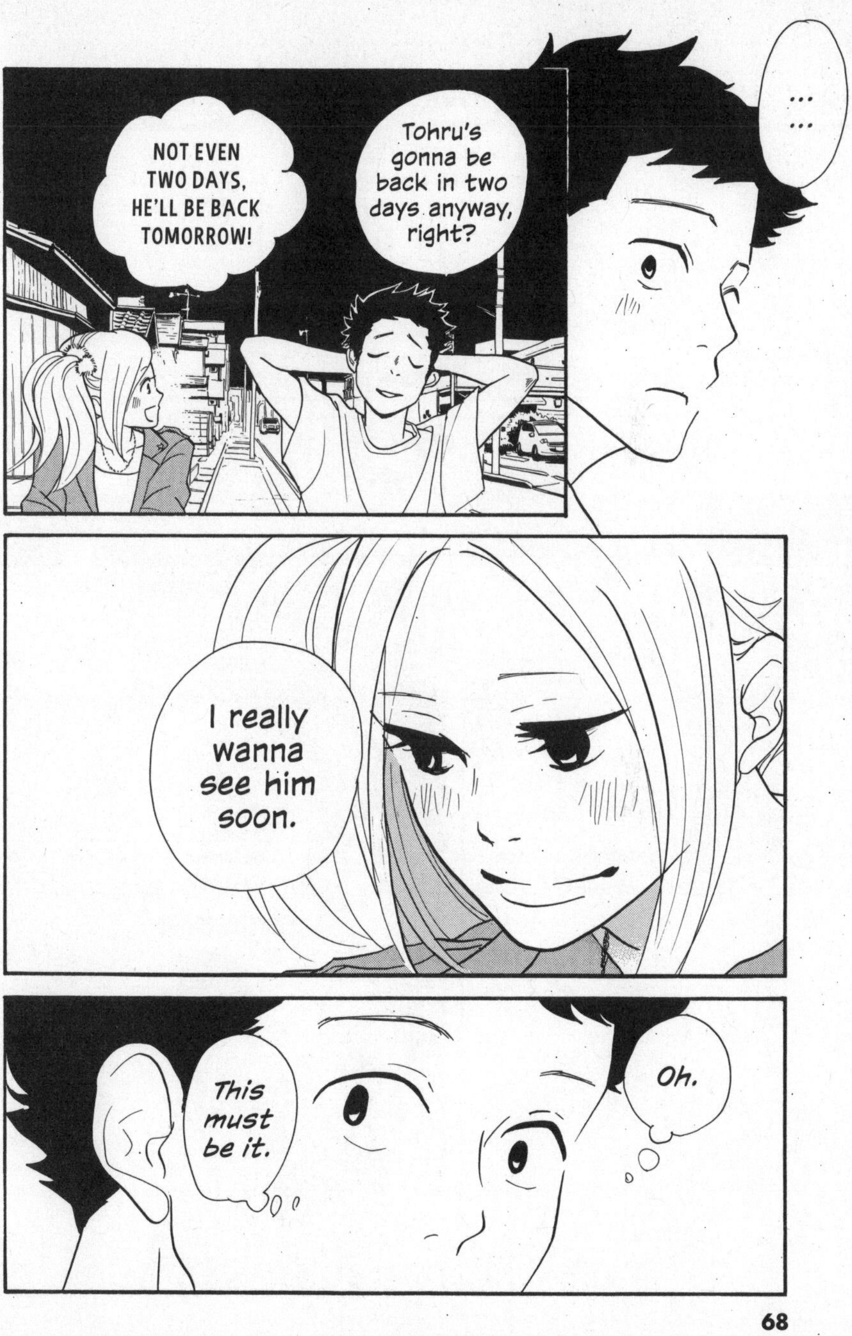
......
Tohru's gonna be back in two days anyway, right?
NOT EVEN TWO DAYS, HE'LL BE BACK TOMORROW!
I really wanna see him soon.
Oh.
This must be it.

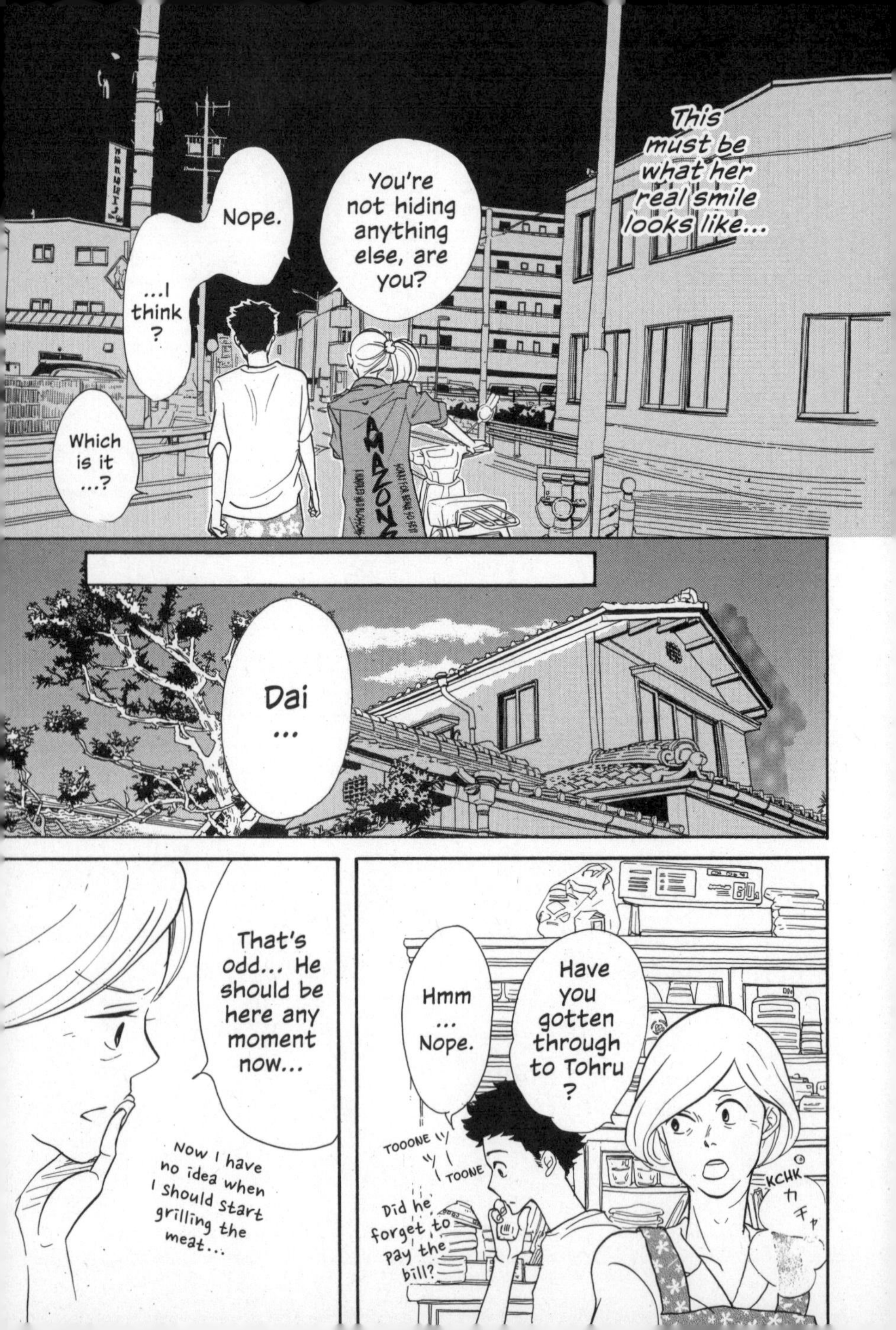

This must be what her real smile looks like...
You're not hiding anything else, are you?
Nope.
...I think?
Which is it ...?
Dai ...
Have you gotten through to Tohru ?
Hmm ... Nope.
TOOONE
TOONE
KCHK カチャ
Did he forget to pay the bill?
That's odd... He should be here any moment now...
Now I have no idea when I should start grilling the meat...

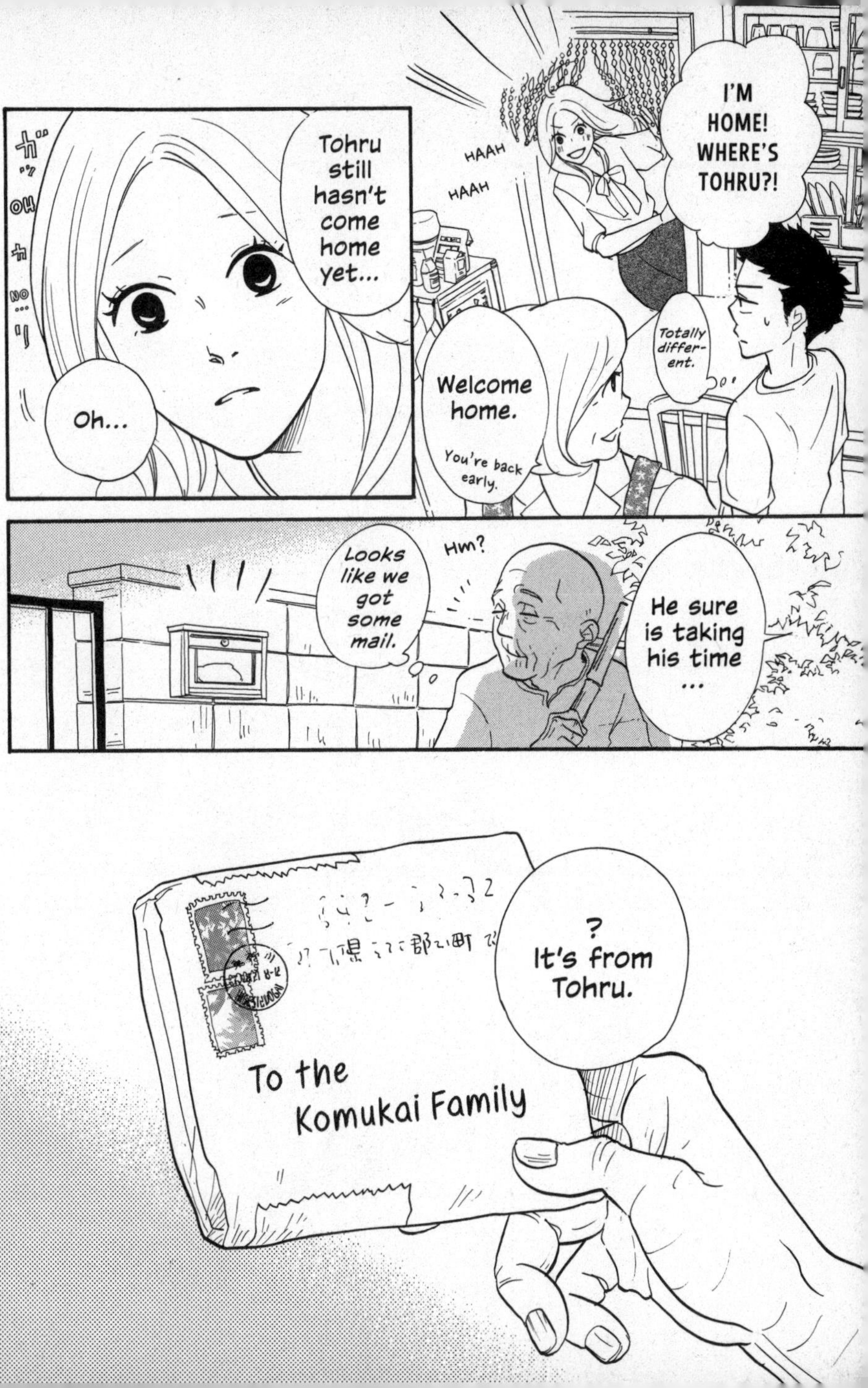
I'M HOME! WHERE'S TOHRU?!
HAAH
HAAH
Totally differ-ent.
Welcome home.
You're back early.
Tohru still hasn't come home yet...
Oh...
He sure is taking his time ...
Hm?
Looks like we got some mail.
? It's from Tohru.
To the Komukai Family

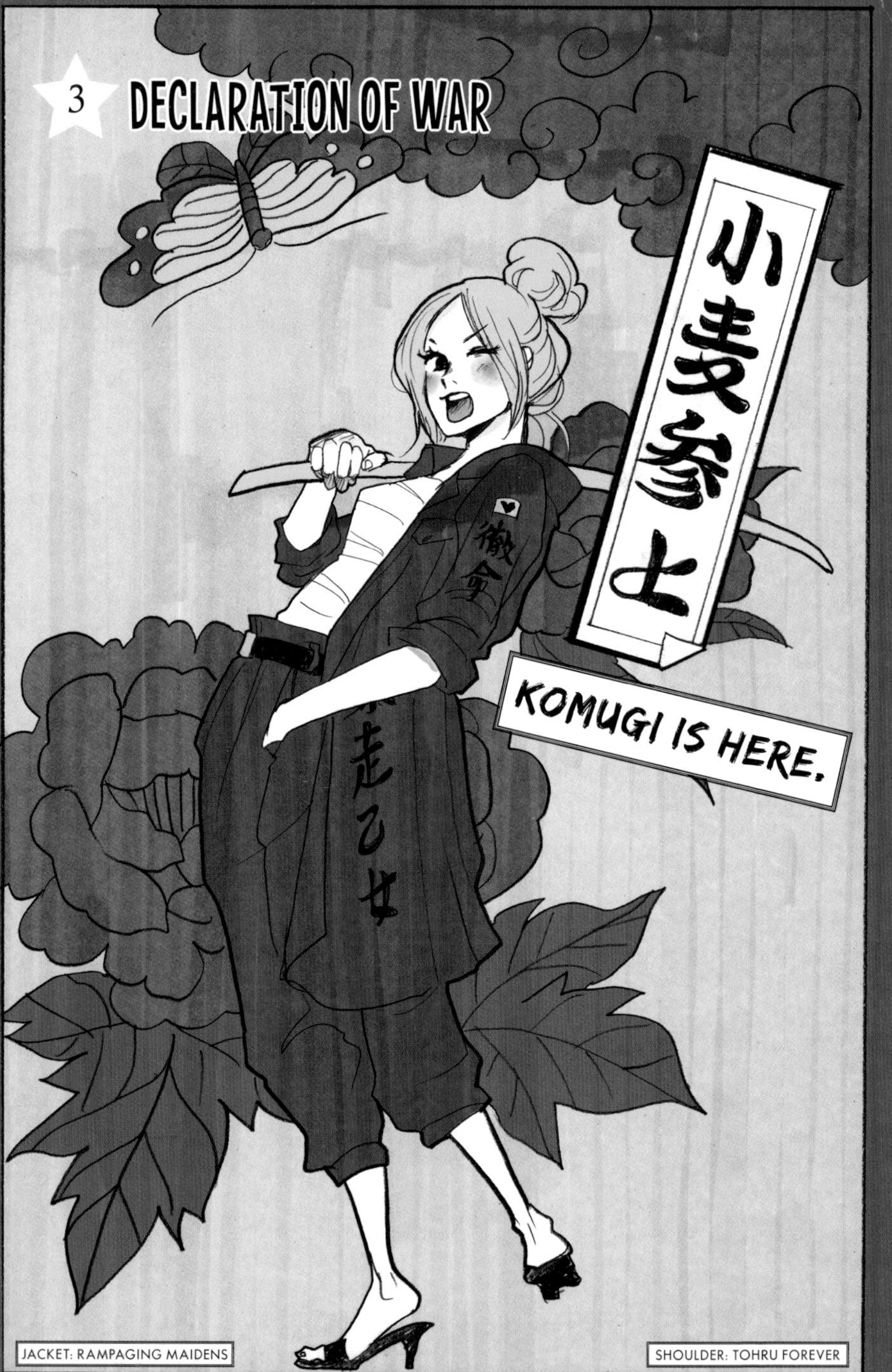
3
DECLARATION OF WAR
小麦参上
KOMUGI IS HERE.
JACKET: RAMPAGING MAIDENS
SHOULDER: TOHRU FOREVER

The Delinquent HOUSEWIFE!

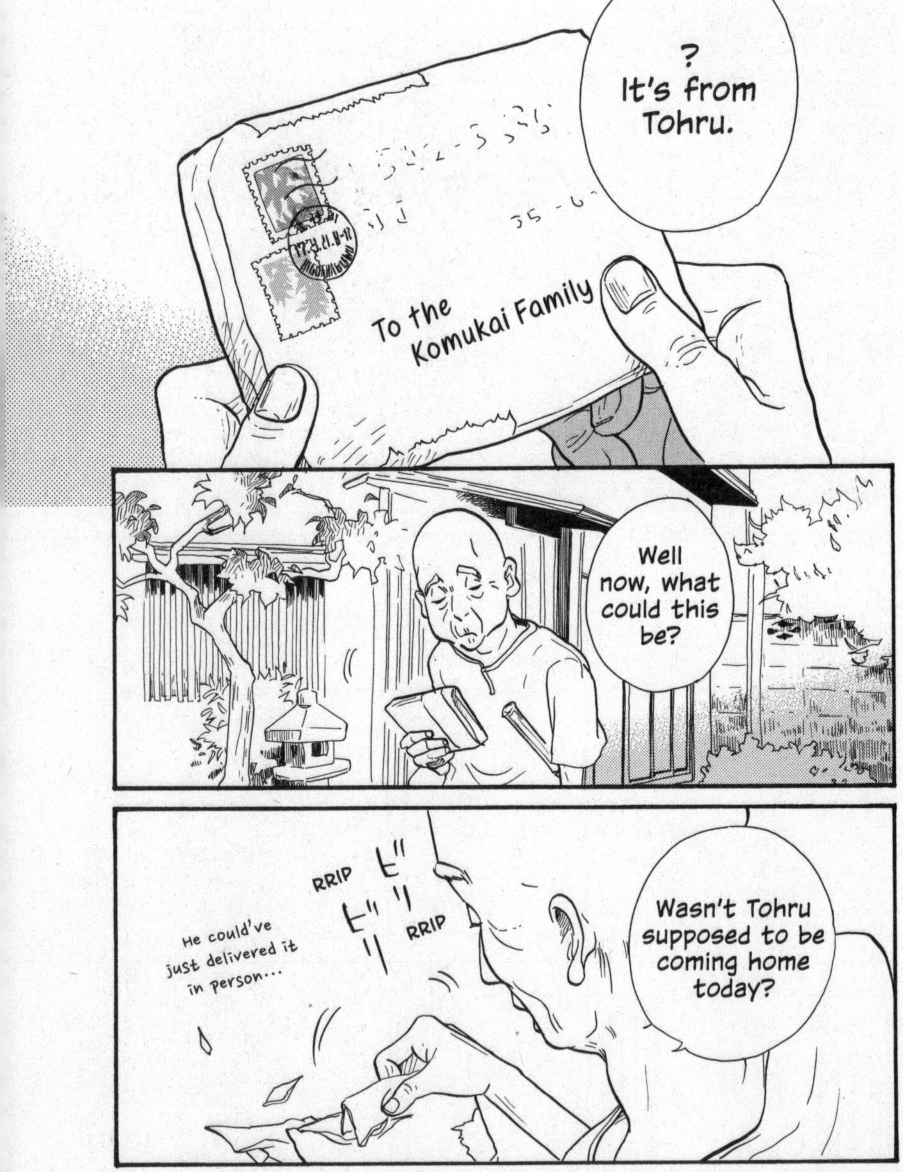
?
It's from Tohru.
To the Komukai Family
Well now, what could this be?
Wasn't Tohru supposed to be coming home today?
RRIP ビリ
RRIP ビリ
He could've just delivered it in person...

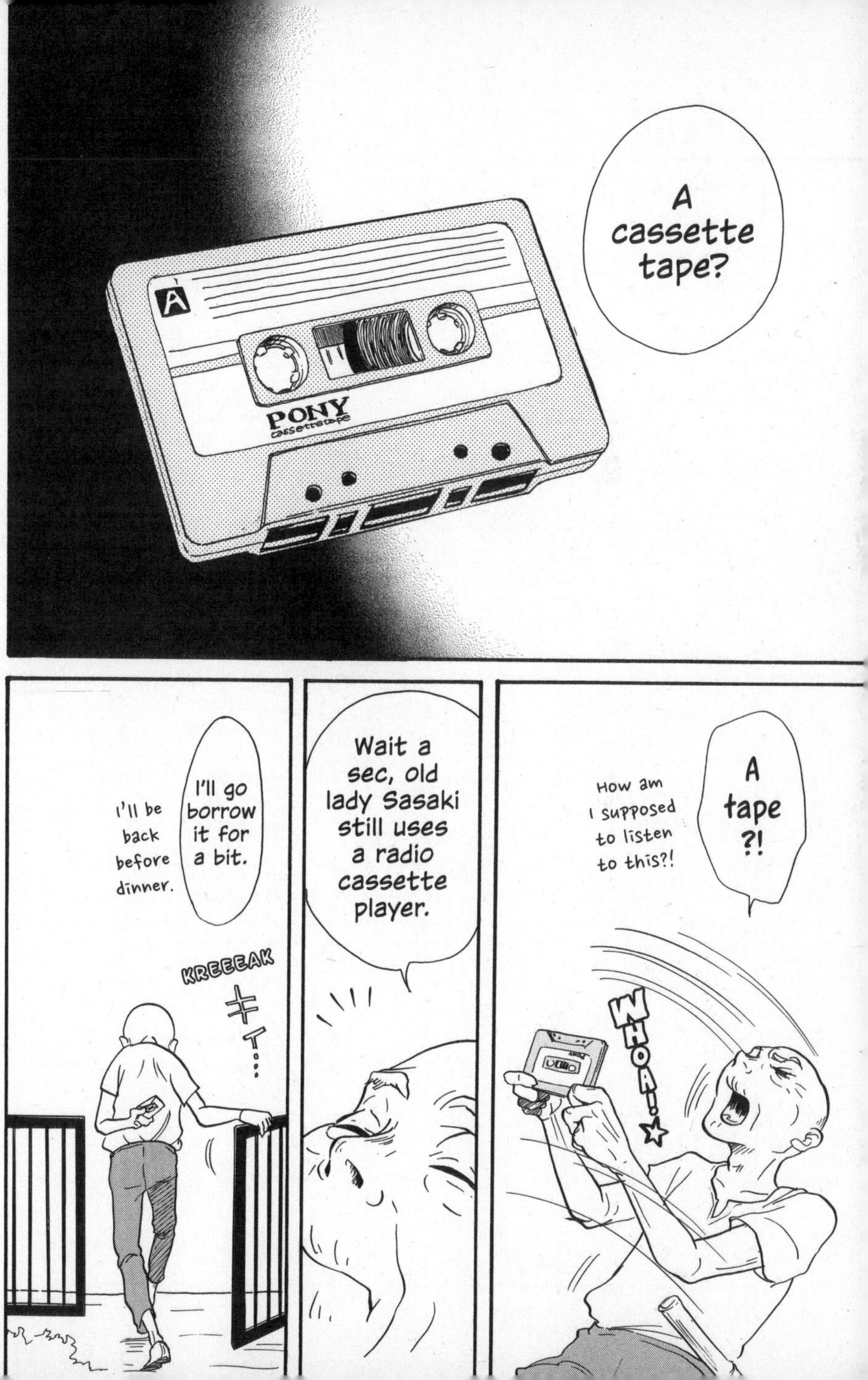
PONY
cassettetape
A cassette tape?
A tape ?!
How am I supposed to listen to this?!
WHOA!☆
Wait a sec, old lady Sasaki still uses a radio cassette player.
I'll go borrow it for a bit.
I'll be back before dinner.
KREEEAK
キィ…

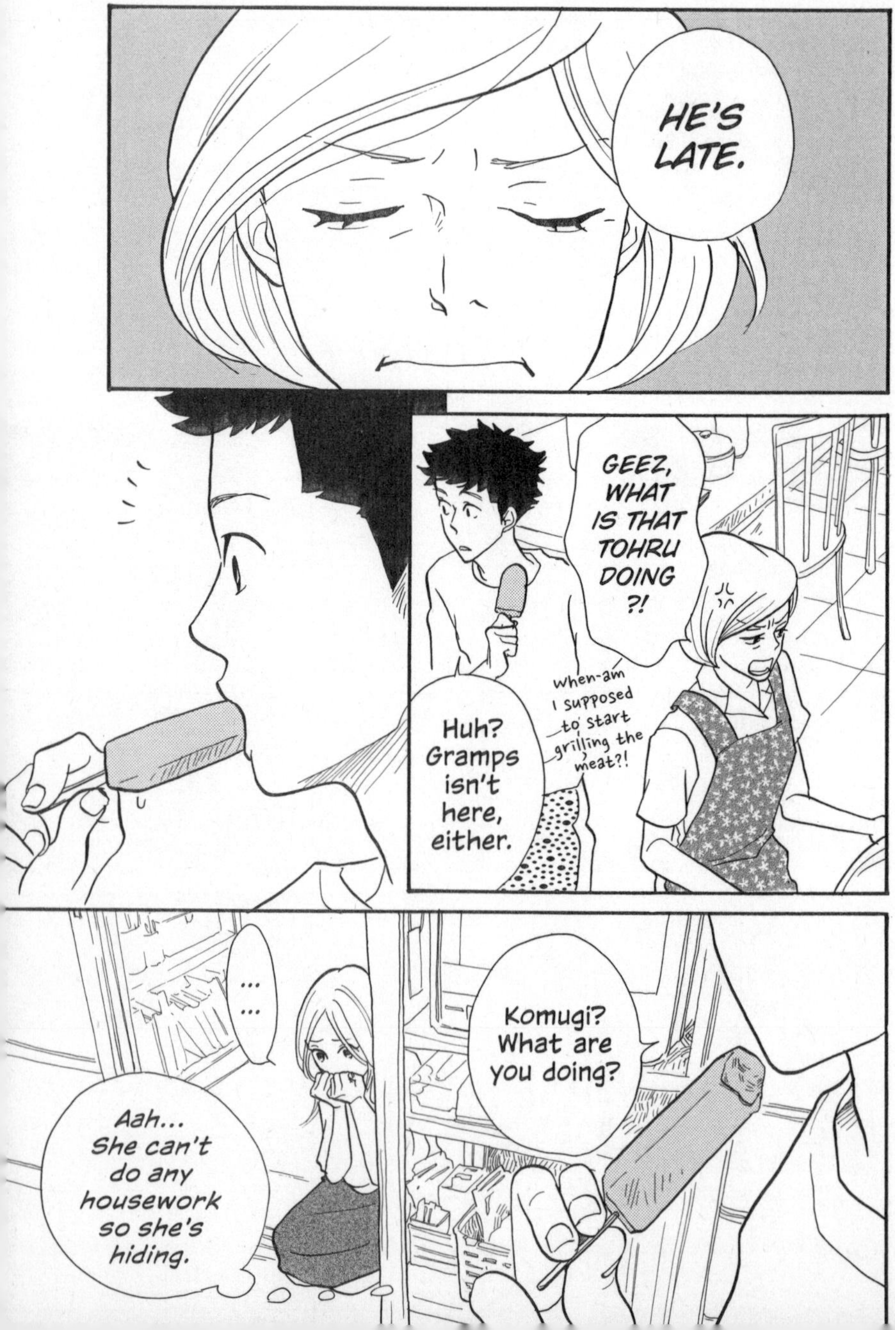
HE'S LATE.
GEEZ, WHAT IS THAT TOHRU DOING?!
When am I supposed to start grilling the meat?!
Huh? Gramps isn't here, either.
Komugi? What are you doing?
......
Aah... She can't do any housework so she's hiding.

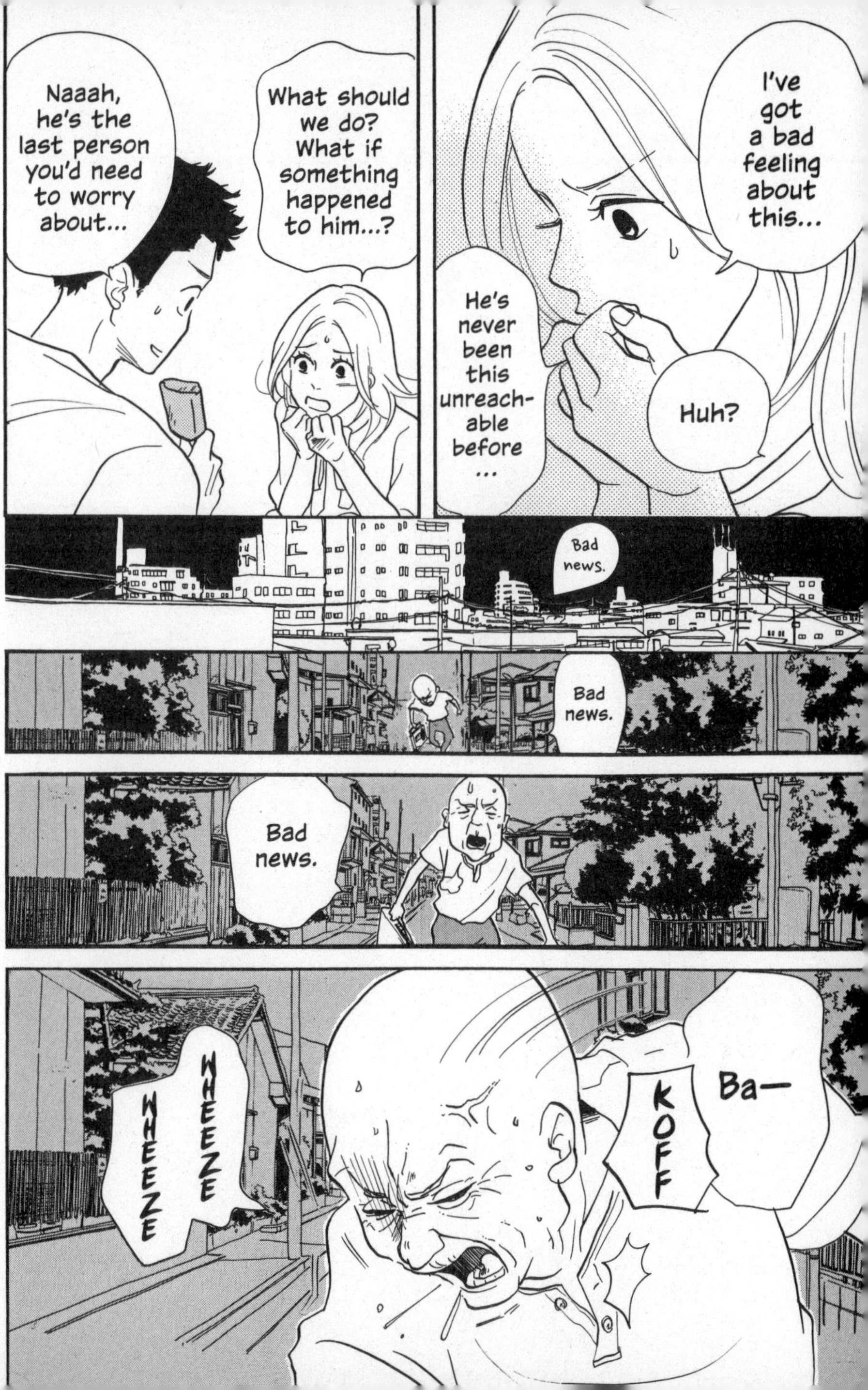
I've got a bad feeling about this...
Huh?
He's never been this unreachable before ...
What should we do? What if something happened to him...?
Naaah, he's the last person you'd need to worry about...
Bad news.
Bad news.
Bad news.
Ba—
KOFF
WHEEZE
WHEEZE

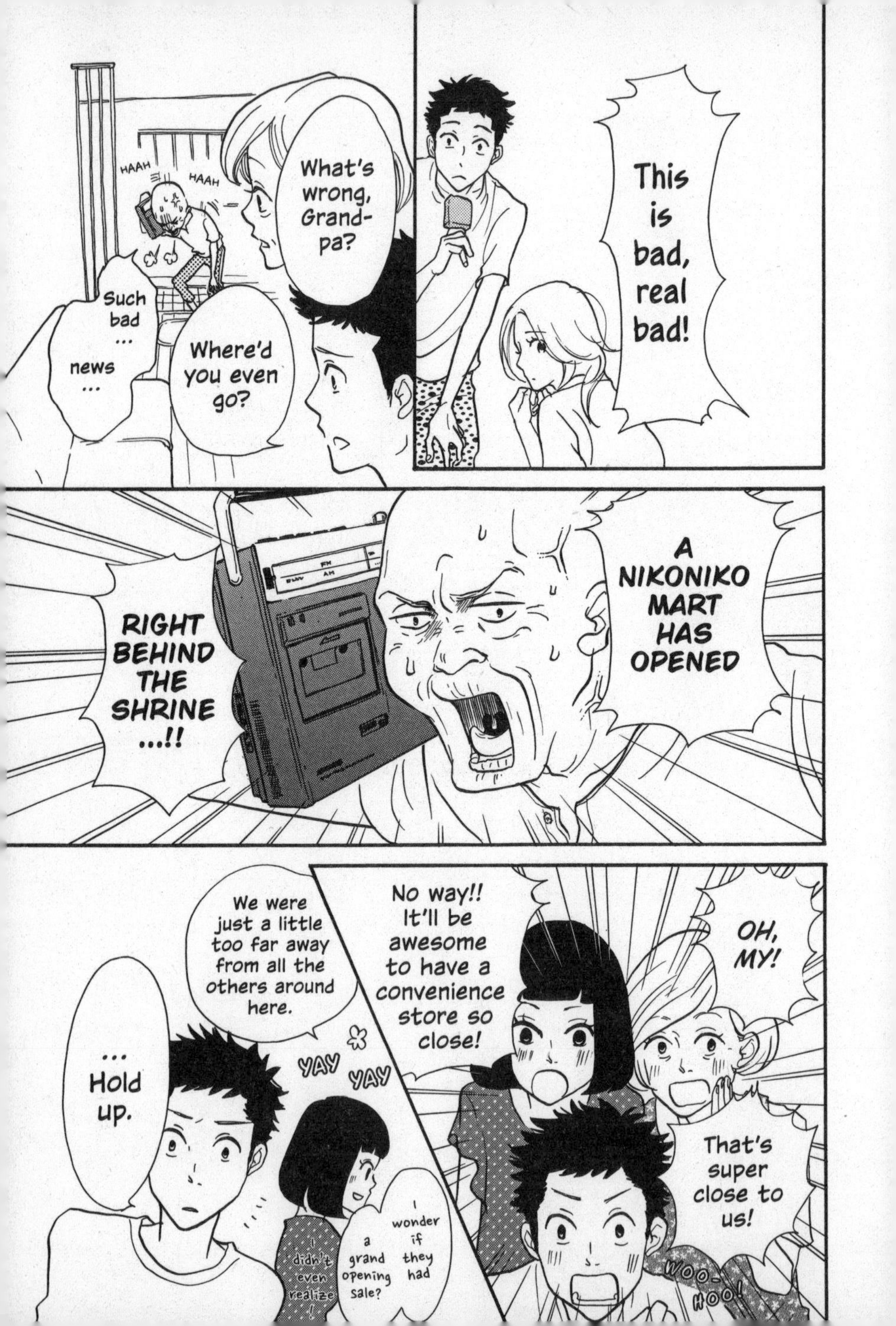
This is bad, real bad!
What's wrong, Grand-pa?
HAAH
HAAH
Where'd you even go?
Such bad ... news ...
A NIKONIKO MART HAS OPENED
RIGHT BEHIND THE SHRINE ...!!
OH, MY!
No way!! It'll be awesome to have a convenience store so close!
That's super close to us!
WOO-HOO!
We were just a little too far away from all the others around here.
YAY
YAY
... Hold up.
I wonder if they had a grand opening sale?
I didn't even realize!

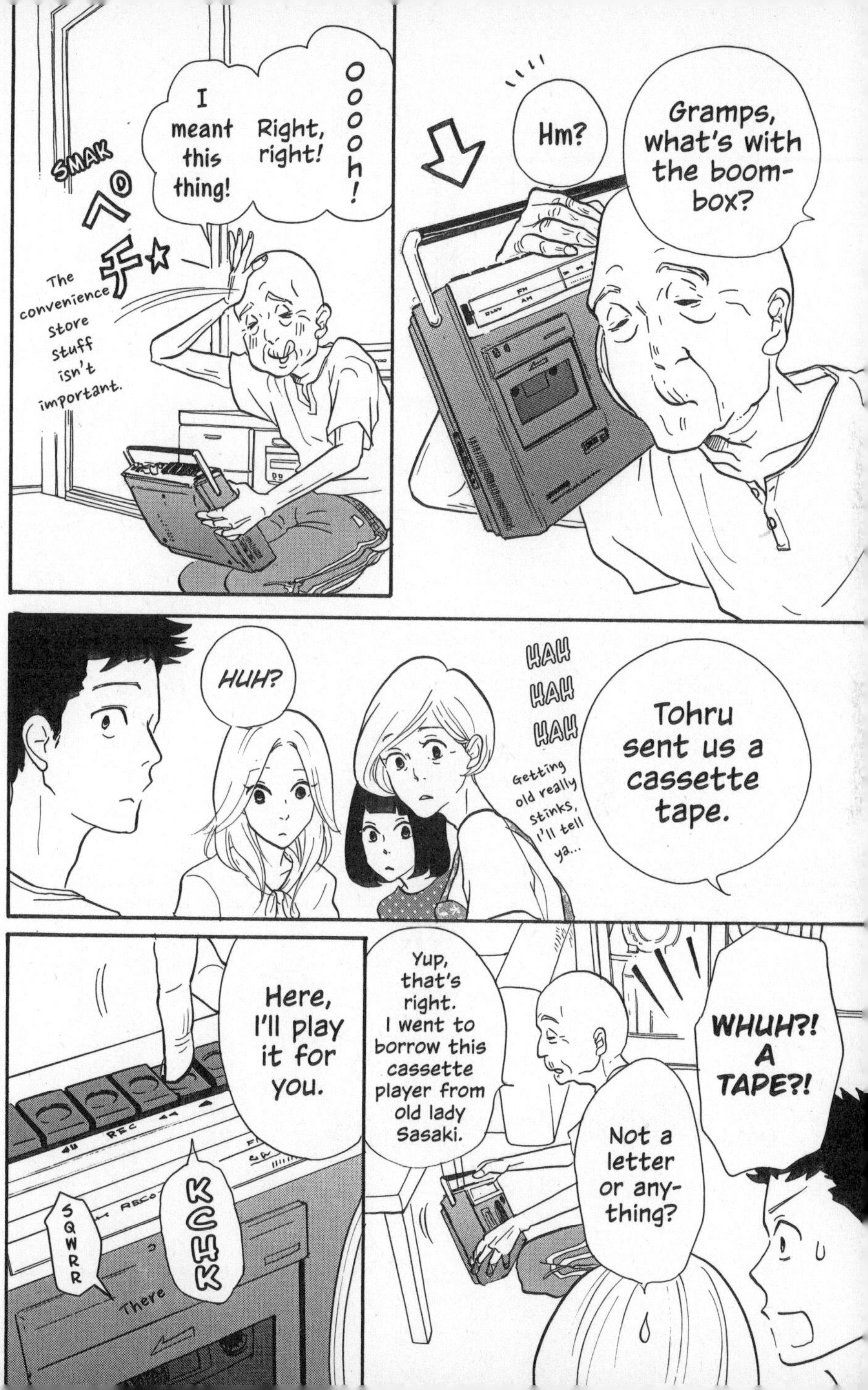
Gramps, what's with the boom-box?
Hm?
Ooooh!
Right, right!
I meant this thing!
SMAK
The convenience store stuff isn't important.
Tohru sent us a cassette tape.
HAH HAH HAH
Getting old really stinks, I'll tell ya...
HUH?
WHUH?! A TAPE?!
Not a letter or any-thing?
Yup, that's right. I went to borrow this cassette player from old lady Sasaki.
Here, I'll play it for you.
KCHK
SQWRR
There

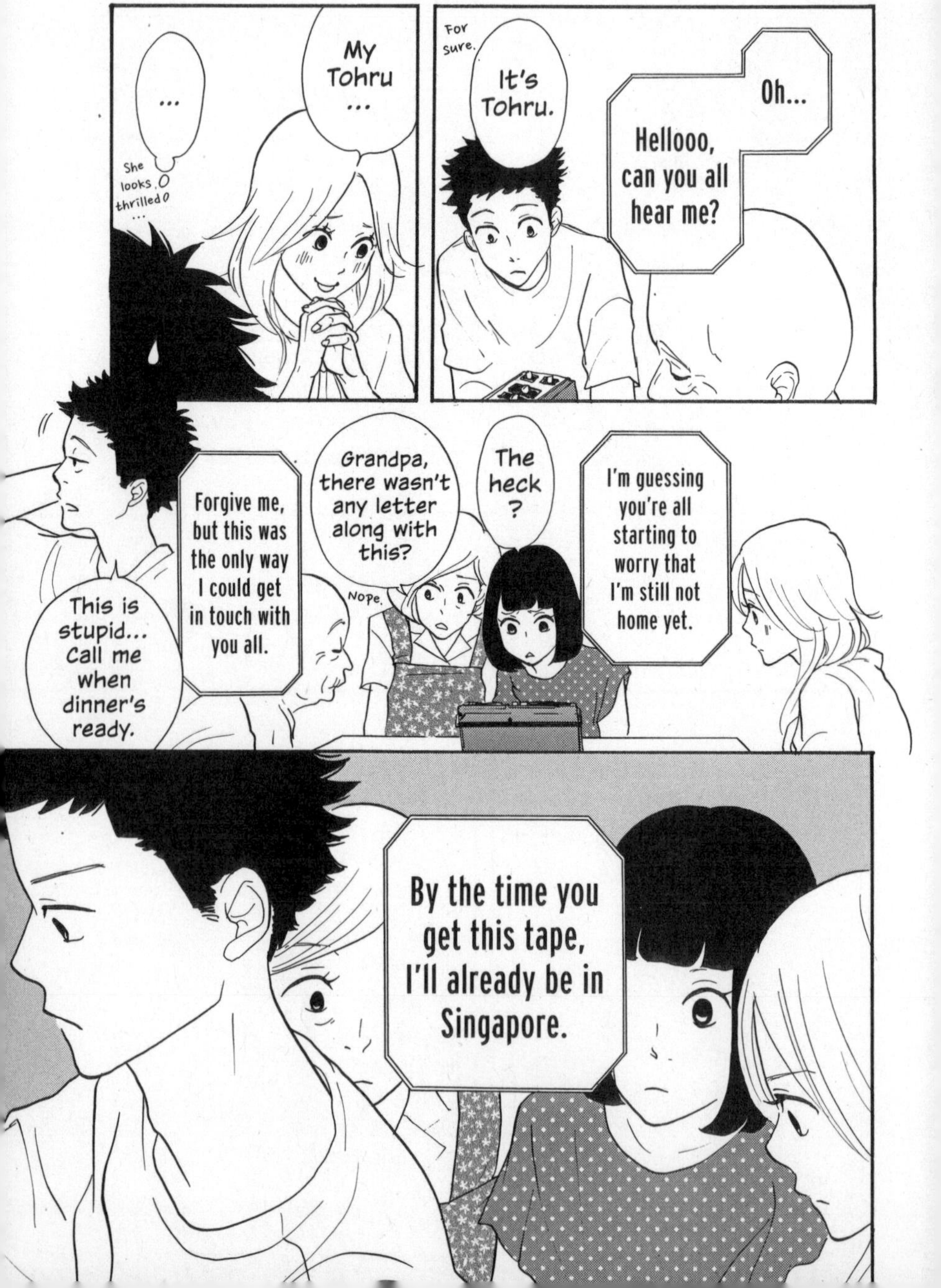
Oh...
Hellooo, can you all hear me?
For sure.
It's Tohru.
My Tohru ...
...
She looks thrilled ...
I'm guessing you're all starting to worry that I'm still not home yet.
The heck?
Grandpa, there wasn't any letter along with this?
Nope.
Forgive me, but this was the only way I could get in touch with you all.
This is stupid... Call me when dinner's ready.
By the time you get this tape, I'll already be in Singapore.

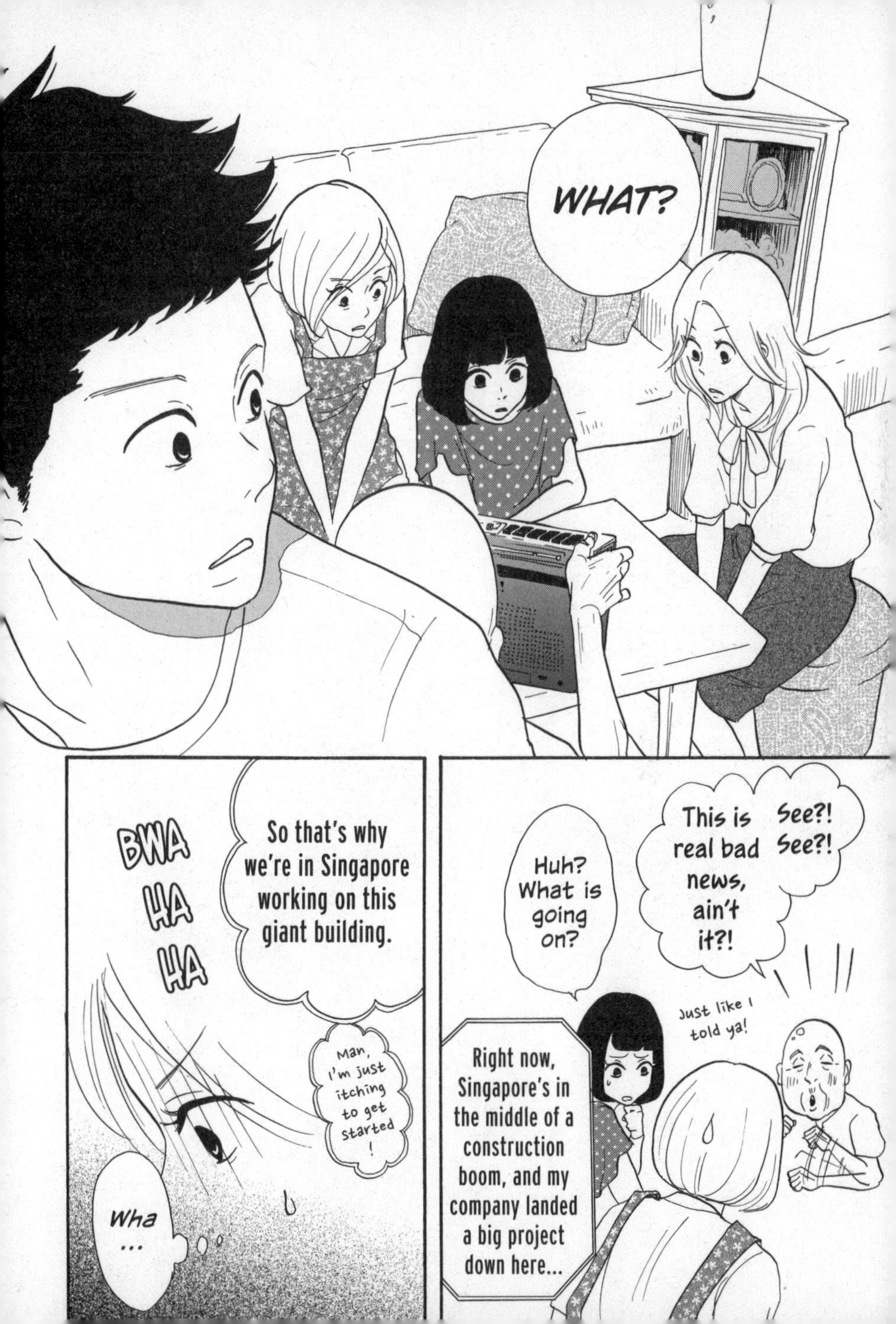
WHAT?
This is real bad news, ain't it?! See?! See?!
Huh? What is going on?
Just like I told ya!
Right now, Singapore's in the middle of a construction boom, and my company landed a big project down here...
So that's why we're in Singapore working on this giant building.
BWA HA HA HA
Man, I'm just itching to get started!
Wha...

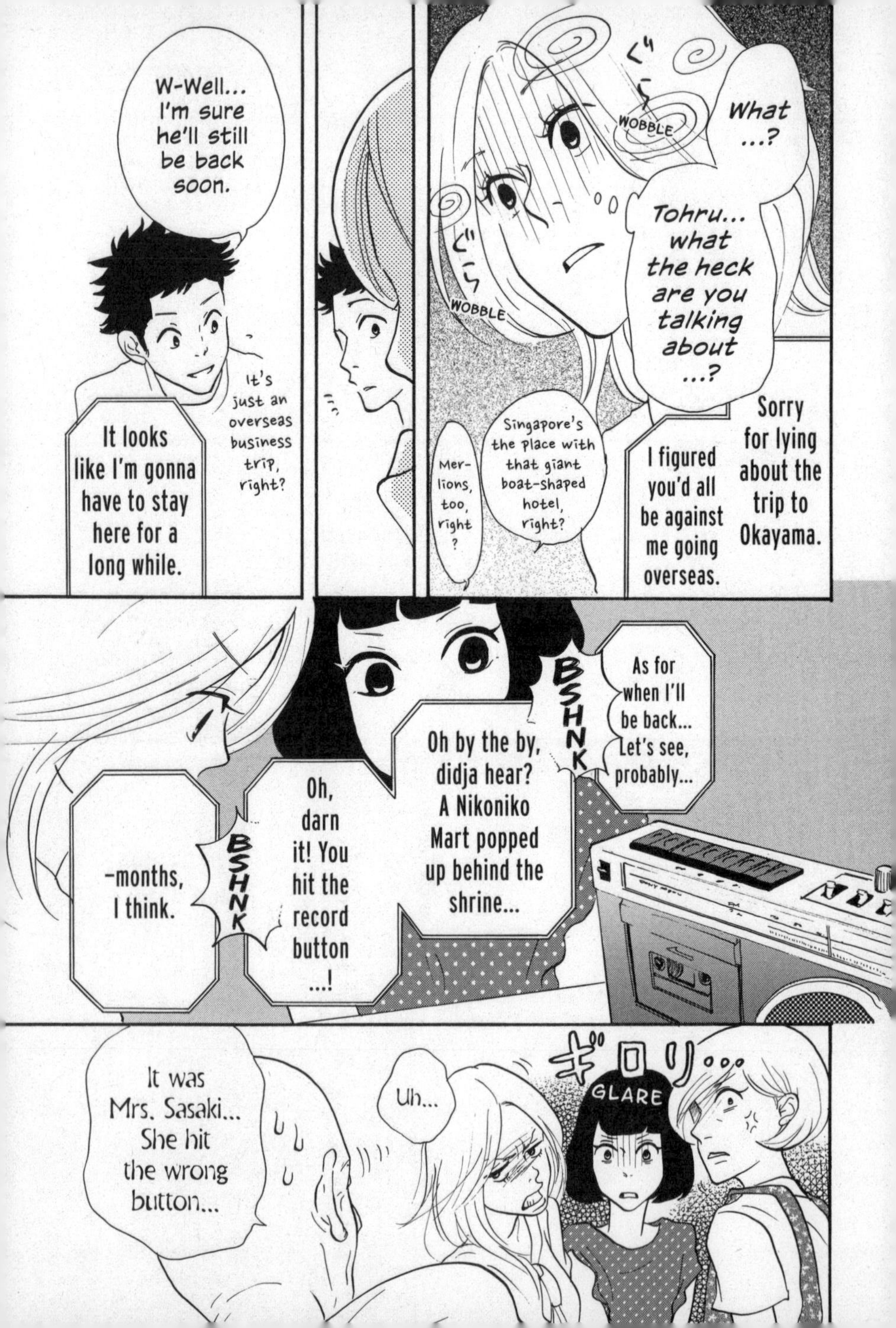
ぐら
WOBBLE
What ...?
ぐら
WOBBLE
Tohru... what the heck are you talking about ...?
Sorry for lying about the trip to Okayama.
I figured you'd all be against me going overseas.
Singapore's the place with that giant boat-shaped hotel, right?
Merlions, too, right?
W-Well... I'm sure he'll still be back soon.
It's just an overseas business trip, right?
It looks like I'm gonna have to stay here for a long while.
As for when I'll be back... Let's see, probably...
BSHNK
Oh by the by, didja hear? A Nikoniko Mart popped up behind the shrine...
Oh, darn it! You hit the record button ...!
BSHNK
-months, I think.
ギロリ...
GLARE
Uh...
It was Mrs. Sasaki... She hit the wrong button...

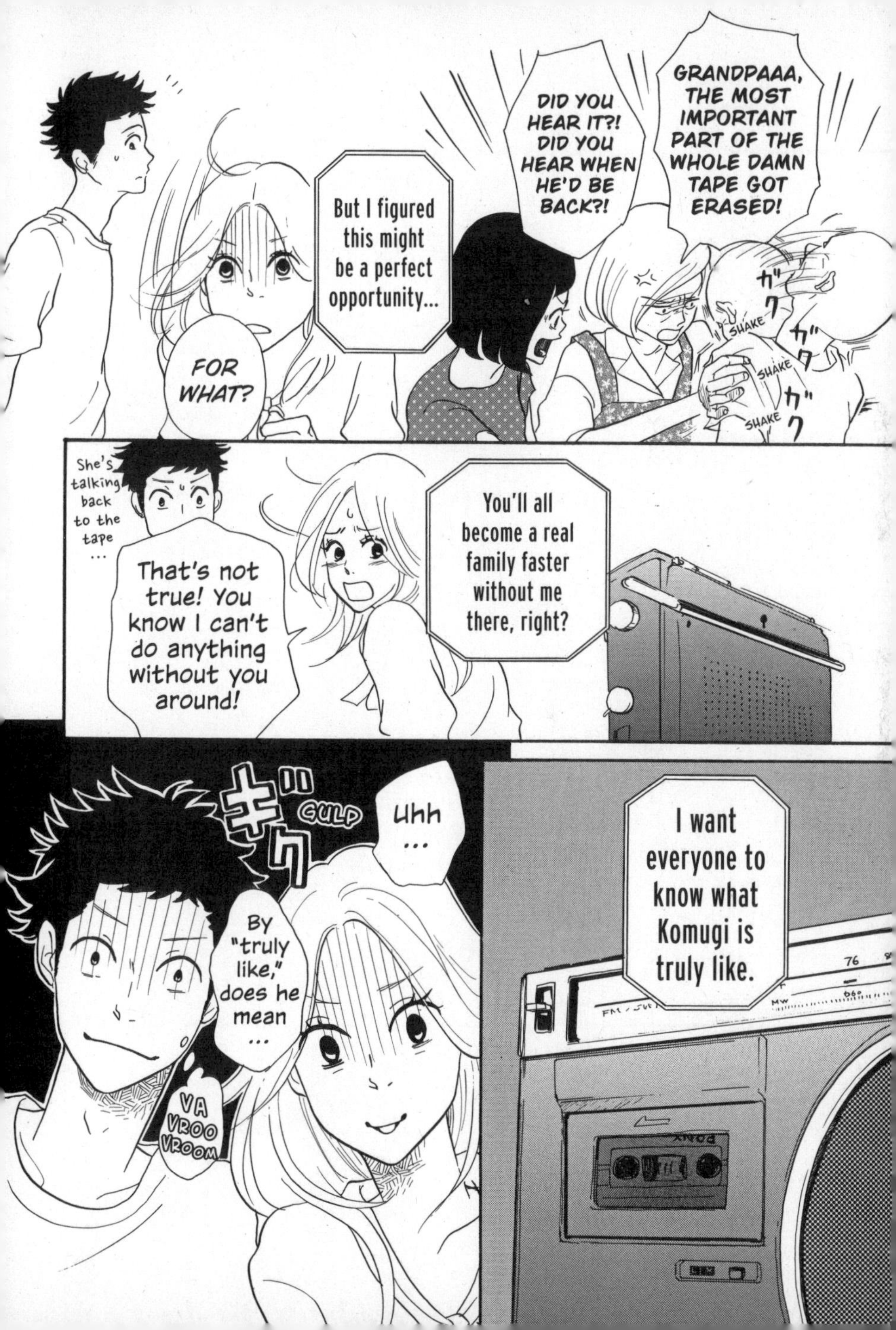
GRANDPAAA, THE MOST IMPORTANT PART OF THE WHOLE DAMN TAPE GOT ERASED!
SHAKE
SHAKE
SHAKE
DID YOU HEAR IT?! DID YOU HEAR WHEN HE'D BE BACK?!
But I figured this might be a perfect opportunity...
FOR WHAT?
You'll all become a real family faster without me there, right?
That's not true! You know I can't do anything without you around!
She's talking back to the tape ...
I want everyone to know what Komugi is truly like.
Uhh ...
GULP
By "truly like," does he mean ...
VA VROO VROOM

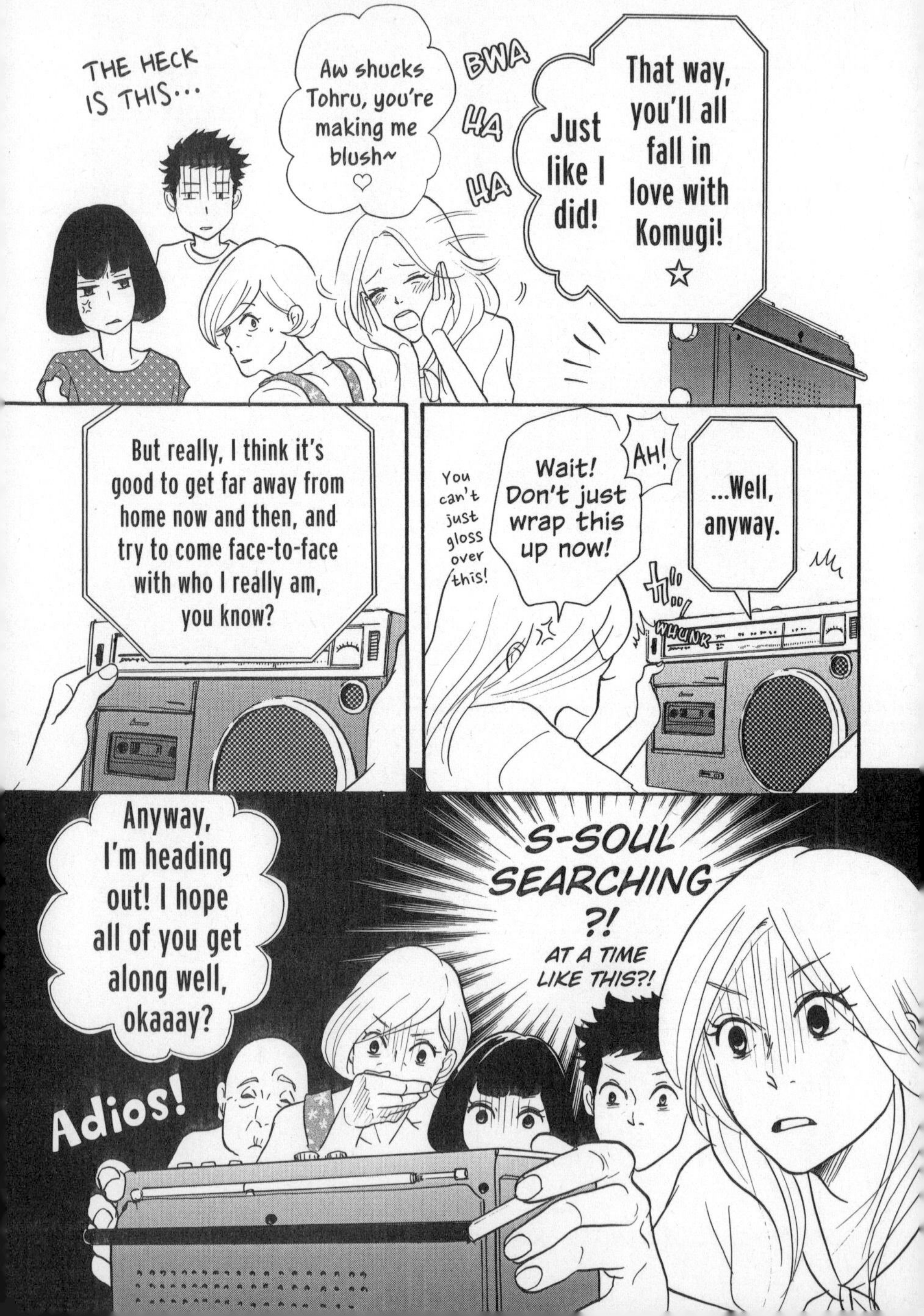

Just like I did! That way, you'll all fall in love with Komugi! ☆
BWA HA HA
Aw shucks Tohru, you're making me blush~ ♡
THE HECK IS THIS...
...Well, anyway.
AH!
WHUNK
Wait! Don't just wrap this up now!
You can't just gloss over this!
But really, I think it's good to get far away from home now and then, and try to come face-to-face with who I really am, you know?
S-SOUL SEARCHING?!
AT A TIME LIKE THIS?!
Anyway, I'm heading out! I hope all of you get along well, okaaay?
Adios!

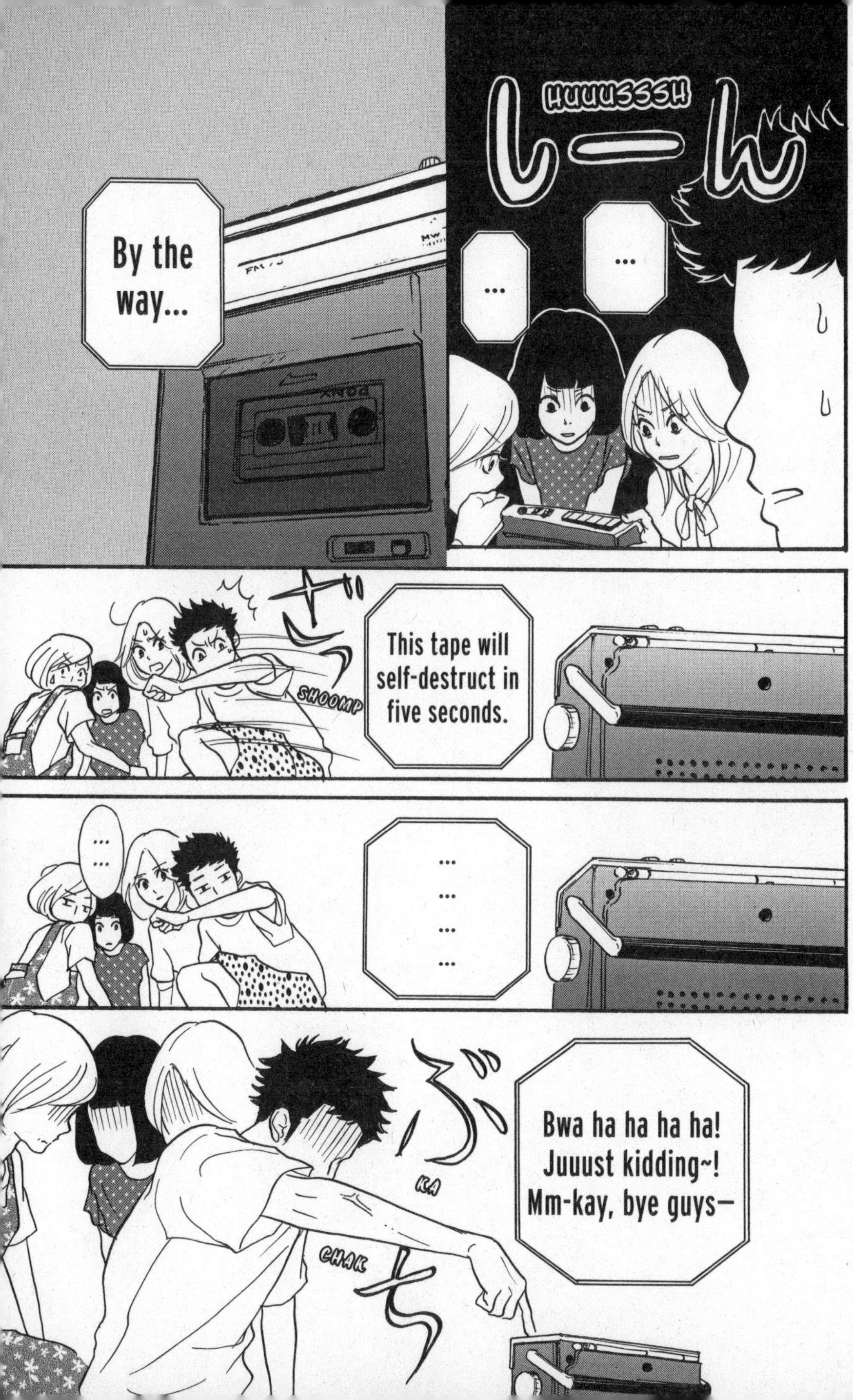

HUUUSSSH
しーん
...
...
By the way...
This tape will self-destruct in five seconds.
SHOOMP
...
...
...
...
...
...
Bwa ha ha ha ha! Juuust kidding~! Mm-kay, bye guys—
KA
CHAK

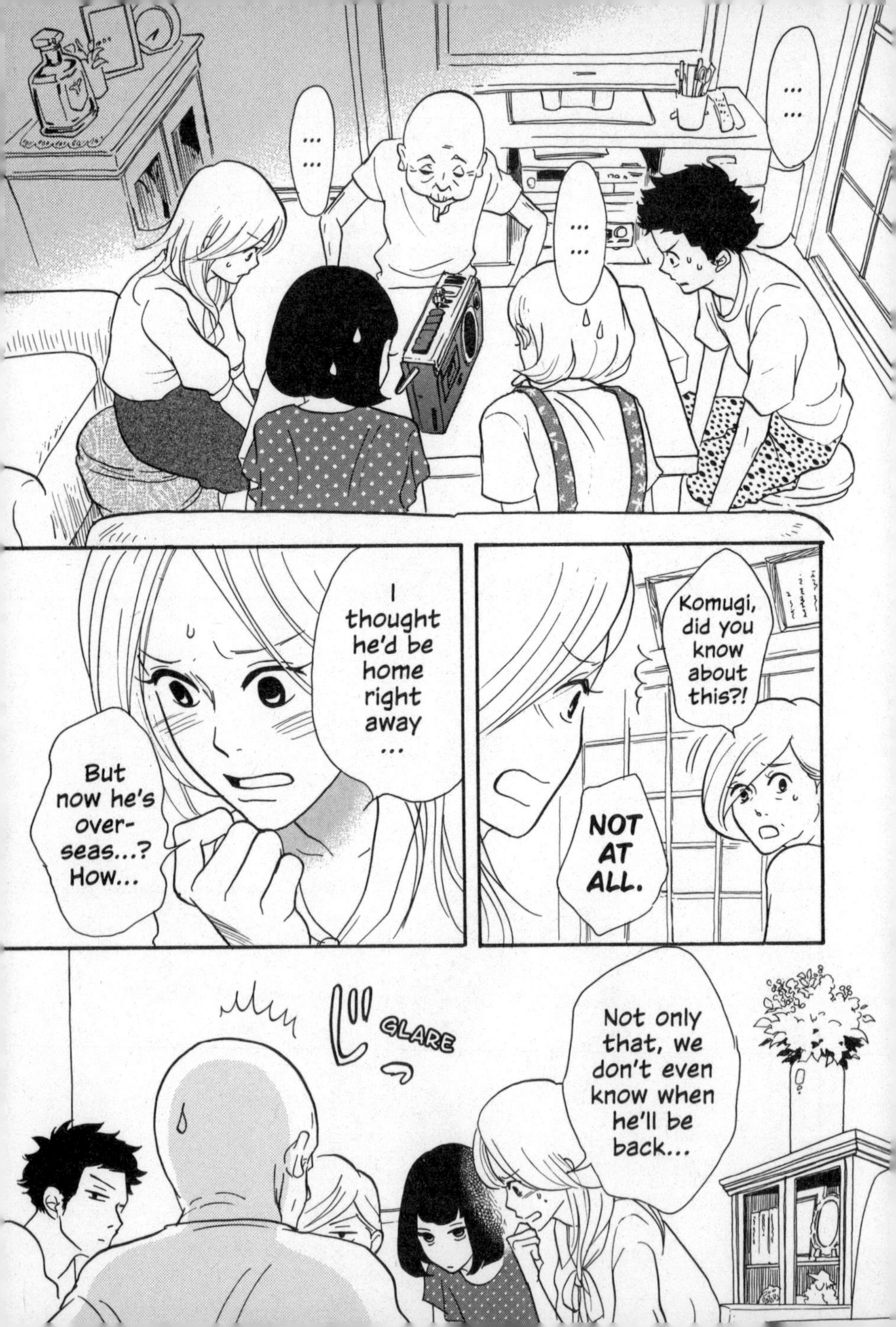
... ...
... ...
... ...
Komugi, did you know about this?!
NOT AT ALL.
I thought he'd be home right away...
But now he's over-seas...? How...
Not only that, we don't even know when he'll be back...
GLARE

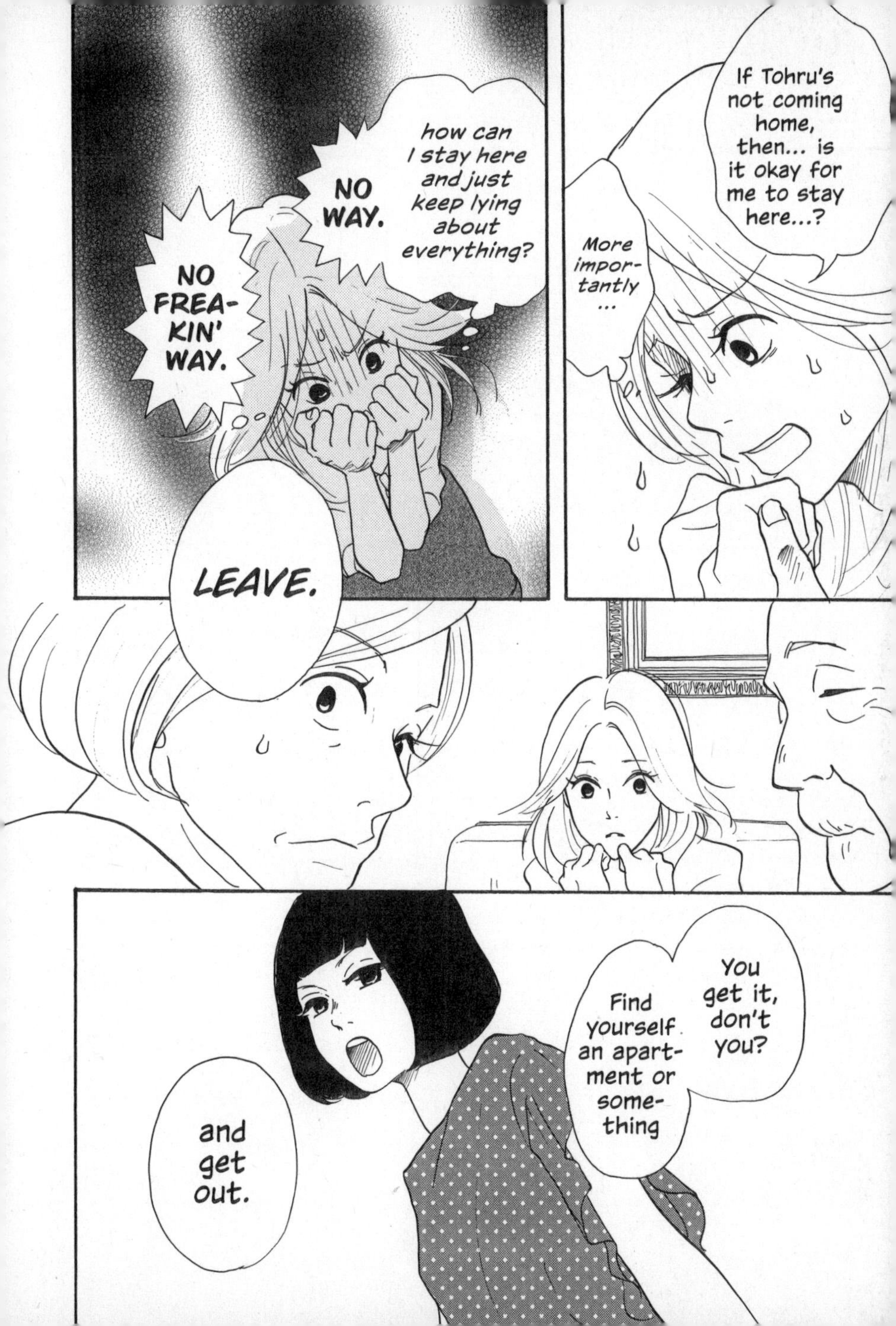
If Tohru's not coming home, then... is it okay for me to stay here...?
More importantly ...
how can I stay here and just keep lying about everything?
NO WAY.
NO FREAKIN' WAY.
LEAVE.
You get it, don't you?
Find yourself an apartment or something
and get out.

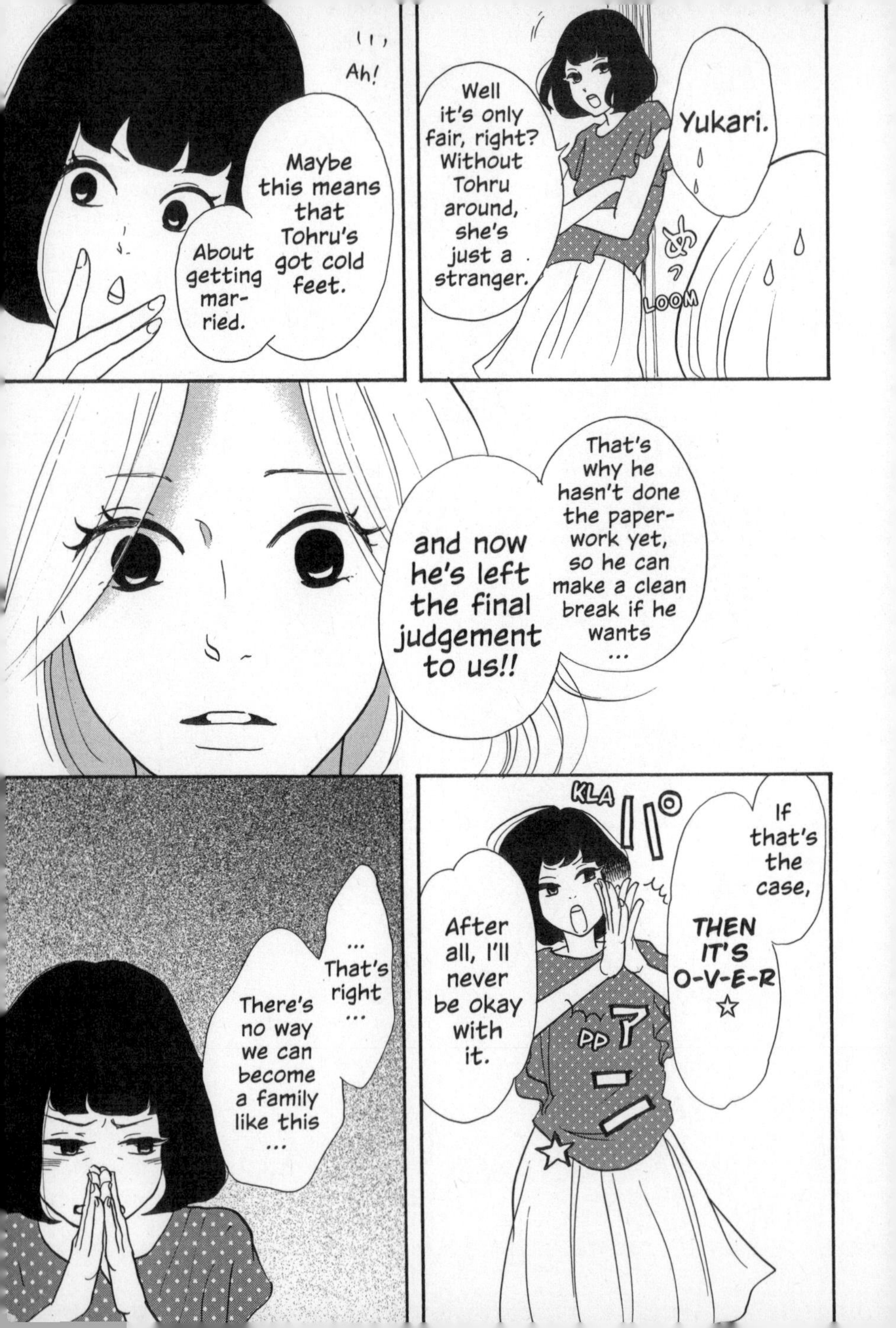
Yukari.
LOOM
Well it's only fair, right? Without Tohru around, she's just a stranger.
Ah!
Maybe this means that Tohru's got cold feet.
About getting mar-ried.
That's why he hasn't done the paper-work yet, so he can make a clean break if he wants ...
and now he's left the final judgement to us!!
KLA
If that's the case,
THEN IT'S O-V-E-R ☆
PP
After all, I'll never be okay with it.
... That's right ...
There's no way we can become a family like this ...

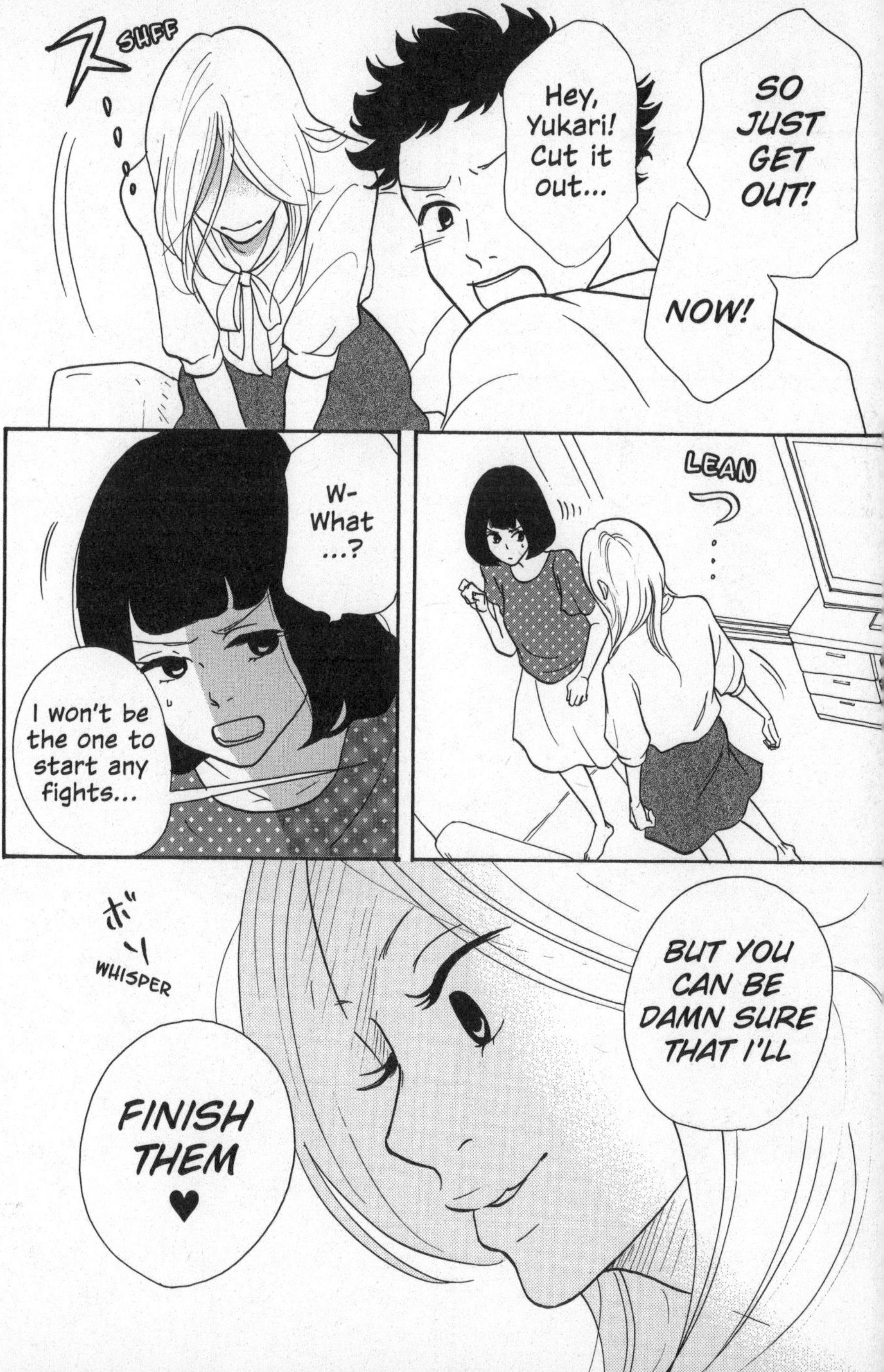
SO JUST GET OUT!
NOW!
Hey, Yukari! Cut it out...
SHFF
LEAN
...
W- What ...?
I won't be the one to start any fights...
BUT YOU CAN BE DAMN SURE THAT I'LL
FINISH THEM ♥
ボソ
WHISPER

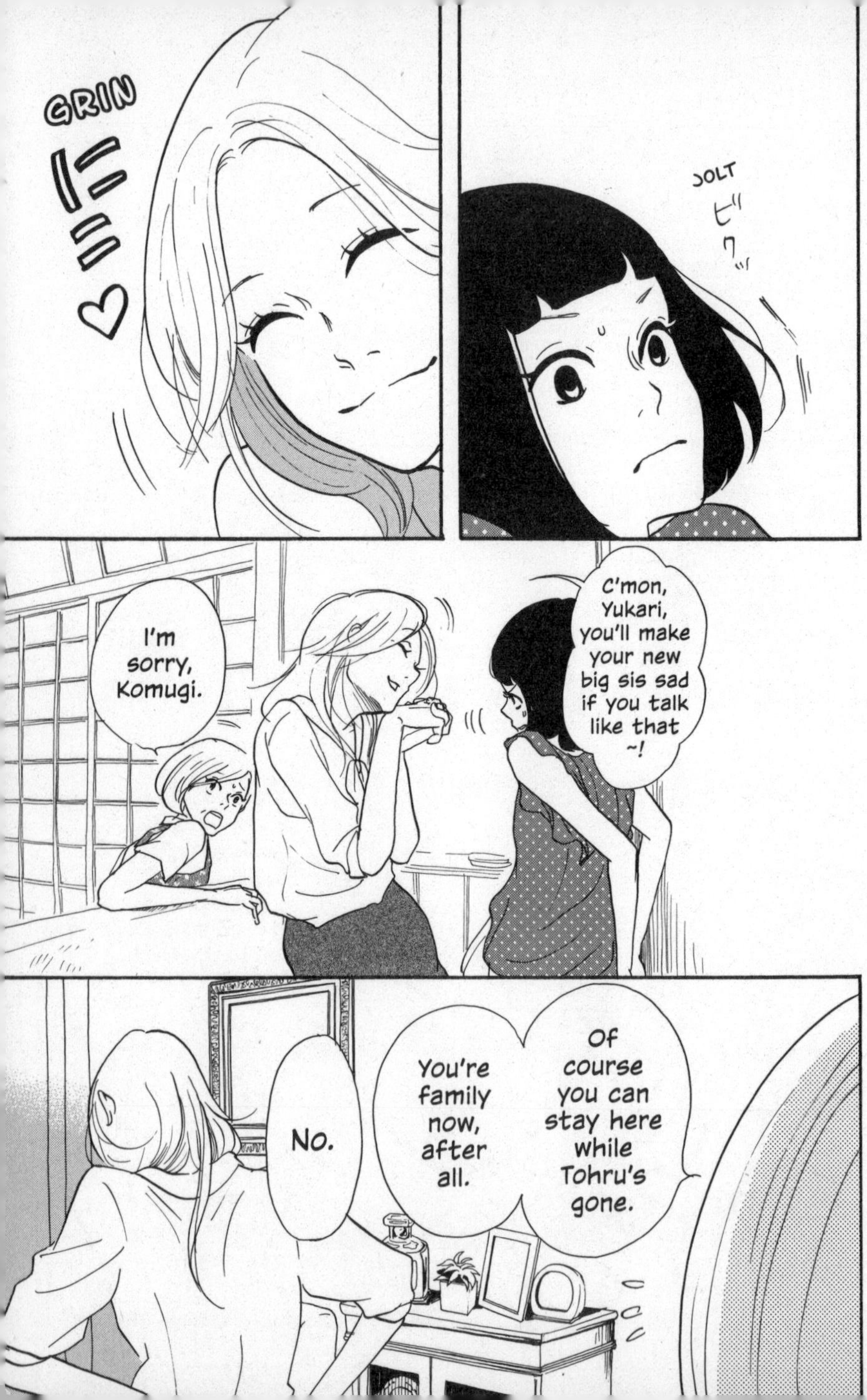
JOLT
GRIN
C'mon, Yukari, you'll make your new big sis sad if you talk like that ~!
I'm sorry, Komugi.
Of course you can stay here while Tohru's gone.
You're family now, after all.
No.

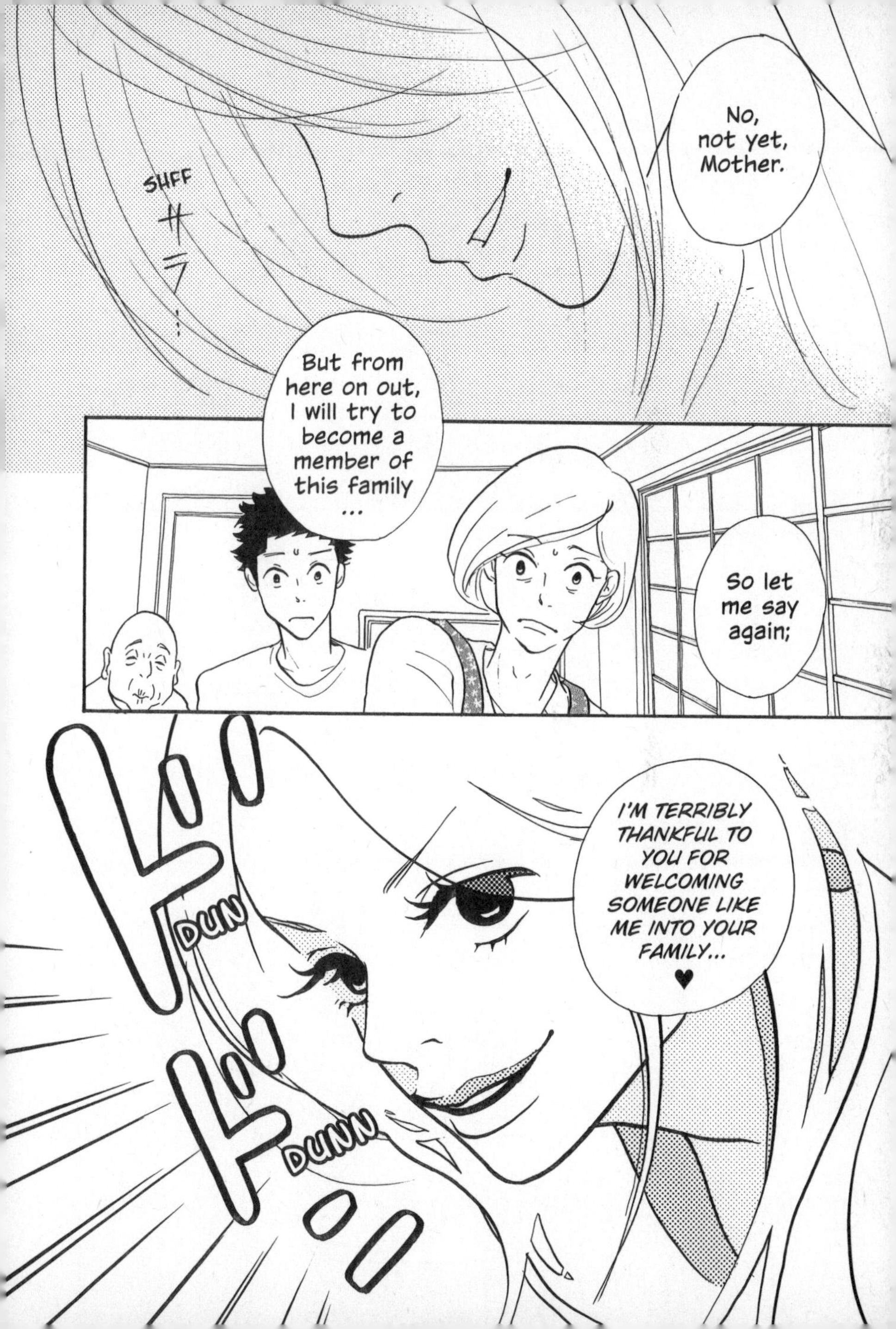
No, not yet, Mother.
SHFF
サラ…
But from here on out, I will try to become a member of this family ...
So let me say again;
I'M TERRIBLY THANKFUL TO YOU FOR WELCOMING SOMEONE LIKE ME INTO YOUR FAMILY... ♥
DUN
DUNN

The Delinquent HOUSEWIFE!

4 TO SAY OR NOT TO SAY

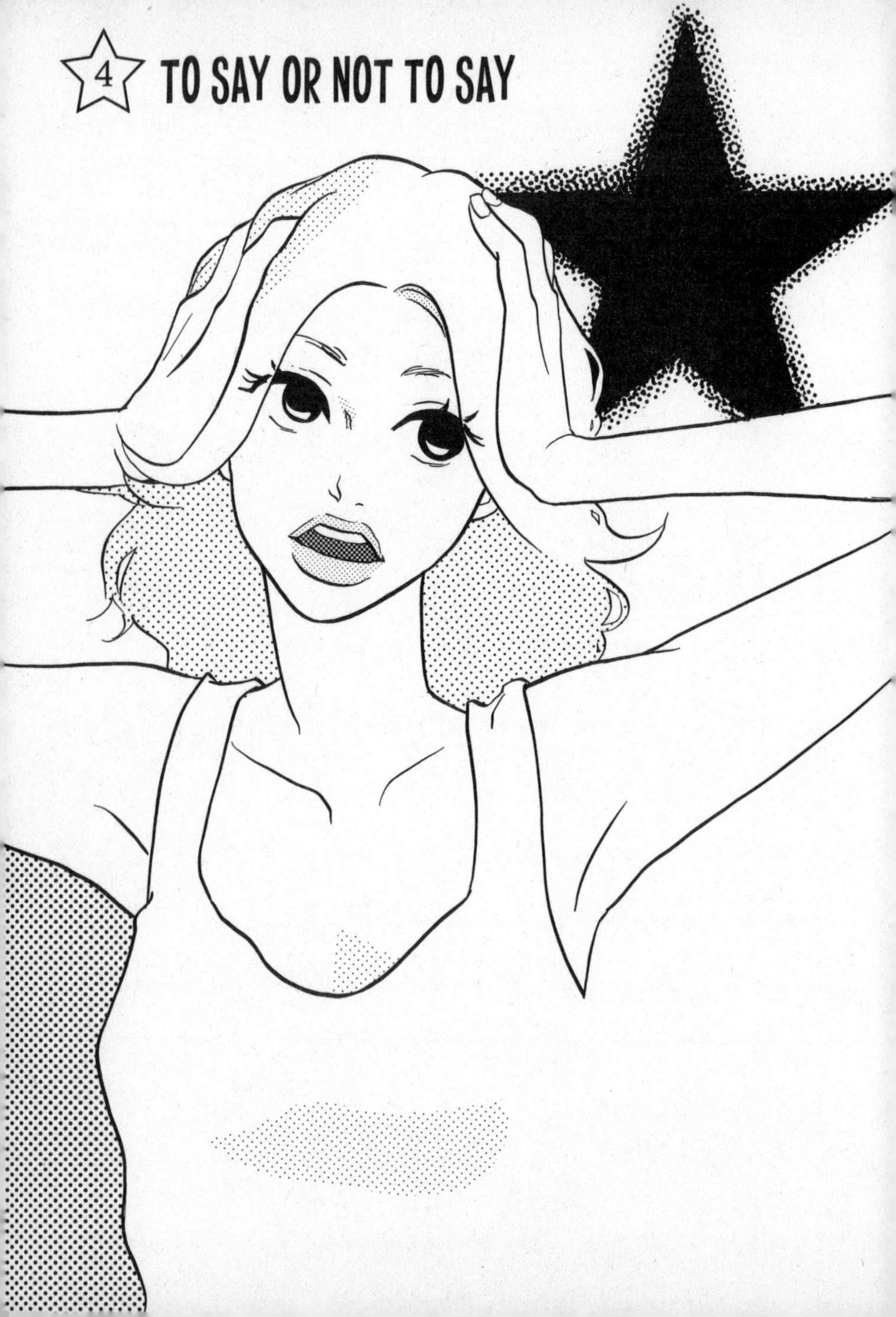

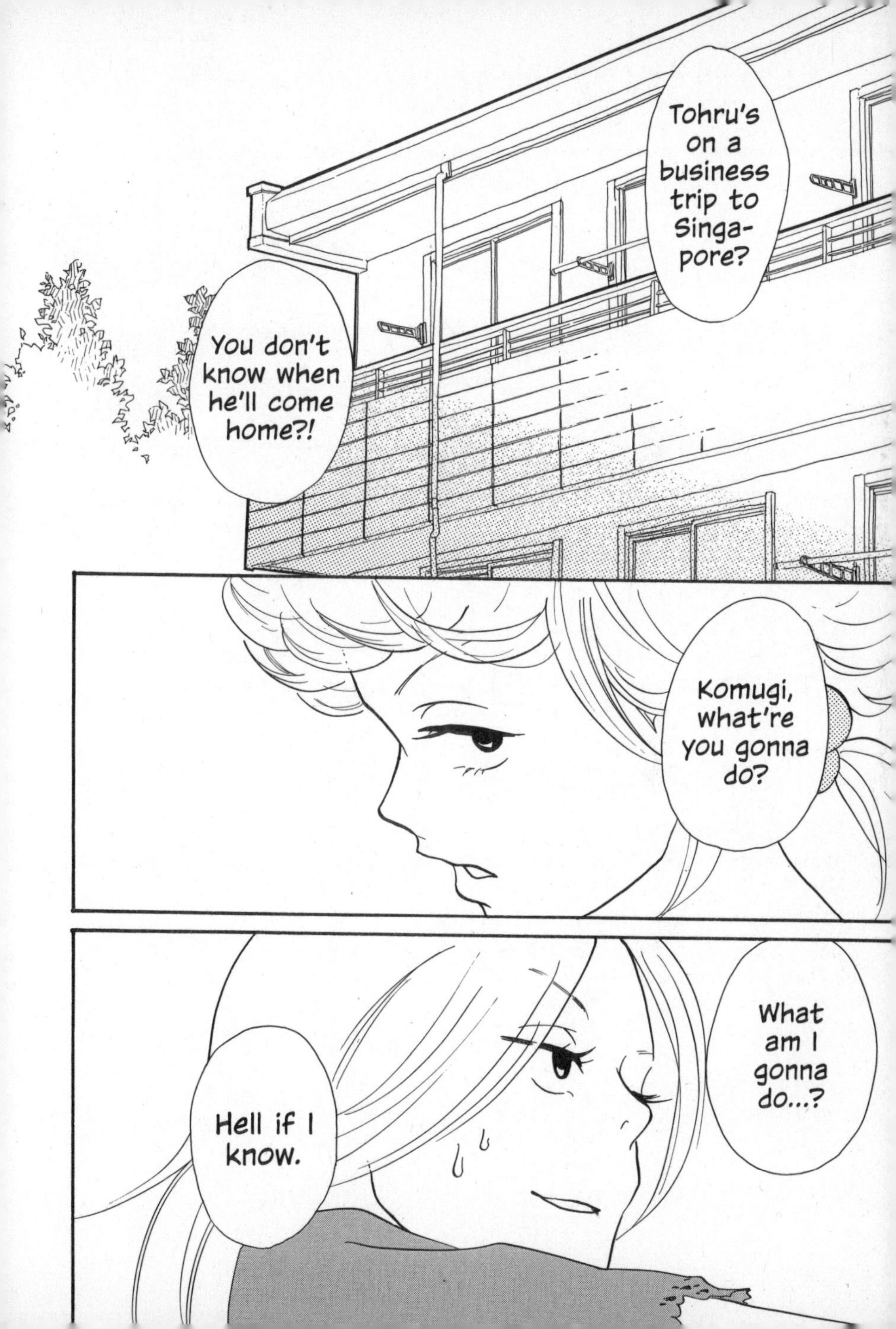
Tohru's on a business trip to Singa-pore?
You don't know when he'll come home?!
Komugi, what're you gonna do?
What am I gonna do...?
Hell if I know.

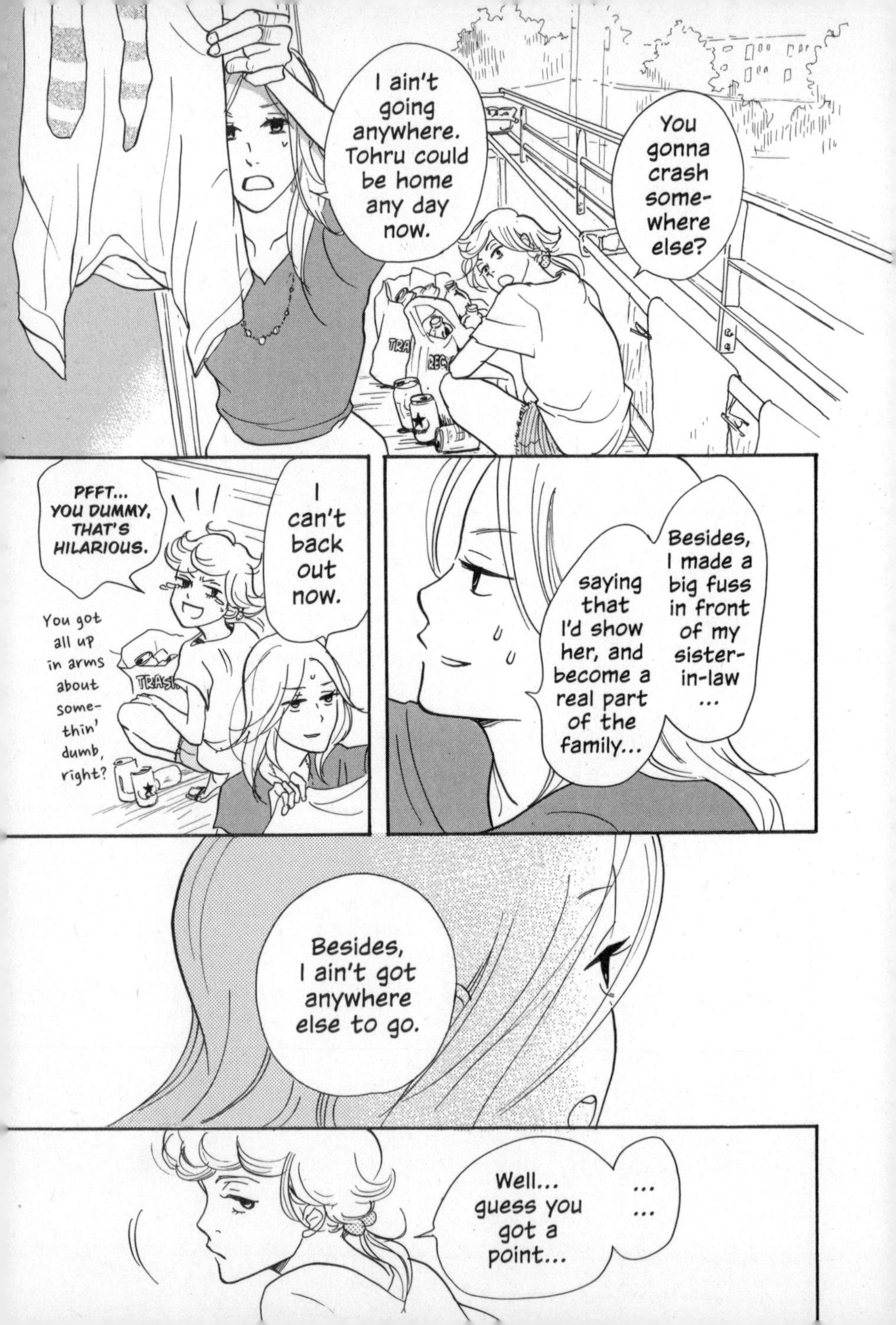
You gonna crash some-where else?
I ain't going anywhere. Tohru could be home any day now.
Besides, I made a big fuss in front of my sister-in-law...
saying that I'd show her, and become a real part of the family...
I can't back out now.
PFFT... YOU DUMMY, THAT'S HILARIOUS.
You got all up in arms about some-thin' dumb, right?
Besides, I ain't got anywhere else to go.
... ...
Well... guess you got a point...

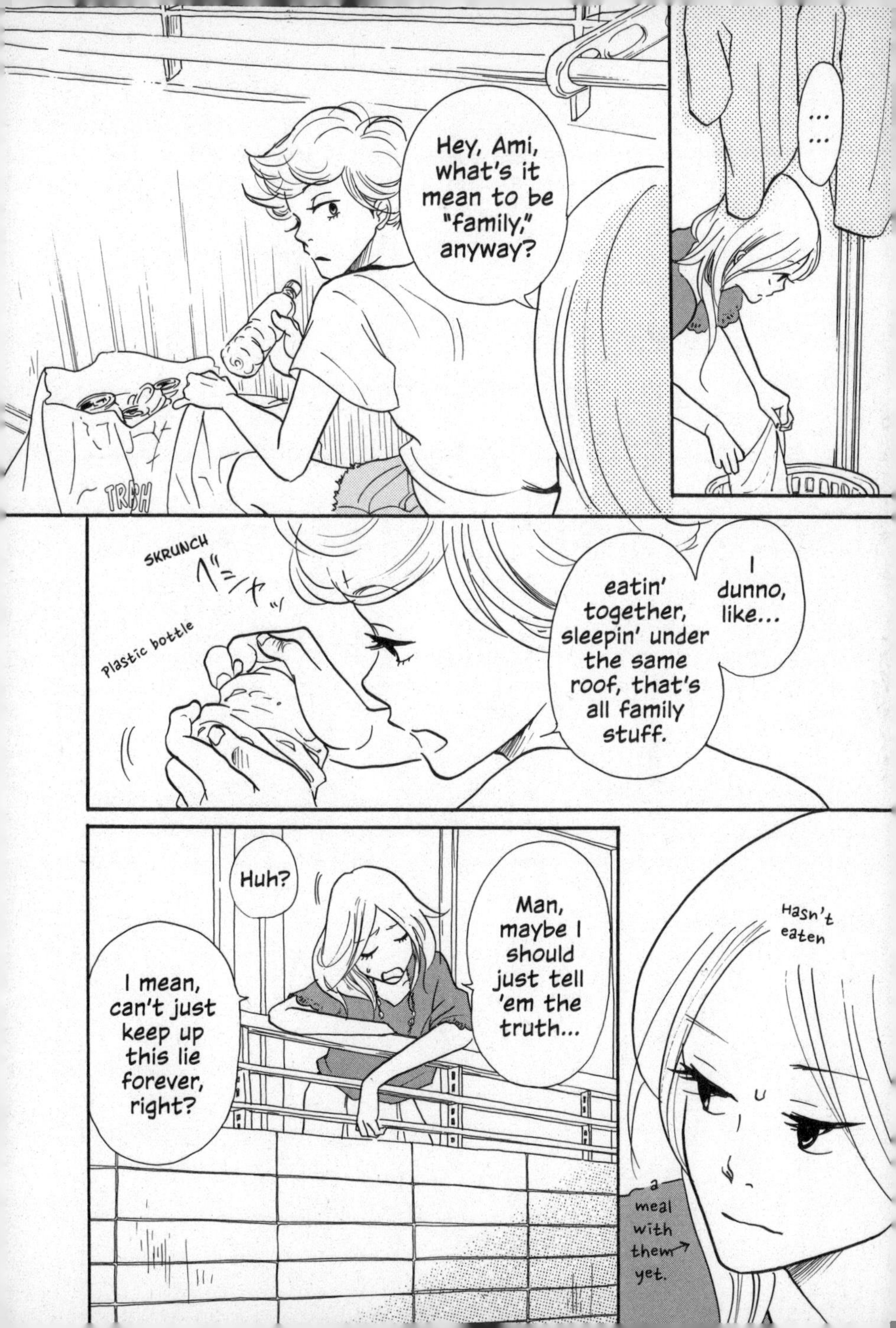
……
Hey, Ami, what's it mean to be "family," anyway?
I dunno, like...
eatin' together, sleepin' under the same roof, that's all family stuff.
SKRUNCH
Plastic bottle
Hasn't eaten a meal with them yet.
Man, maybe I should just tell 'em the truth...
Huh?
I mean, can't just keep up this lie forever, right?

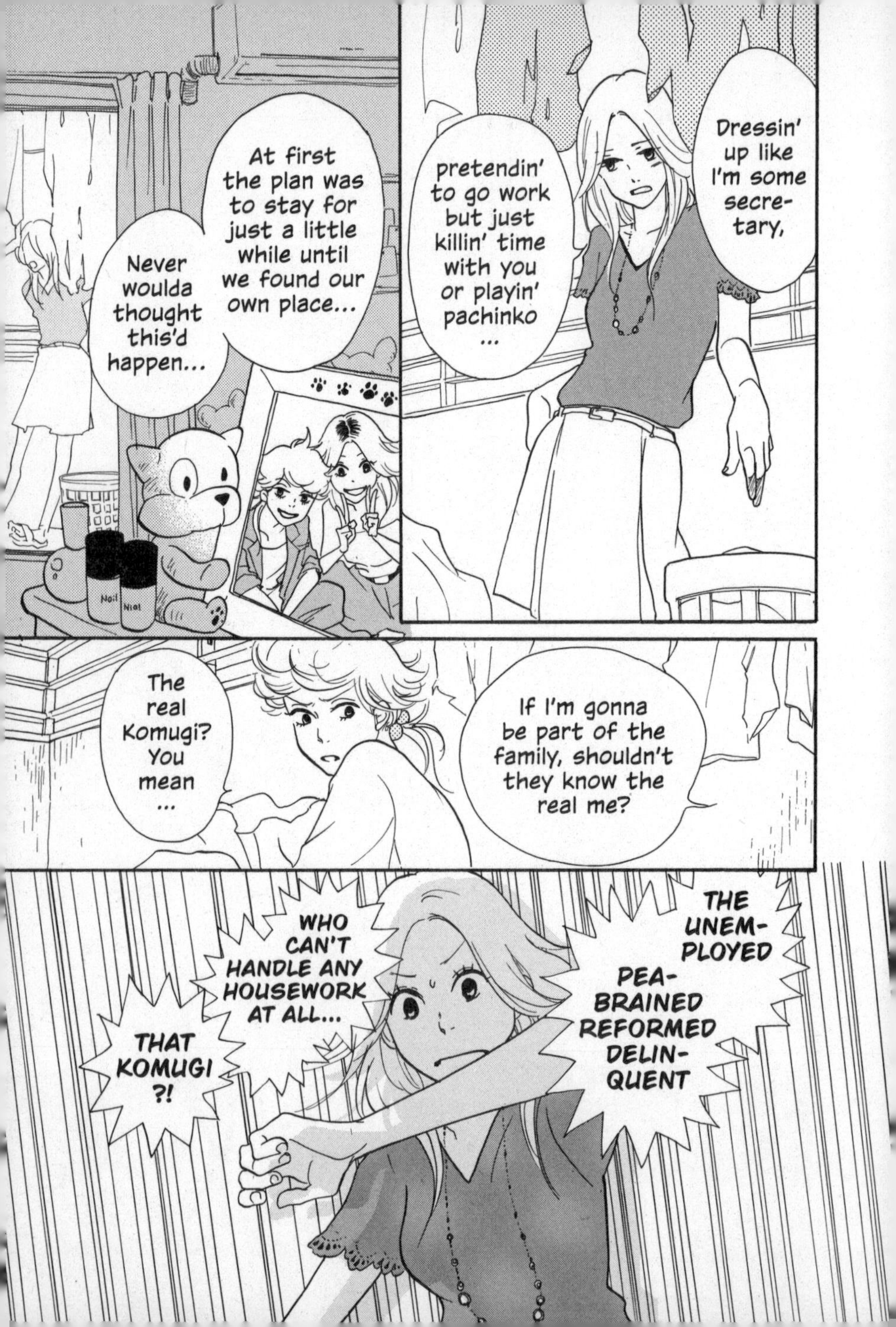
Dressin' up like I'm some secre-tary,
pretendin' to go work but just killin' time with you or playin' pachinko ...
At first the plan was to stay for just a little while until we found our own place...
Never woulda thought this'd happen...
If I'm gonna be part of the family, shouldn't they know the real me?
The real Komugi? You mean ...
THE UNEMPLOYED PEA-BRAINED REFORMED DELIN-QUENT
WHO CAN'T HANDLE ANY HOUSEWORK AT ALL...
THAT KOMUGI ?!

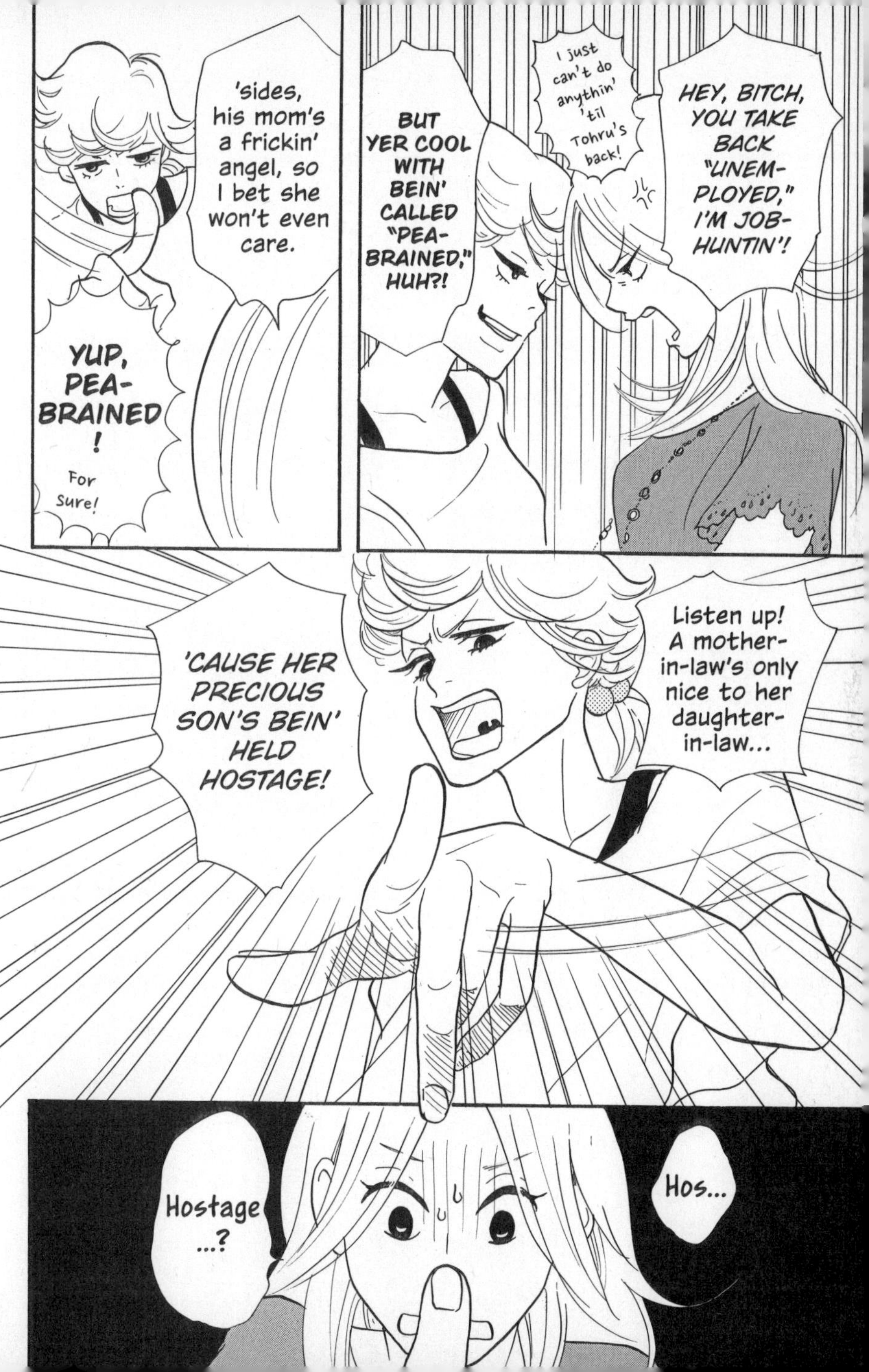
HEY, BITCH, YOU TAKE BACK "UNEMPLOYED," I'M JOB-HUNTIN'!
I just can't do anythin' 'til Tohru's back!
BUT YER COOL WITH BEIN' CALLED "PEA-BRAINED," HUH?!
'sides, his mom's a frickin' angel, so I bet she won't even care.
YUP, PEA-BRAINED!
For sure!
Listen up! A mother-in-law's only nice to her daughter-in-law...
'CAUSE HER PRECIOUS SON'S BEIN' HELD HOSTAGE!
Hos...
Hostage ...?

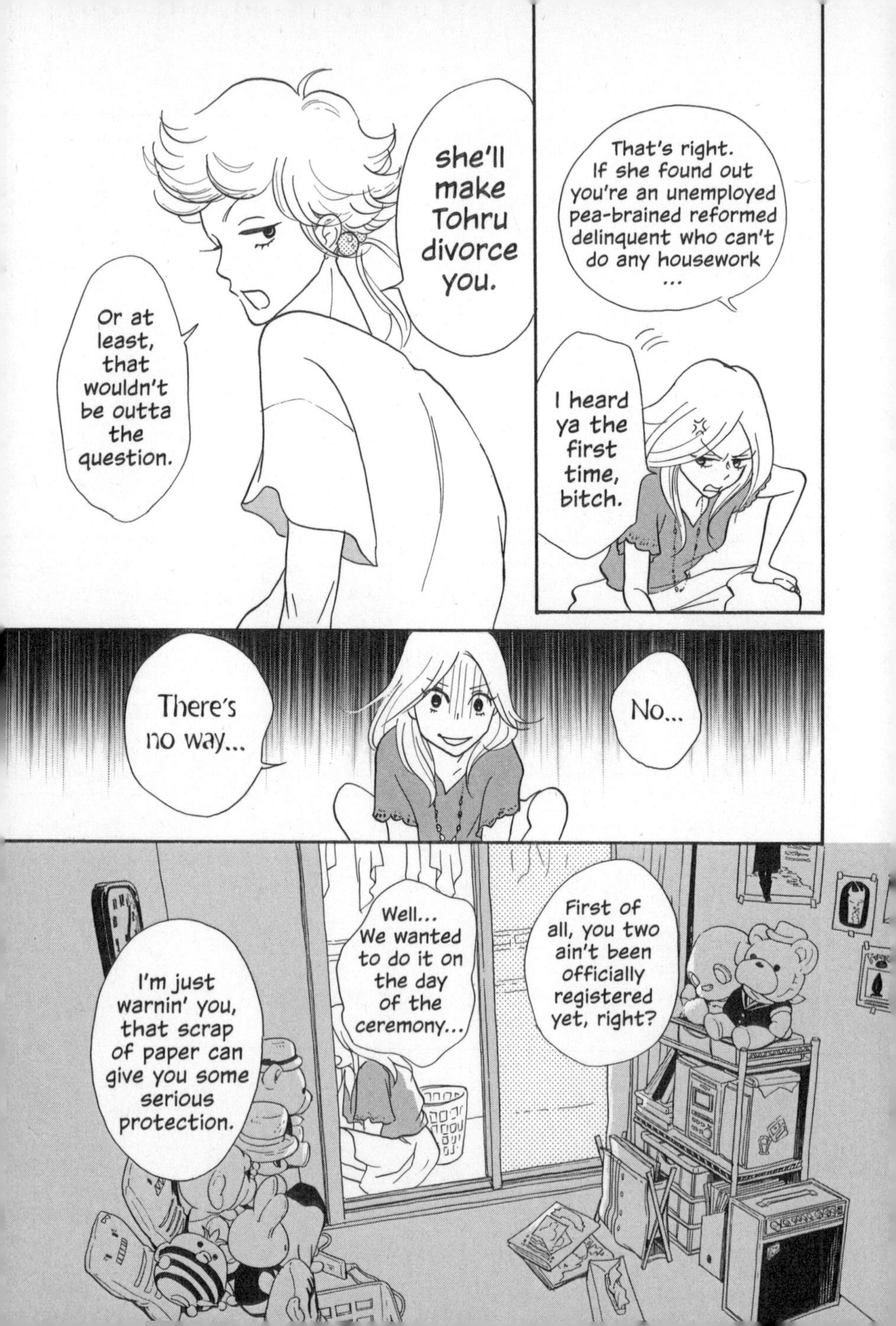
That's right. If she found out you're an unemployed pea-brained reformed delinquent who can't do any housework ...
I heard ya the first time, bitch.
she'll make Tohru divorce you.
Or at least, that wouldn't be outta the question.
No...
There's no way...
First of all, you two ain't been officially registered yet, right?
Well... We wanted to do it on the day of the ceremony...
I'm just warnin' you, that scrap of paper can give you some serious protection.

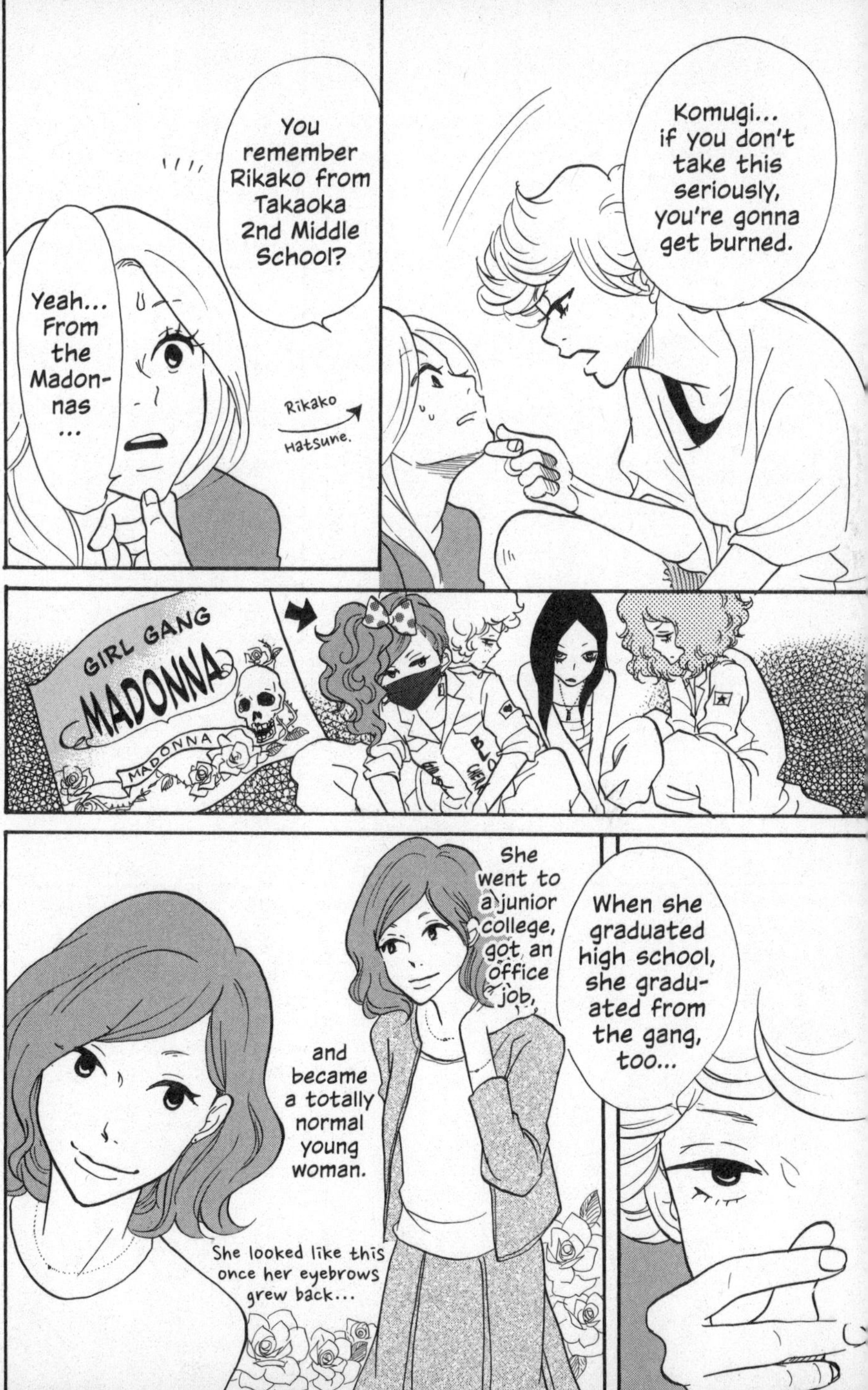

Komugi... if you don't take this seriously, you're gonna get burned.
You remember Rikako from Takaoka 2nd Middle School?
Yeah... From the Madonnas...
Rikako Hatsune.
GIRL GANG
MADONNA
MADONNA
When she graduated high school, she graduated from the gang, too...
She went to a junior college, got an office job,
and became a totally normal young woman.
She looked like this once her eyebrows grew back...

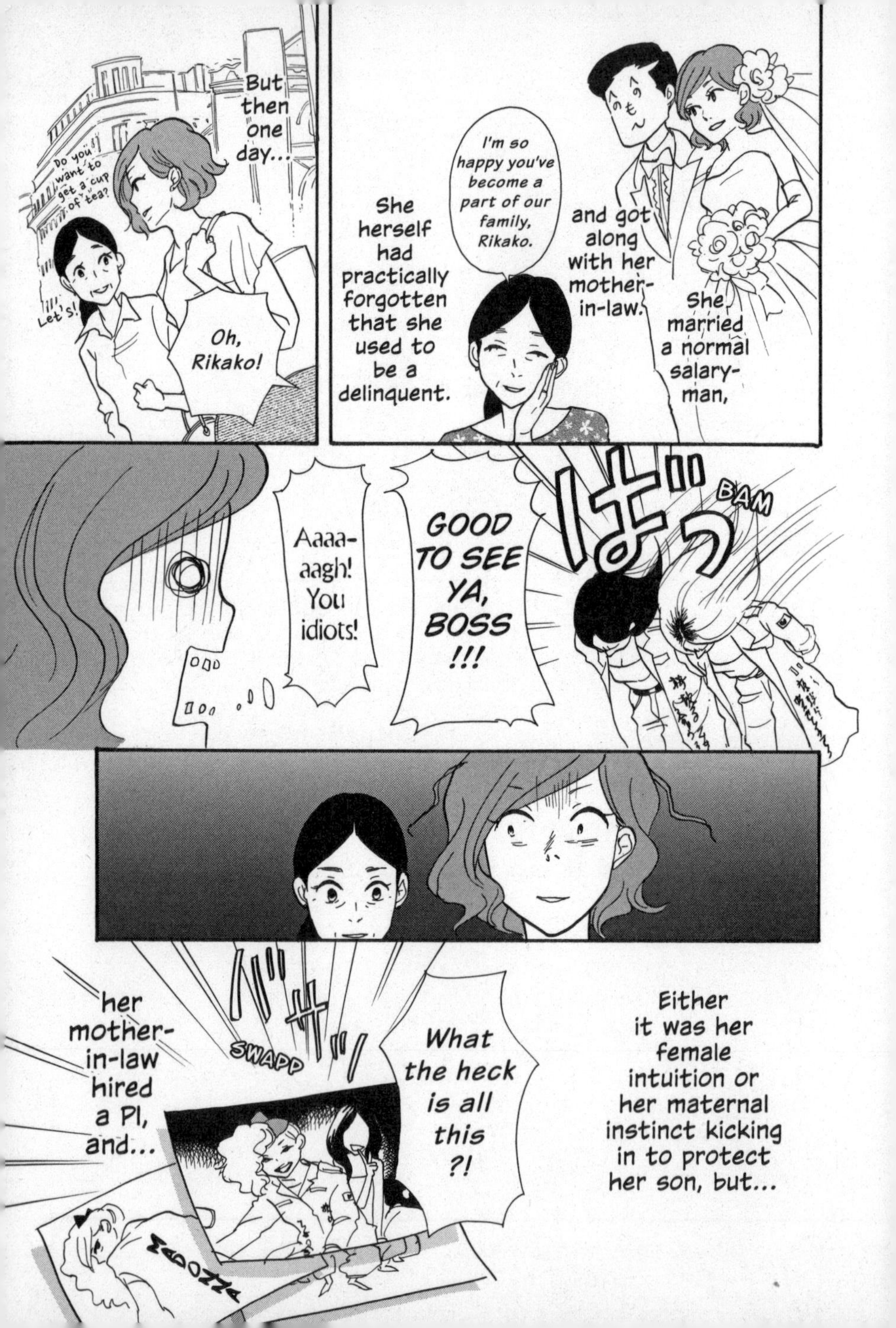

She married a normal salaryman,
and got along with her mother-in-law.
I'm so happy you've become a part of our family, Rikako.
She herself had practically forgotten that she used to be a delinquent.
But then one day...
Oh, Rikako!
Do you want to get a cup of tea?
Let's!
ぼっ
BAM
GOOD TO SEE YA, BOSS!!!
Aaaa-aagh! You idiots!
Either it was her female intuition or her maternal instinct kicking in to protect her son, but...
her mother-in-law hired a PI, and...
バサッ
SWAPP
What the heck is all this?!

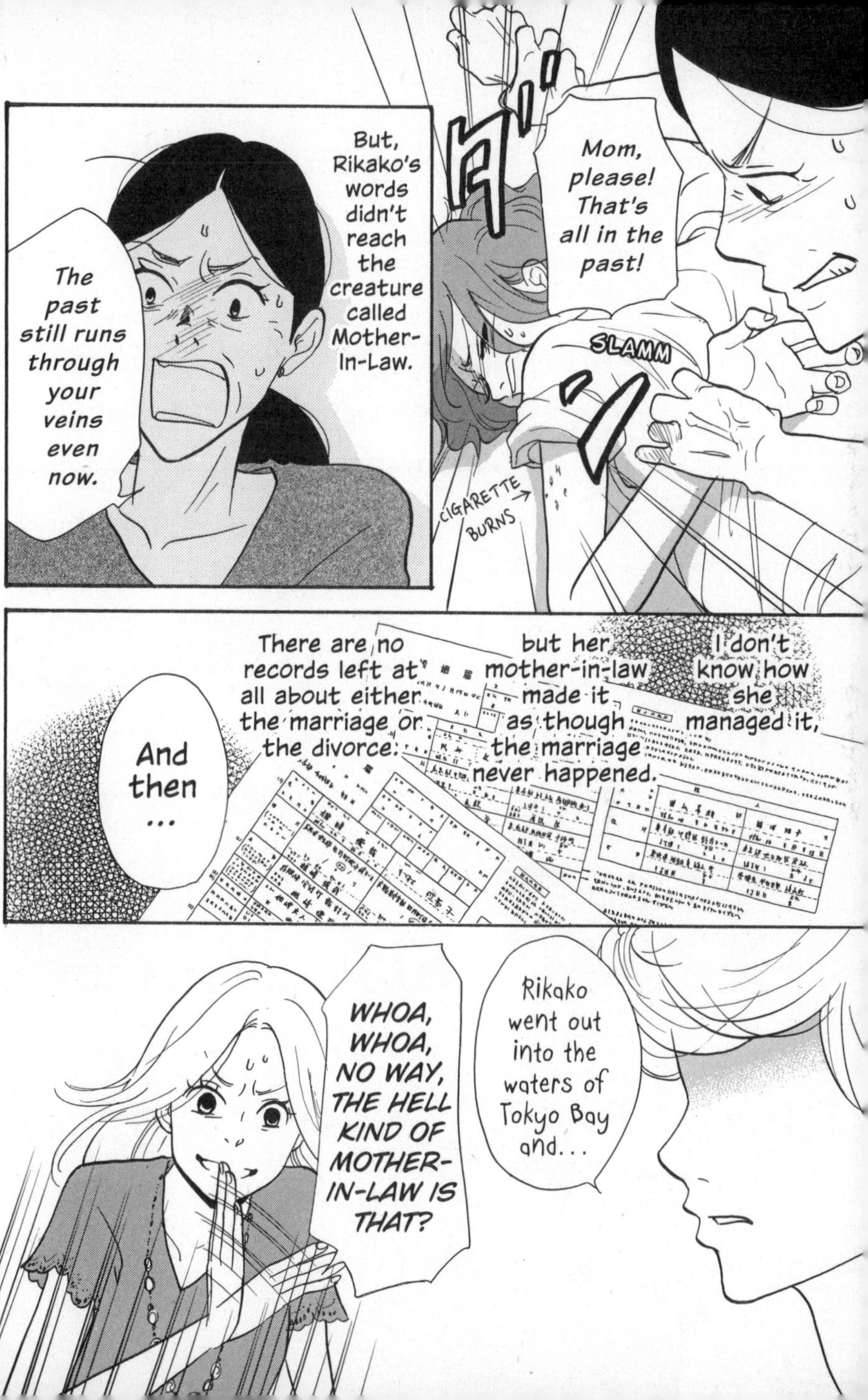
Mom, please! That's all in the past!
SLAMM
CIGARETTE BURNS
But, Rikako's words didn't reach the creature called Mother-In-Law.
The past still runs through your veins even now.
I don't know how she managed it,
but her mother-in-law made it as though the marriage never happened.
There are no records left at all about either the marriage or the divorce.
And then...
Rikako went out into the waters of Tokyo Bay and...
WHOA, WHOA, NO WAY, THE HELL KIND OF MOTHER-IN-LAW IS THAT?

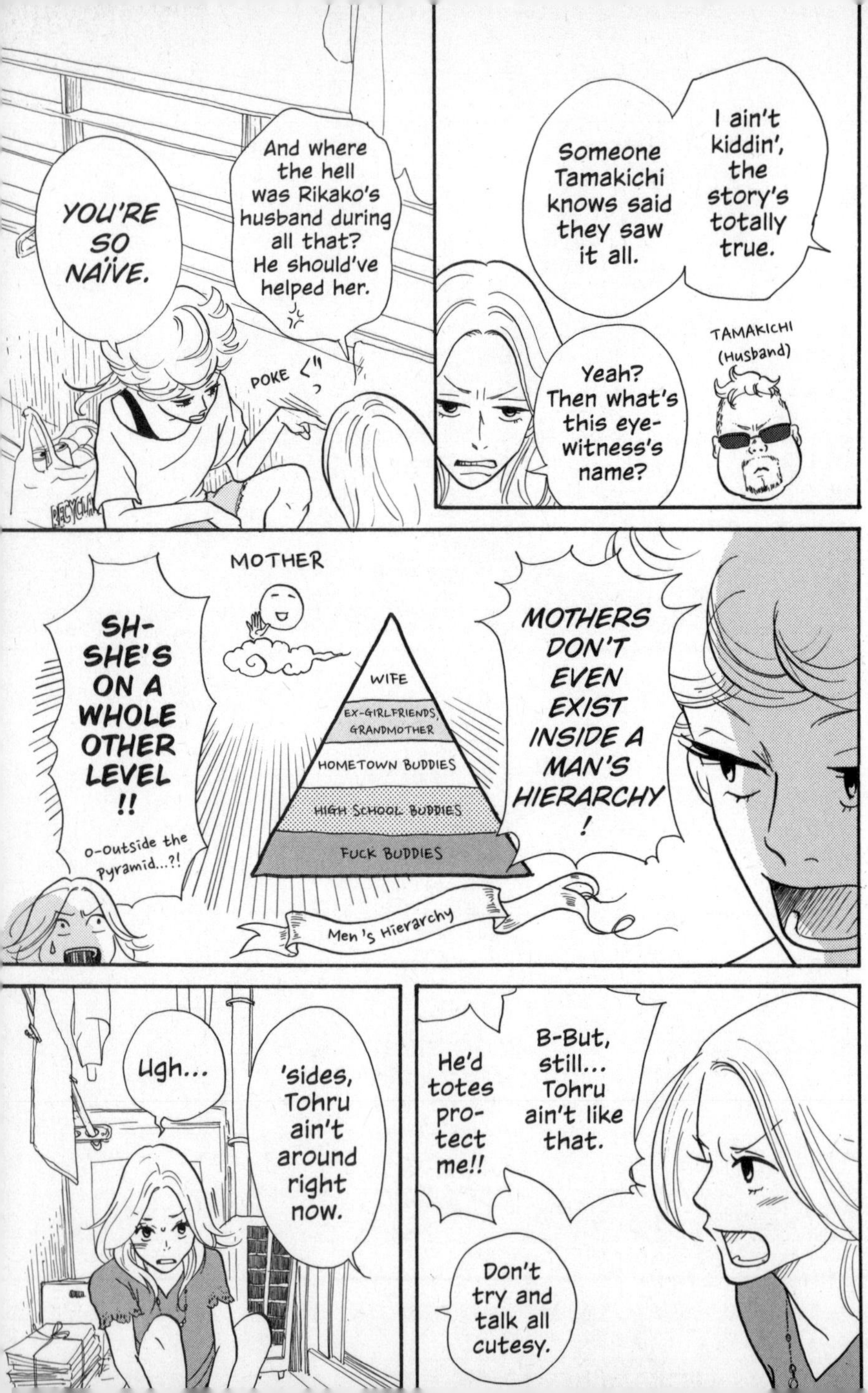
I ain't kiddin', the story's totally true.
Someone Tamakichi knows said they saw it all.
Yeah? Then what's this eye-witness's name?
TAMAKICHI (Husband)
And where the hell was Rikako's husband during all that? He should've helped her.
YOU'RE SO NAÏVE.
POKE
MOTHERS DON'T EVEN EXIST INSIDE A MAN'S HIERARCHY!
MOTHER
WIFE
EX-GIRLFRIENDS, GRANDMOTHER
HOMETOWN BUDDIES
HIGH SCHOOL BUDDIES
FUCK BUDDIES
Men's Hierarchy
SH-SHE'S ON A WHOLE OTHER LEVEL!!
O-Outside the Pyramid...?!
B-But, still... Tohru ain't like that.
He'd totes pro-tect me!!
Don't try and talk all cutesy.
'sides, Tohru ain't around right now.
Ugh...

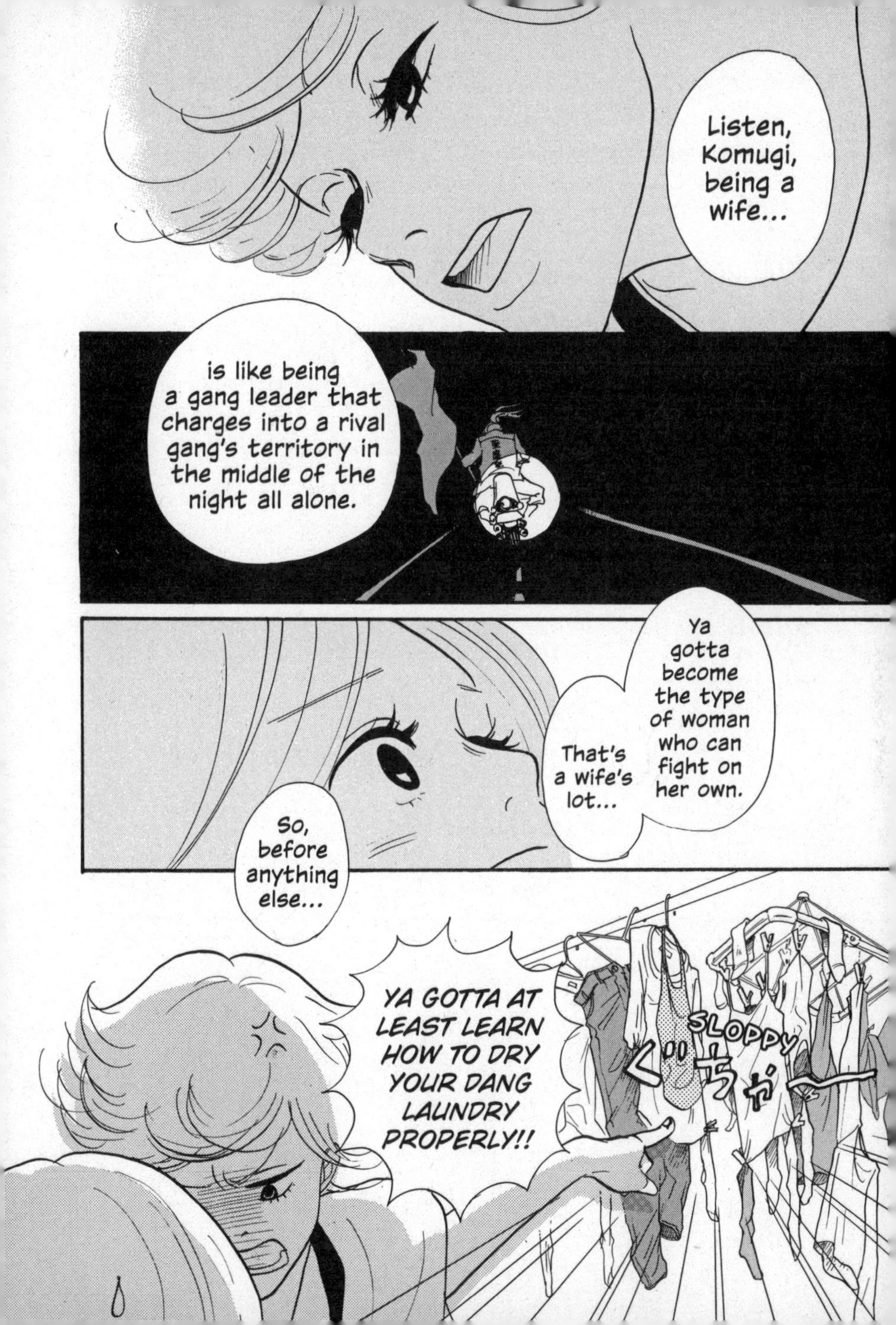
Listen, Komugi, being a wife...
is like being a gang leader that charges into a rival gang's territory in the middle of the night all alone.
Ya gotta become the type of woman who can fight on her own.
That's a wife's lot...
So, before anything else...
YA GOTTA AT LEAST LEARN HOW TO DRY YOUR DANG LAUNDRY PROPERLY!!
SLOPPY
ぐちゃー

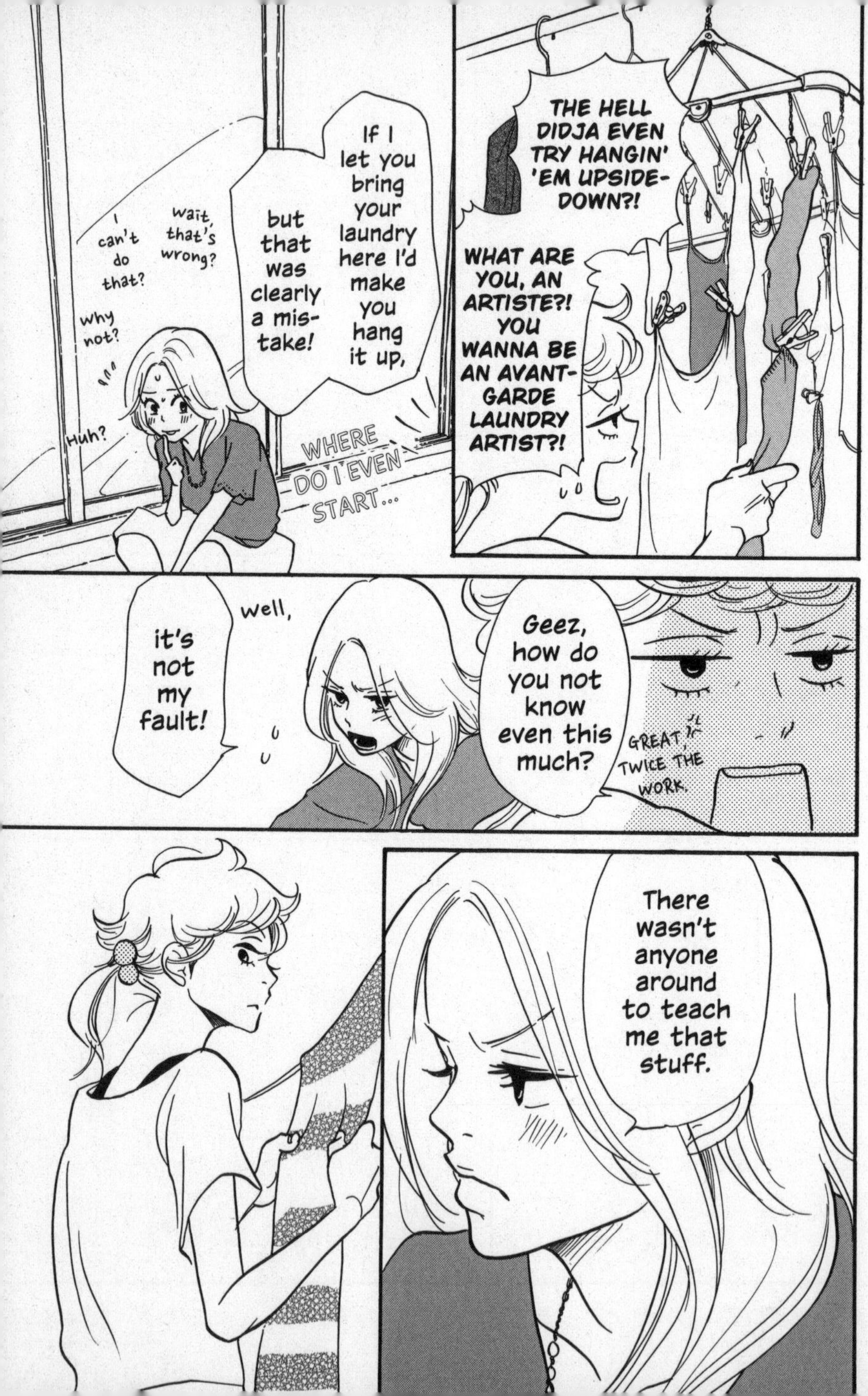
THE HELL DIDJA EVEN TRY HANGIN' 'EM UPSIDE-DOWN?!
WHAT ARE YOU, AN ARTISTE?! YOU WANNA BE AN AVANT-GARDE LAUNDRY ARTIST?!
If I let you bring your laundry here I'd make you hang it up,
but that was clearly a mistake!
WHERE DO I EVEN START...
wait, that's wrong?
I can't do that?
why not?
Huh?
Geez, how do you not know even this much?
GREAT, TWICE THE WORK
well,
it's not my fault!
There wasn't anyone around to teach me that stuff.

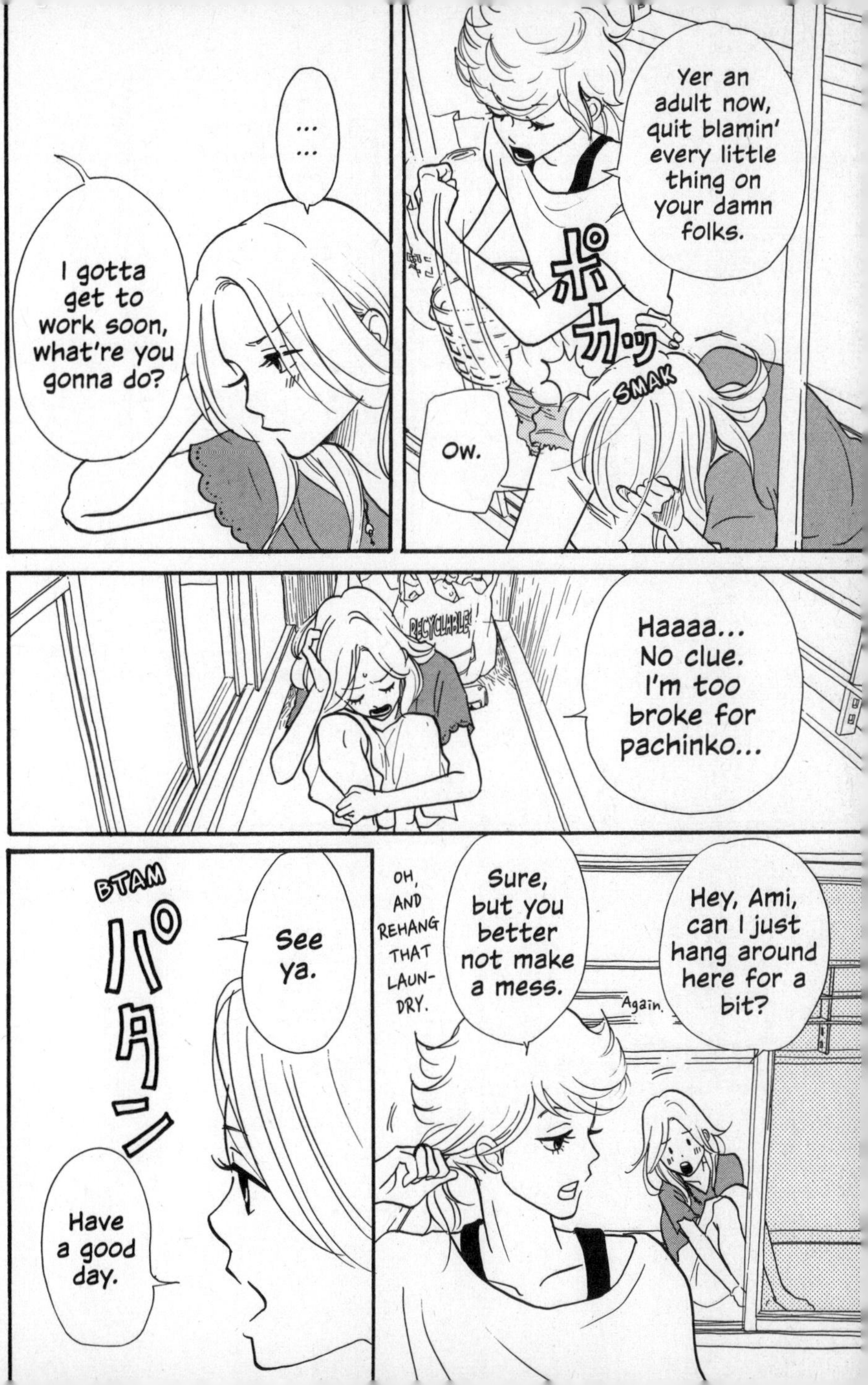
Yer an adult now, quit blamin' every little thing on your damn folks.
ポカッ
SMAK
Ow.
……
I gotta get to work soon, what're you gonna do?
Haaaa... No clue. I'm too broke for pachinko...
Hey, Ami, can I just hang around here for a bit?
Again.
Sure, but you better not make a mess.
OH, AND REHANG THAT LAUN-DRY.
See ya.
BTAM
パターン
Have a good day.

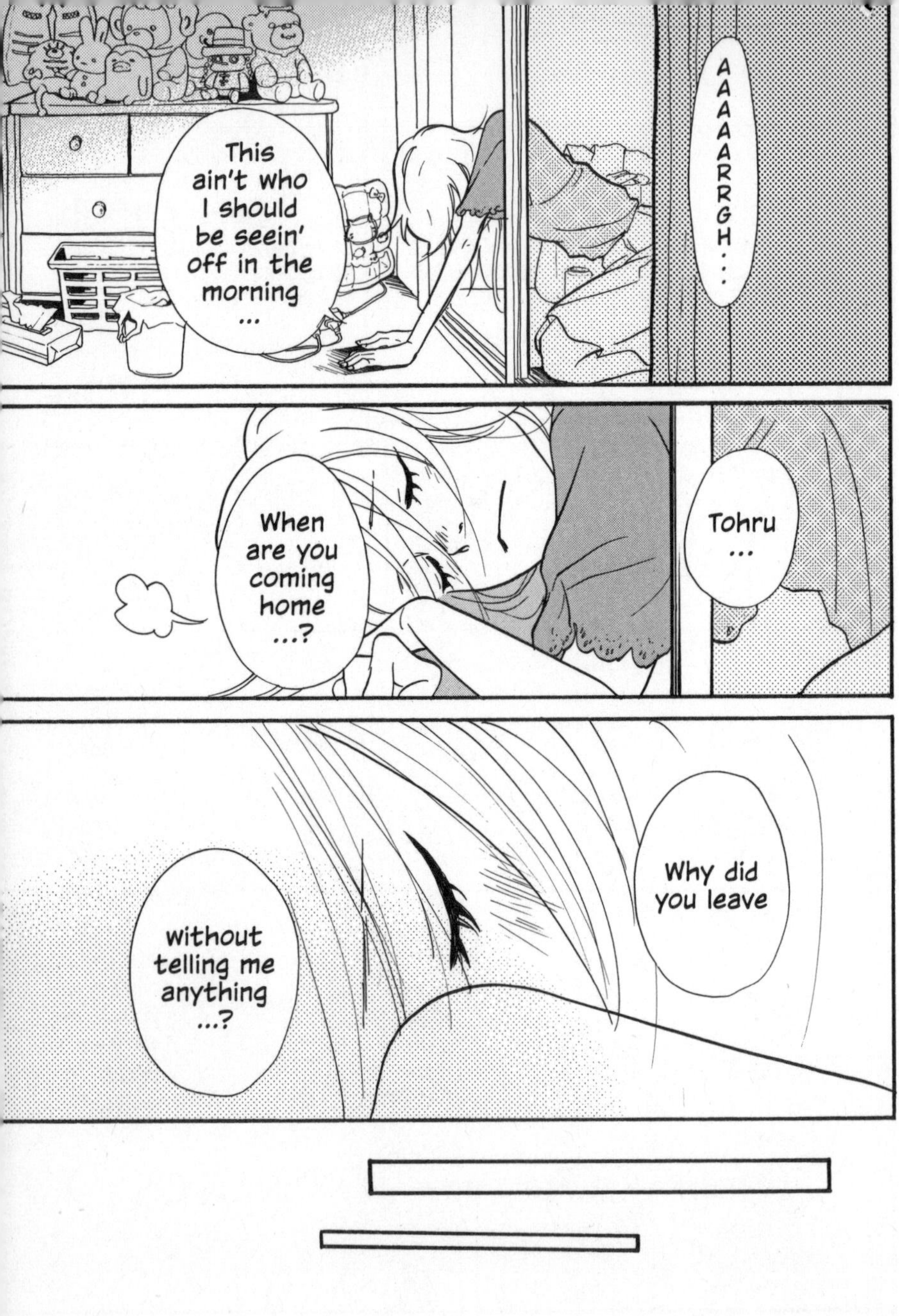
AAAAARRGH...
This ain't who I should be seein' off in the morning ...
Tohru ...
When are you coming home ...?
Why did you leave
without telling me anything ...?

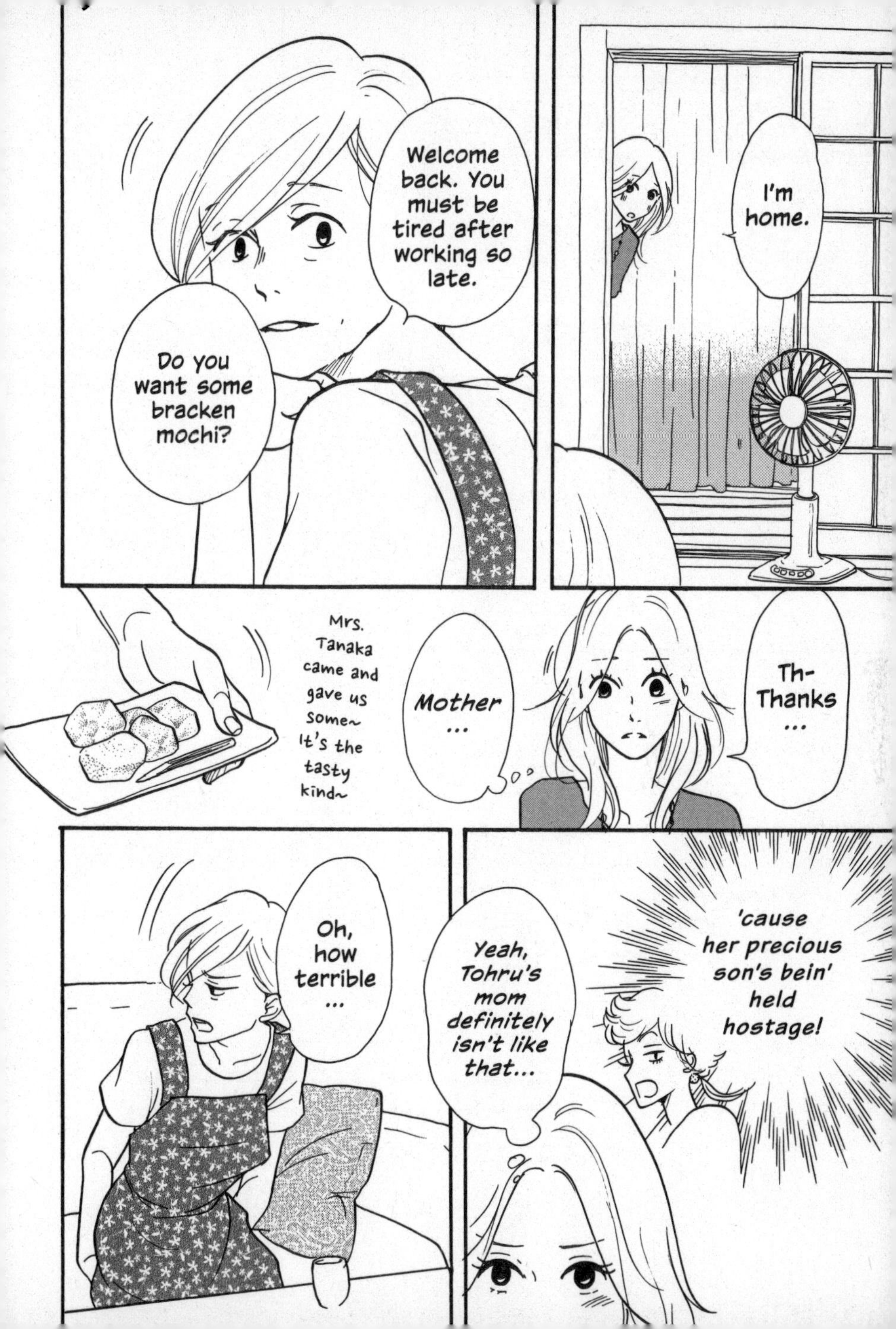
I'm home.
Welcome back. You must be tired after working so late.
Do you want some bracken mochi?
Th- Thanks...
Mother...
Mrs. Tanaka came and gave us some~ It's the tasty kind~
'cause her precious son's bein' held hostage!
Yeah, Tohru's mom definitely isn't like that...
Oh, how terrible...

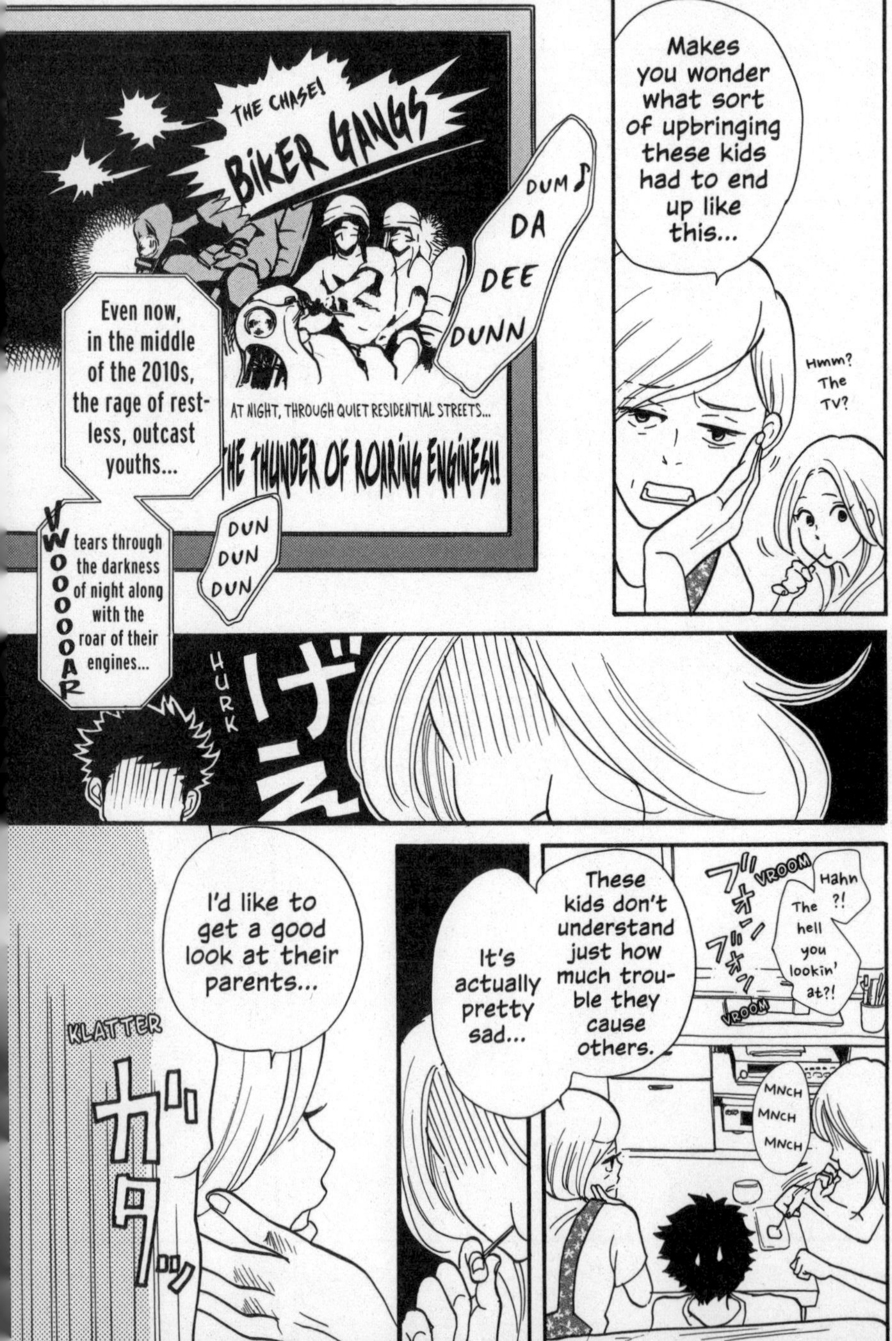
Makes you wonder what sort of upbringing these kids had to end up like this...
Hmm? The TV?
THE CHASE!
BIKER GANGS
DUM♪ DA DEE DUNN
Even now, in the middle of the 2010s, the rage of restless, outcast youths...
AT NIGHT, THROUGH QUIET RESIDENTIAL STREETS...
THE THUNDER OF ROARING ENGINES!!
DUN DUN DUN
VWOOOOOOAR tears through the darkness of night along with the roar of their engines...
HURK
VROOM
Hahn ?!
The hell you lookin' at?!
VROOM
MNCH MNCH MNCH
These kids don't understand just how much trouble they cause others.
It's actually pretty sad...
I'd like to get a good look at their parents...
KLATTER

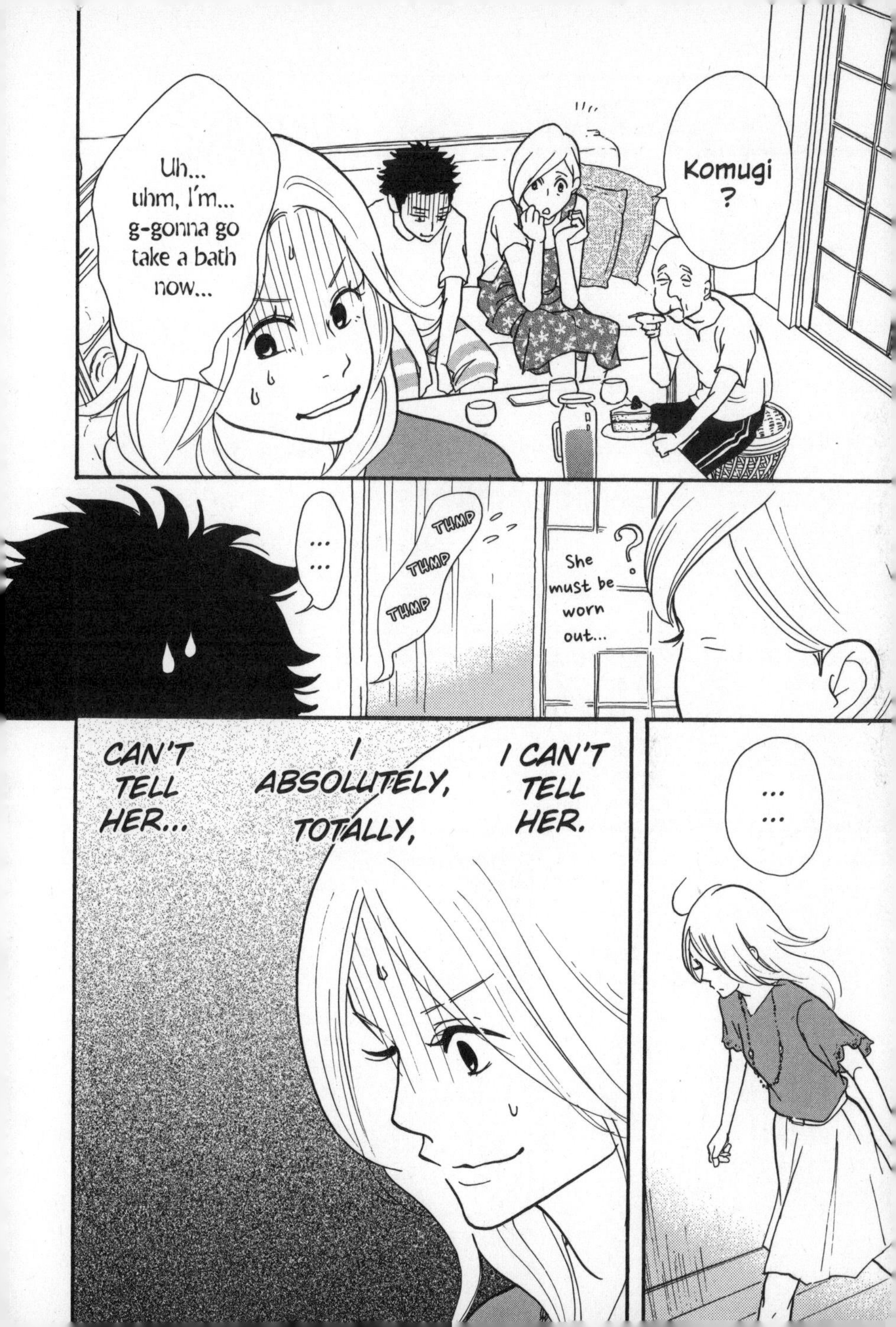
Komugi ?
Uh... uhm, I'm... g-gonna go take a bath now...
She must be worn out...
THMP THMP THMP
... ...
... ...
I CAN'T TELL HER.
I ABSOLUTELY, TOTALLY,
CAN'T TELL HER...

5 MY SISTER-IN-LAW IS IN 8TH GRADE

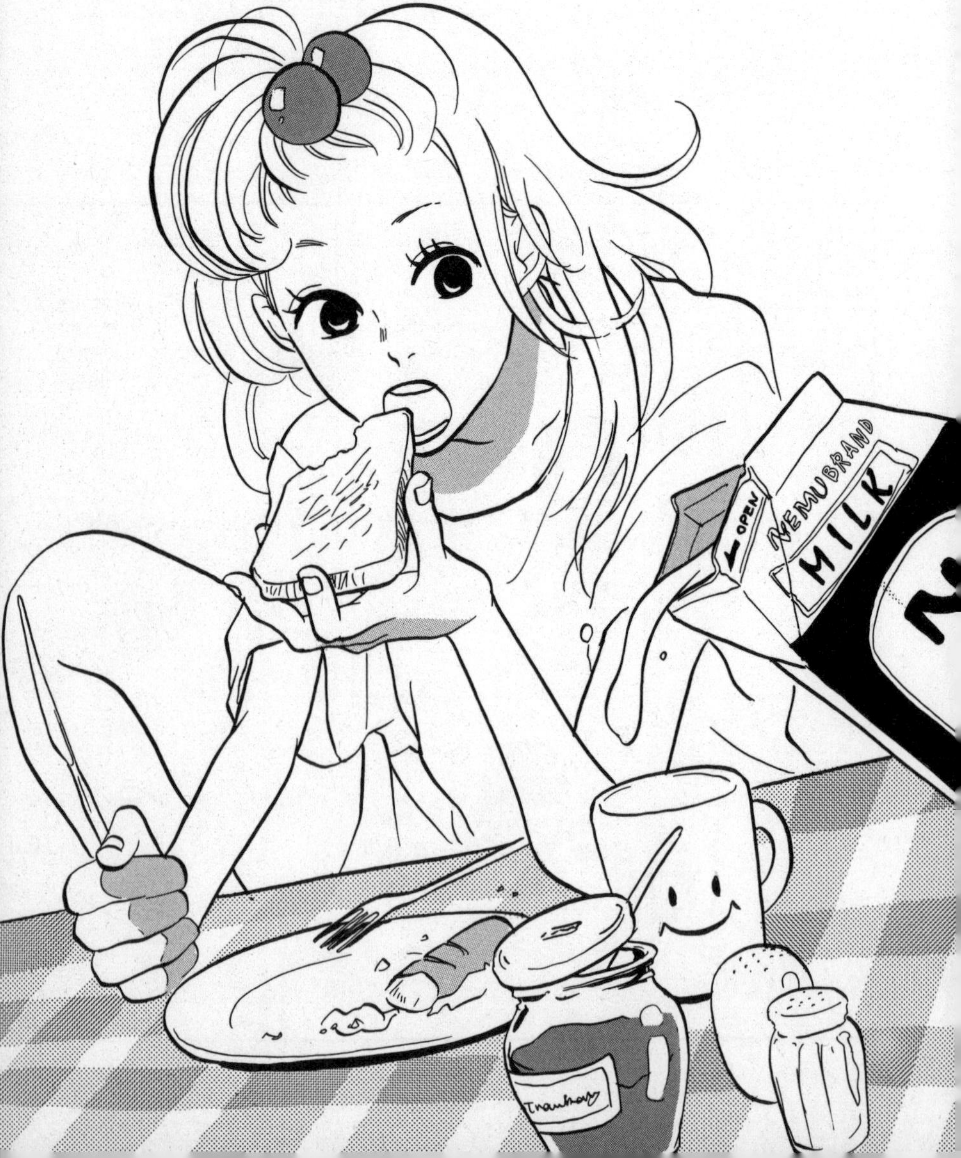
OPEN
NEMUBRAND
MILK

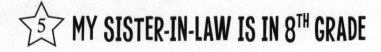

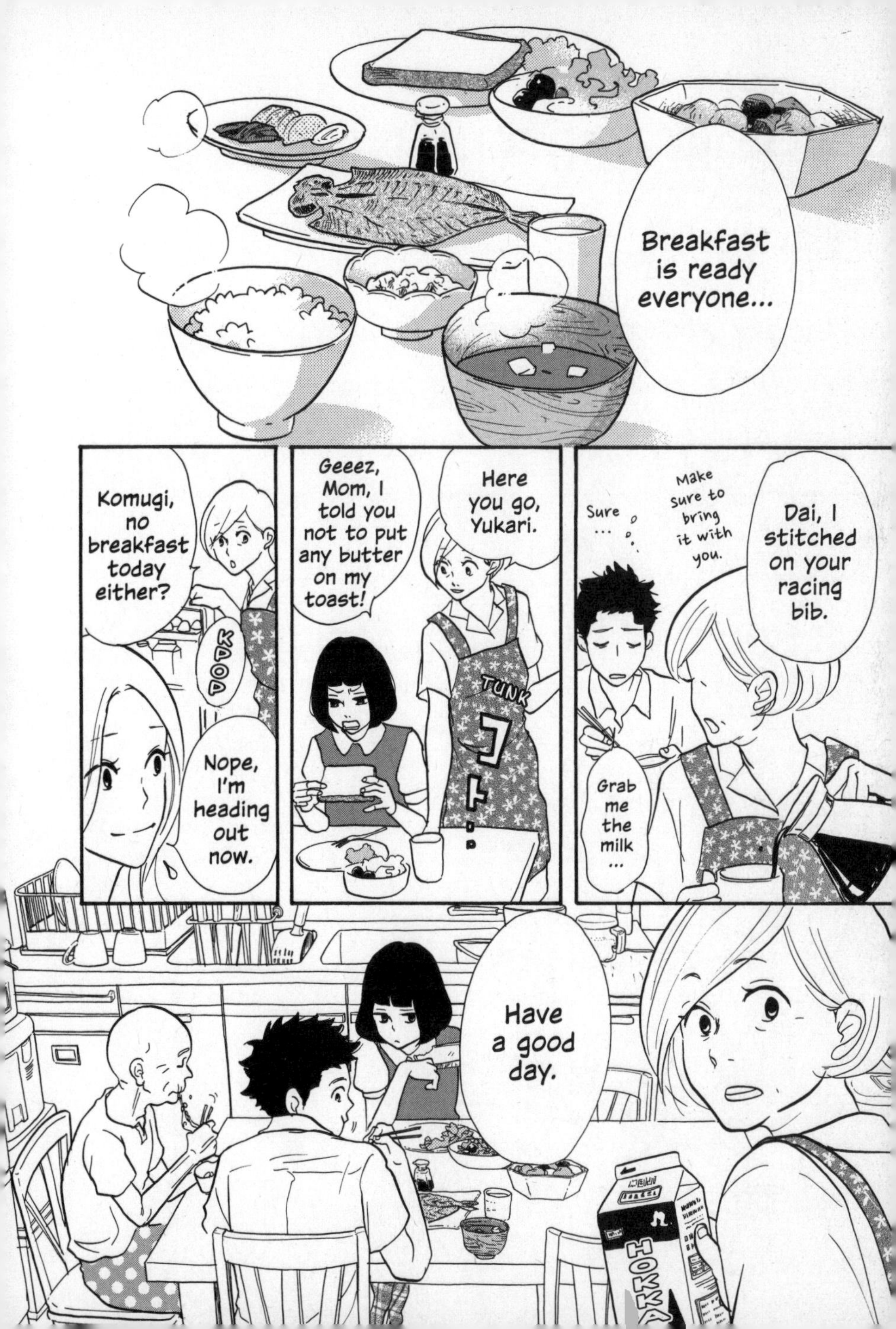
Breakfast is ready everyone...
Dai, I stitched on your racing bib.
Make sure to bring it with you.
Sure...
Grab me the milk...
Here you go, Yukari.
Geeez, Mom, I told you not to put any butter on my toast!
TUNK
コト
Komugi, no breakfast today either?
KPOP
Nope, I'm heading out now.
Have a good day.
HOKKA

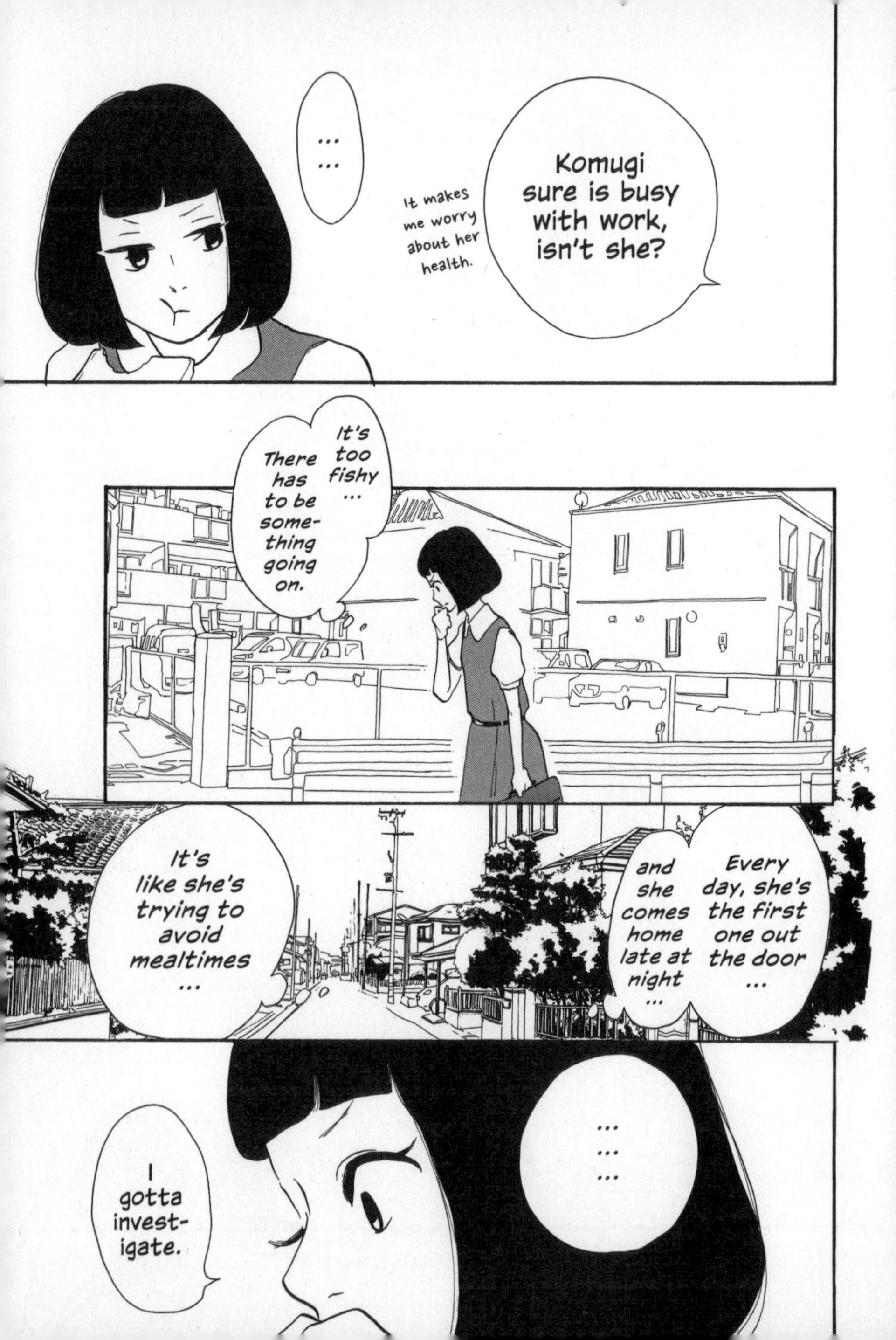
Komugi sure is busy with work, isn't she?
It makes me worry about her health.
... ...
It's too fishy ...
There has to be some-thing going on.
Every day, she's the first one out the door ...
and she comes home late at night ...
It's like she's trying to avoid mealtimes ...
... ...
I gotta invest-igate.

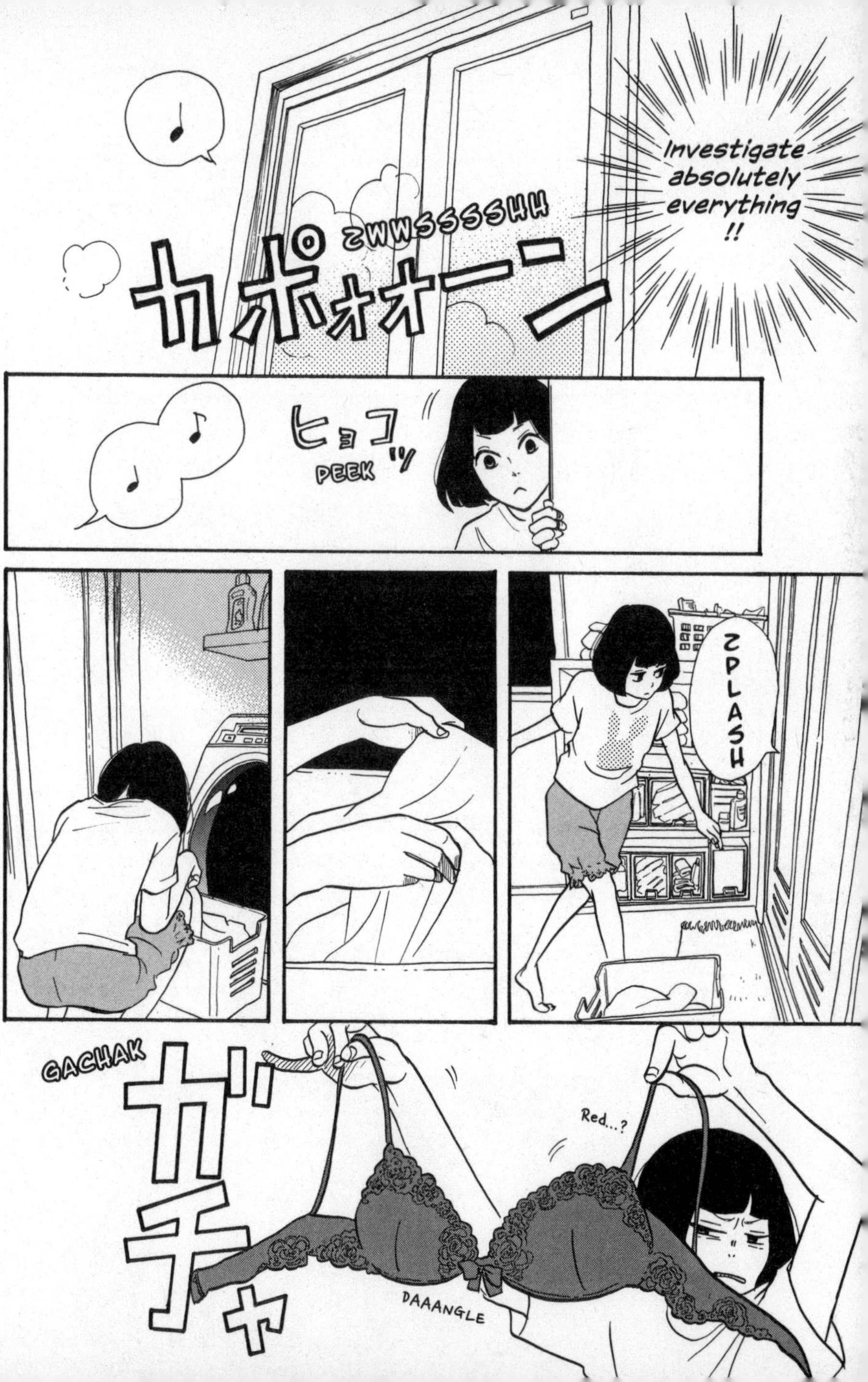
Investigate absolutely everything !!
カポォオーン
SWWSSSSSHH
♪
ヒョコッ
PEEK
♪ ♪
SPLASH
Red...?
ガチャ
GACHAK
DAAANGLE

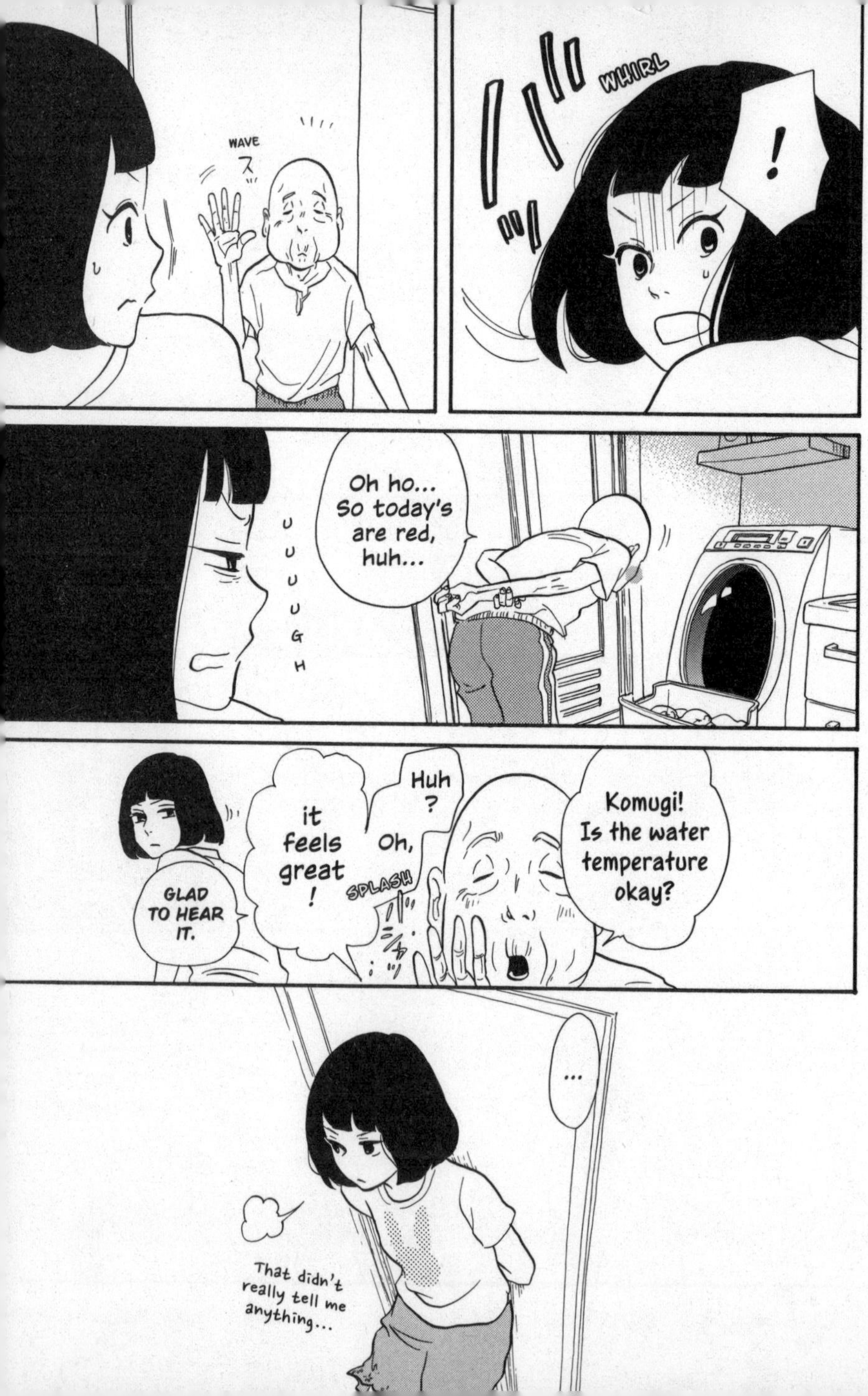
WHIRL
!
WAVE
ス
Oh ho... So today's are red, huh...
UUUUUGH
Komugi! Is the water temperature okay?
Huh?
Oh, it feels great!
SPLASH
GLAD TO HEAR IT.
...
That didn't really tell me anything...

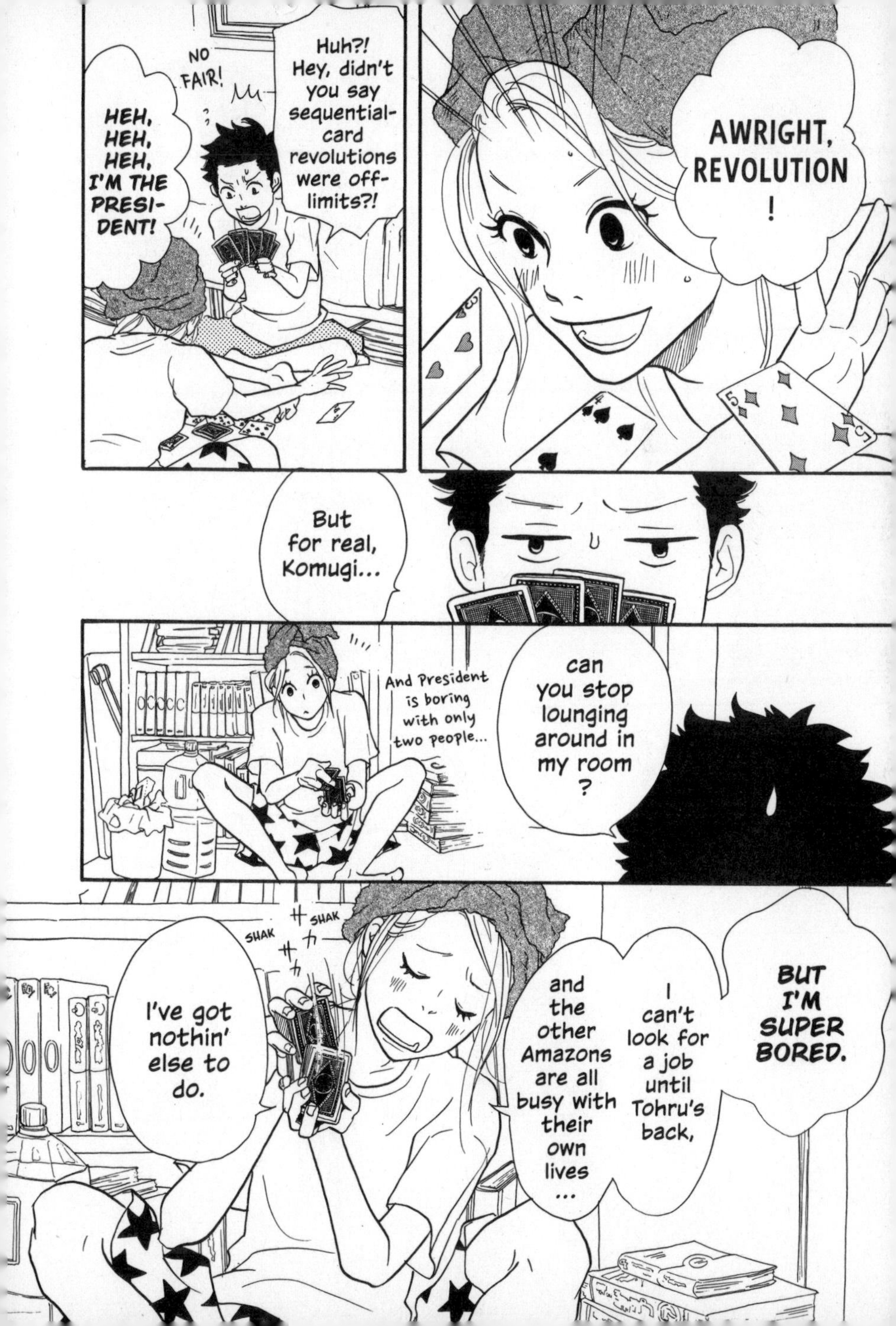
AWRIGHT, REVOLUTION!
Huh?! Hey, didn't you say sequential-card revolutions were off-limits?!
NO FAIR!
HEH, HEH, HEH, I'M THE PRESIDENT!
But for real, Komugi...
can you stop lounging around in my room?
And President is boring with only two people...
BUT I'M SUPER BORED.
I can't look for a job until Tohru's back,
and the other Amazons are all busy with their own lives...
SHAK
SHAK
I've got nothin' else to do.

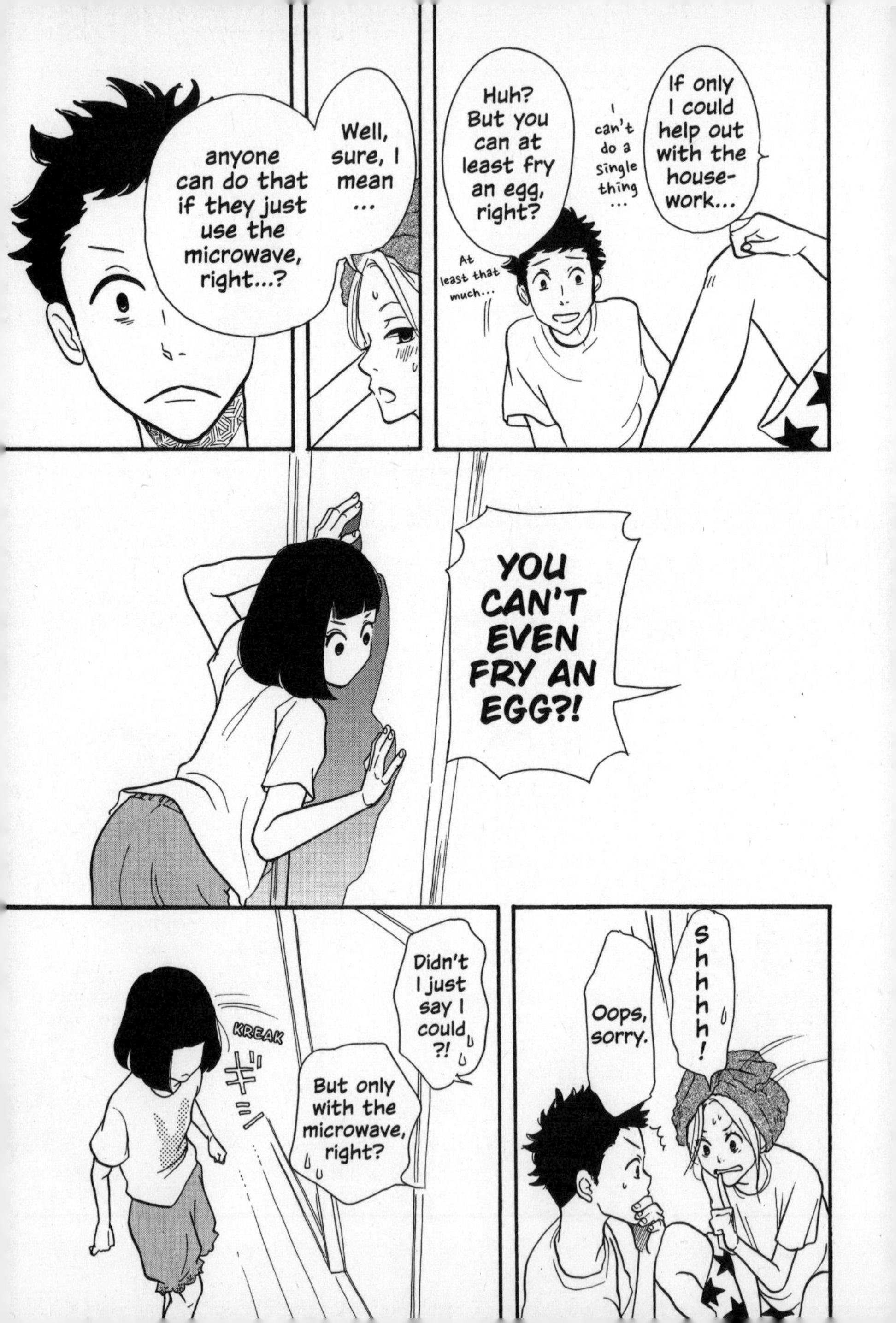
If only I could help out with the house-work...
I can't do a single thing...
Huh? But you can at least fry an egg, right?
At least that much...
Well, sure, I mean...
anyone can do that if they just use the microwave, right...?
YOU CAN'T EVEN FRY AN EGG?!
Shhhh!
Oops, sorry.
Didn't I just say I could?!
But only with the microwave, right?
KREAK
ギー

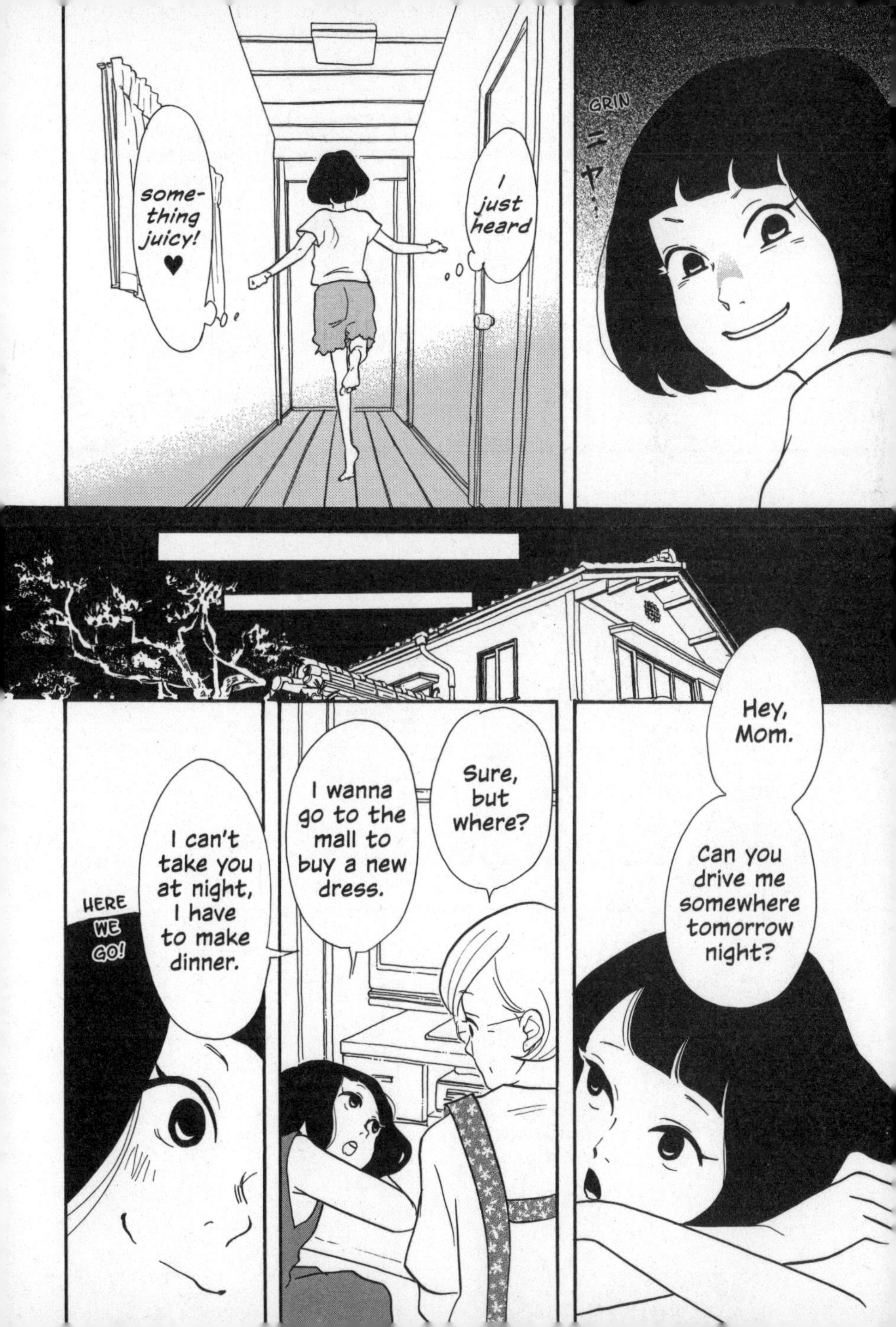
GRIN
ニヤ…
I just heard
something-thing juicy! ♥
Hey, Mom.
Can you drive me somewhere tomorrow night?
Sure, but where?
I wanna go to the mall to buy a new dress.
I can't take you at night, I have to make dinner.
HERE WE GO!

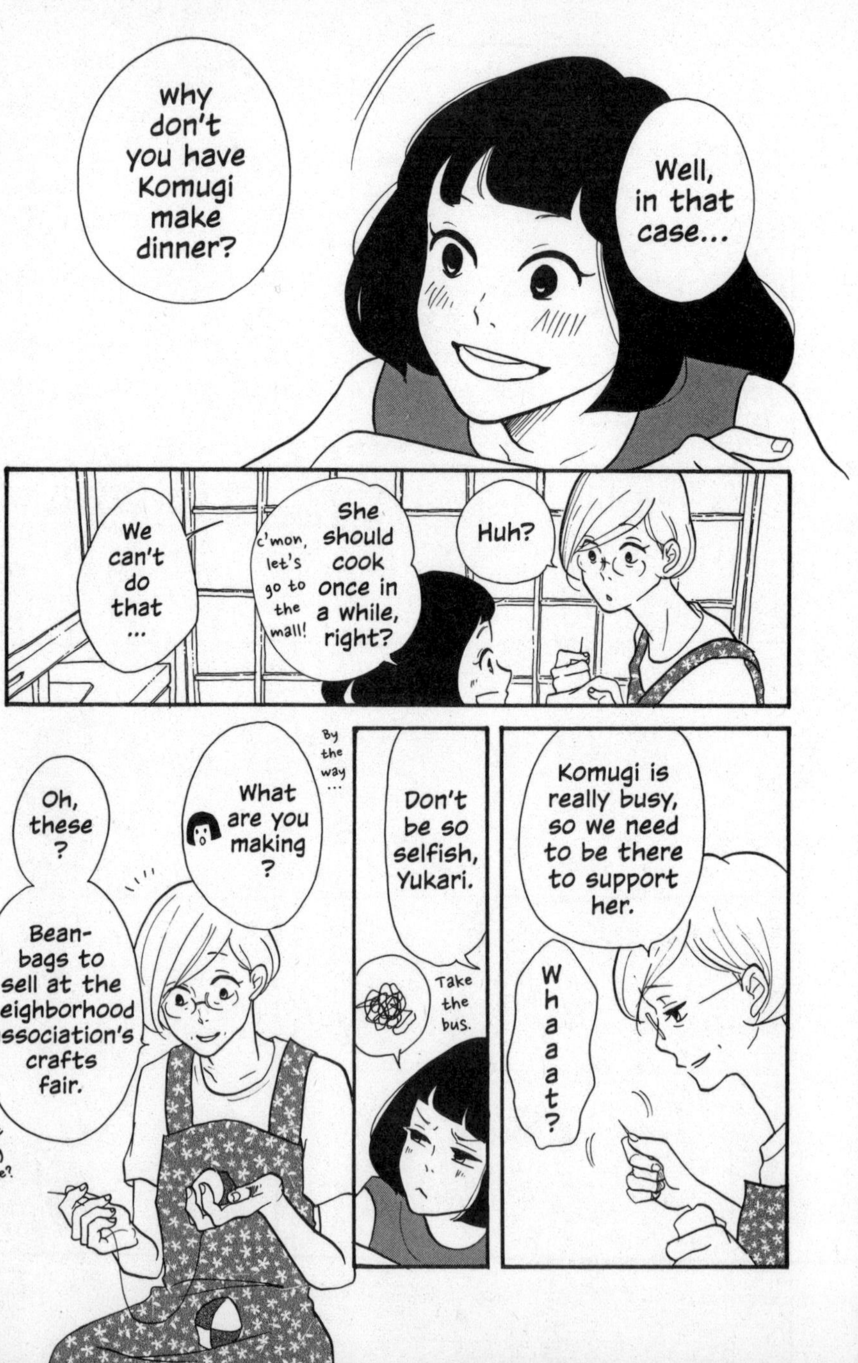
Well, in that case...
Why don't you have Komugi make dinner?
Huh?
She should cook once in a while, right?
c'mon, let's go to the mall!
We can't do that ...
Komugi is really busy, so we need to be there to support her.
Whaaaat?
Don't be so selfish, Yukari.
Take the bus.
By the way ...
What are you making?
Oh, these?
Bean-bags to sell at the neighborhood association's crafts fair.
Aren't they cute?

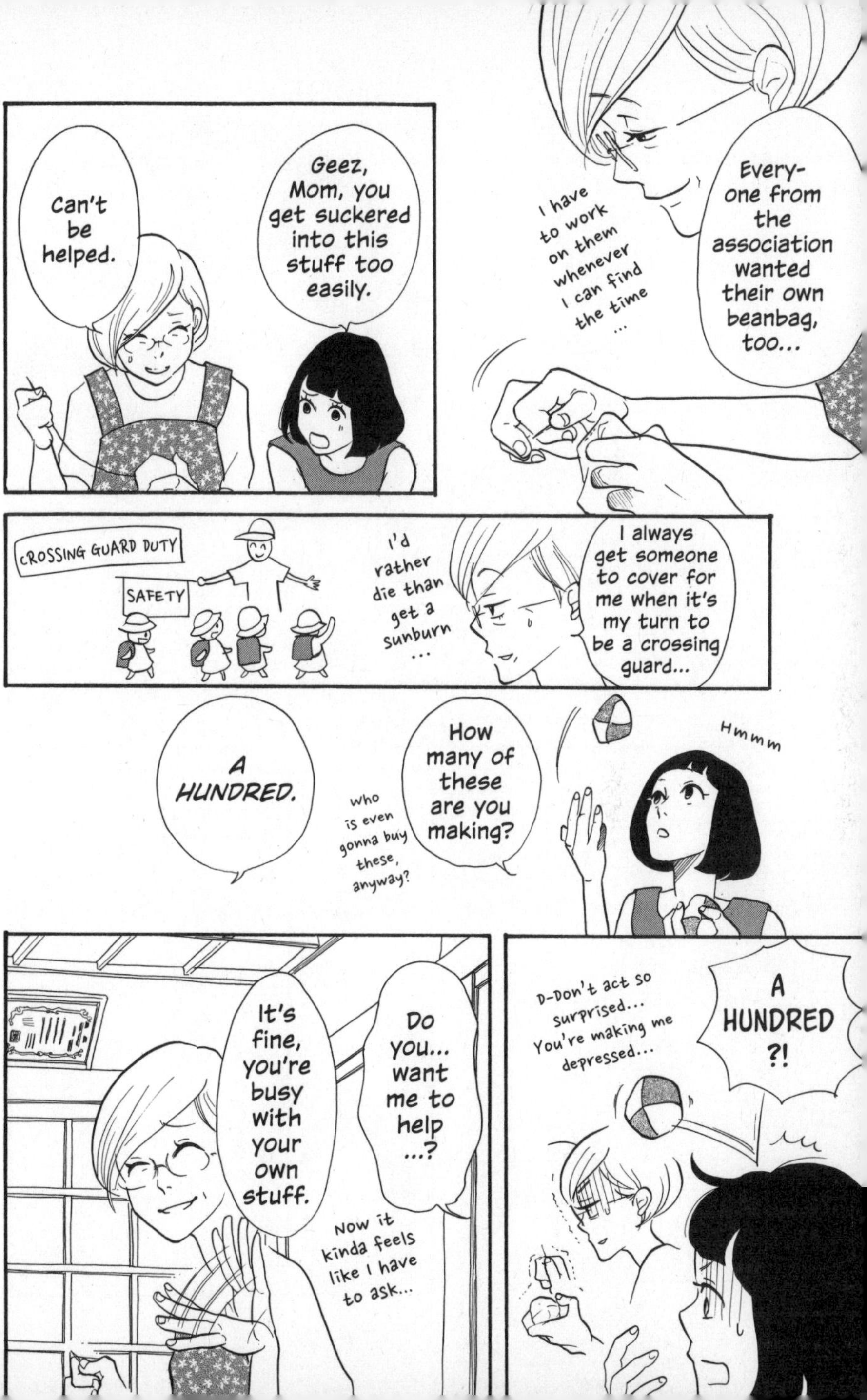
Every-one from the association wanted their own beanbag, too...
I have to work on them whenever I can find the time ...
Geez, Mom, you get suckered into this stuff too easily.
Can't be helped.
I always get someone to cover for me when it's my turn to be a crossing guard...
I'd rather die than get a sunburn ...
CROSSING GUARD DUTY
SAFETY
Hmmm
How many of these are you making?
Who is even gonna buy these, anyway?
A HUNDRED.
A HUNDRED ?!
D-Don't act so surprised... You're making me depressed...
Do you... want me to help ...?
Now it kinda feels like I have to ask...
It's fine, you're busy with your own stuff.

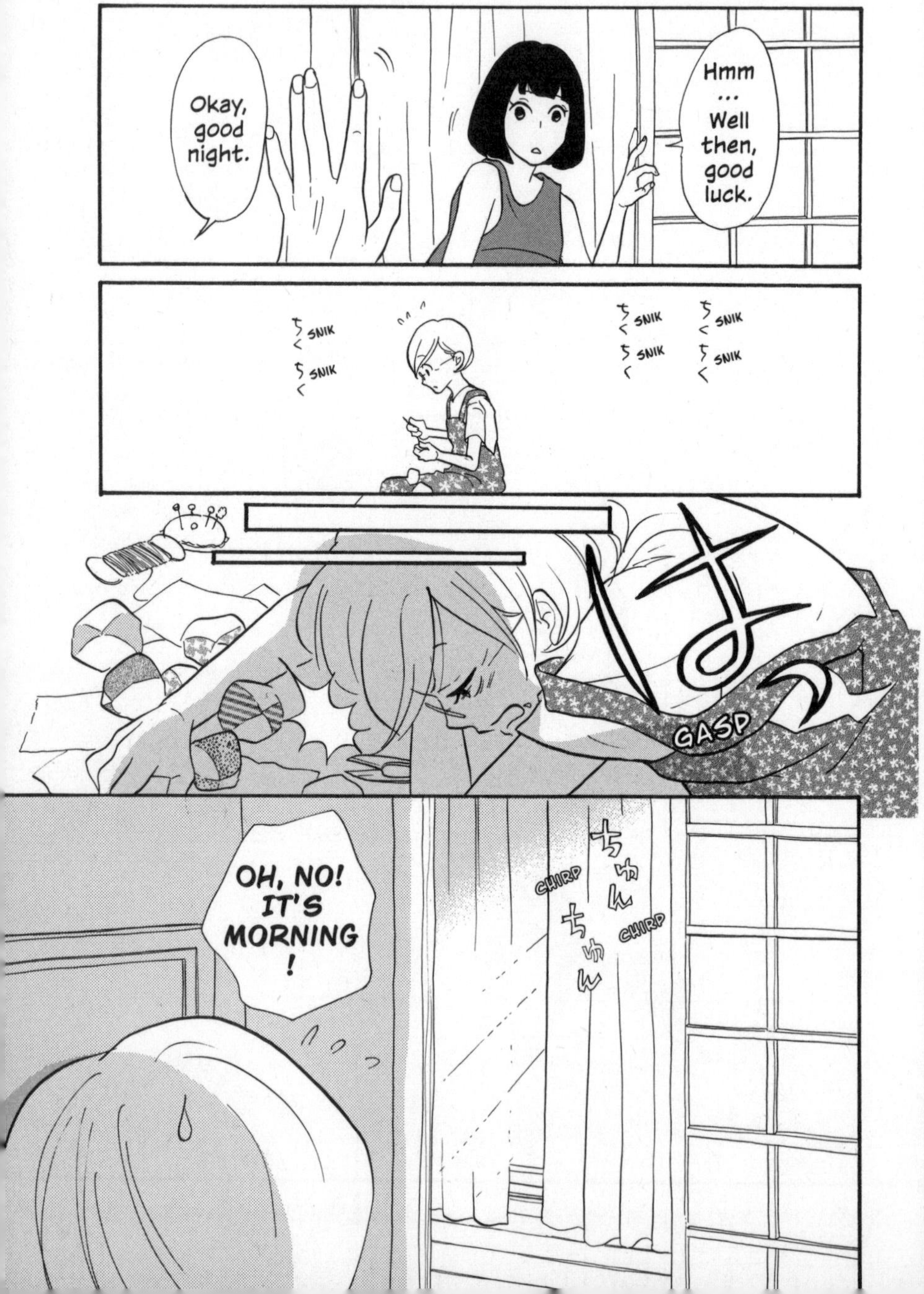
Hmm ... Well then, good luck.
Okay, good night.
ちく SNIK
ちく SNIK
ちく SNIK
ちく SNIK
ちく SNIK
ちく SNIK
はっ
GASP
ちゅん CHIRP
ちゅん CHIRP
OH, NO! IT'S MORNING!

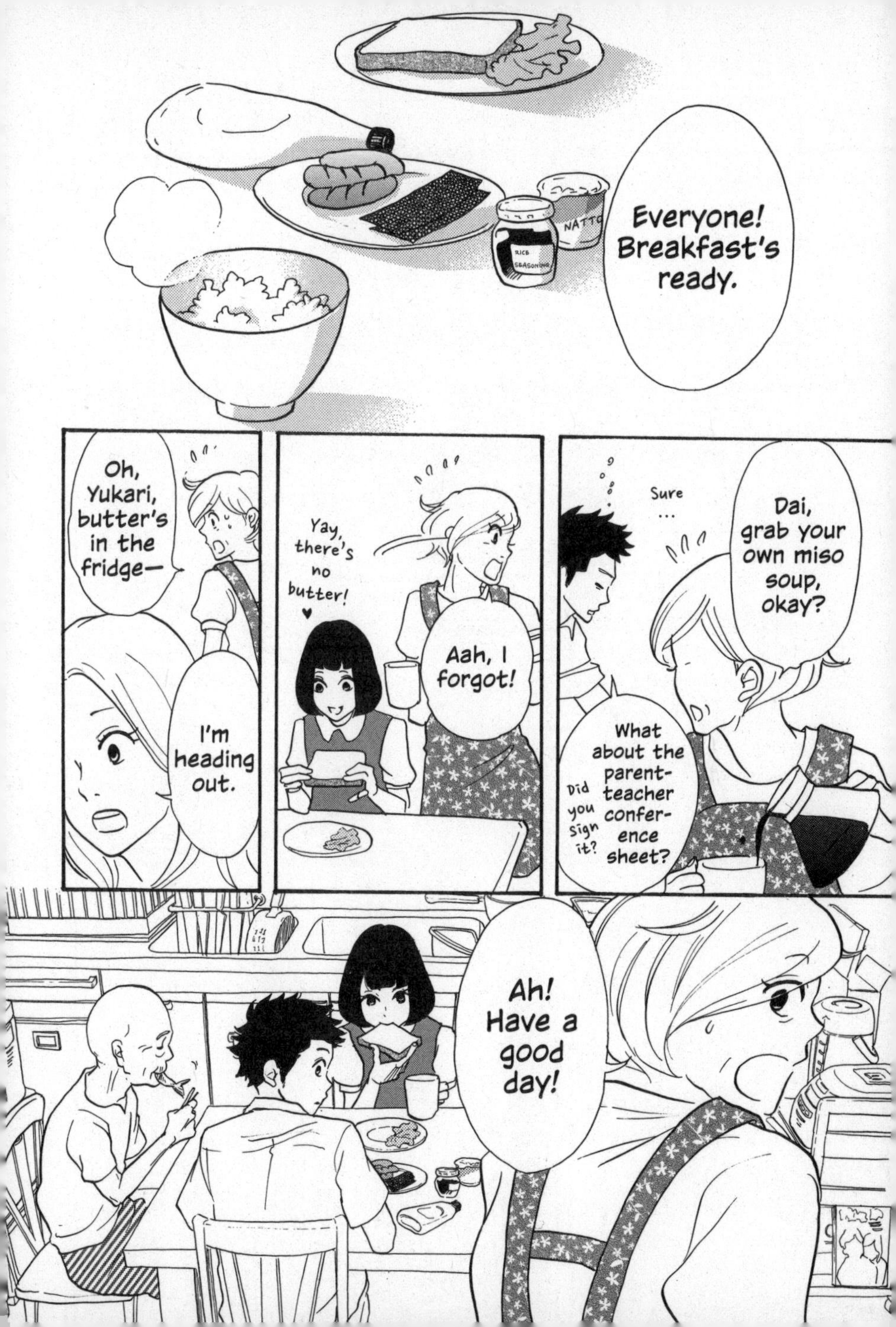
NATTO
RICE SEASONING
Everyone! Breakfast's ready.
Dai, grab your own miso soup, okay?
Sure ...
What about the parent-teacher conference sheet?
Did you sign it?
Yay, there's no butter! ♥
Aah, I forgot!
Oh, Yukari, butter's in the fridge—
I'm heading out.
Ah! Have a good day!

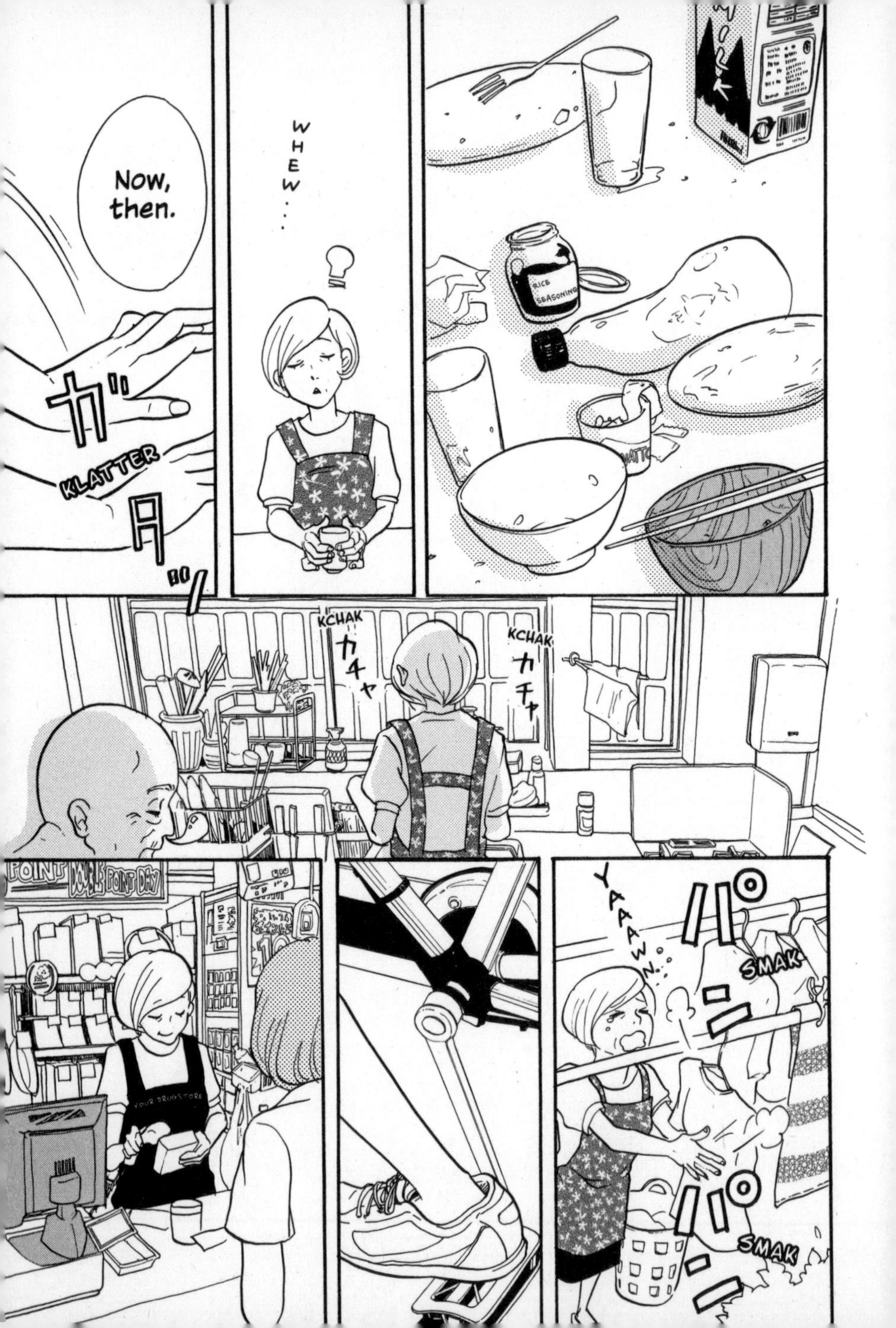
RICE SEASONING
WHEW...
Now, then.
KLATTER
KCHAK
カチャ
KCHAK
カチャ
YAAAWN...
SMAK
SMAK
POINTS
DOUBLE POINT DAY
YOUR DRUGSTORE

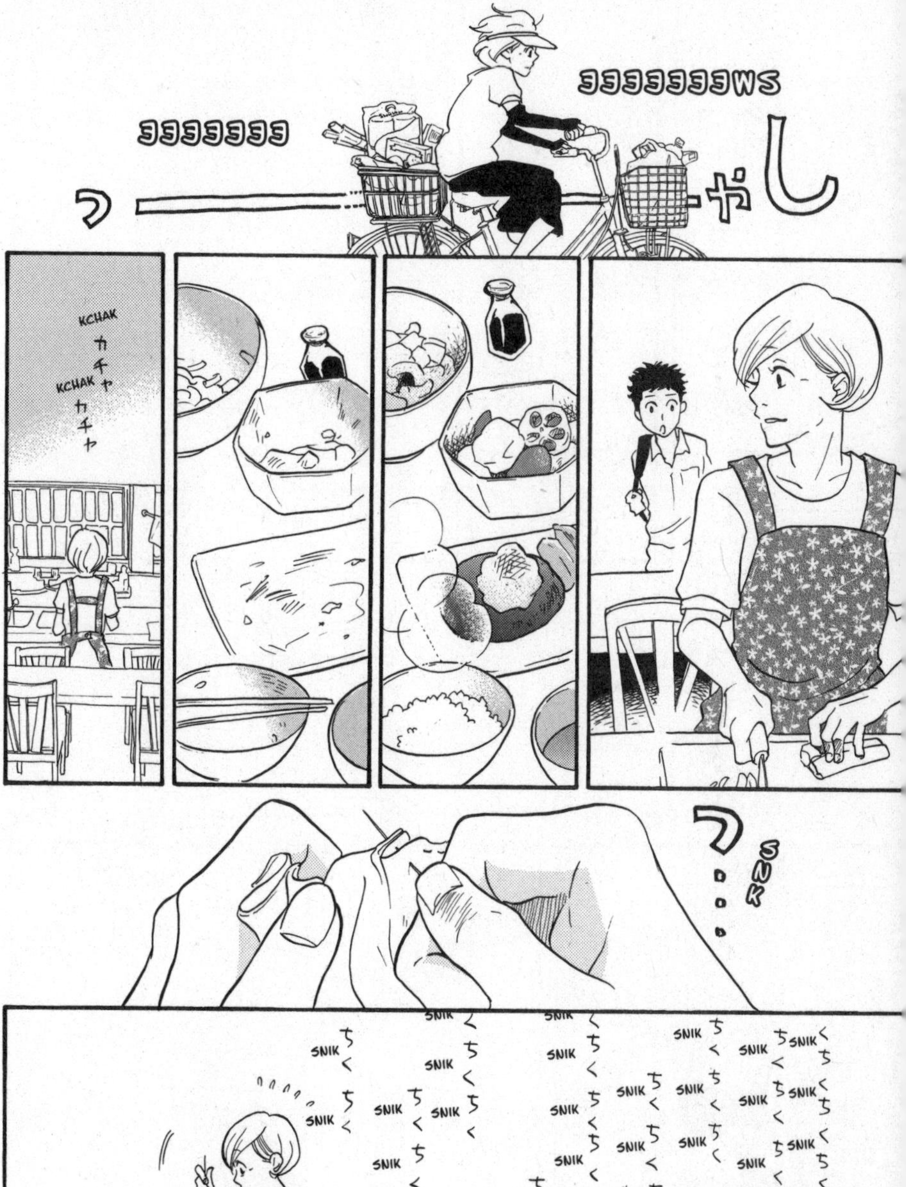

しゃーーーーっ
SWEEEEEEEEE
EEEEEEE
KCHAK
カチャ
KCHAK
カチャ
っ・・・
SNK
ちくちく
SNIK
ちくちく
SNIK

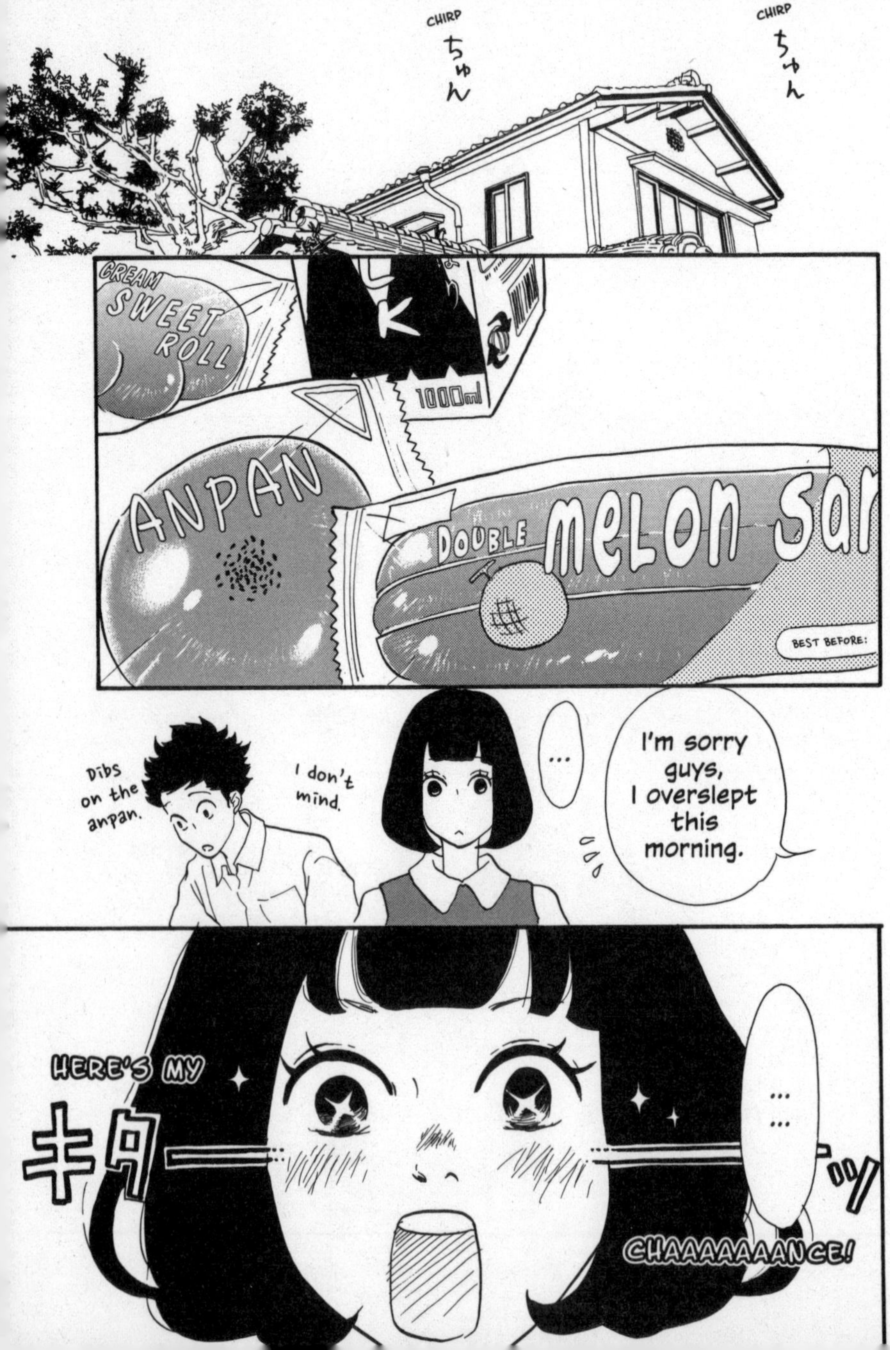
CHIRP
ちゅん
CHIRP
ちゅん
CREAM SWEET ROLL
1000ml
ANPAN
DOUBLE melon sar
BEST BEFORE:
I'm sorry guys, I overslept this morning.
...
I don't mind.
Dibs on the anpan.
...
...
HERE'S MY
キター
CHAAAAAAAANCE!

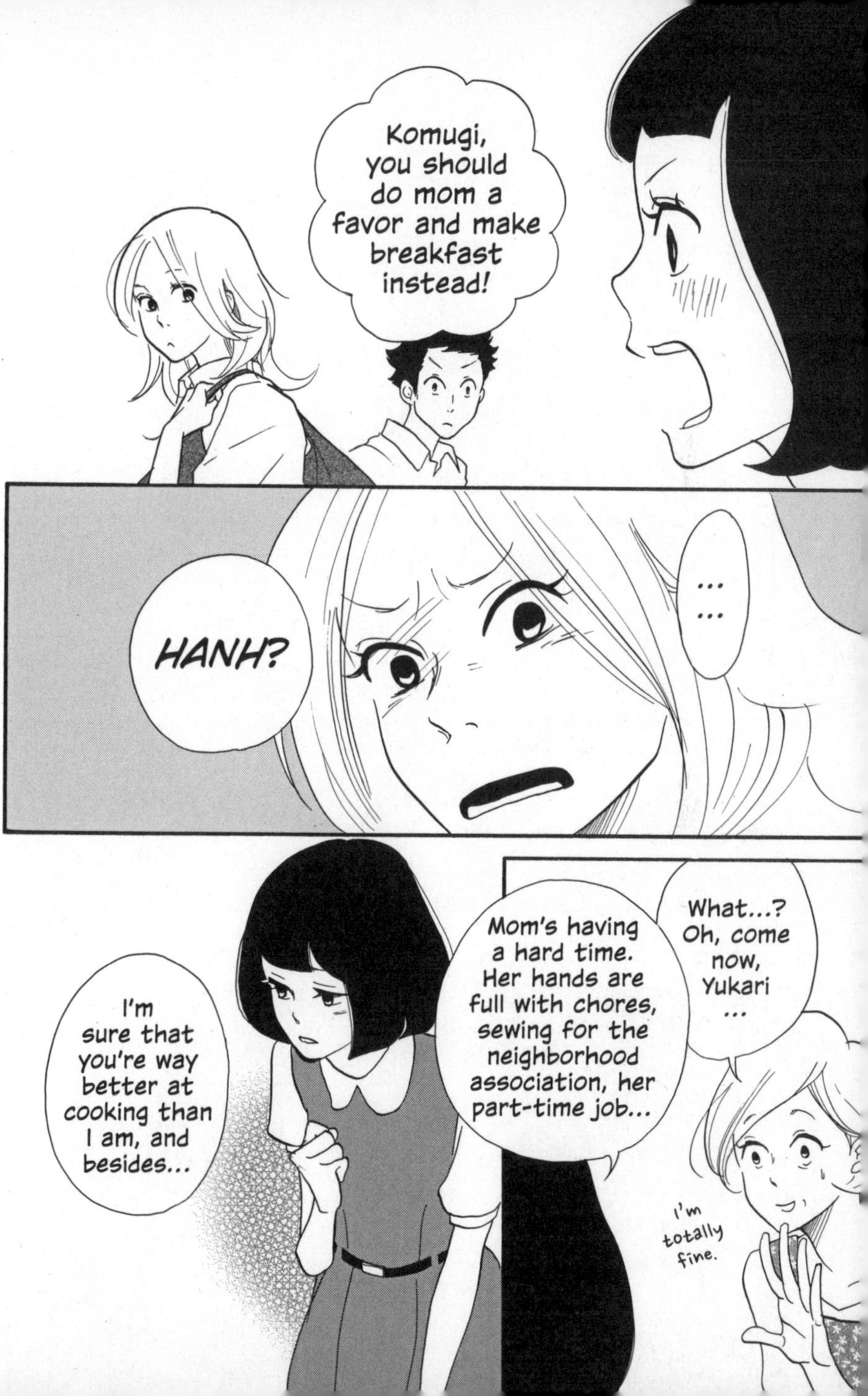
Komugi, you should do mom a favor and make breakfast instead!
... ...
HANH?
What...? Oh, come now, Yukari ...
I'm totally fine.
Mom's having a hard time. Her hands are full with chores, sewing for the neighborhood association, her part-time job...
I'm sure that you're way better at cooking than I am, and besides...

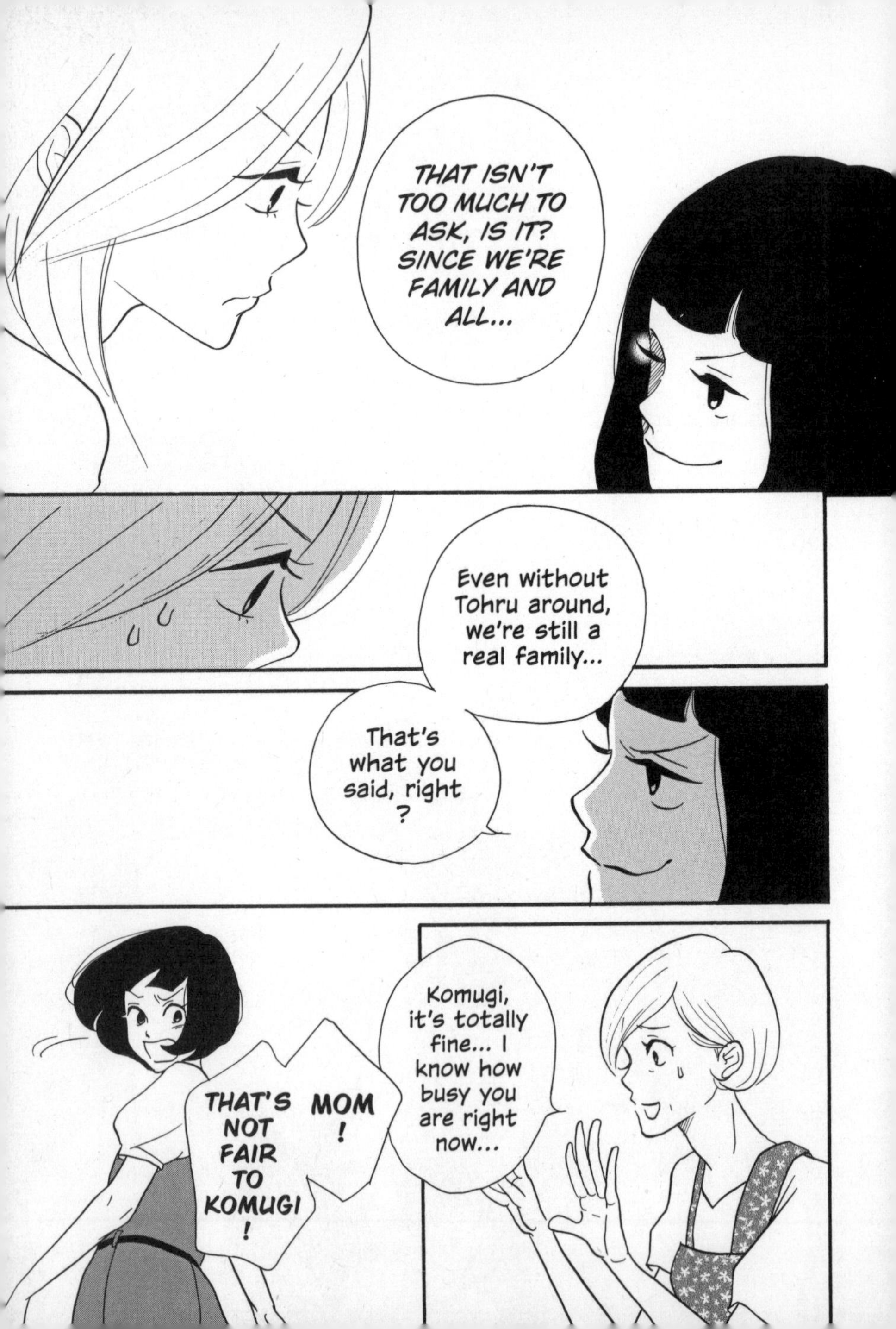
THAT ISN'T TOO MUCH TO ASK, IS IT? SINCE WE'RE FAMILY AND ALL...
Even without Tohru around, we're still a real family...
That's what you said, right?
Komugi, it's totally fine... I know how busy you are right now...
MOM! THAT'S NOT FAIR TO KOMUGI!

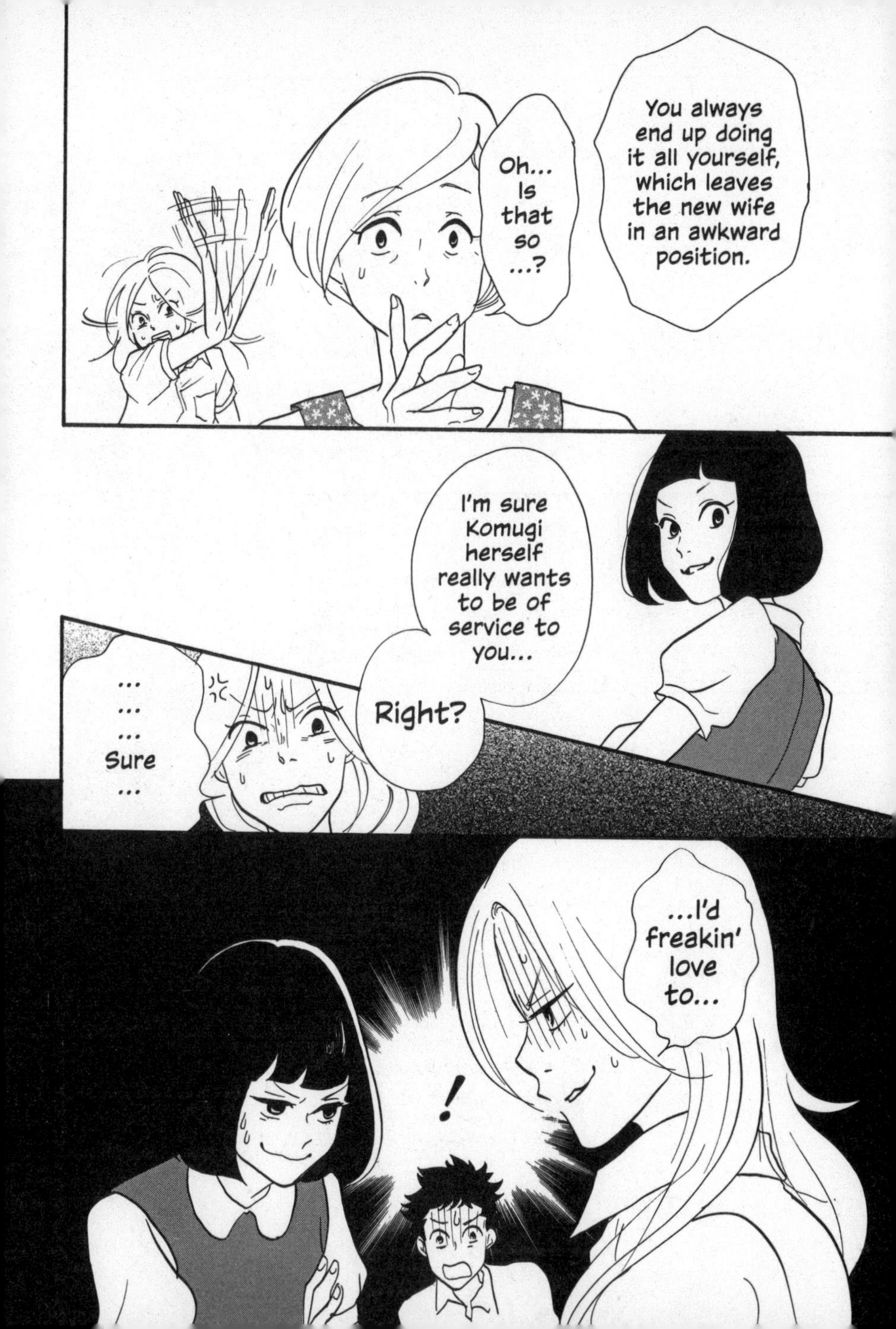
You always end up doing it all yourself, which leaves the new wife in an awkward position.
Oh... Is that so ...?
I'm sure Komugi herself really wants to be of service to you...
Right?
... ... Sure ...
...I'd freakin' love to...
!

6 HER FIRST... ♥

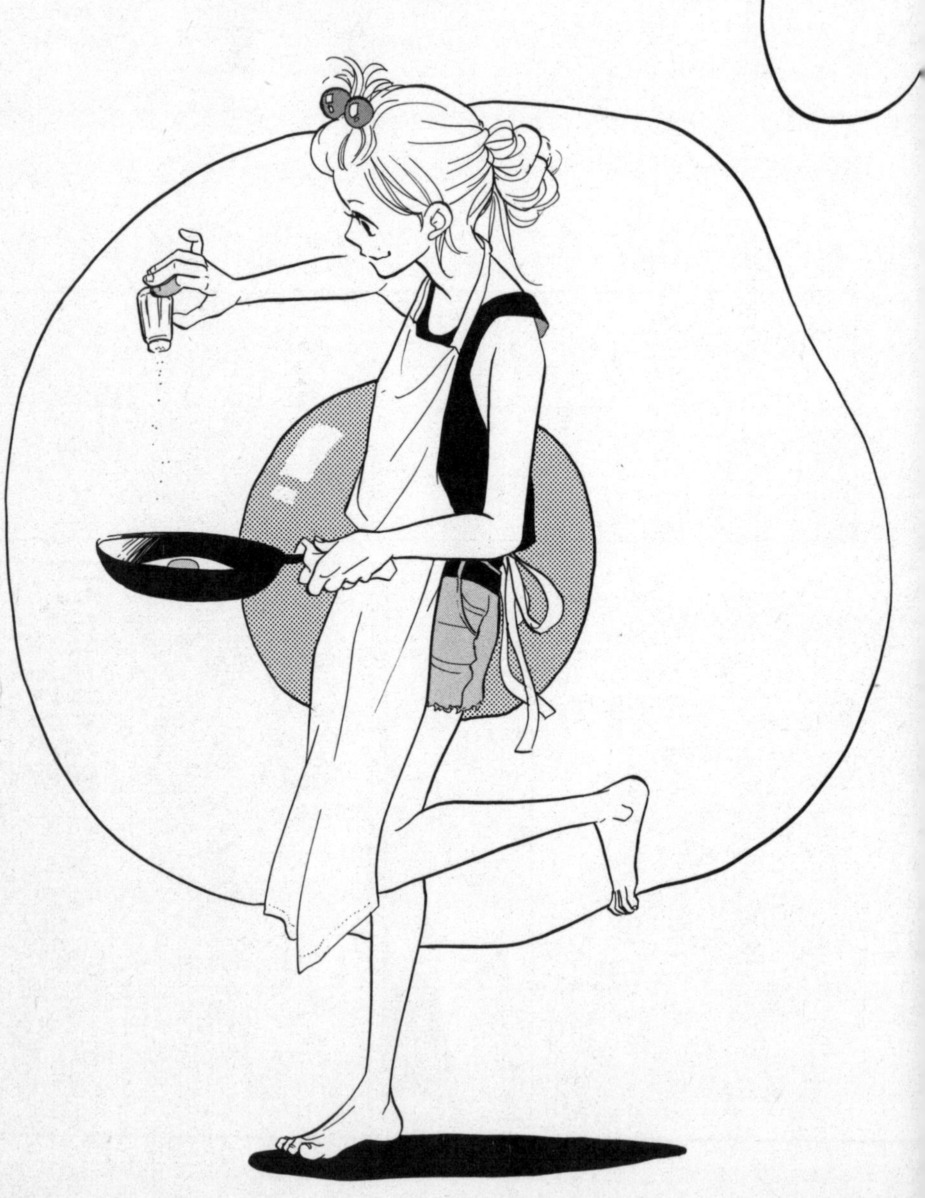

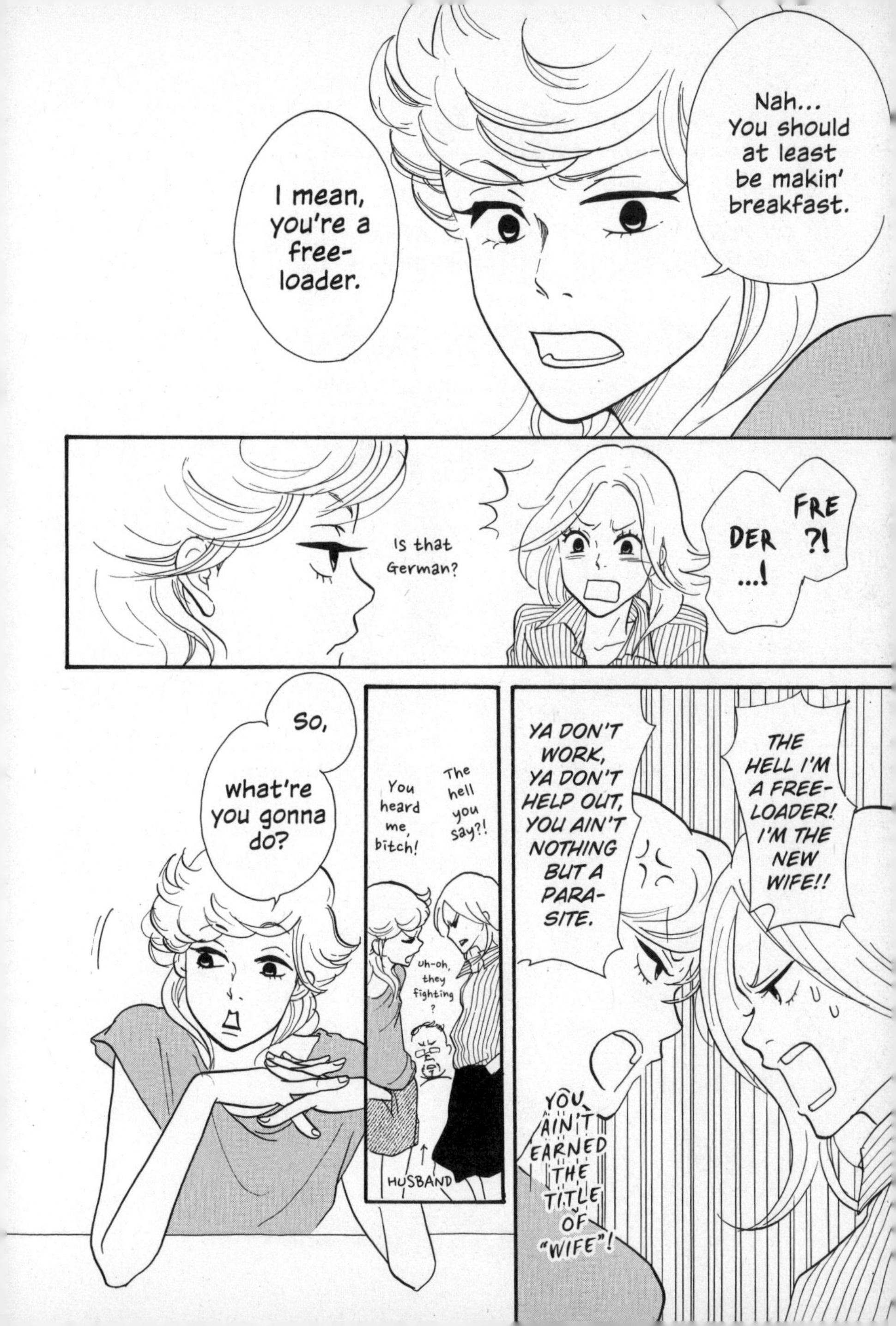
Nah... You should at least be makin' breakfast.
I mean, you're a free-loader.
FRE ?!
DER ...!
Is that German?
THE HELL I'M A FREE-LOADER! I'M THE NEW WIFE!!
YA DON'T WORK, YA DON'T HELP OUT, YOU AIN'T NOTHING BUT A PARA-SITE.
YOU AIN'T EARNED THE TITLE OF "WIFE"!
The hell you say?!
You heard me, bitch!
Uh-oh, they fighting?
HUSBAND
So, what're you gonna do?

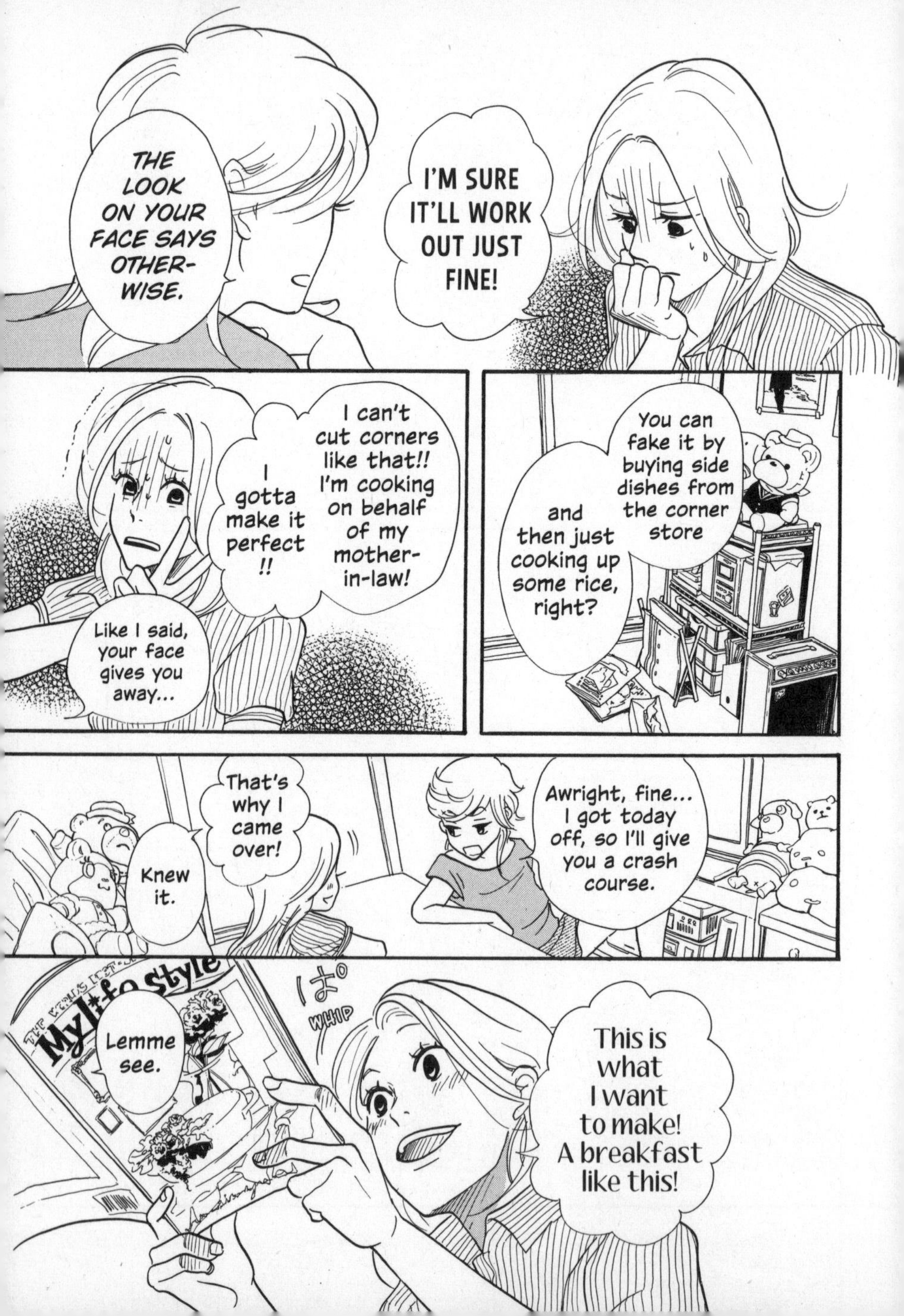
I'M SURE IT'LL WORK OUT JUST FINE!
THE LOOK ON YOUR FACE SAYS OTHER-WISE.
You can fake it by buying side dishes from the corner store
and then just cooking up some rice, right?
I can't cut corners like that!! I'm cooking on behalf of my mother-in-law!
I gotta make it perfect!!
Like I said, your face gives you away...
Awright, fine... I got today off, so I'll give you a crash course.
That's why I came over!
Knew it.
ぱ
WHIP
This is what I want to make! A breakfast like this!
Lemme see.

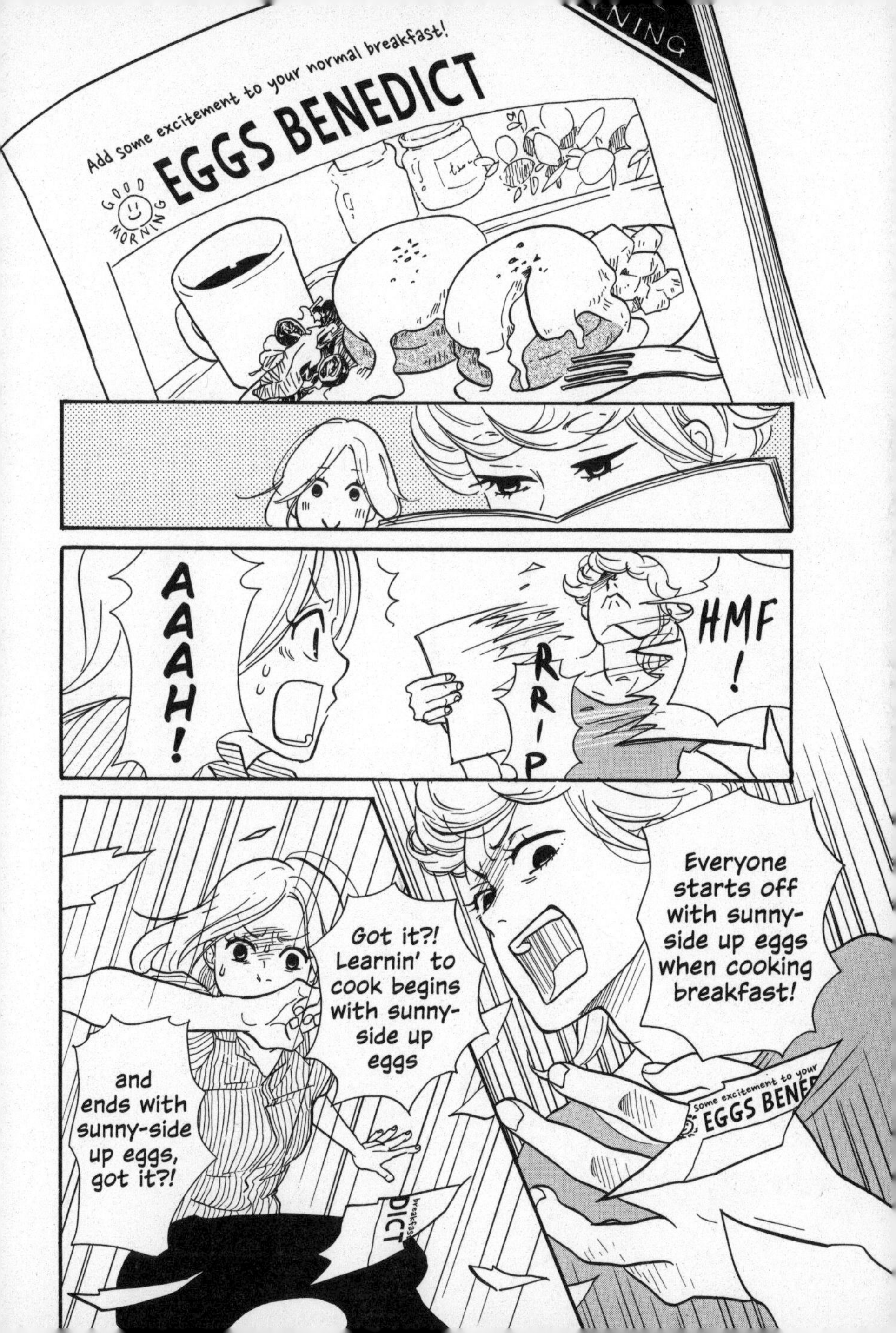
NING
Add some excitement to your normal breakfast!
GOOD MORNING
EGGS BENEDICT
HMF!
RRIP
AAAAH!
Everyone starts off with sunny-side up eggs when cooking breakfast!
Some excitement to your
EGGS BENE
Got it?! Learnin' to cook begins with sunny-side up eggs
and ends with sunny-side up eggs, got it?!
DICT
breakfast

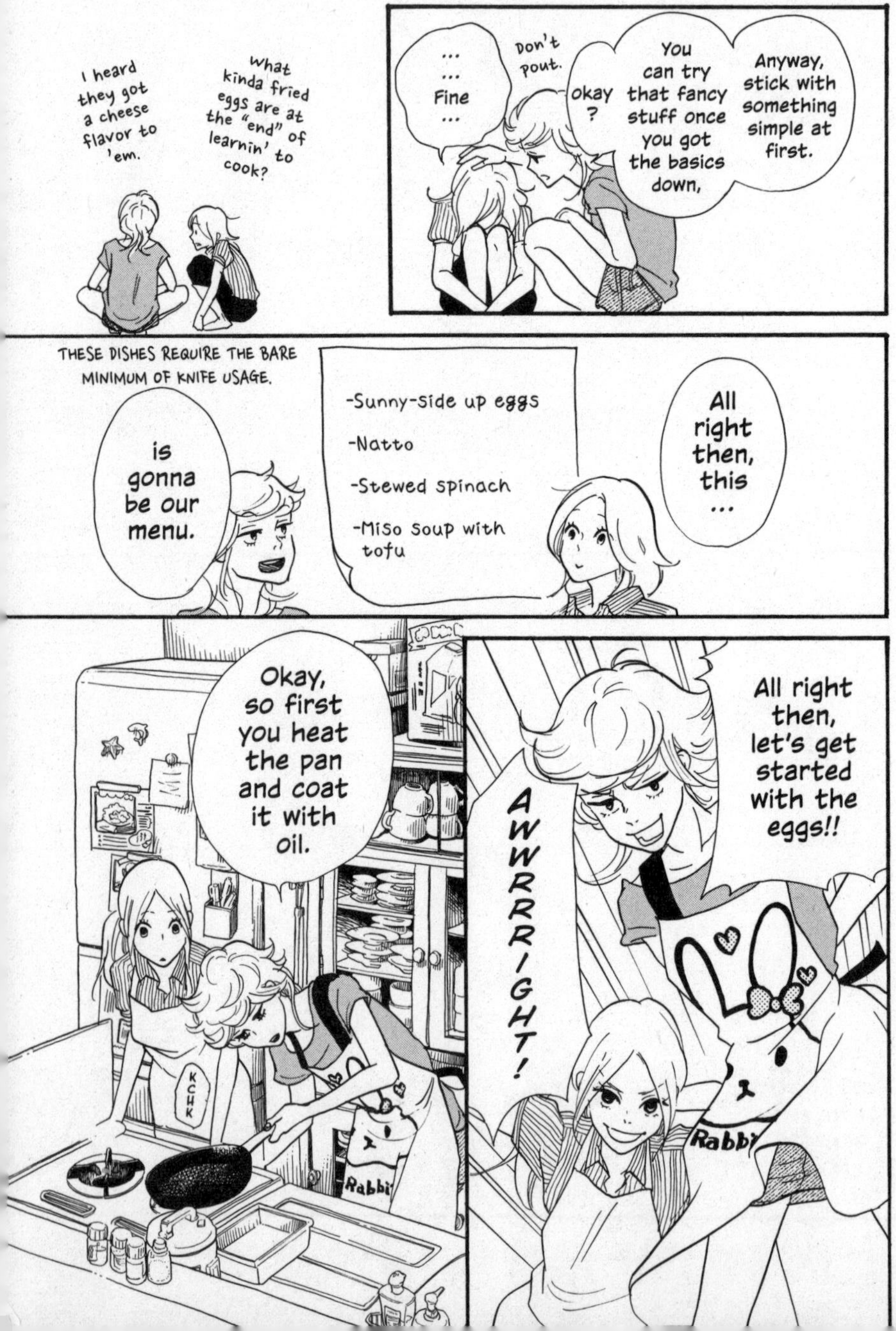
Anyway, stick with something simple at first.
You can try that fancy stuff once you got the basics down, okay?
Don't pout.
... ... Fine ...
what kinda fried eggs are at the "end" of learnin' to cook?
I heard they got a cheese flavor to 'em.
All right then, this...
-Sunny-side up eggs
-Natto
-Stewed spinach
-Miso soup with tofu
is gonna be our menu.
THESE DISHES REQUIRE THE BARE MINIMUM OF KNIFE USAGE.
All right then, let's get started with the eggs!!
AWWRRRIGHT!
Rabbi
Okay, so first you heat the pan and coat it with oil.
KCHK
Rabbi

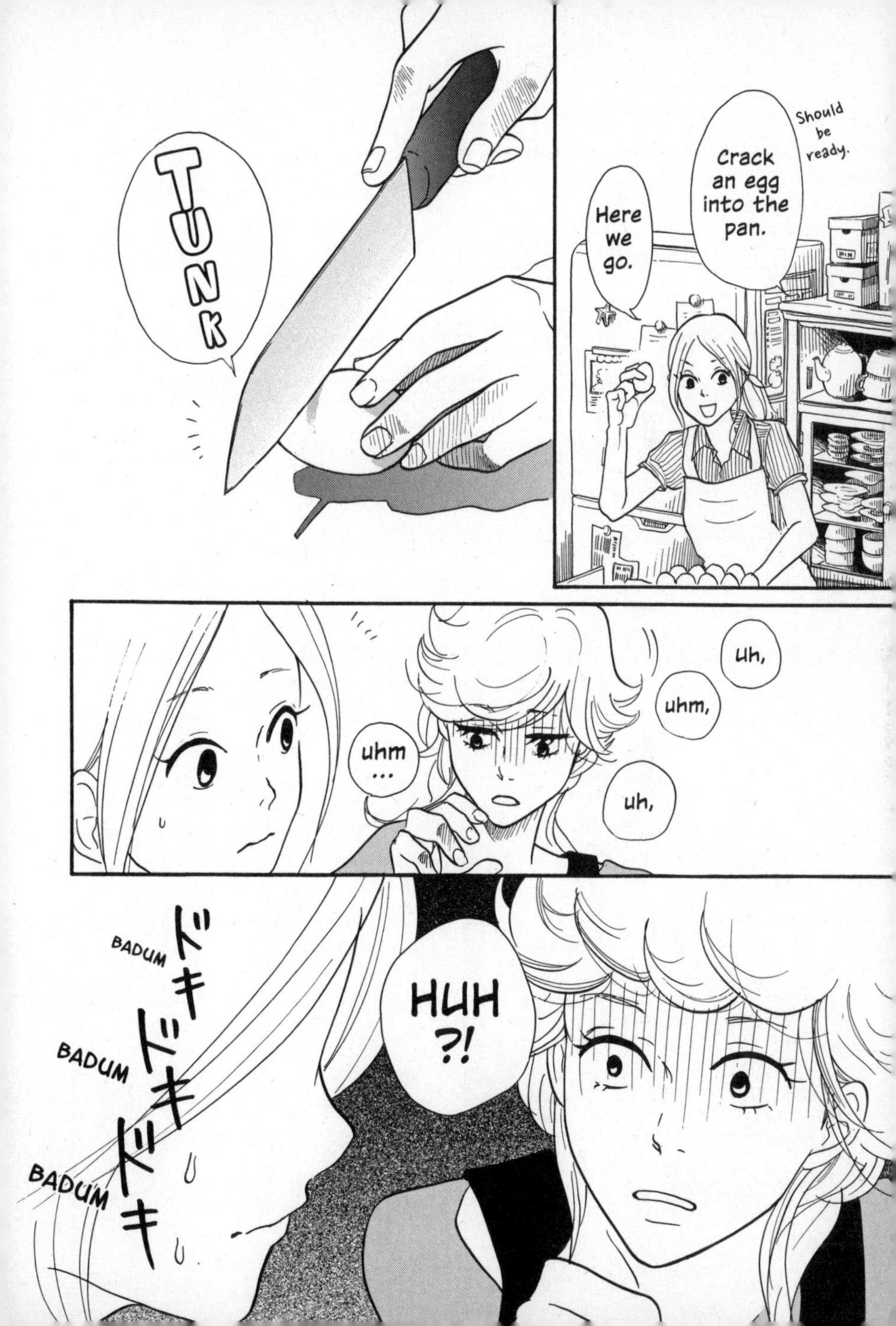
Should be ready.
Crack an egg into the pan.
Here we go.
TUNK
uh,
uhm,
uh,
uhm ...
HUH ?!
ドキ
BADUM
ドキ
BADUM
ドキ
BADUM

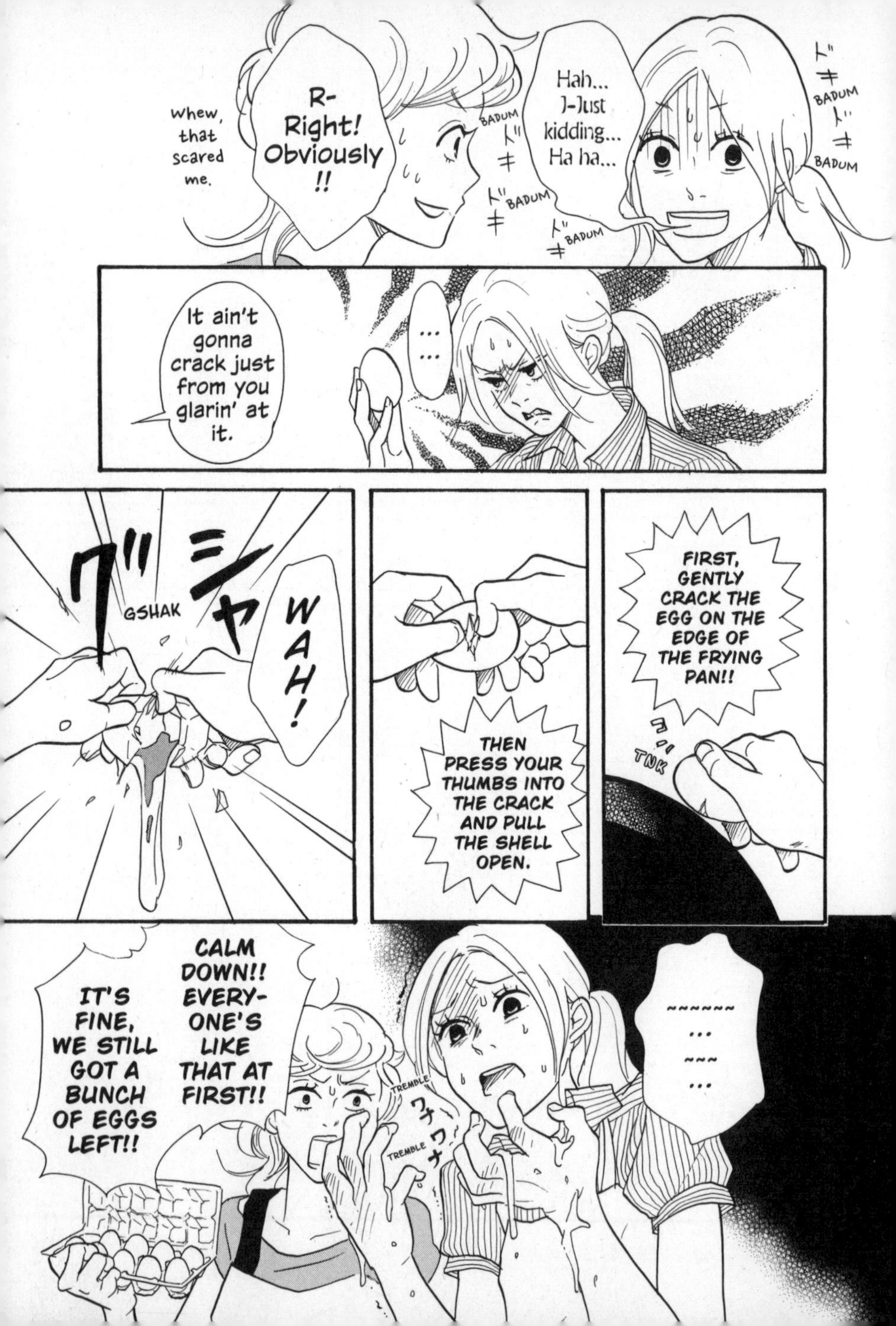
Hah... J-Just kidding... Ha ha...
ドキ BADUM ドキ BADUM
R- Right! Obviously !!
ドキ BADUM ドキ BADUM ドキ BADUM
Whew, that scared me.
......
It ain't gonna crack just from you glarin' at it.
FIRST, GENTLY CRACK THE EGG ON THE EDGE OF THE FRYING PAN!!
コツ TNK
THEN PRESS YOUR THUMBS INTO THE CRACK AND PULL THE SHELL OPEN.
グシャ GSHAK
WAH!
~~~~~~ ... ~~~ ...
ワナワナ TREMBLE TREMBLE
CALM DOWN!! EVERY-ONE'S LIKE THAT AT FIRST!!
IT'S FINE, WE STILL GOT A BUNCH OF EGGS LEFT!!
~~~~~~

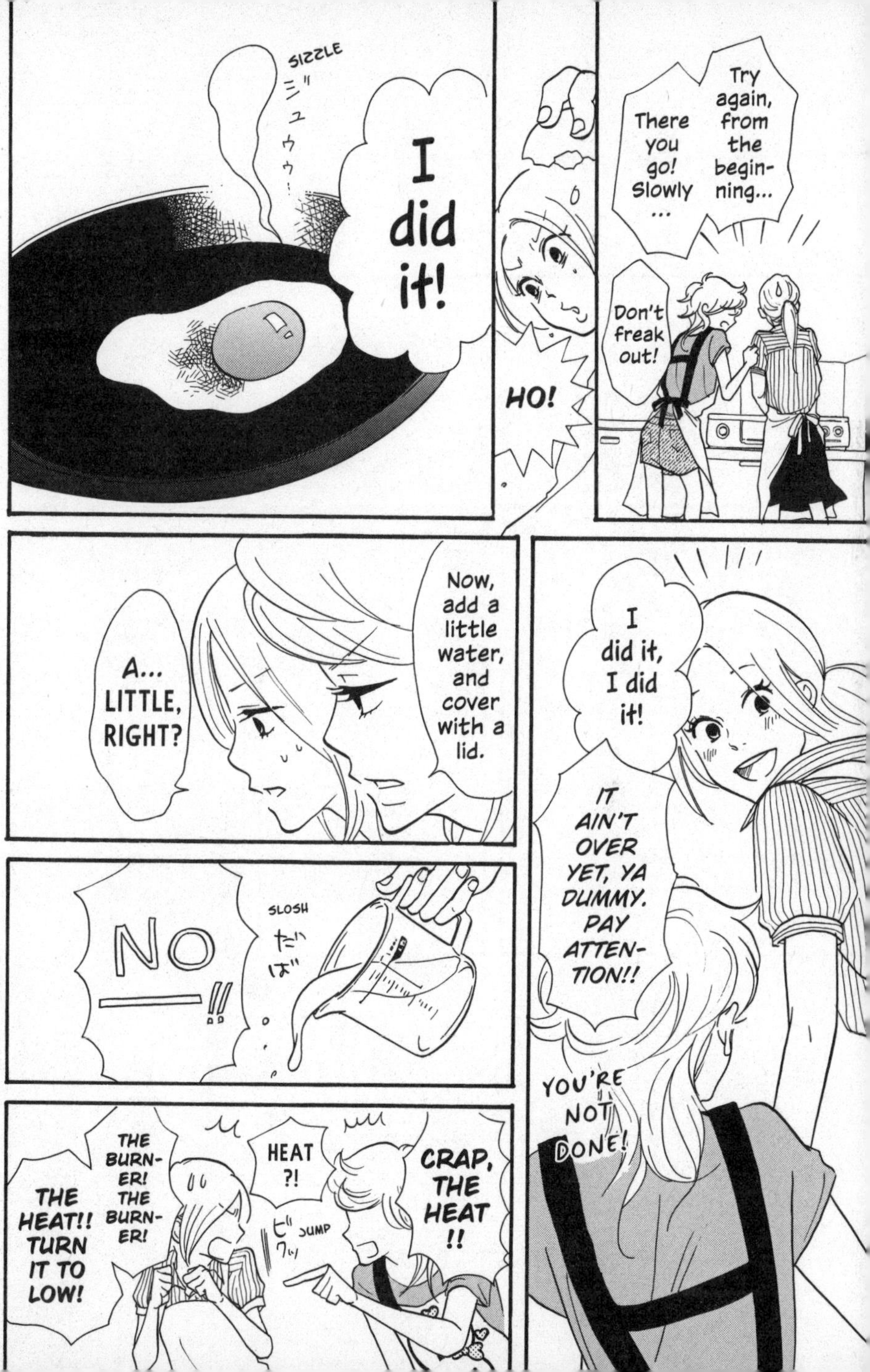

Try again, from the beginning...
There you go! Slowly ...
Don't freak out!
HO!
SIZZLE
ジュウウ〜
I did it!
I did it, I did it!
IT AIN'T OVER YET, YA DUMMY. PAY ATTENTION!!
YOU'RE NOT DONE!
Now, add a little water, and cover with a lid.
A... LITTLE, RIGHT?
SLOSH
だば
NO—!!
CRAP, THE HEAT!!
ビクッ
JUMP
HEAT?!
THE BURNER! THE BURNER!
THE HEAT!! TURN IT TO LOW!

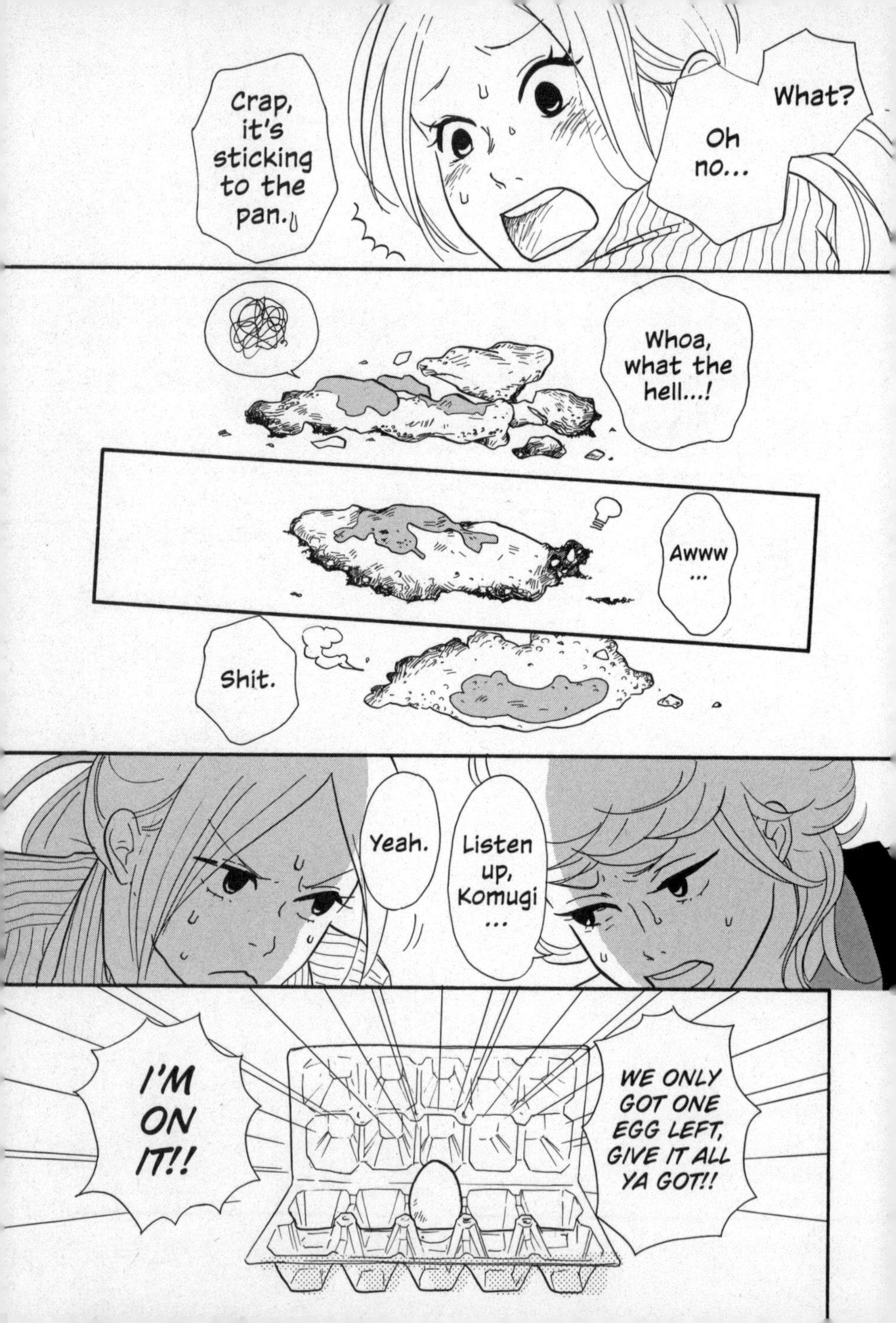
What? Oh no...
Crap, it's sticking to the pan.
Whoa, what the hell...!
Awww...
Shit.
Listen up, Komugi...
Yeah.
WE ONLY GOT ONE EGG LEFT, GIVE IT ALL YA GOT!!
I'M ON IT!!

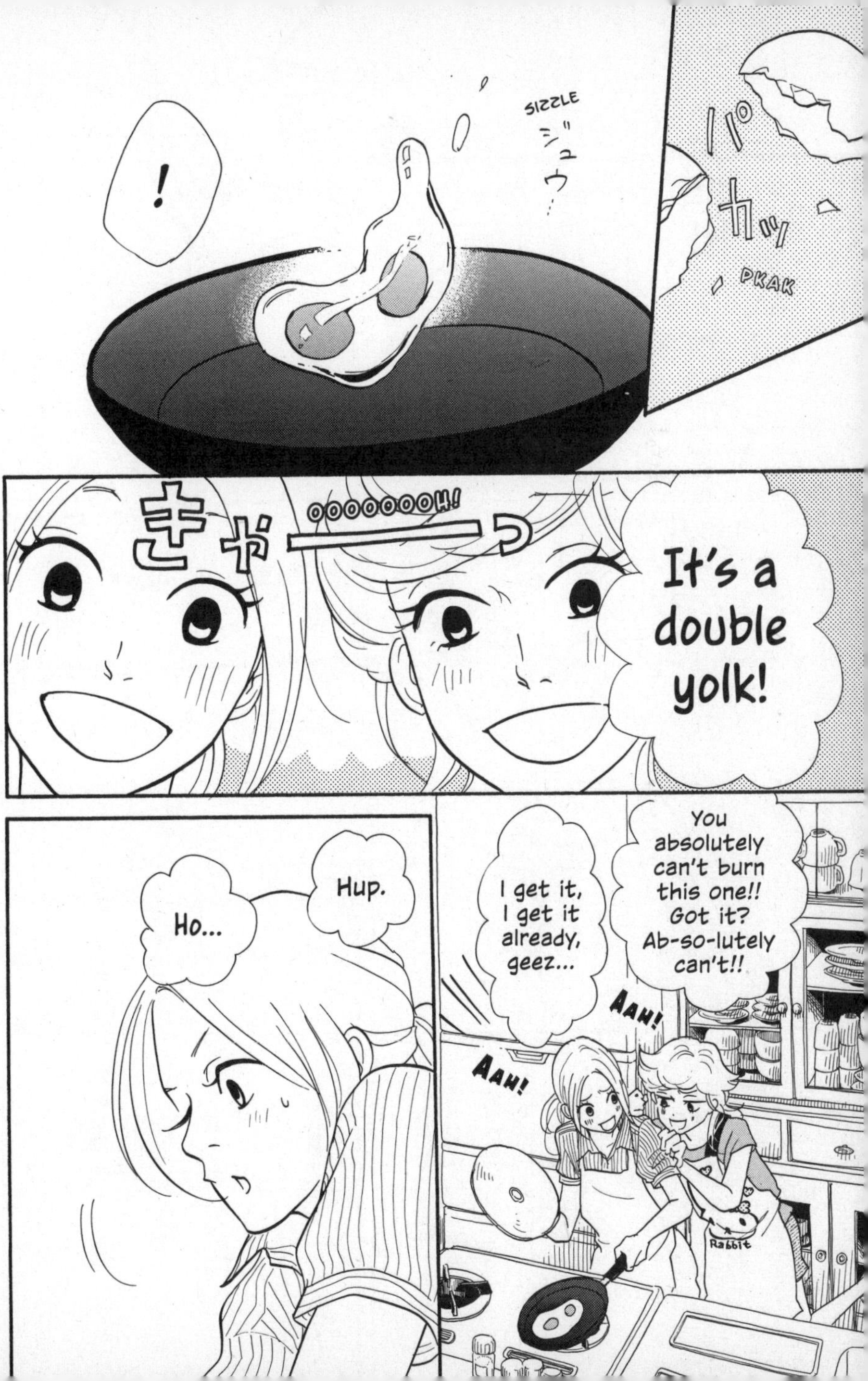
パカッ
PKAK
ジュウ…
SIZZLE
!
きゃーっ
OOOOOOOOH!
It's a double yolk!
You absolutely can't burn this one!! Got it? Ab-so-lutely can't!!
I get it, I get it already, geez...
AAH!
AAH!
Rabbit
Hup.
Ho...

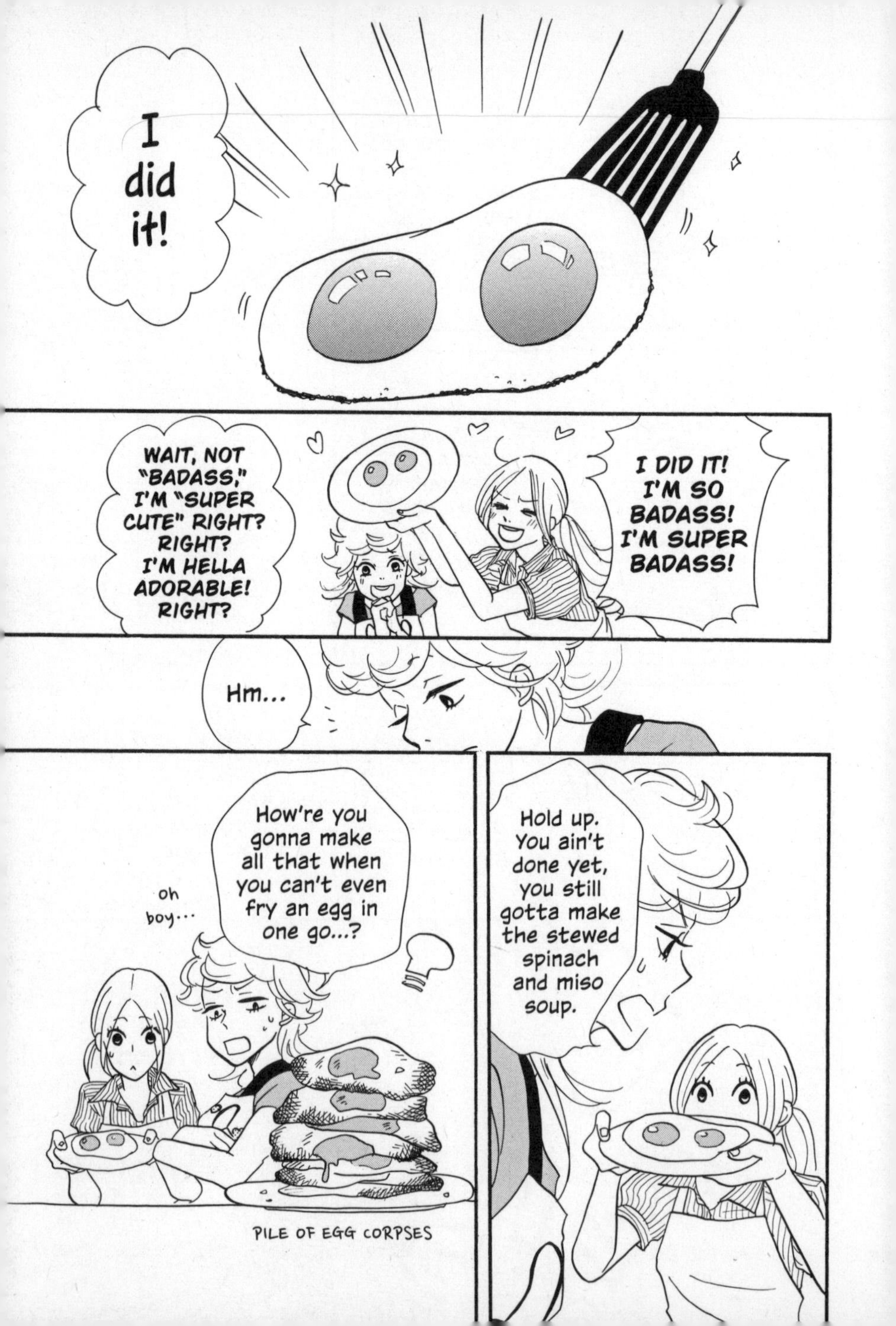
I did it!
I DID IT! I'M SO BADASS! I'M SUPER BADASS!
WAIT, NOT "BADASS," I'M "SUPER CUTE" RIGHT? RIGHT? I'M HELLA ADORABLE! RIGHT?
Hm...
Hold up. You ain't done yet, you still gotta make the stewed spinach and miso soup.
How're you gonna make all that when you can't even fry an egg in one go...?
oh boy...
PILE OF EGG CORPSES

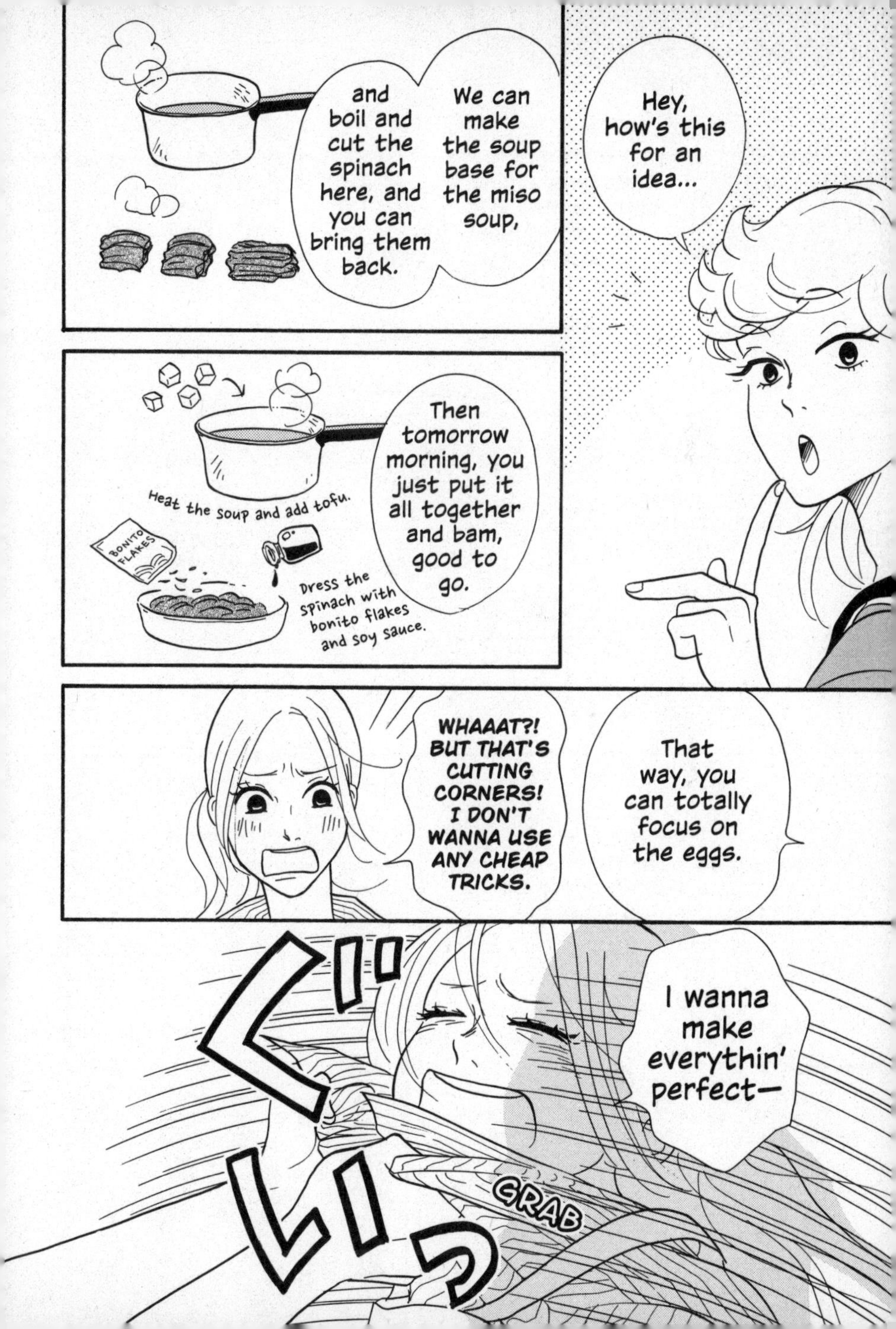
Hey, how's this for an idea...
We can make the soup base for the miso soup,
and boil and cut the spinach here, and you can bring them back.
Then tomorrow morning, you just put it all together and bam, good to go.
Heat the soup and add tofu.
BONITO FLAKES
Dress the spinach with bonito flakes and soy sauce.
That way, you can totally focus on the eggs.
WHAAAT?! BUT THAT'S CUTTING CORNERS! I DON'T WANNA USE ANY CHEAP TRICKS.
I wanna make everythin' perfect—
ぐいっ
GRAB

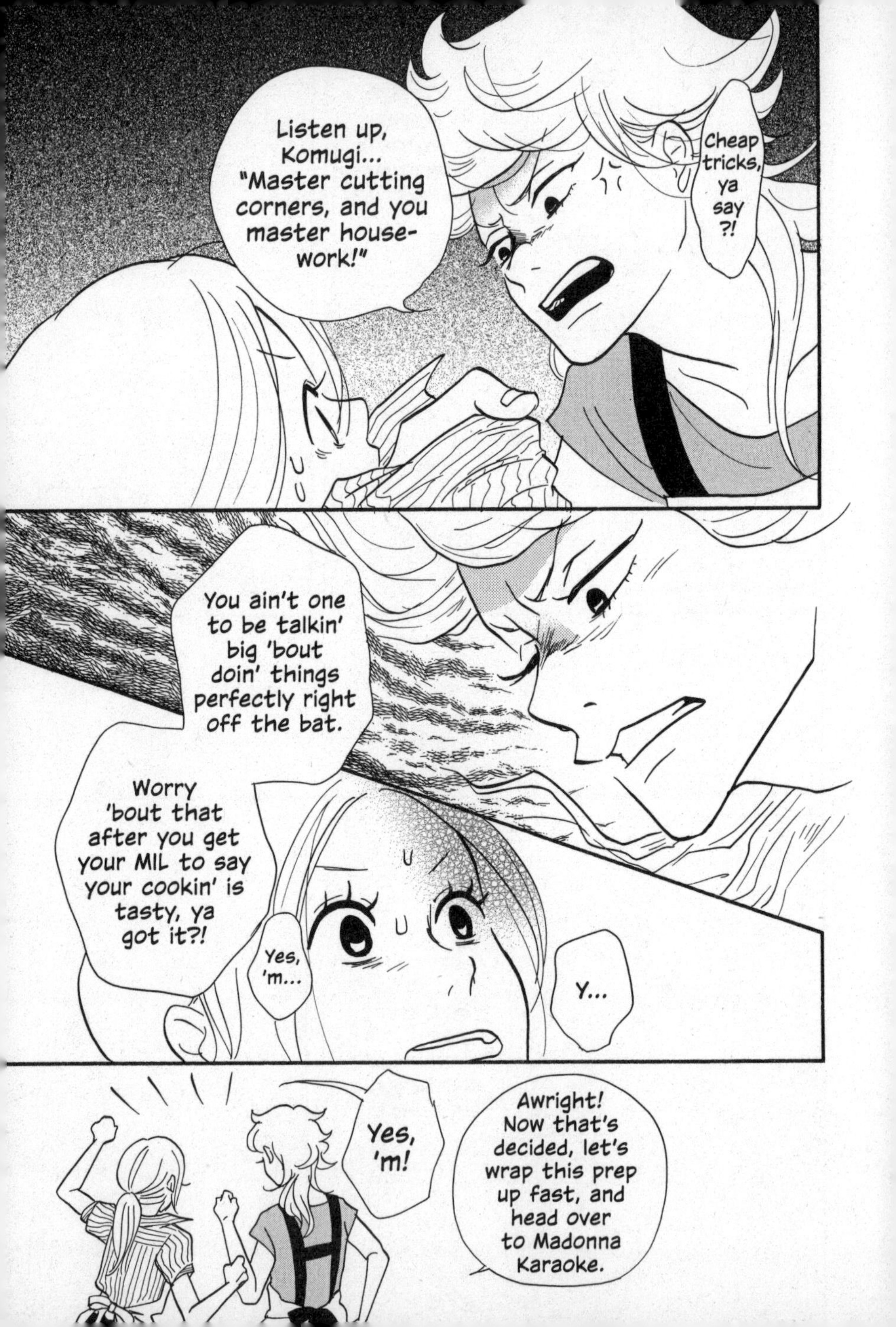
Cheap tricks, ya say?!
Listen up, Komugi... "Master cutting corners, and you master house-work!"
You ain't one to be talkin' big 'bout doin' things perfectly right off the bat.
Worry 'bout that after you get your MIL to say your cookin' is tasty, ya got it?!
Y...
Yes, 'm...
Awright! Now that's decided, let's wrap this prep up fast, and head over to Madonna Karaoke.
Yes, 'm!

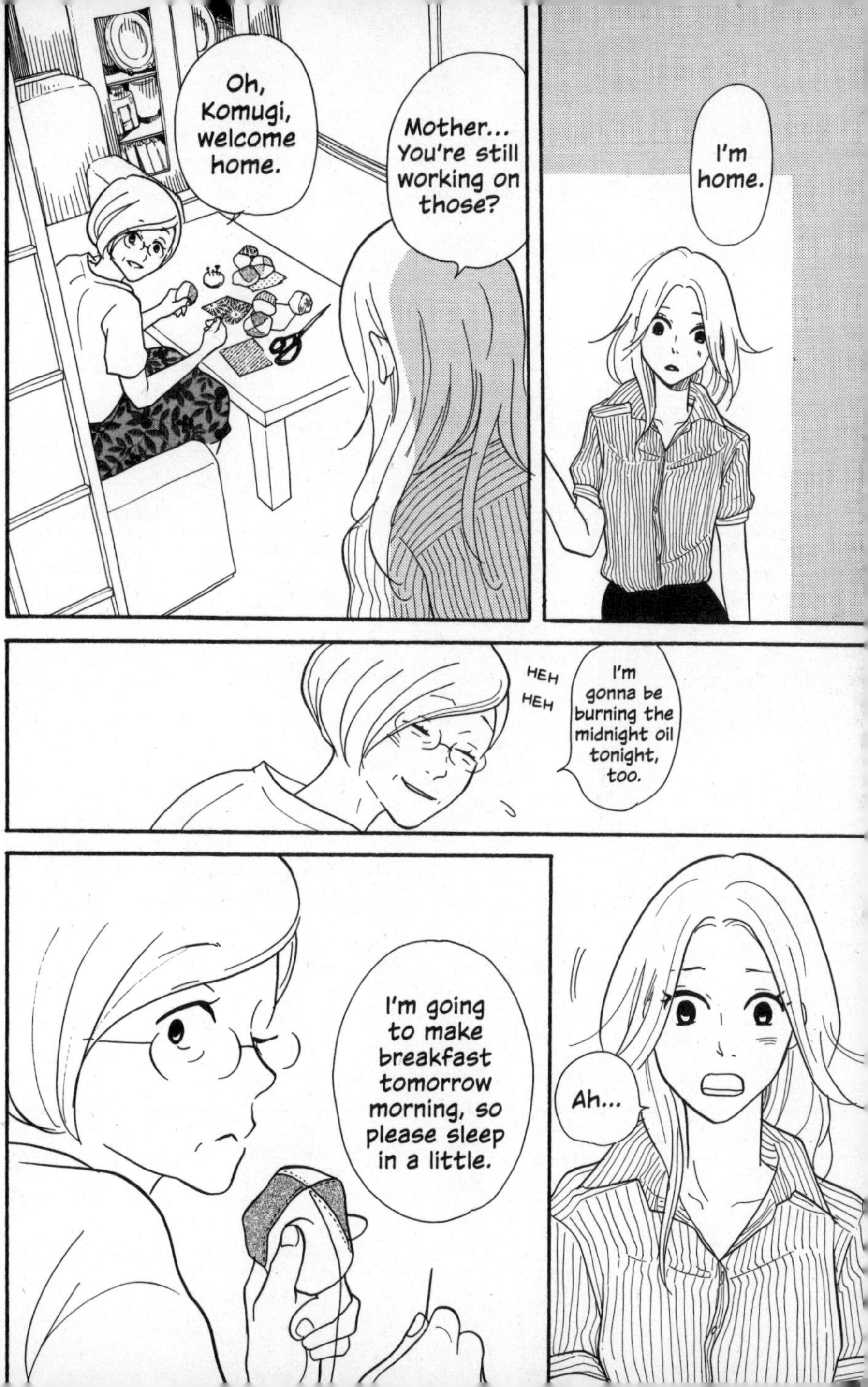
I'm home.
Mother... You're still working on those?
Oh, Komugi, welcome home.
HEH HEH
I'm gonna be burning the midnight oil tonight, too.
Ah...
I'm going to make breakfast tomorrow morning, so please sleep in a little.

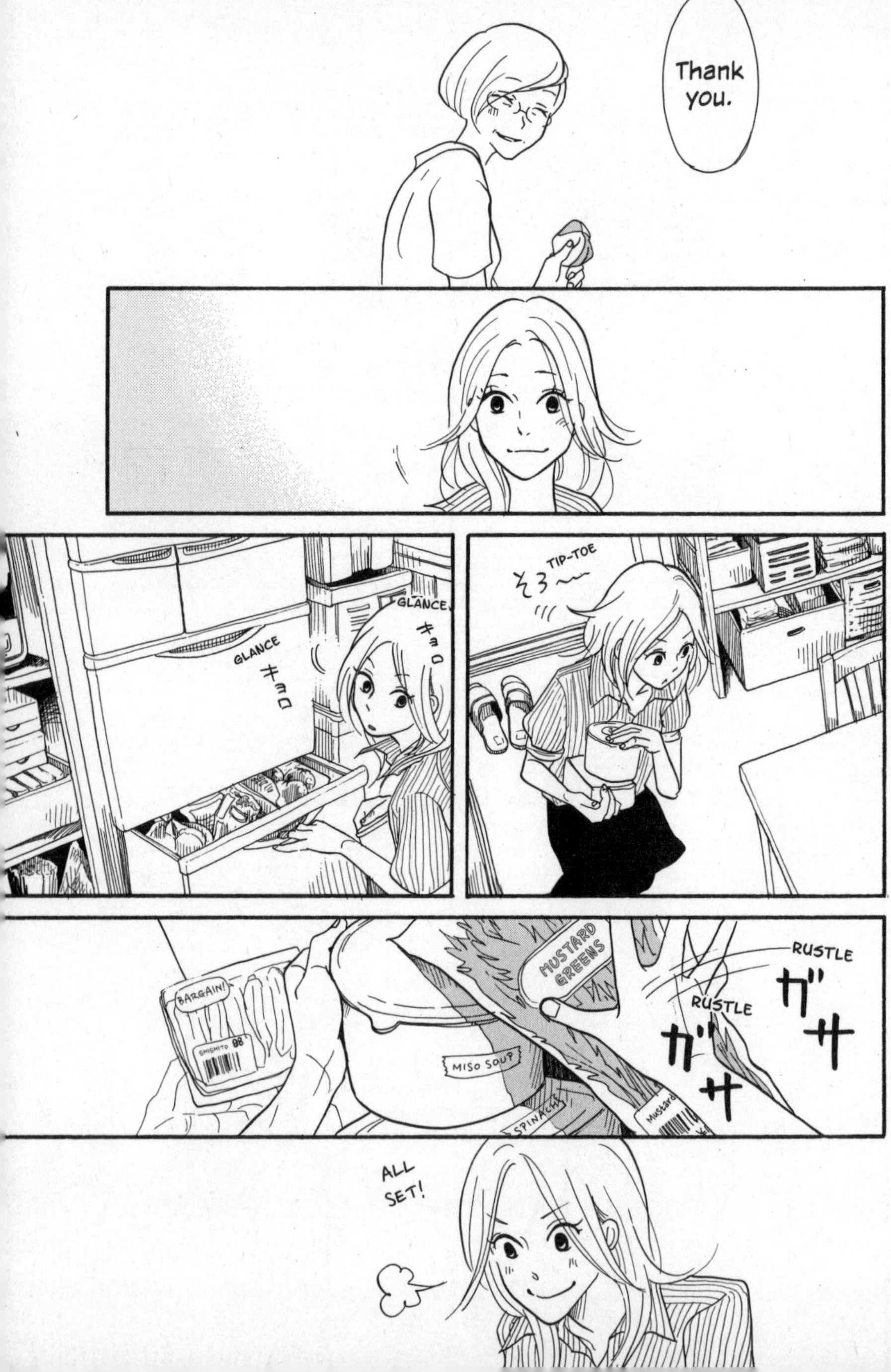

Thank you.
TIP-TOE
そろ〜〜
GLANCE
キョロ
GLANCE
キョロ
RUSTLE
ガサ
RUSTLE
ガサ
MUSTARD GREENS
BARGAIN!
SHISHITO 88
MISO SOUP
SPINACH
Mustard
ALL SET!

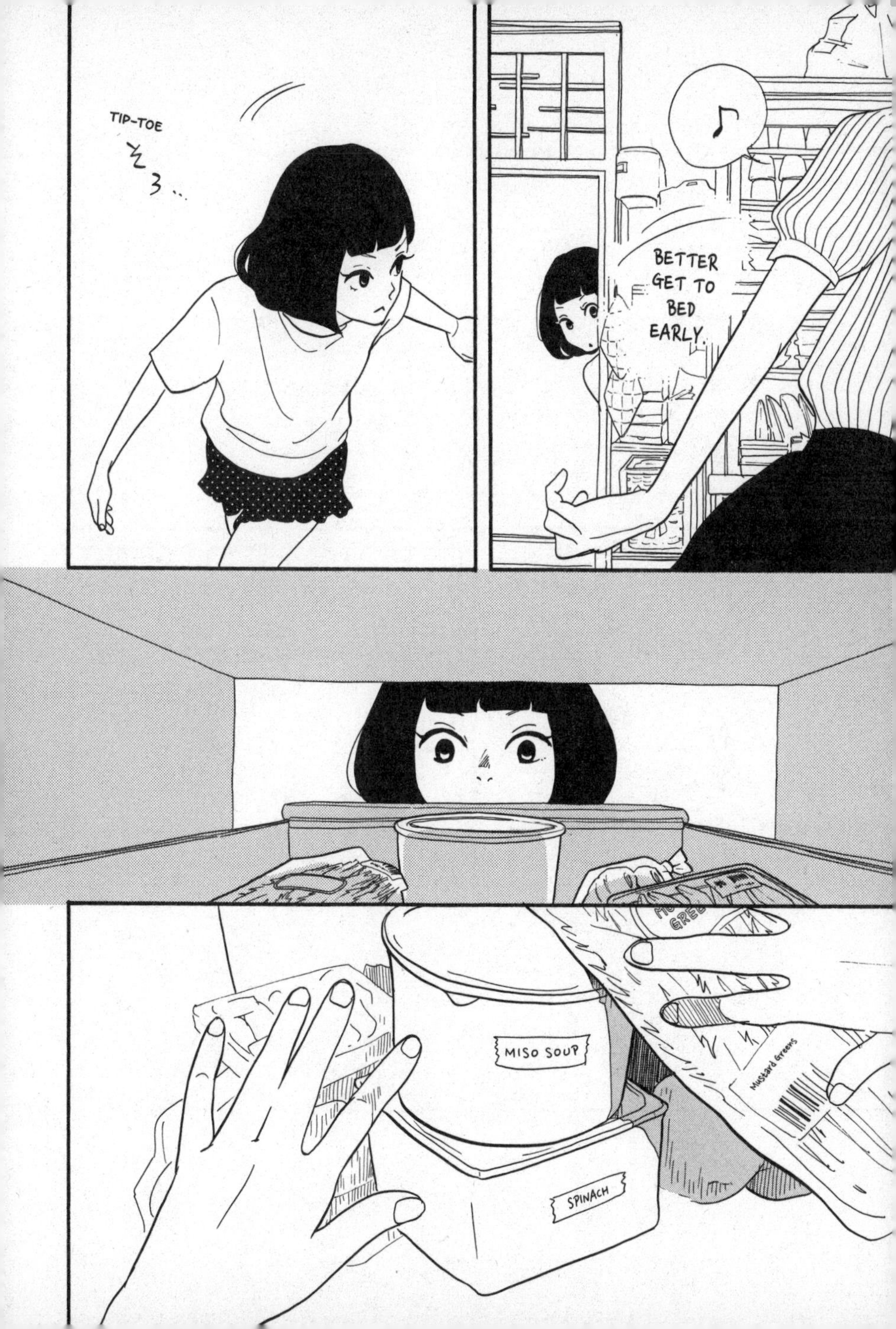
♪
BETTER GET TO BED EARLY.
TIP-TOE
MISO SOUP
Mustard Greens
SPINACH

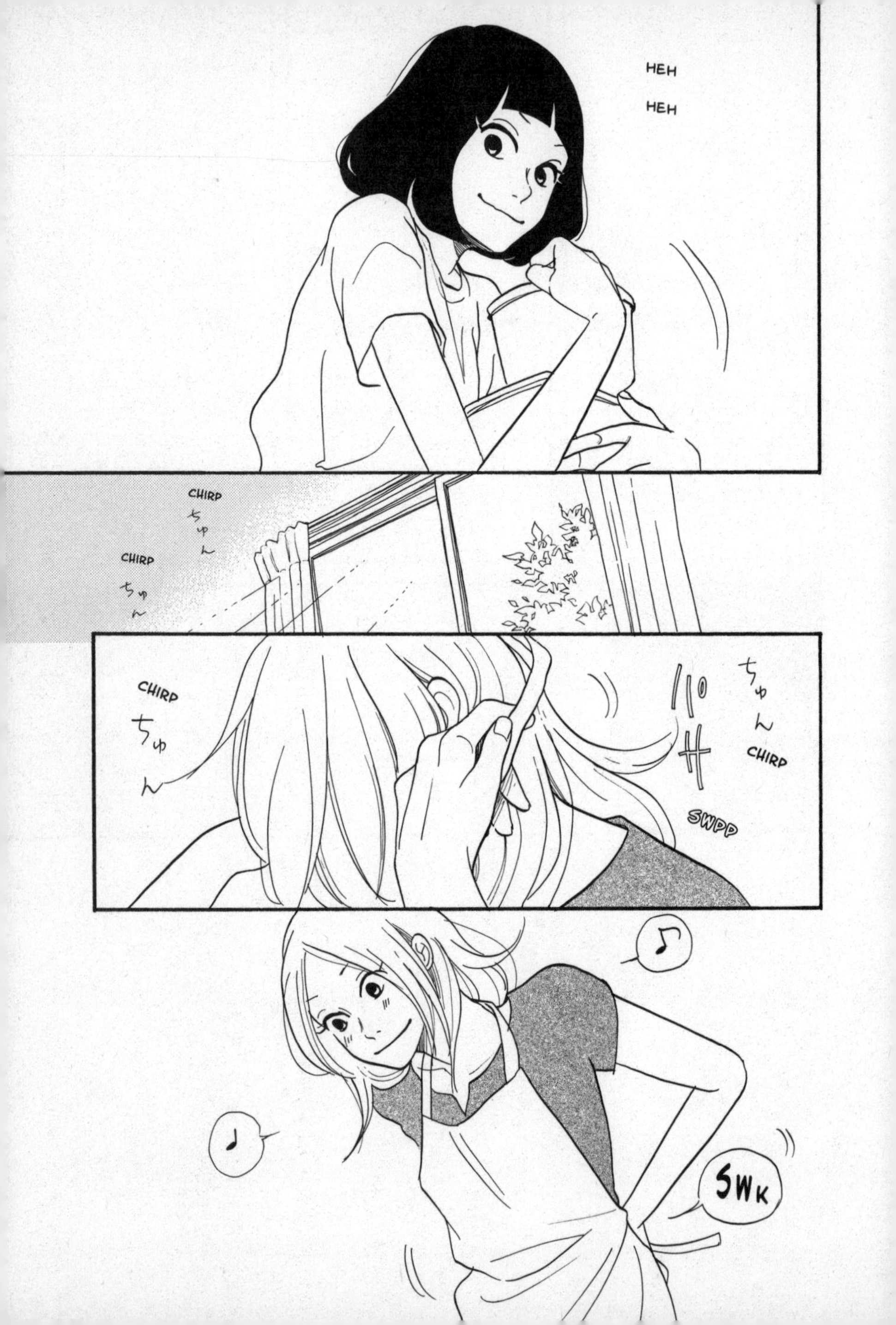
HEH
HEH
CHIRP
ちゅん
CHIRP
ちゅん
ちゅん
CHIRP
SWPP
CHIRP
ちゅん
♪
SWK
♪

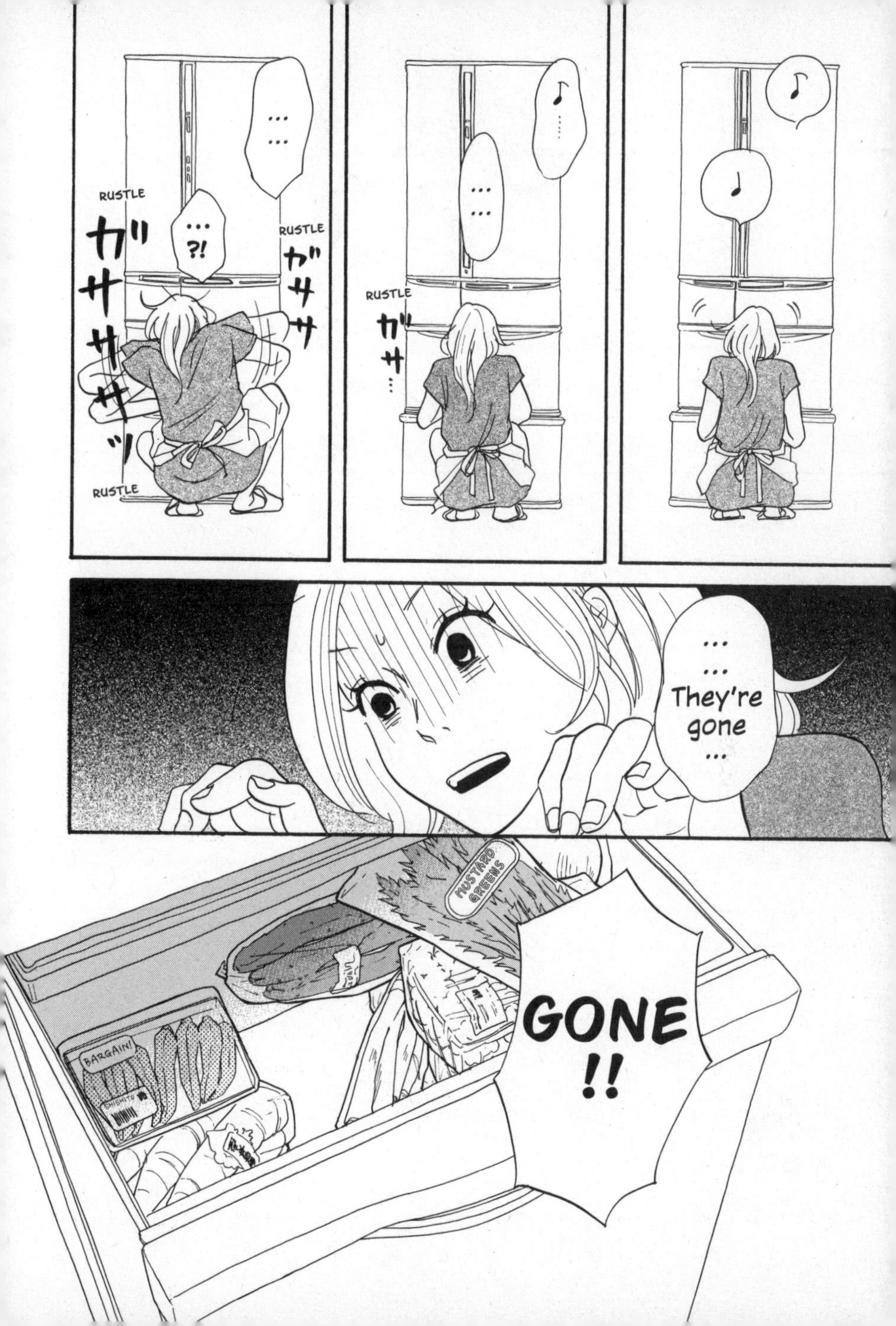
♪
♪
♪ ......
......
RUSTLE
ガサ…
......
...?!
RUSTLE
RUSTLE
ガササ
RUSTLE
......
......
They're gone
...
MUSTARD GREENS
BARGAIN!
GONE !!

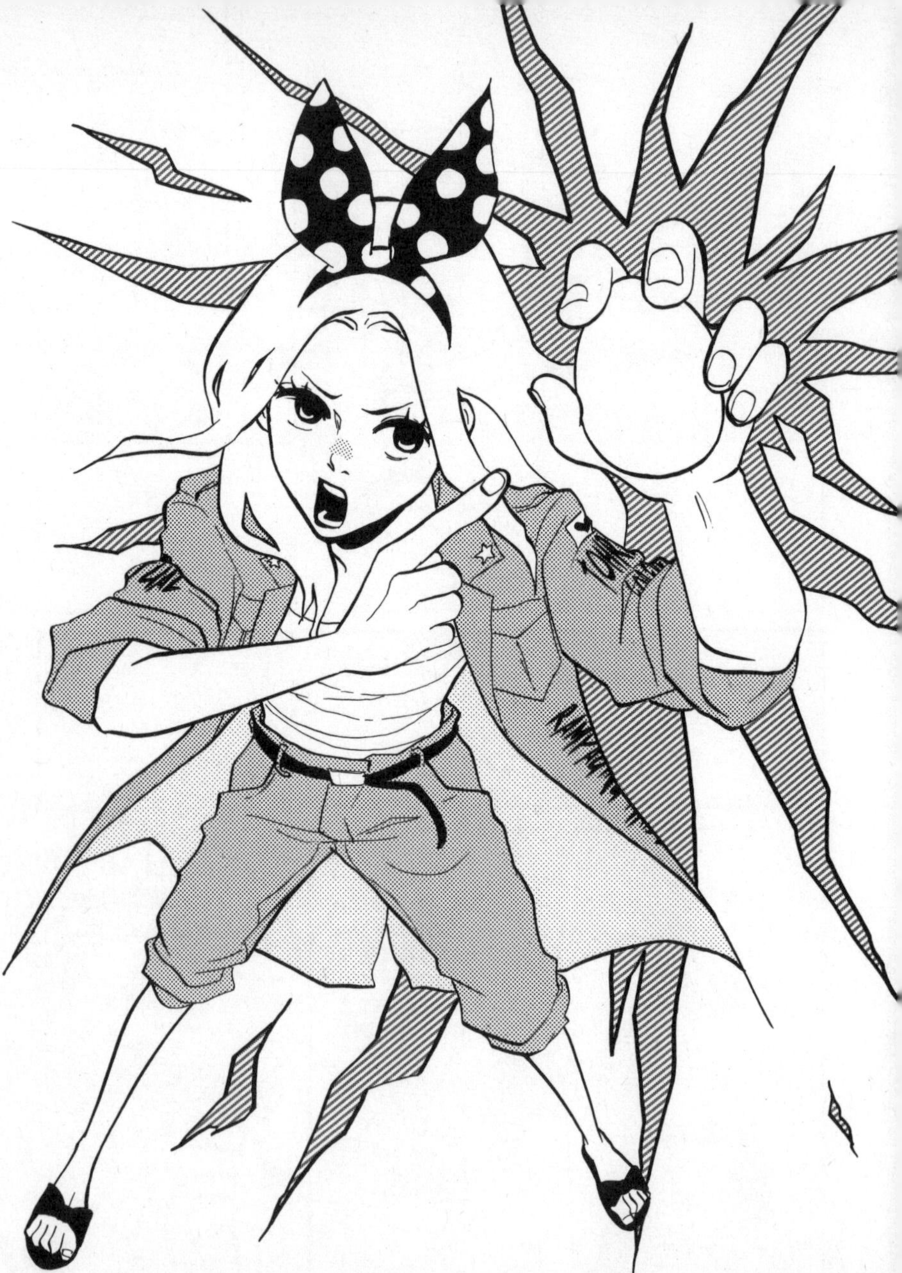

7 WIFE AND BROTHER-IN-LAW JOINT OPERATION

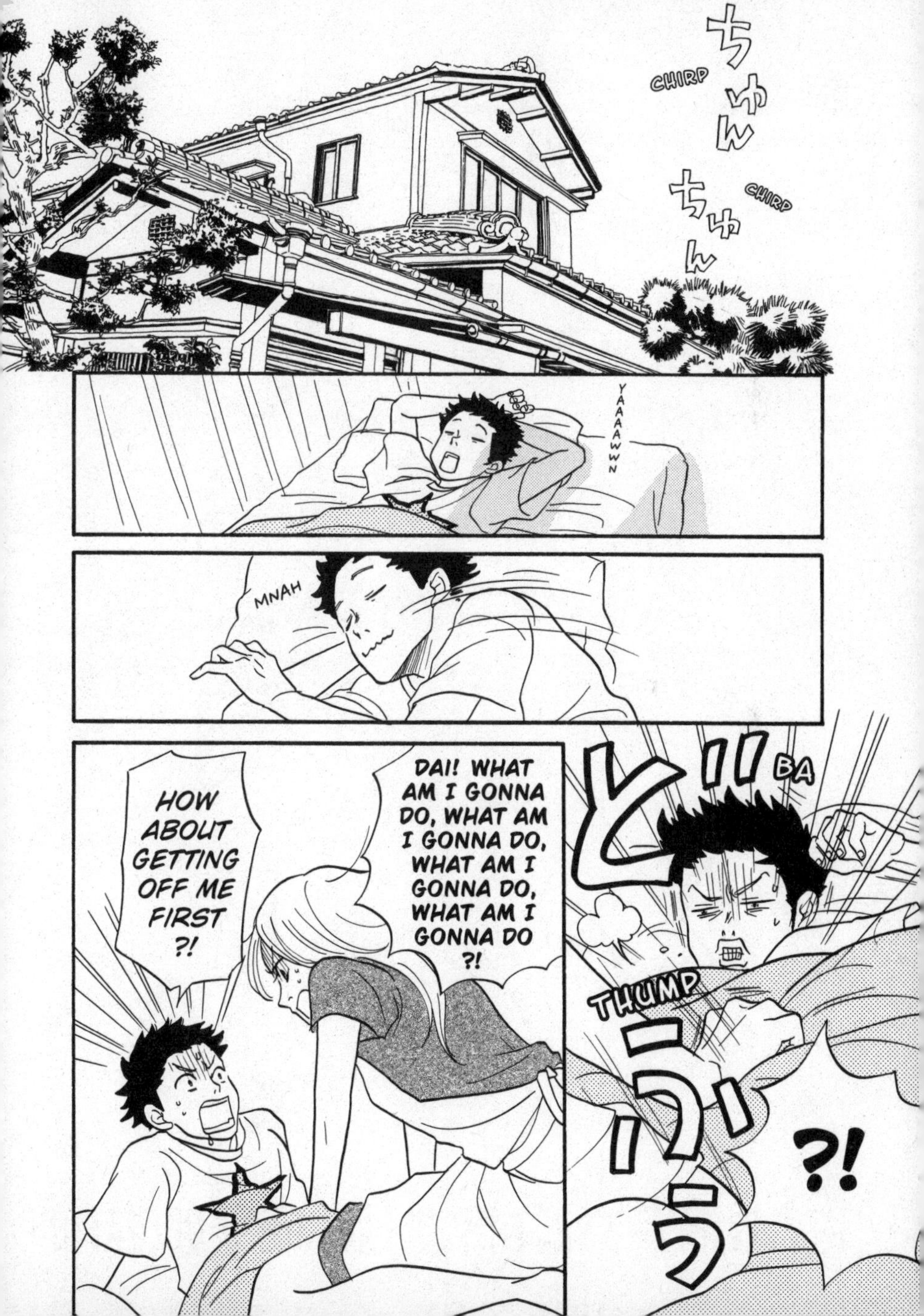
ちゅん
CHIRP
ちゅん
CHIRP
YAAAAAWWN
MNAH
BA
THUMP
?!
DAI! WHAT AM I GONNA DO, WHAT AM I GONNA DO, WHAT AM I GONNA DO, WHAT AM I GONNA DO?!
HOW ABOUT GETTING OFF ME FIRST?!

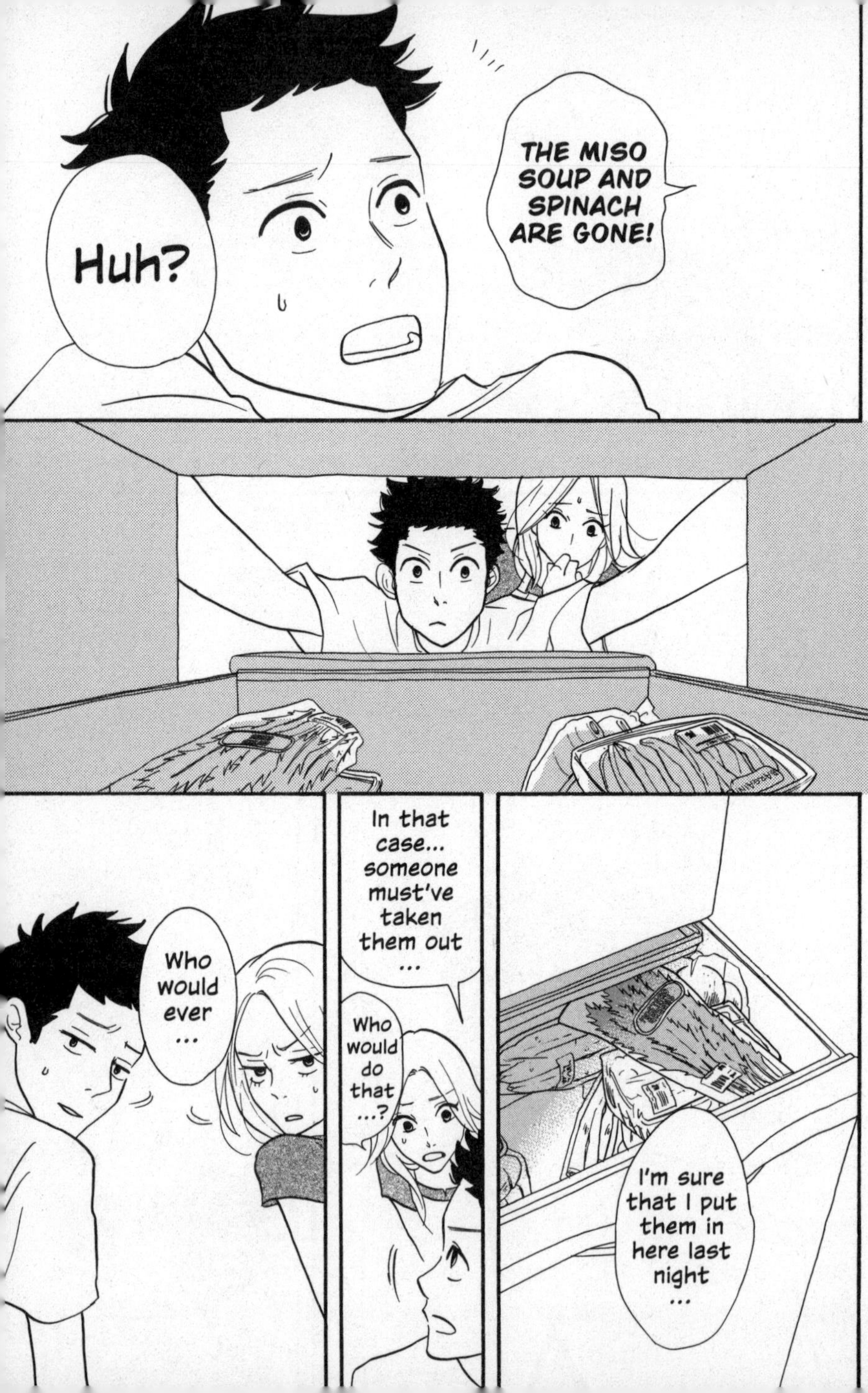
THE MISO SOUP AND SPINACH ARE GONE!
Huh?
I'm sure that I put them in here last night ...
In that case... someone must've taken them out ...
Who would do that ...?
Who would ever ...

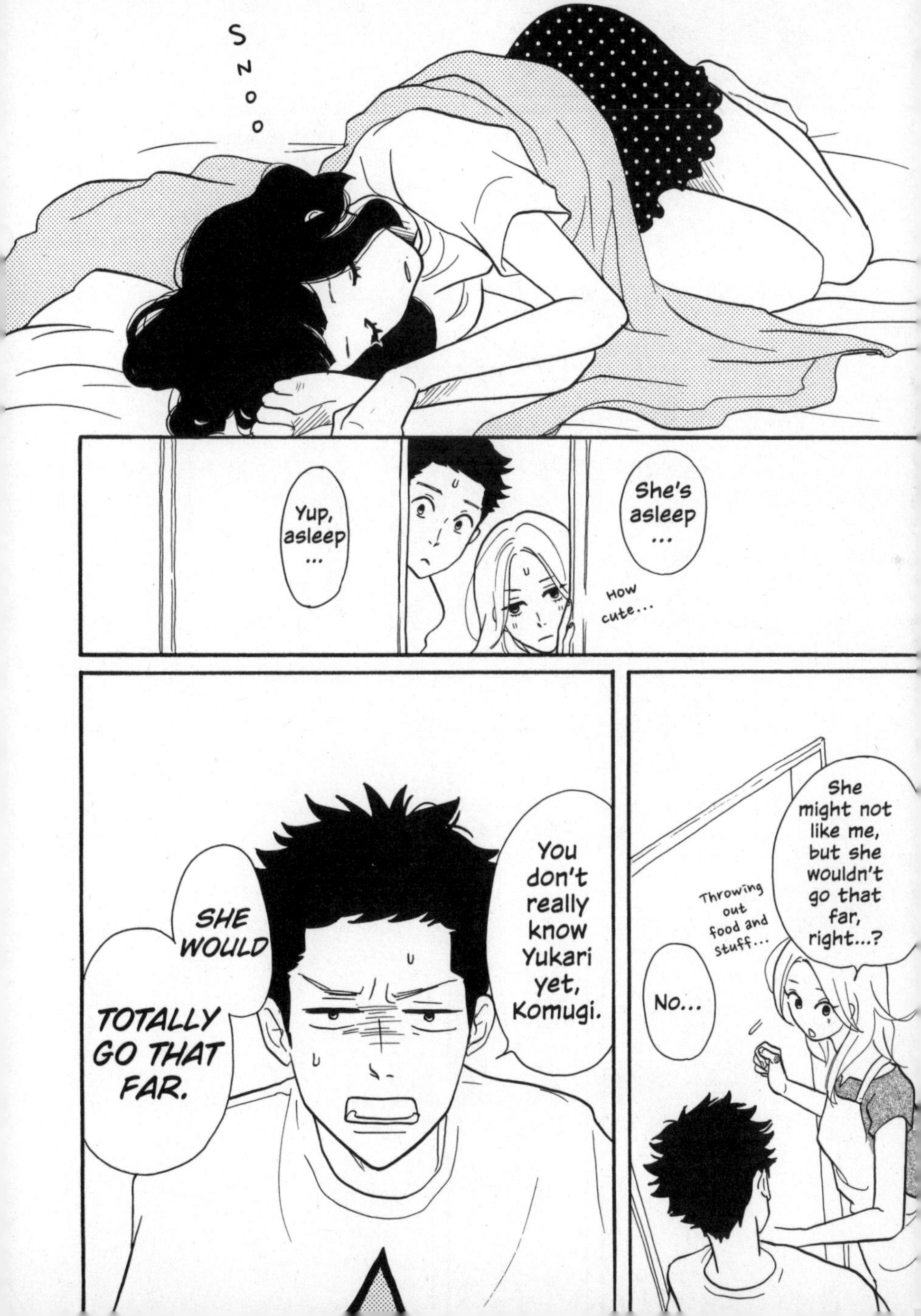
SNOOO
She's asleep...
How cute...
Yup, asleep...
She might not like me, but she wouldn't go that far, right...?
Throwing out food and stuff...
No...
You don't really know Yukari yet, Komugi.
SHE WOULD TOTALLY GO THAT FAR.

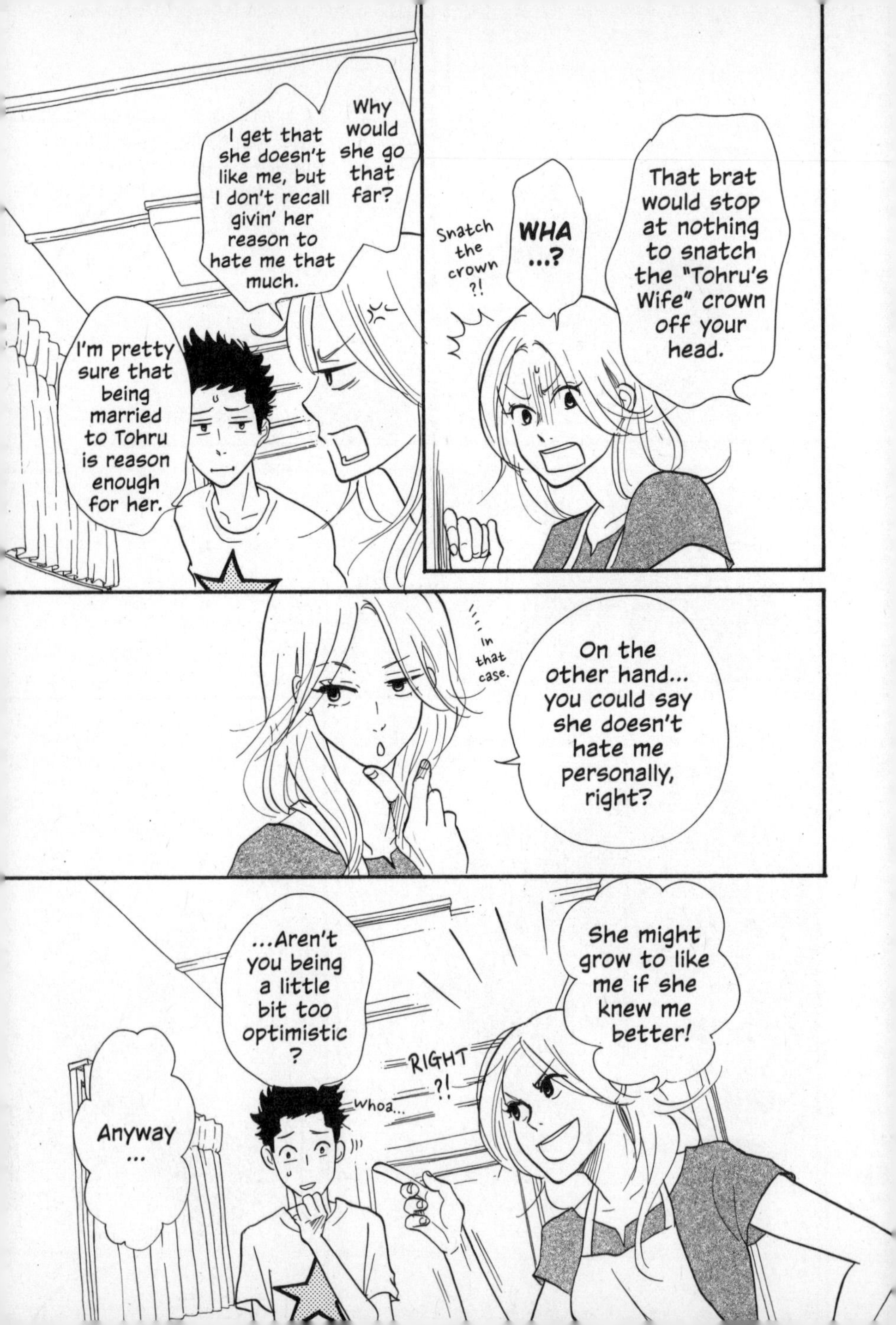

That brat would stop at nothing to snatch the "Tohru's Wife" crown off your head.
WHA ...?
Snatch the crown ?!
Why would she go that far?
I get that she doesn't like me, but I don't recall givin' her reason to hate me that much.
I'm pretty sure that being married to Tohru is reason enough for her.
On the other hand... you could say she doesn't hate me personally, right?
In that case.
She might grow to like me if she knew me better!
...Aren't you being a little bit too optimistic ?
RIGHT ?!
Whoa...
Anyway ...

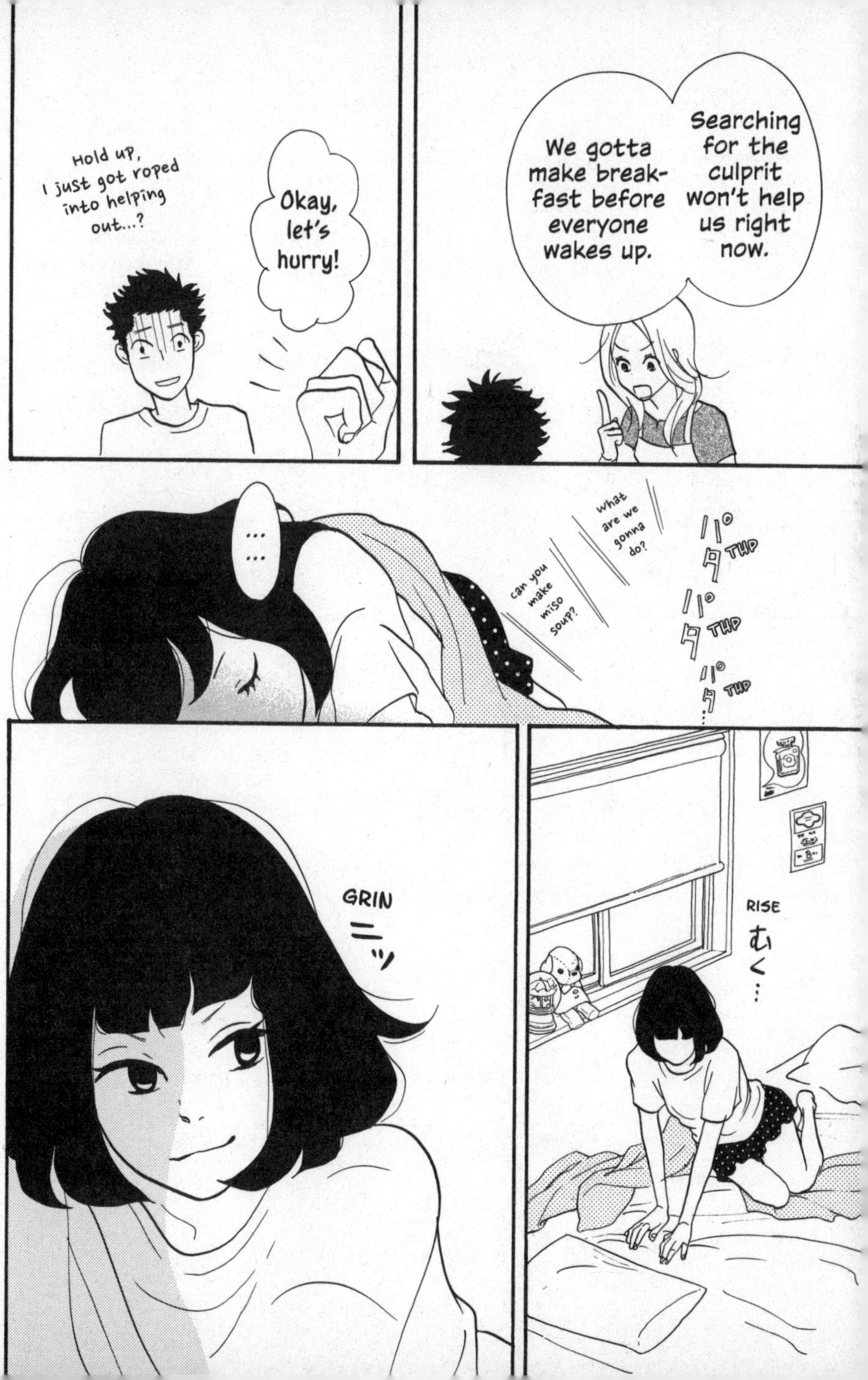
Searching for the culprit won't help us right now.
We gotta make breakfast before everyone wakes up.
Okay, let's hurry!
Hold up, I just got roped into helping out...?
パタ THP
パタ THP
パタ THP
what are we gonna do?
can you make miso soup?
……
RISE
むく…
GRIN
ニッ

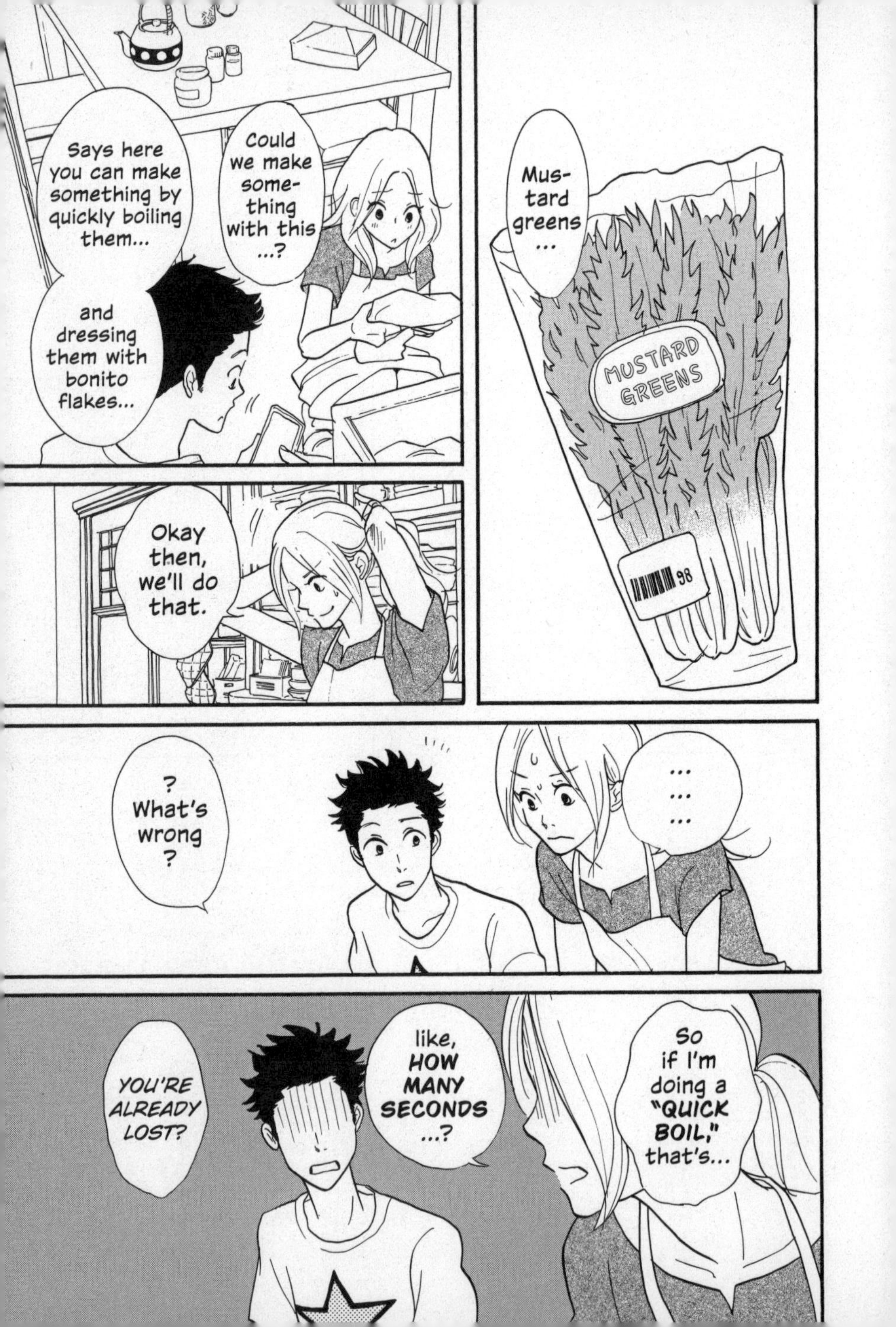
Mus-tard greens ...
MUSTARD GREENS
98
Could we make some-thing with this ...?
Says here you can make something by quickly boiling them...
and dressing them with bonito flakes...
Okay then, we'll do that.
... ...
? What's wrong ?
So if I'm doing a "QUICK BOIL," that's...
like, HOW MANY SECONDS ...?
YOU'RE ALREADY LOST?

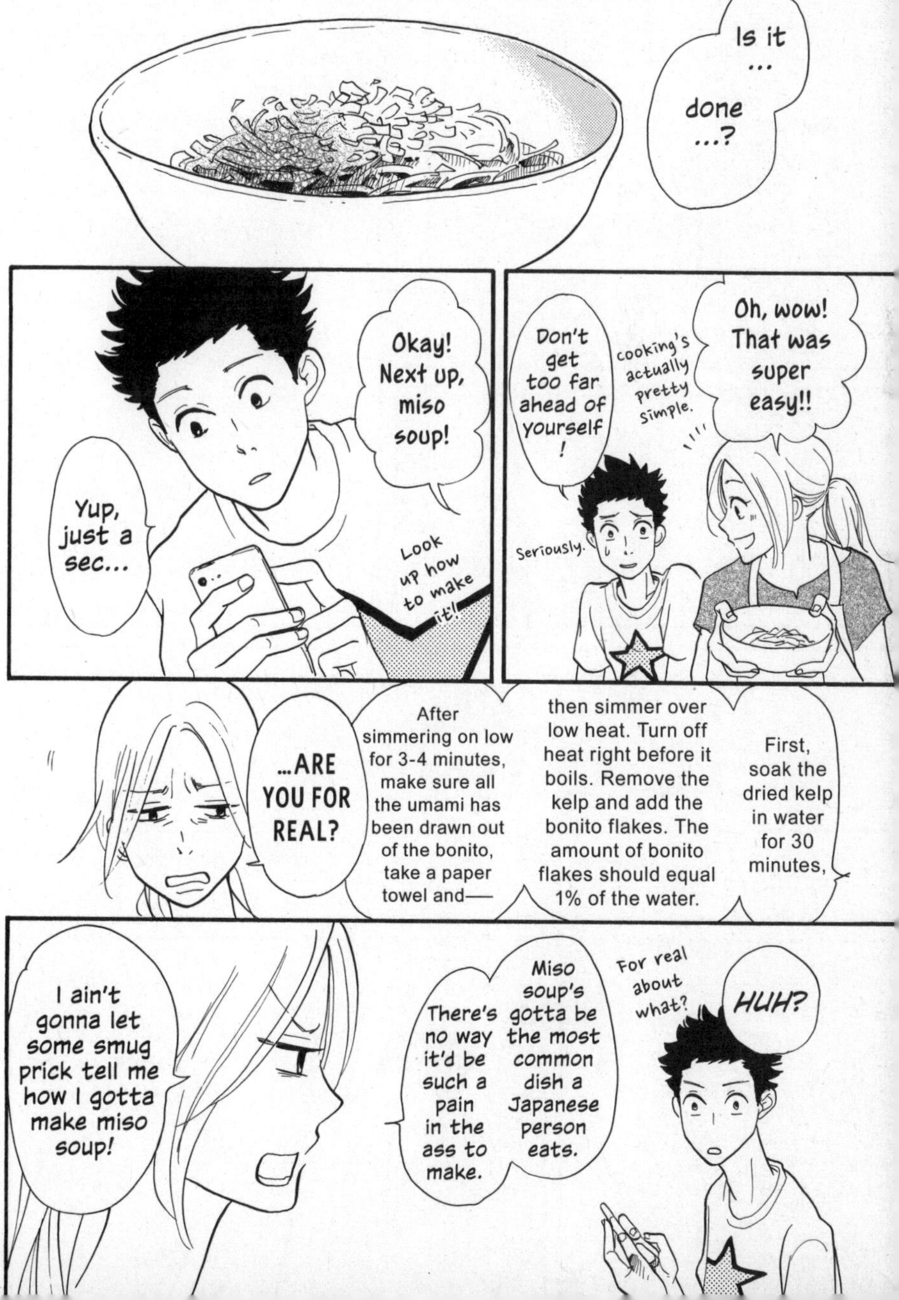
Is it ... done ...?
Oh, wow! That was super easy!!
cooking's actually pretty simple.
Don't get too far ahead of yourself!
Seriously.
Okay! Next up, miso soup!
Look up how to make it!
Yup, just a sec...
First, soak the dried kelp in water for 30 minutes,
then simmer over low heat. Turn off heat right before it boils. Remove the kelp and add the bonito flakes. The amount of bonito flakes should equal 1% of the water.
After simmering on low for 3-4 minutes, make sure all the umami has been drawn out of the bonito, take a paper towel and—
...ARE YOU FOR REAL?
HUH?
For real about what?
Miso soup's gotta be the most common dish a Japanese person eats.
There's no way it'd be such a pain in the ass to make.
I ain't gonna let some smug prick tell me how I gotta make miso soup!

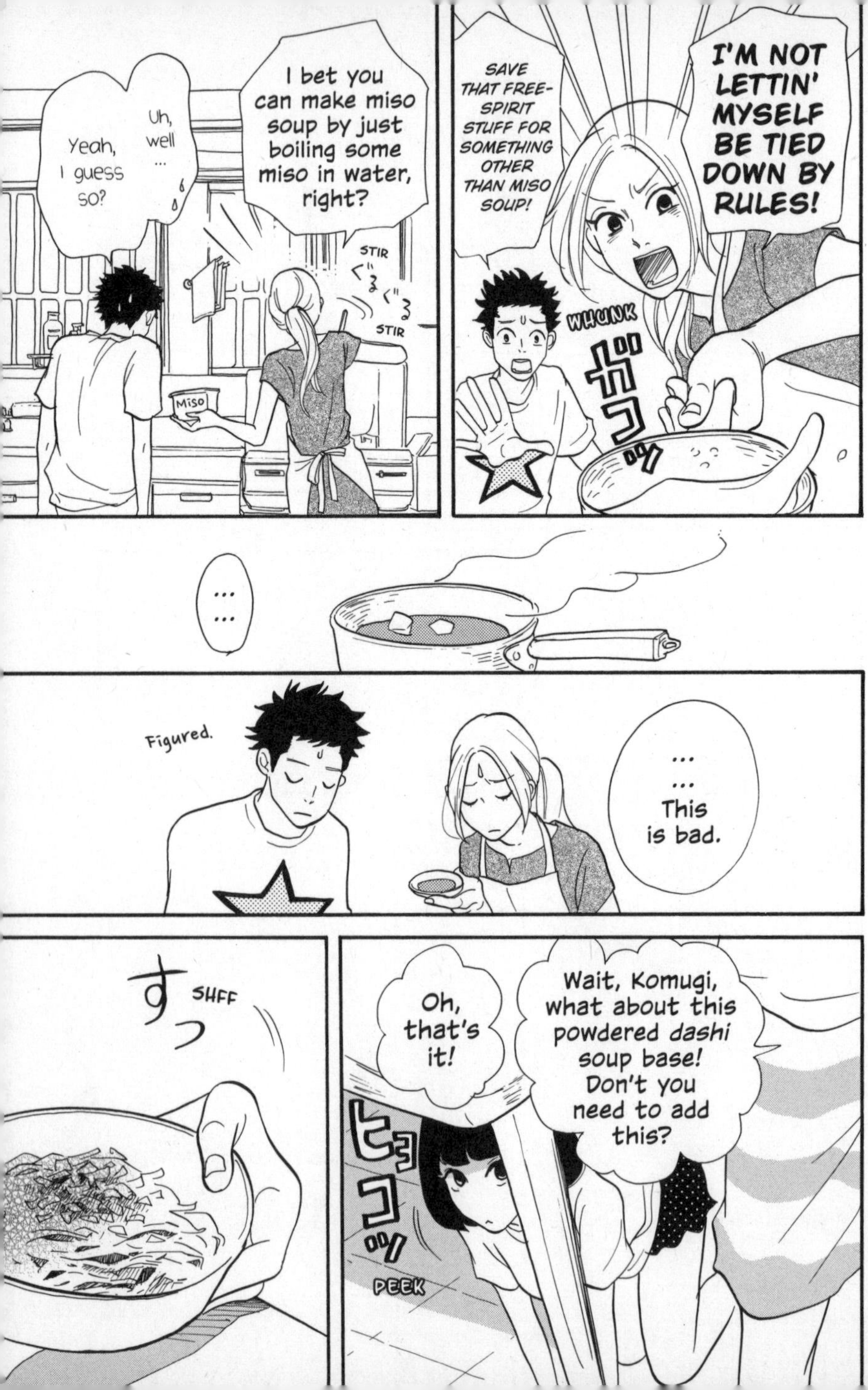
I'M NOT LETTIN' MYSELF BE TIED DOWN BY RULES!
SAVE THAT FREE-SPIRIT STUFF FOR SOMETHING OTHER THAN MISO SOUP!
WHUNK
ガコッ
I bet you can make miso soup by just boiling some miso in water, right?
Uh, well ...
Yeah, I guess so?
STIR
ぐるぐる
STIR
Miso
... ...
... ... This is bad.
Figured.
Wait, Komugi, what about this powdered dashi soup base! Don't you need to add this?
Oh, that's it!
ヒョコッ
PEEK
すっ
SHFF

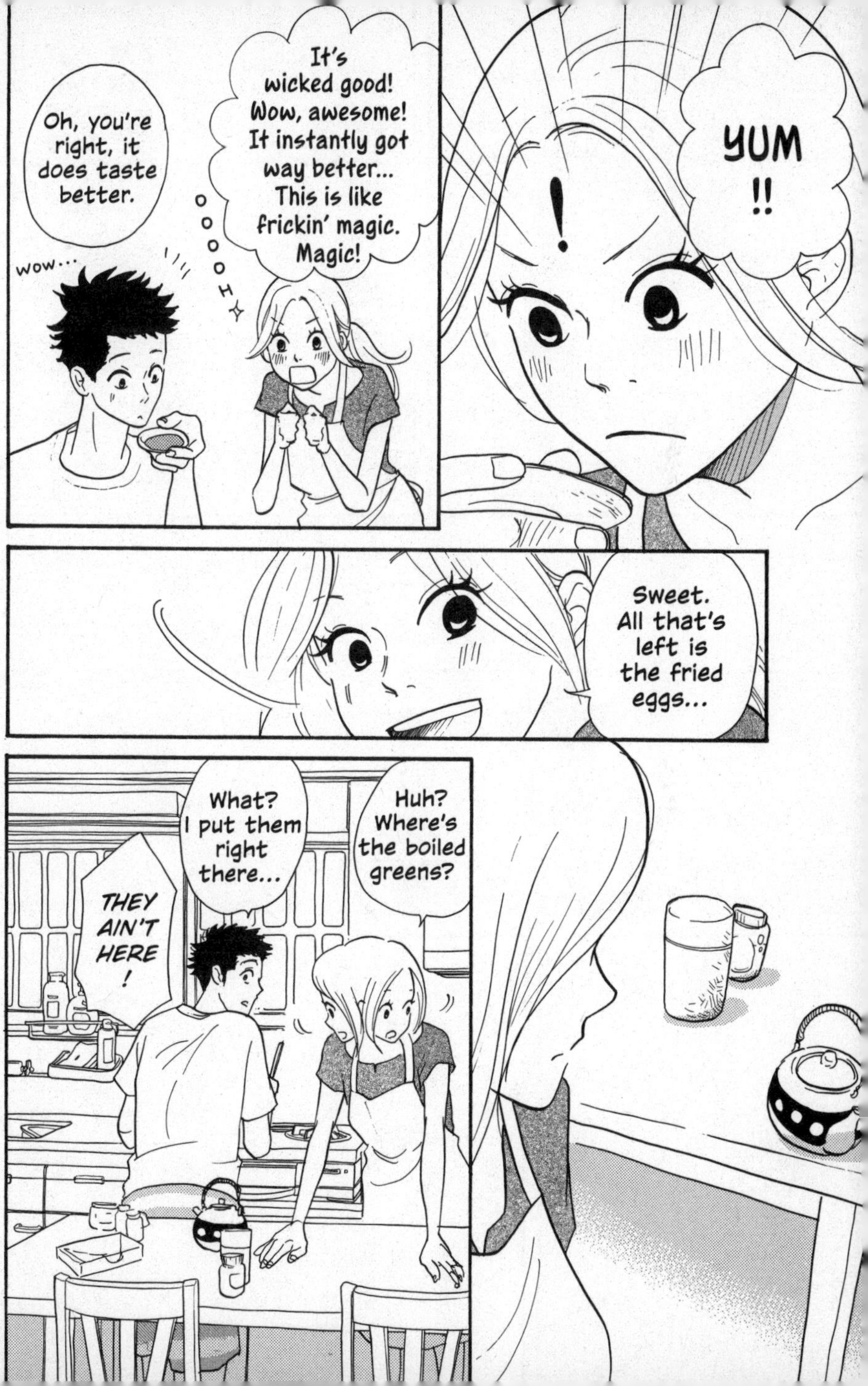
YUM !!
!
It's wicked good! Wow, awesome! It instantly got way better... This is like frickin' magic. Magic!
Oh, you're right, it does taste better.
OOOOH
WOW...
Sweet. All that's left is the fried eggs...
Huh? Where's the boiled greens?
What? I put them right there...
THEY AIN'T HERE!

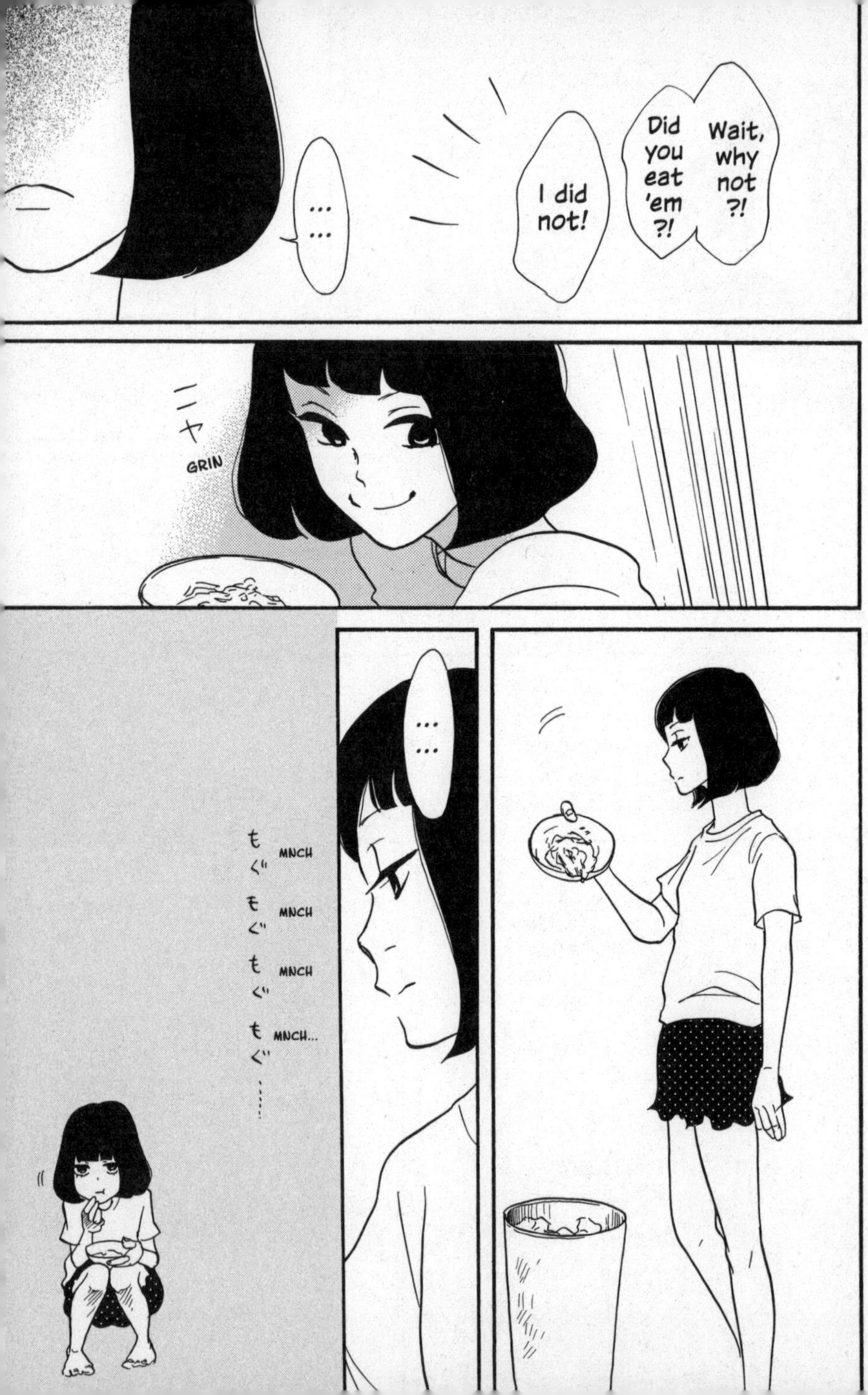

Wait, why not ?!
Did you eat 'em ?!
I did not!
……
ニヤ
GRIN
……
もぐもぐもぐもぐ……
MNCH
MNCH
MNCH
MNCH...

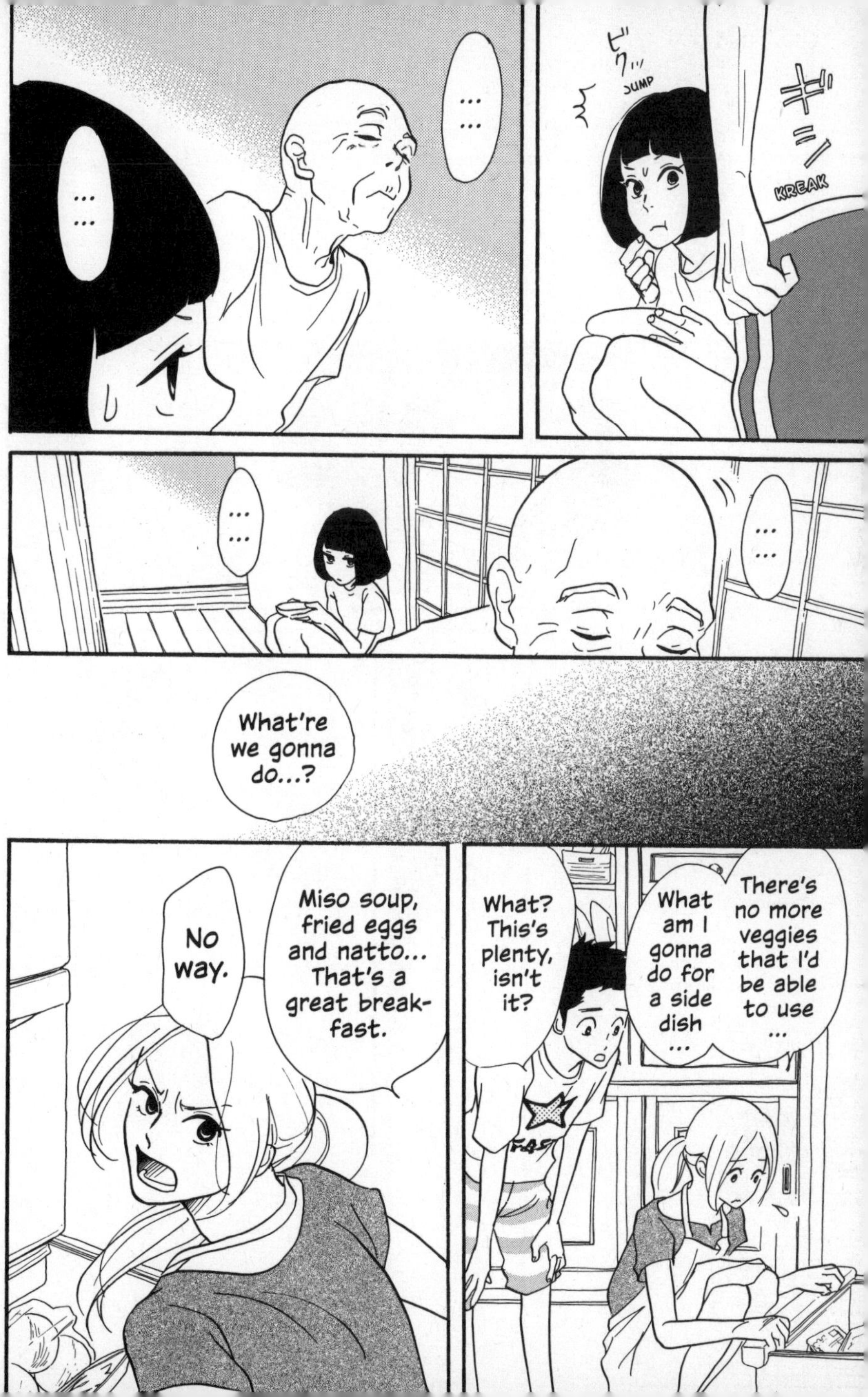
ビクッ
JUMP
ギシッ
KREAK
……
……
……
……
What're we gonna do…?
There's no more veggies that I'd be able to use …
What am I gonna do for a side dish …
What? This's plenty, isn't it?
Miso soup, fried eggs and natto… That's a great break-fast.
No way.

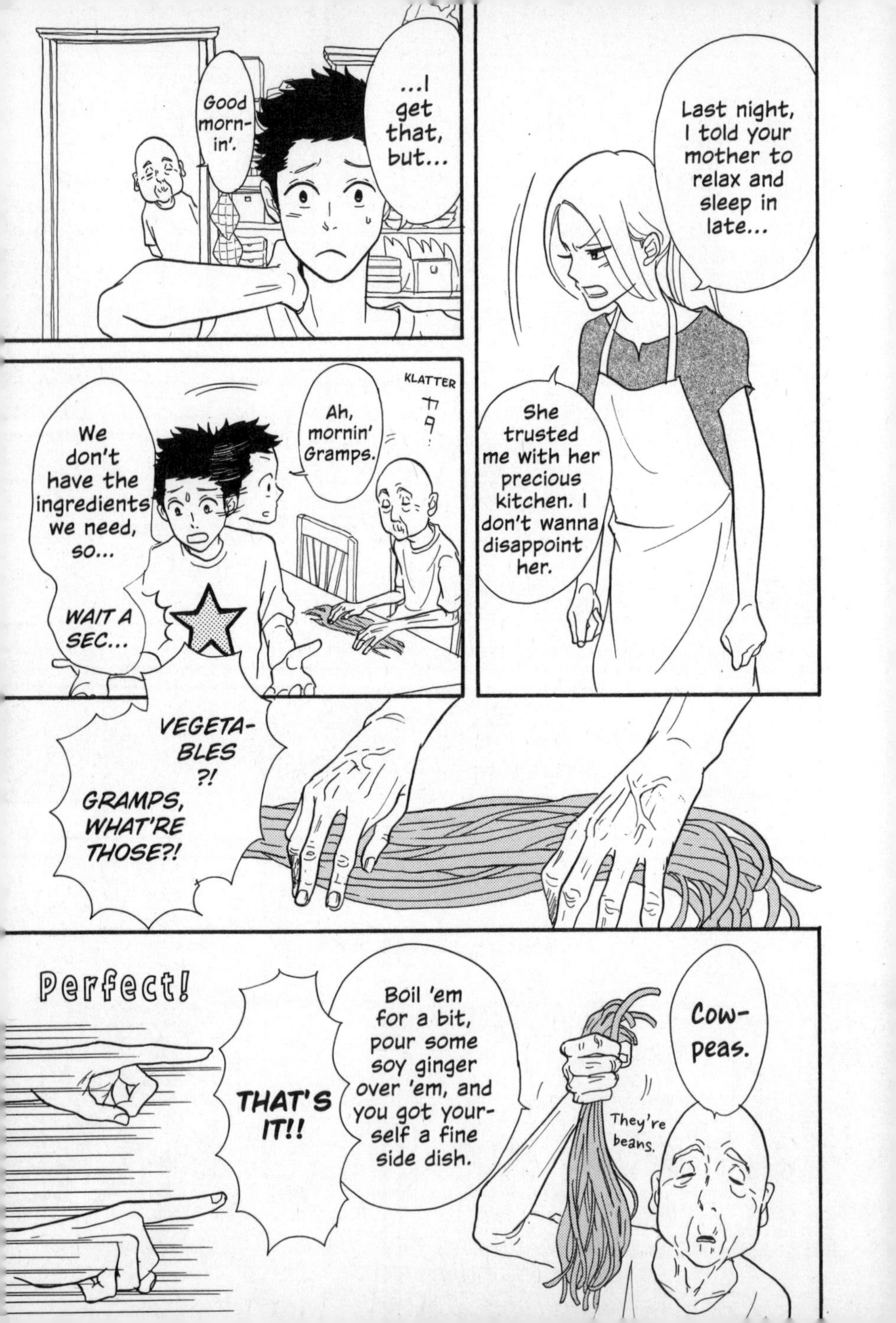
Last night, I told your mother to relax and sleep in late...
She trusted me with her precious kitchen. I don't wanna disappoint her.
...I get that, but...
Good mornin'.
KLATTER
Ah, mornin' Gramps.
We don't have the ingredients we need, so...
WAIT A SEC...
VEGETA-BLES?!
GRAMPS, WHAT'RE THOSE?!
Cow-peas.
They're beans.
Boil 'em for a bit, pour some soy ginger over 'em, and you got your-self a fine side dish.
THAT'S IT!!
Perfect!

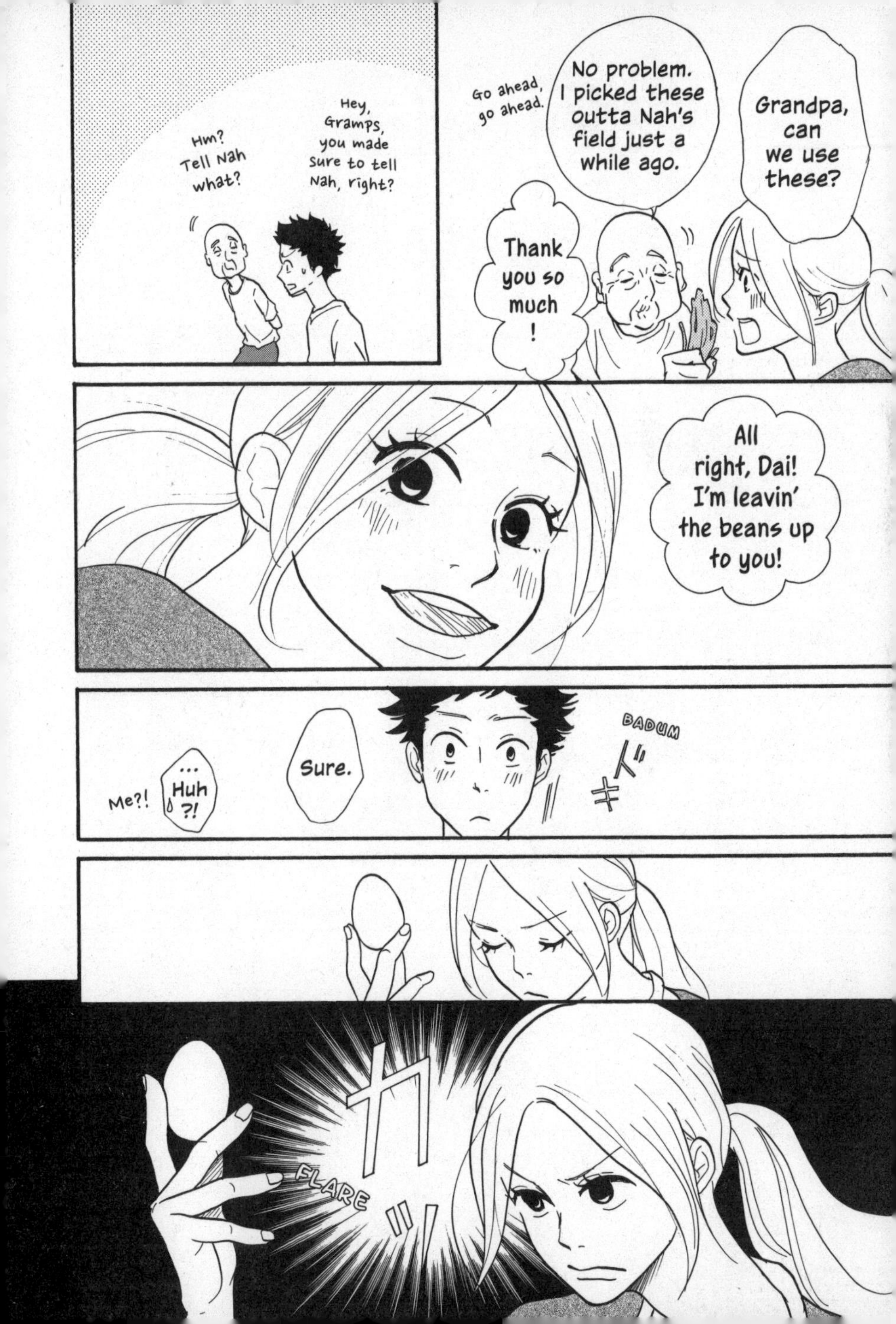
Grandpa, can we use these?
No problem. I picked these outta Nah's field just a while ago.
Go ahead, go ahead.
Thank you so much!
Hey, Gramps, you made sure to tell Nah, right?
Hm? Tell Nah what?
All right, Dai! I'm leavin' the beans up to you!
BADUM
Sure.
... Huh?!
Me?!
FLARE

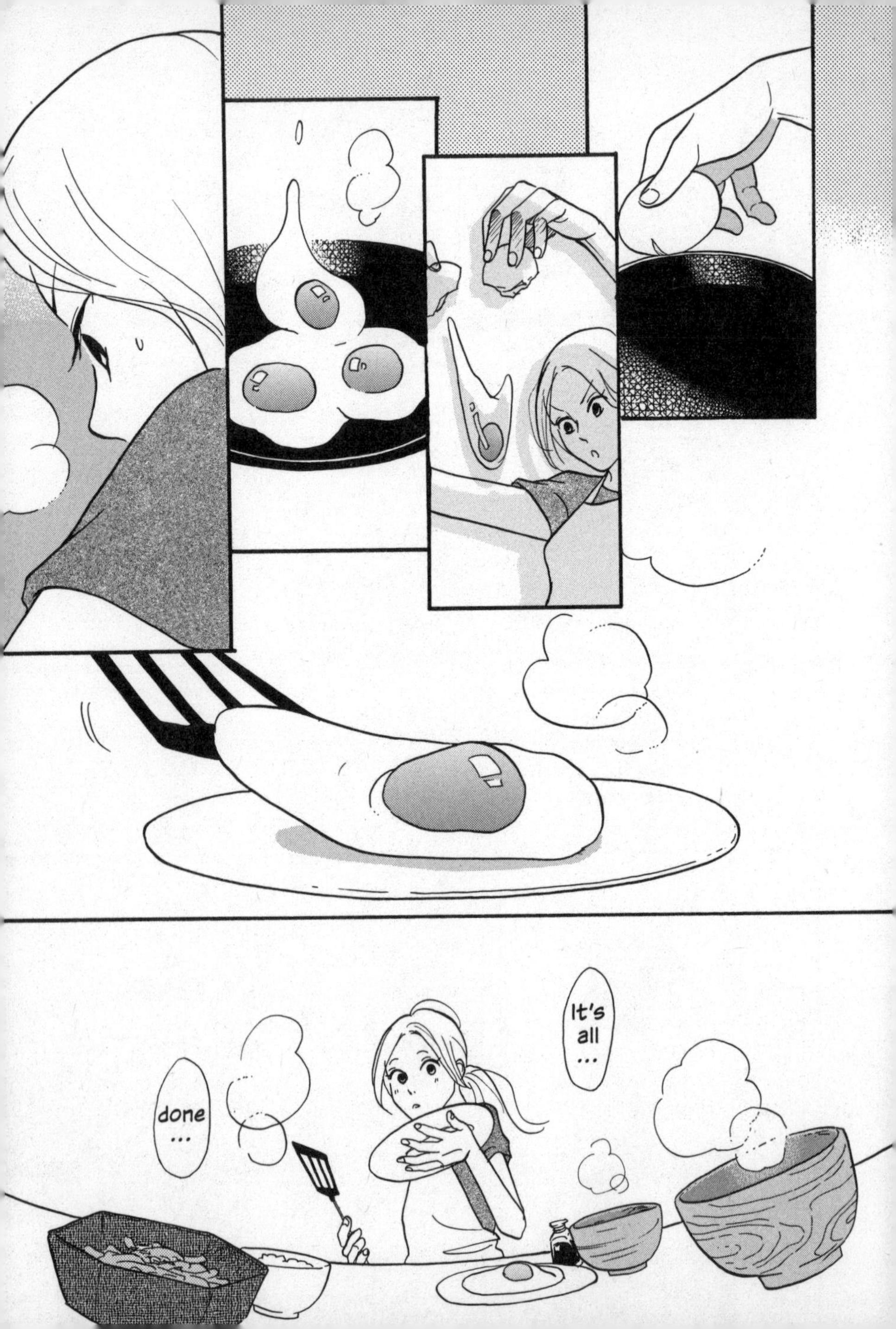
It's all ...
done ...

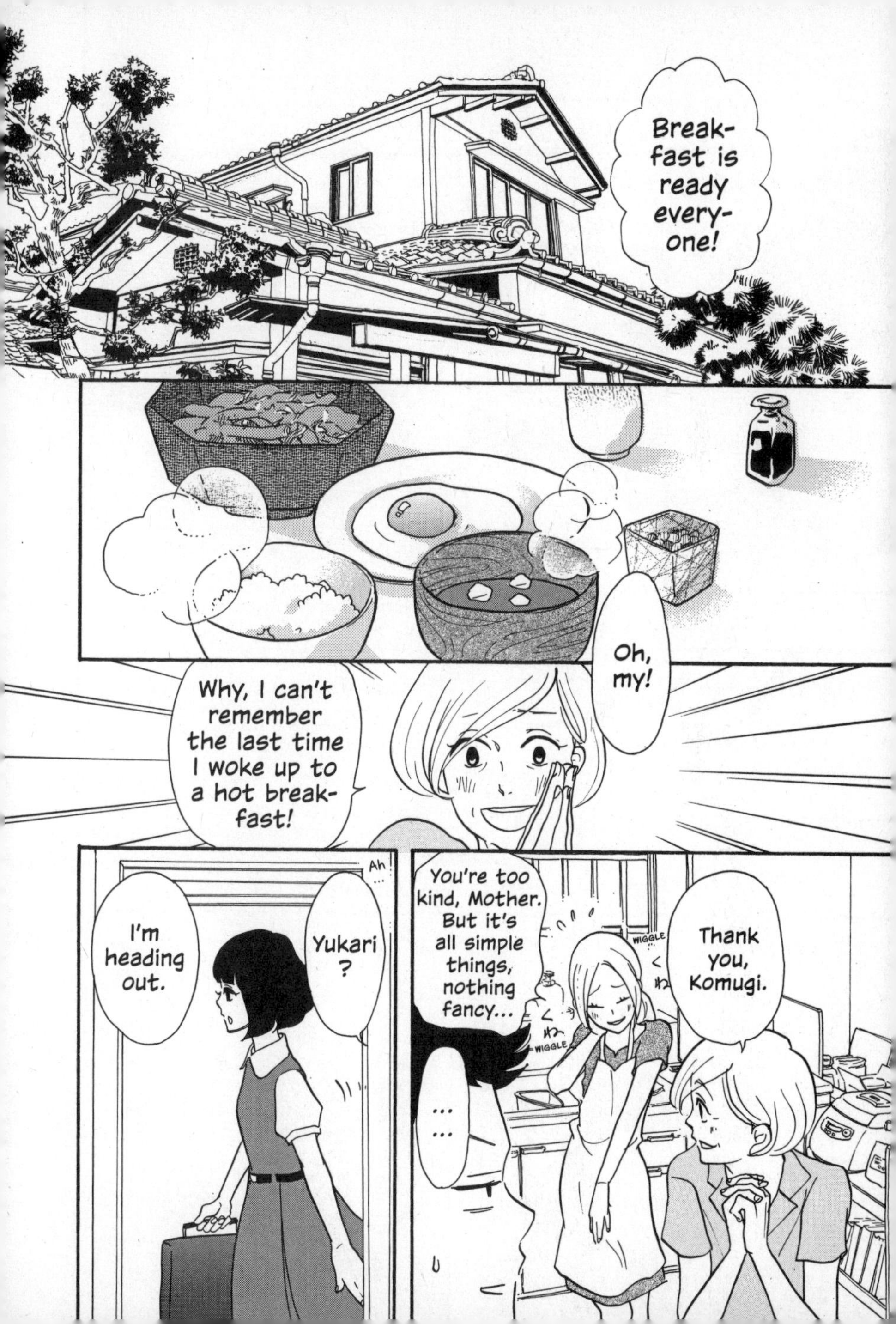
Break-fast is ready every-one!
Oh, my!
Why, I can't remember the last time I woke up to a hot break-fast!
Thank you, Komugi.
WIGGLE
You're too kind, Mother. But it's all simple things, nothing fancy...
WIGGLE
... ...
Ah ...
Yukari ?
I'm heading out.

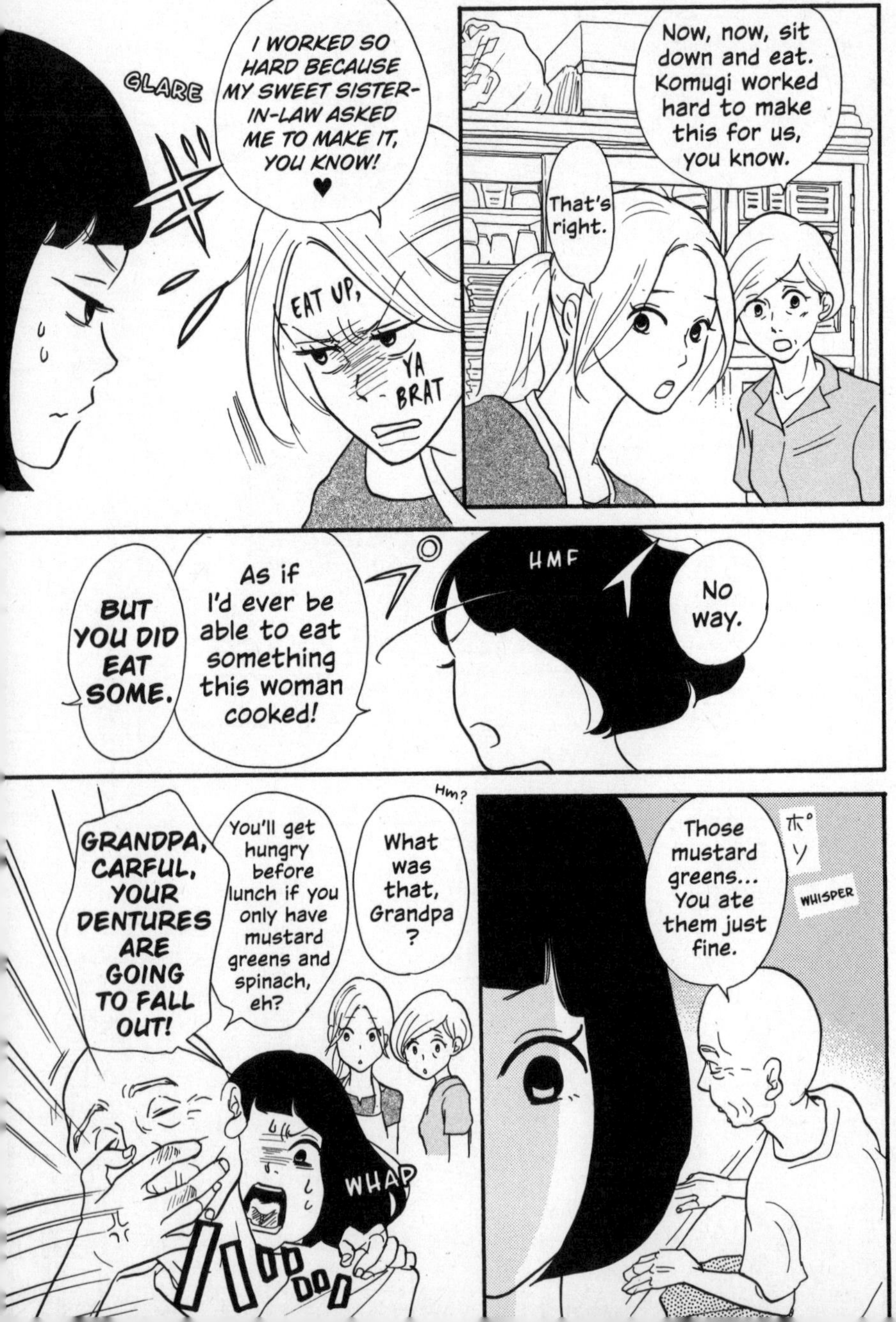
Now, now, sit down and eat. Komugi worked hard to make this for us, you know.
That's right.
GLARE
I WORKED SO HARD BECAUSE MY SWEET SISTER-IN-LAW ASKED ME TO MAKE IT, YOU KNOW! ♥
EAT UP, YA BRAT
No way.
HMF
As if I'd ever be able to eat something this woman cooked!
BUT YOU DID EAT SOME.
ポソ
WHISPER
Those mustard greens... You ate them just fine.
Hm?
What was that, Grandpa?
You'll get hungry before lunch if you only have mustard greens and spinach, eh?
GRANDPA, CARFUL, YOUR DENTURES ARE GOING TO FALL OUT!
WHAP

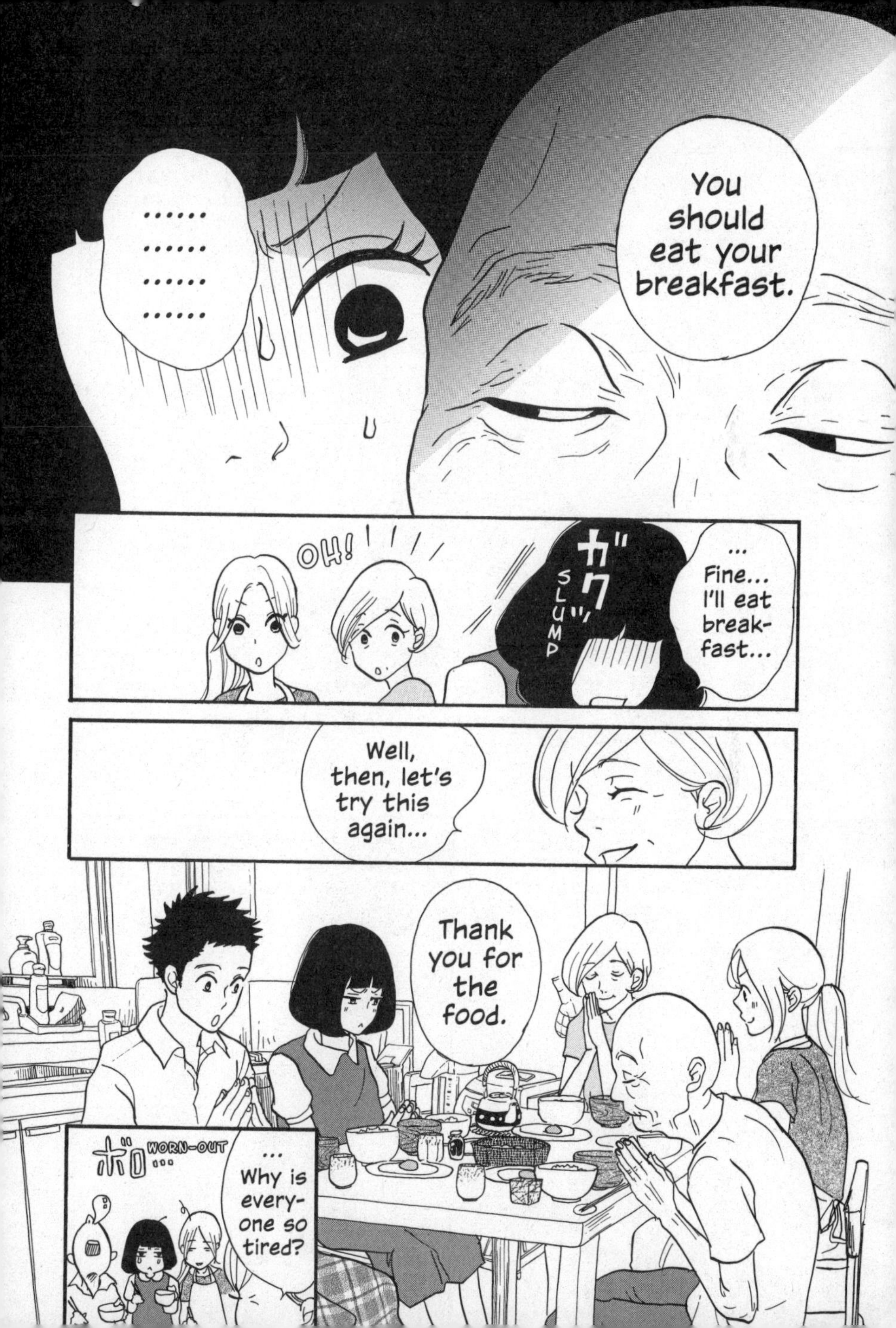

You should eat your breakfast.
......
......
......
......
... Fine... I'll eat break-fast...
ガク SLUMP
OH!
Well, then, let's try this again...
Thank you for the food.
... Why is every-one so tired?
ボロ WORN-OUT ...

The Delinquent HOUSEWIFE!

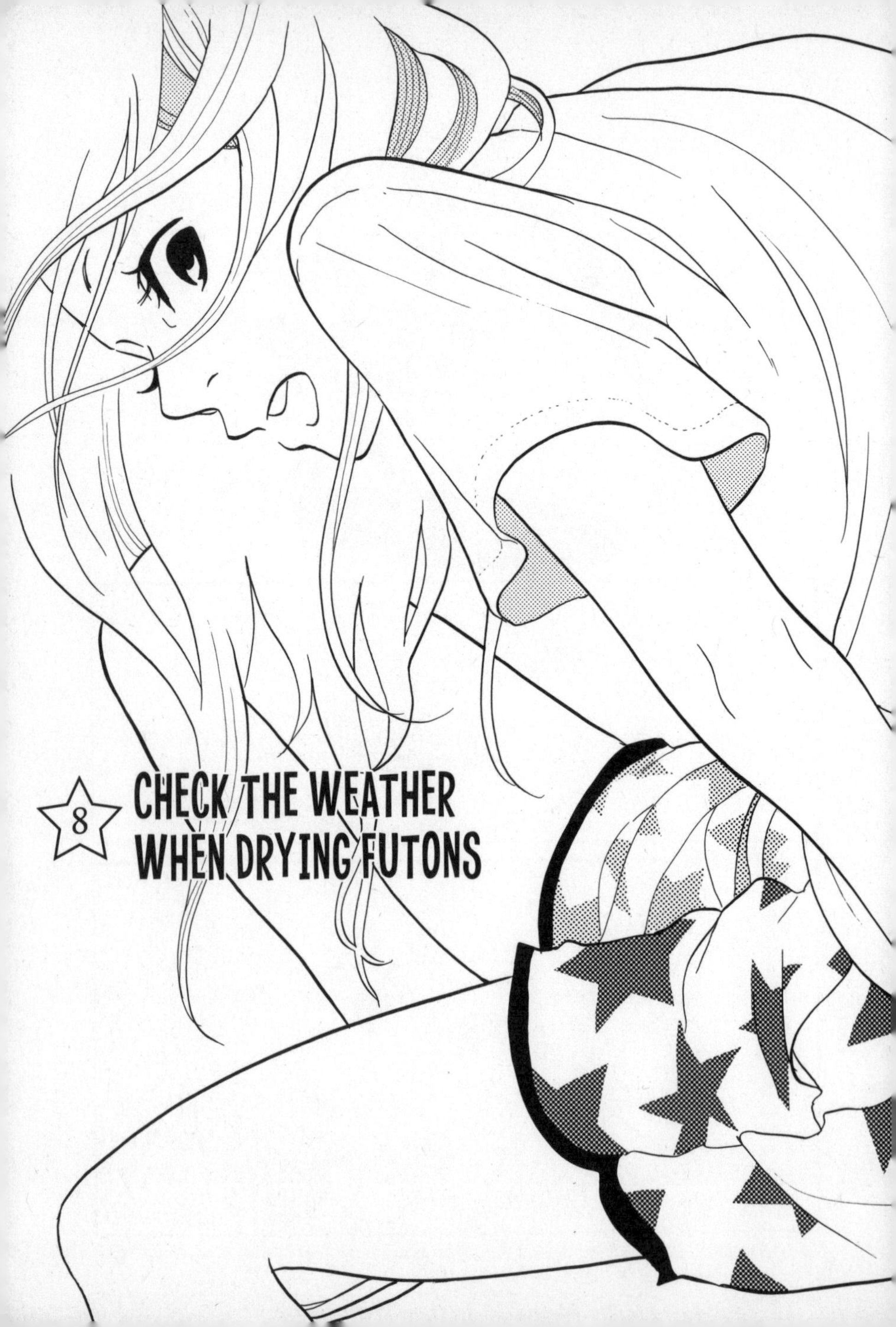
8
CHECK THE WEATHER
WHEN DRYING FUTONS

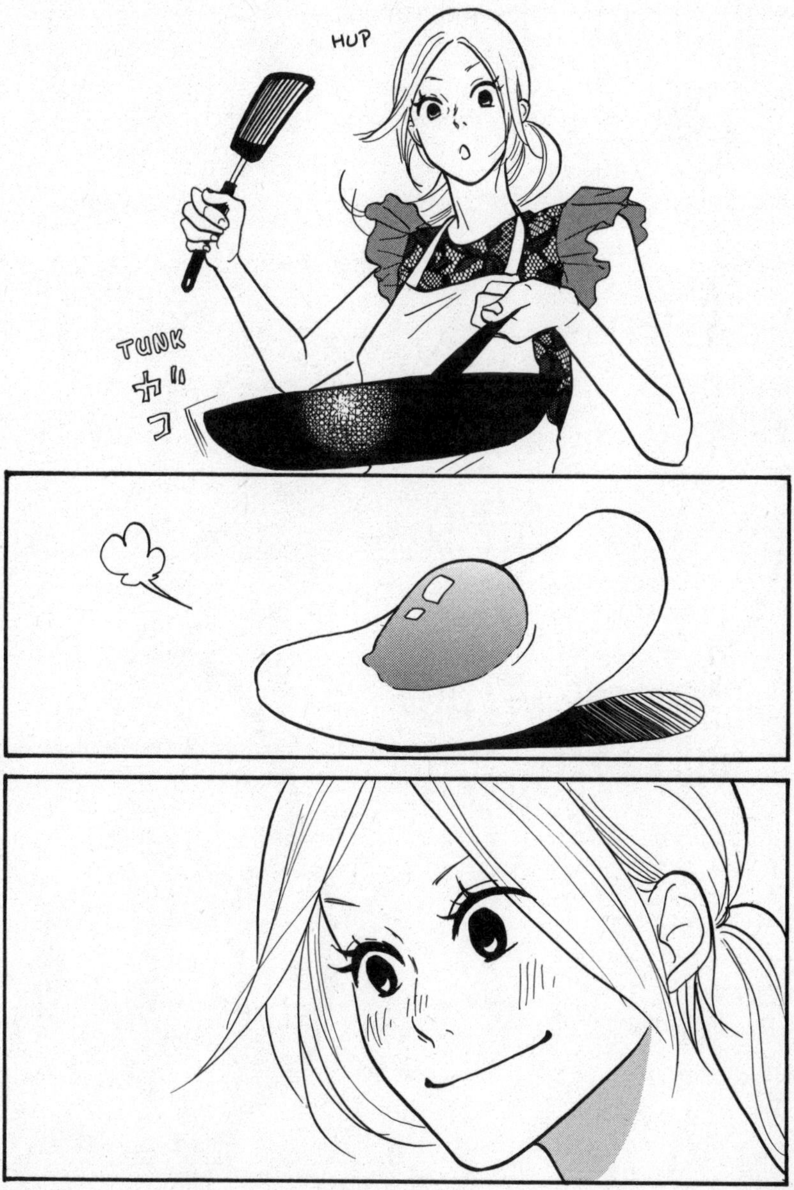
HUP
TUNK
ガコ

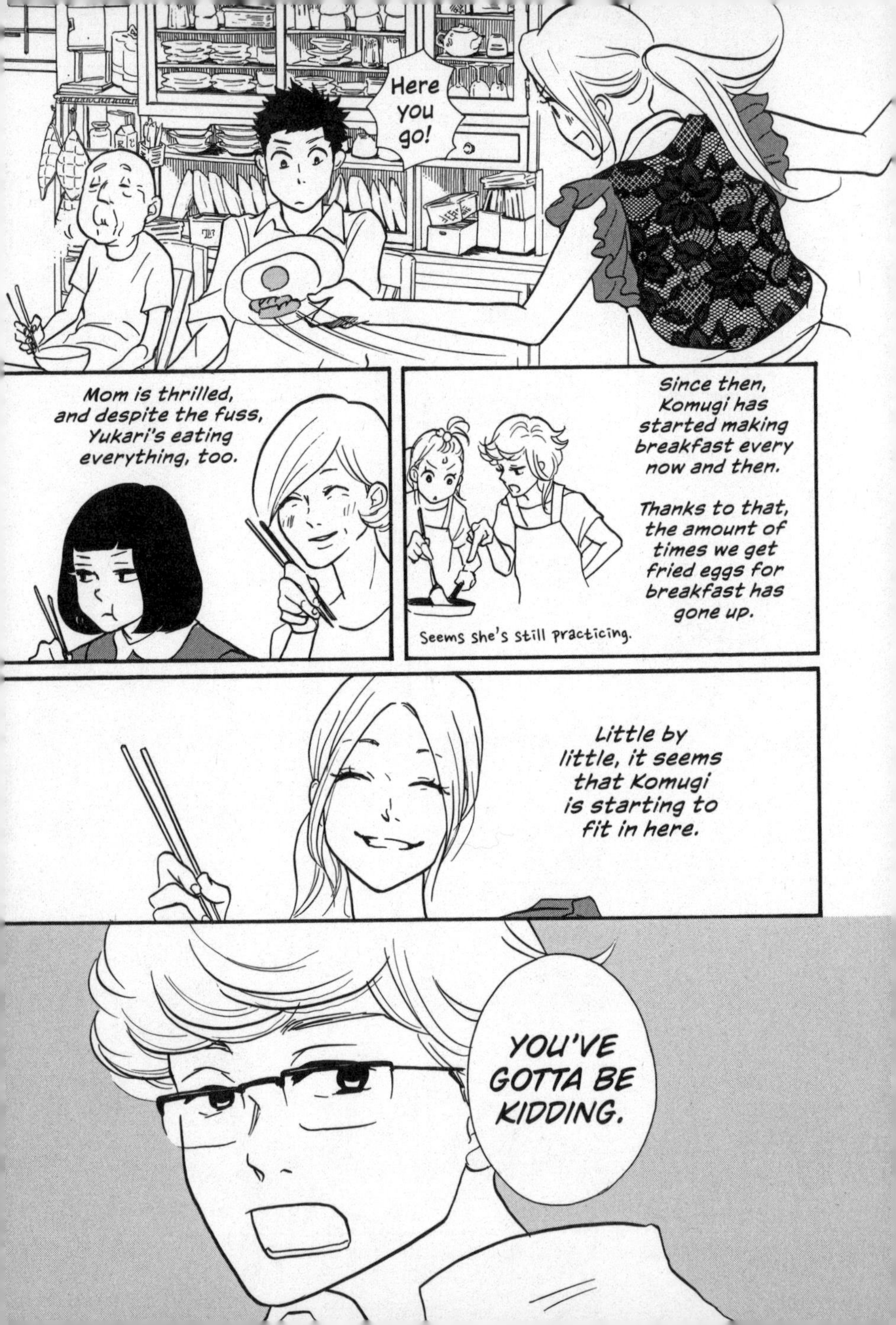
Here you go!
Since then, Komugi has started making breakfast every now and then.
Thanks to that, the amount of times we get fried eggs for breakfast has gone up.
Seems she's still practicing.
Mom is thrilled, and despite the fuss, Yukari's eating everything, too.
Little by little, it seems that Komugi is starting to fit in here.
YOU'VE GOTTA BE KIDDING.

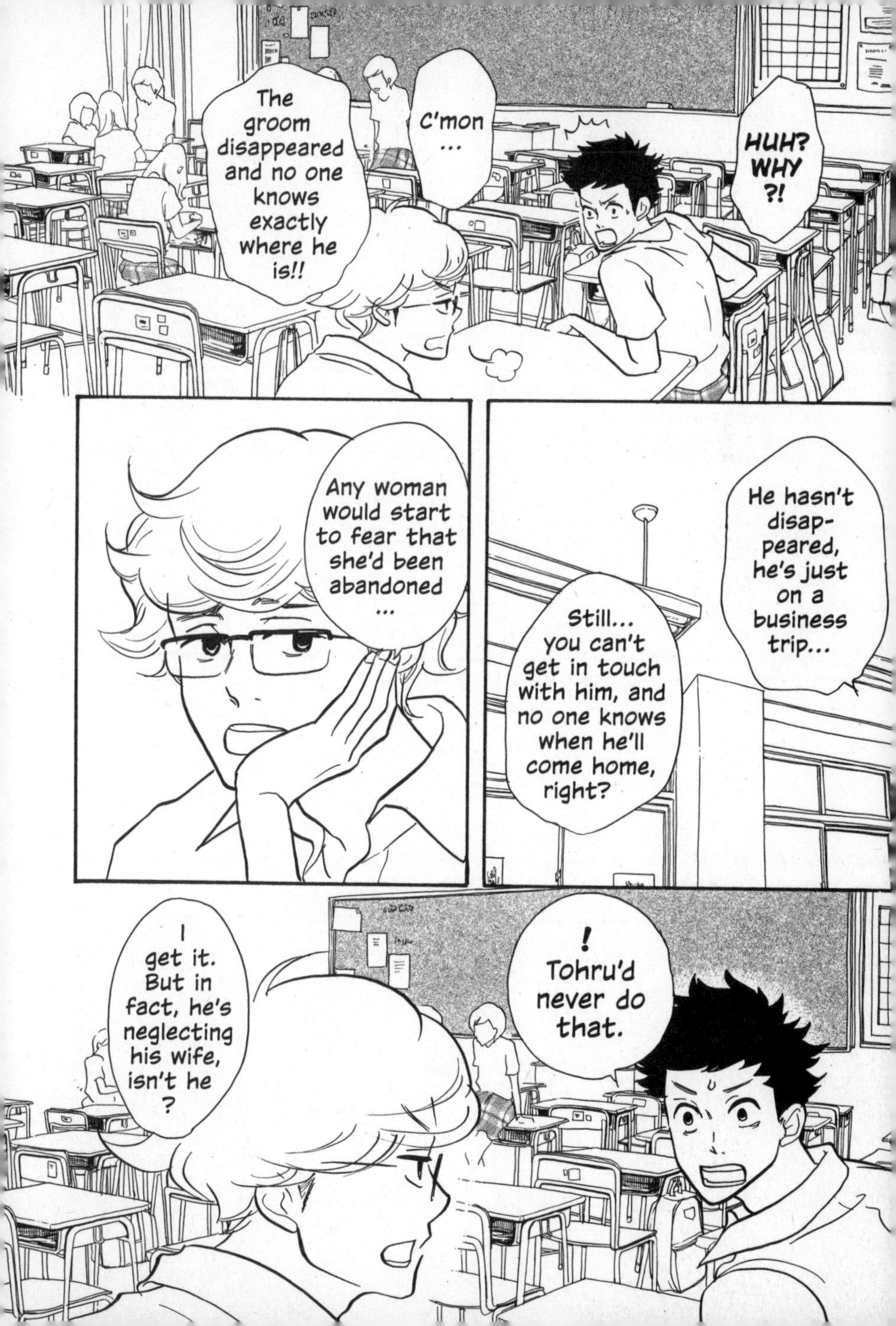
HUH? WHY?!
C'mon...
The groom disappeared and no one knows exactly where he is!!
He hasn't disappeared, he's just on a business trip...
Still... you can't get in touch with him, and no one knows when he'll come home, right?
Any woman would start to fear that she'd been abandoned...
! Tohru'd never do that.
I get it. But in fact, he's neglecting his wife, isn't he?

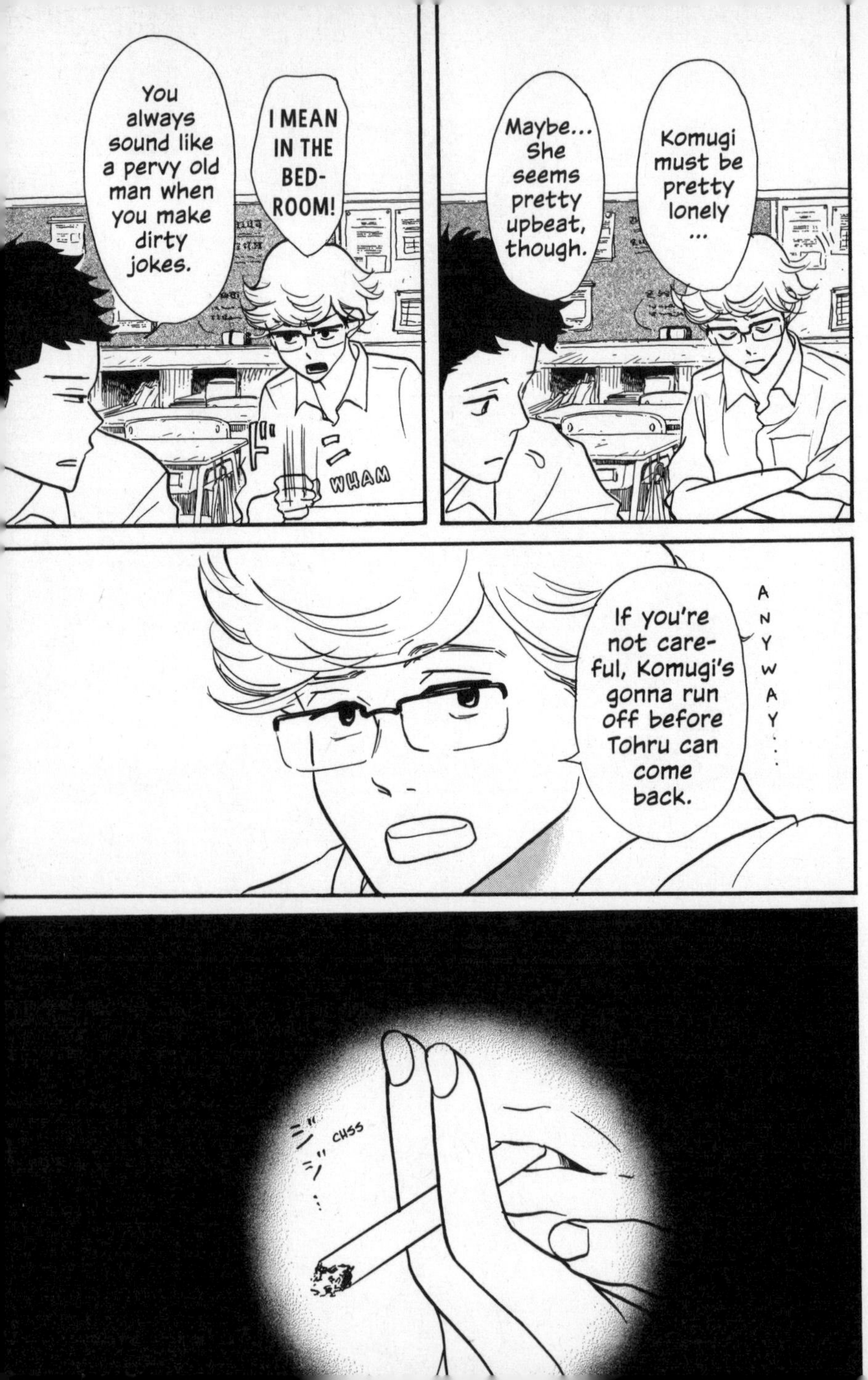

Komugi must be pretty lonely ...
Maybe... She seems pretty upbeat, though.
I MEAN IN THE BED-ROOM!
WHAM
You always sound like a pervy old man when you make dirty jokes.
ANYWAY...
If you're not care-ful, Komugi's gonna run off before Tohru can come back.
CHSS

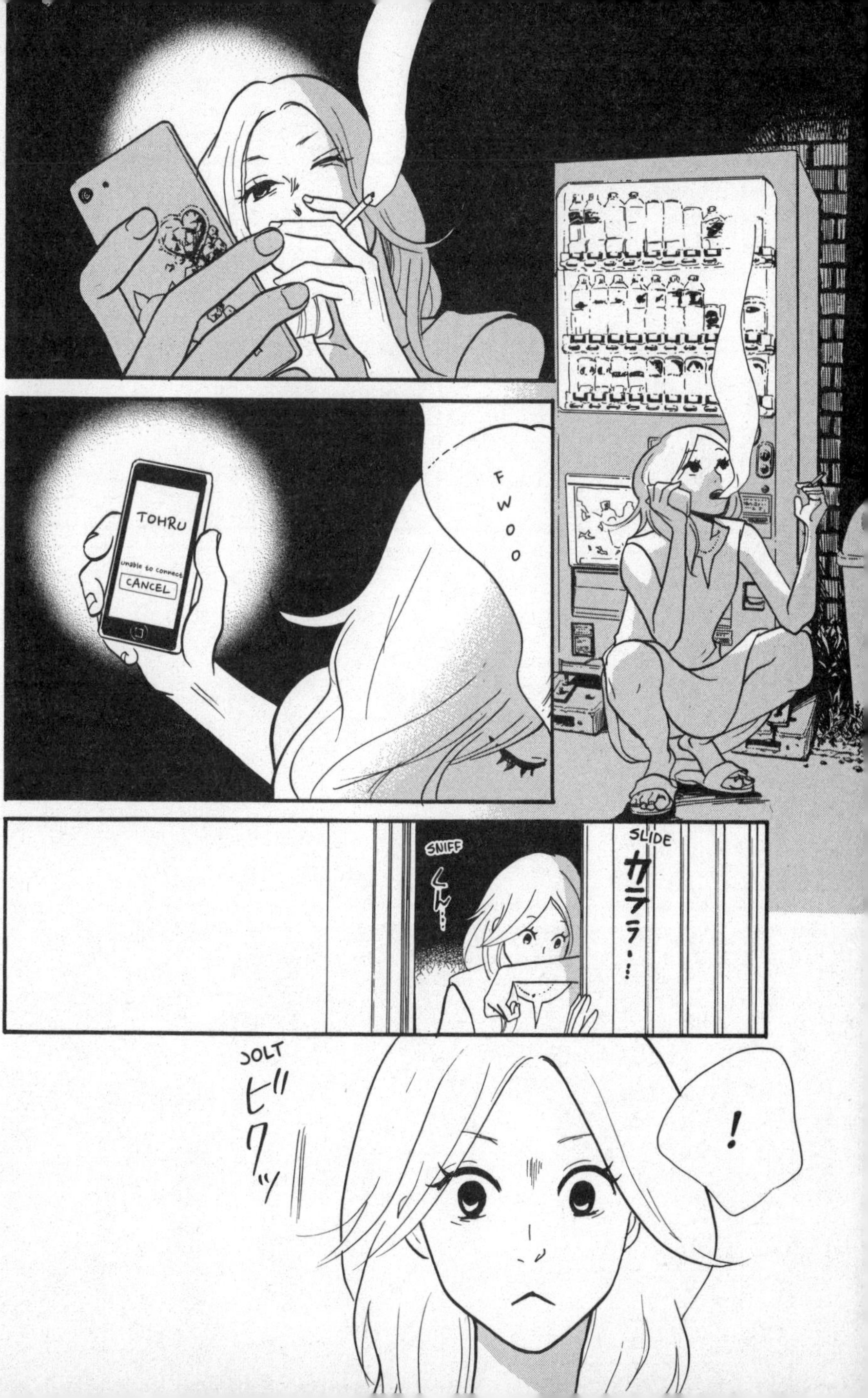
TOHRU
unable to connect
CANCEL
FWOO
SLIDE
カララ…
SNIFF
くん…
JOLT
ビクッ
!

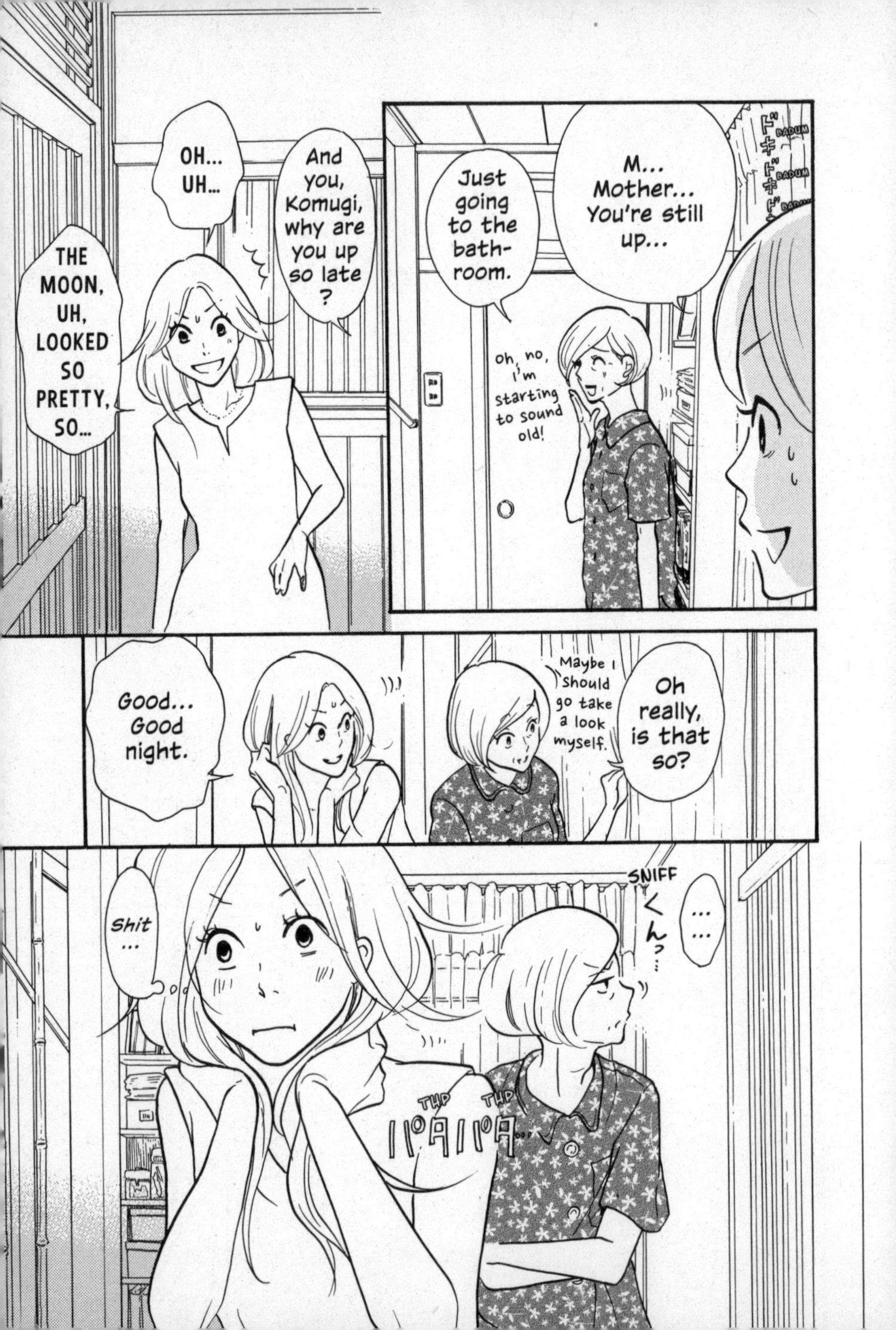

BADUM BADUM BADUM...
M... Mother... You're still up...
Just going to the bathroom.
Oh, no, I'm starting to sound old!
And you, Komugi, why are you up so late?
OH... UH...
THE MOON, UH, LOOKED SO PRETTY, SO...
Oh really, is that so?
Maybe I should go take a look myself.
Good... Good night.
SNIFF
......
Shit...
THP THP

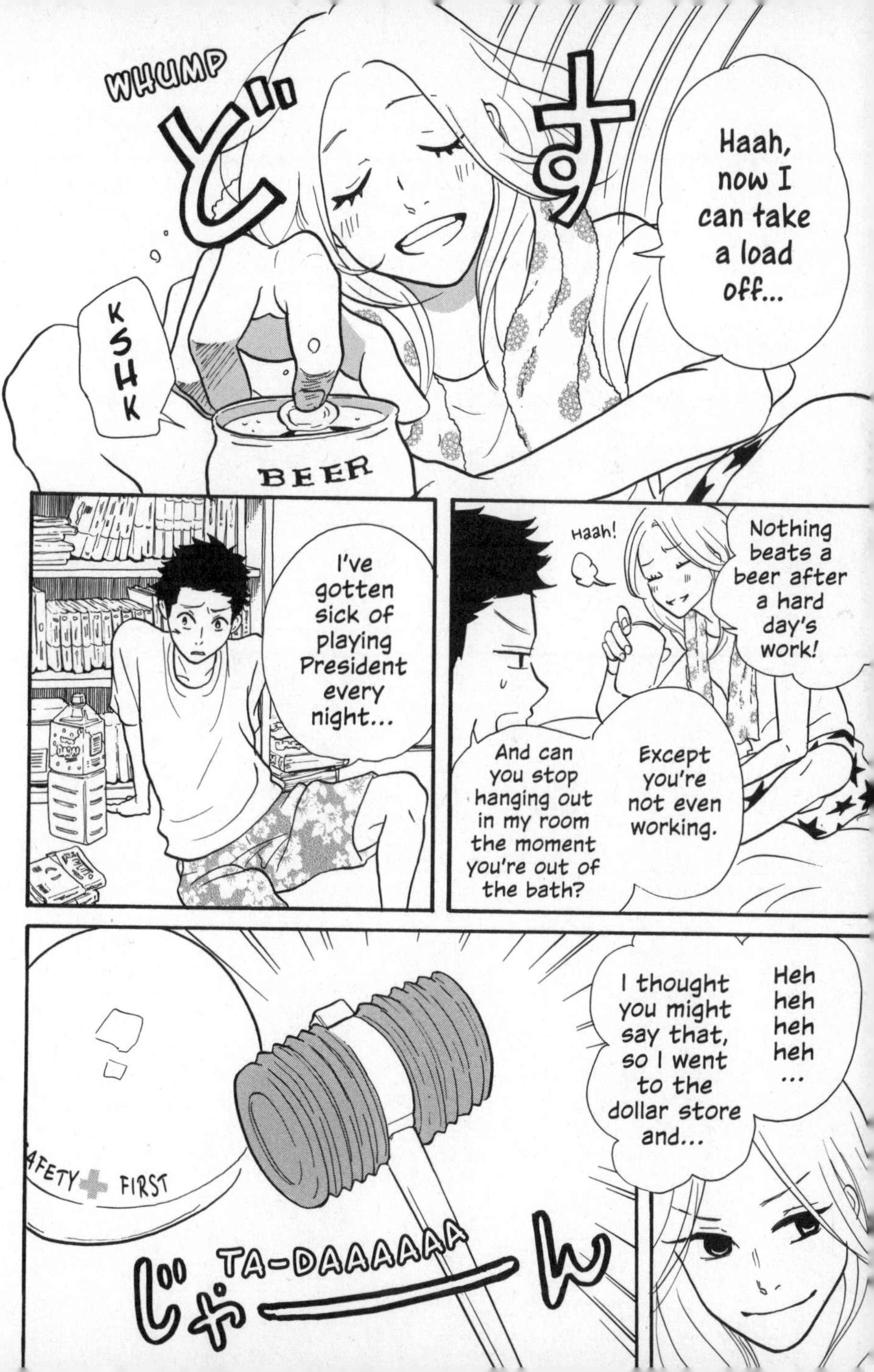
Haah, now I can take a load off...
WHUMP
どす
KSHK
BEER
Nothing beats a beer after a hard day's work!
Haah!
Except you're not even working.
And can you stop hanging out in my room the moment you're out of the bath?
I've gotten sick of playing President every night...
Heh heh heh heh ...
I thought you might say that, so I went to the dollar store and...
AFETY FIRST
TA-DAAAAAA
じゃーん

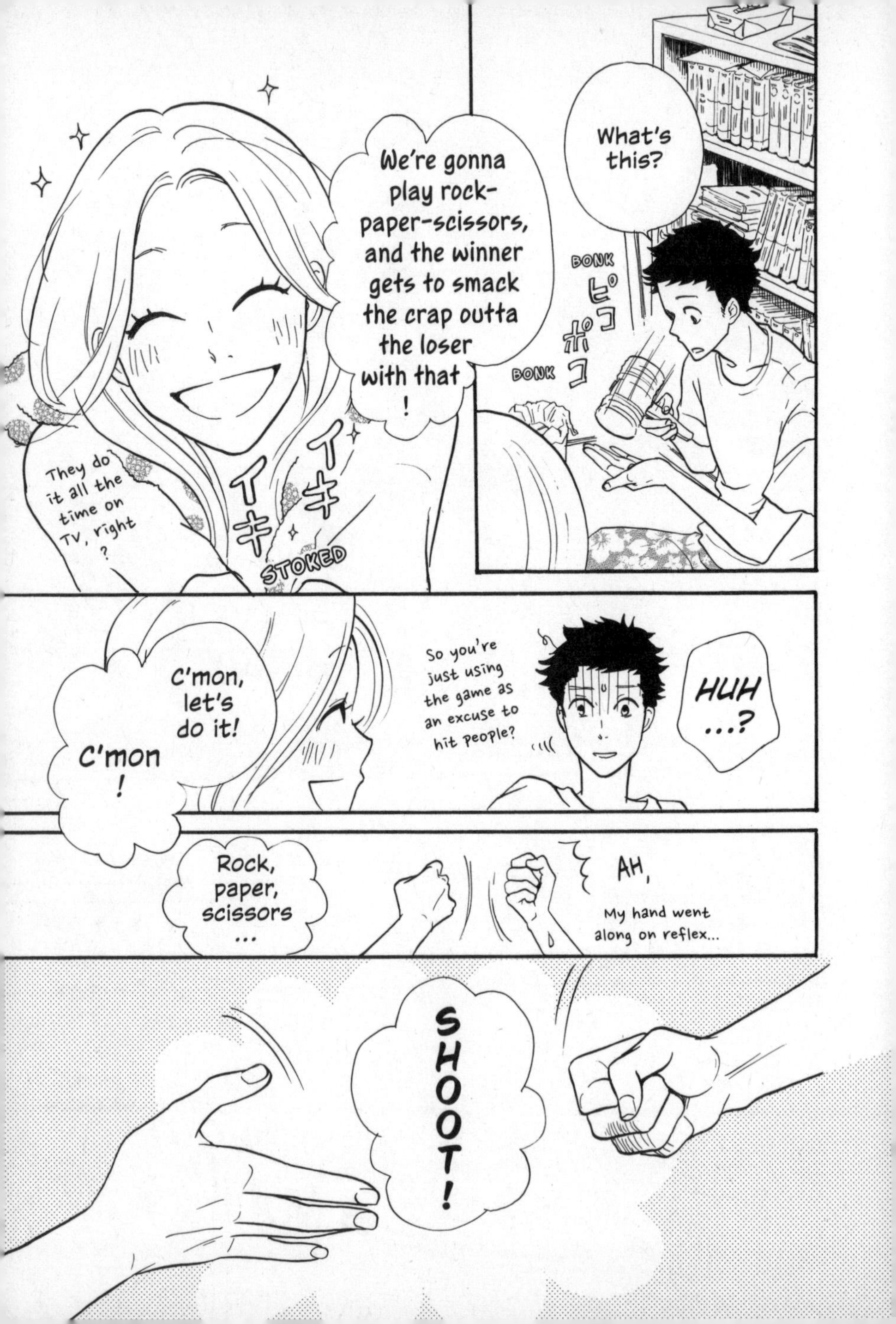
What's this?
BONK ピコ
BONK ポコ
We're gonna play rock-paper-scissors, and the winner gets to smack the crap outta the loser with that!
They do it all the time on TV, right?
イキイキ
STOKED
HUH...?
So you're just using the game as an excuse to hit people?
C'mon, let's do it!
C'mon!
AH,
My hand went along on reflex...
Rock, paper, scissors...
SHOOT!

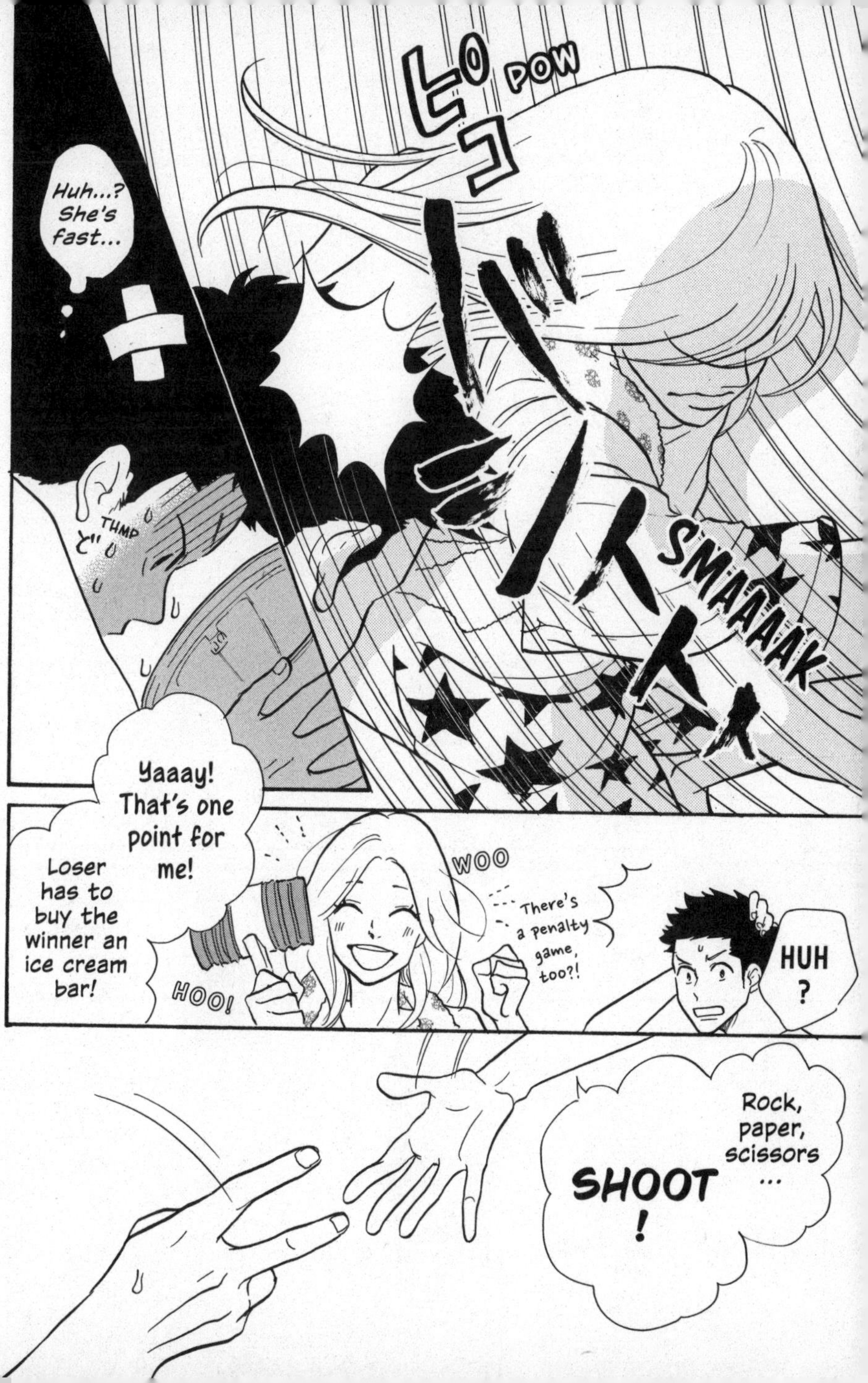
POW
SMAAAAK
Huh...? She's fast...
THMP
HUH?
There's a penalty game, too?!
WOO
Yaaay! That's one point for me!
Loser has to buy the winner an ice cream bar!
HOO!
Rock, paper, scissors... SHOOT!

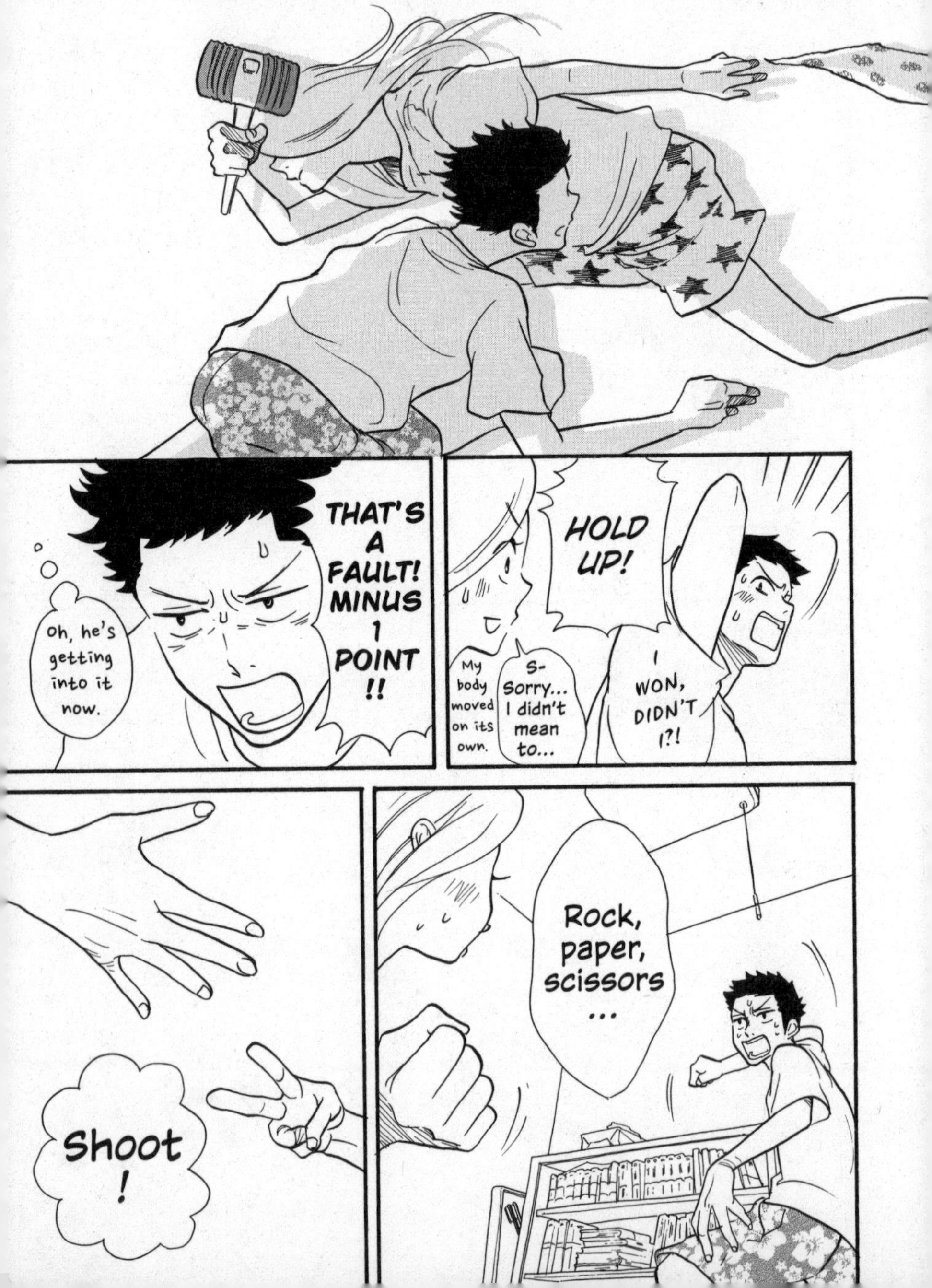
HOLD UP!
I WON, DIDN'T I?!
S-Sorry... I didn't mean to...
My body moved on its own.
THAT'S A FAULT! MINUS 1 POINT!!
Oh, he's getting into it now.
Rock, paper, scissors...
Shoot!

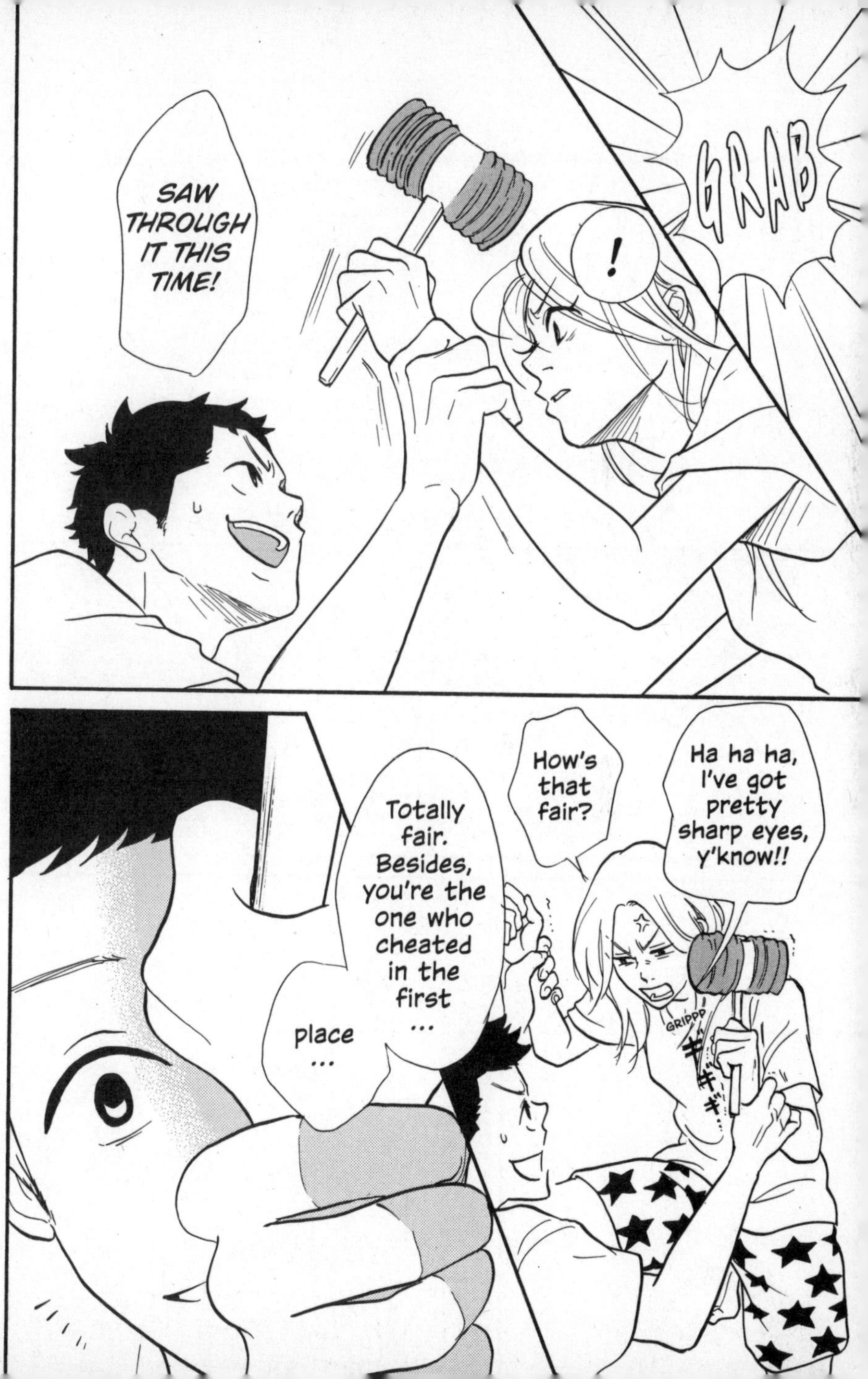
GRAB
!
SAW THROUGH IT THIS TIME!
Ha ha ha, I've got pretty sharp eyes, y'know!!
How's that fair?
GRIPPP
Totally fair. Besides, you're the one who cheated in the first ...
place ...

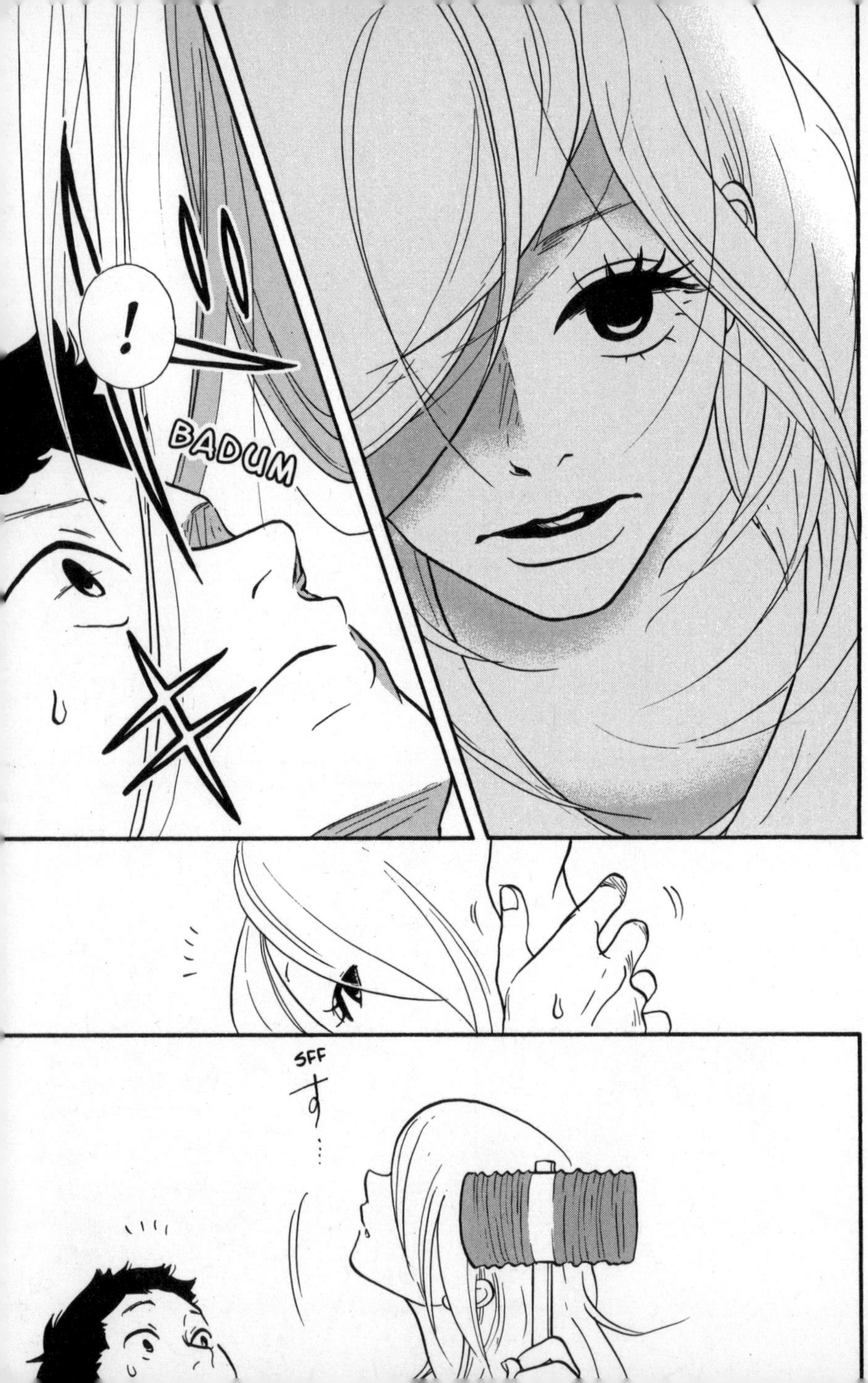
!
BADUM
SFF
す…

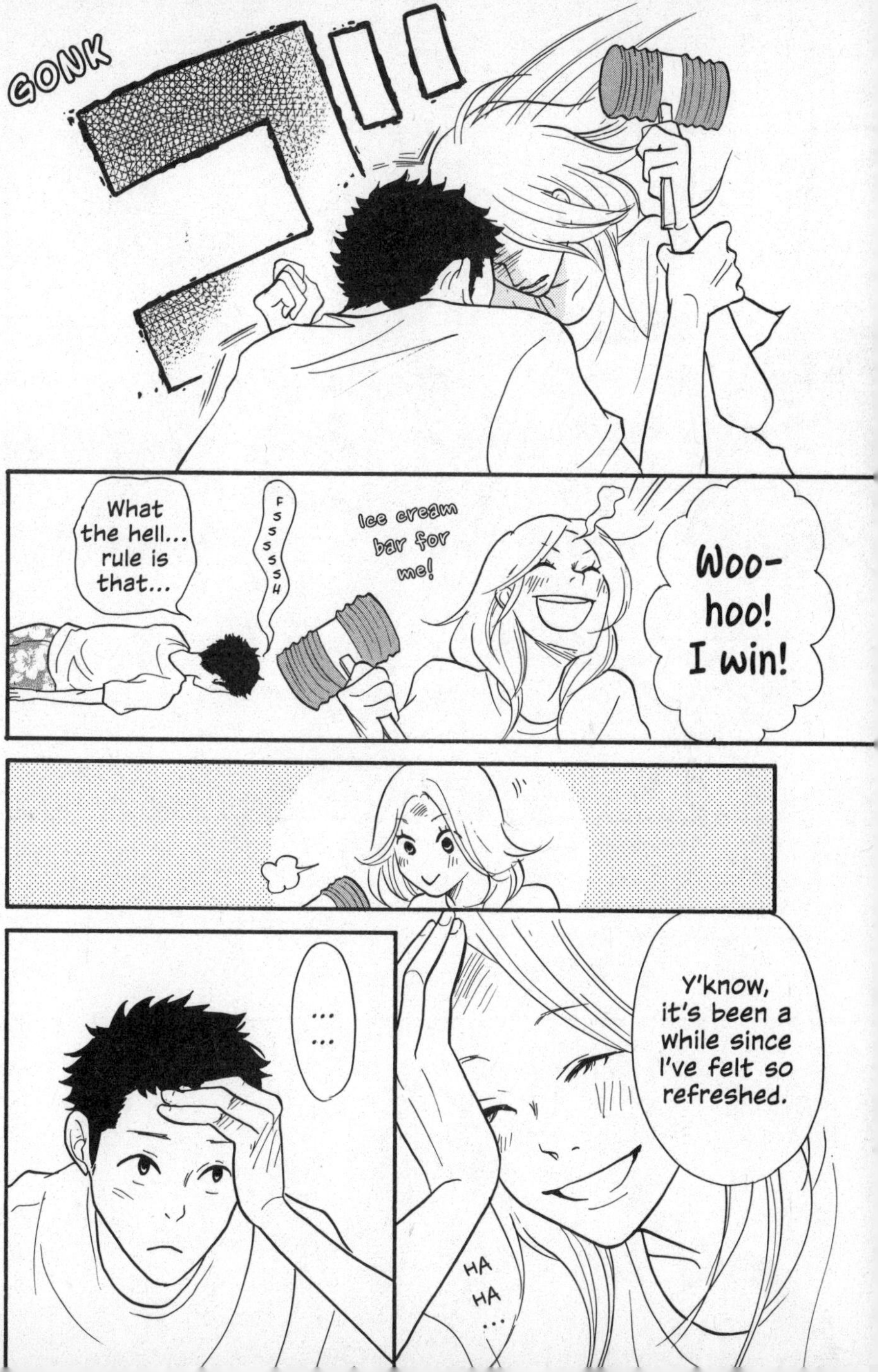
GONK
Woo-hoo! I win!
Ice cream bar for me!
FSSSSSH
What the hell... rule is that...
Y'know, it's been a while since I've felt so refreshed.
HA HA ...
... ...

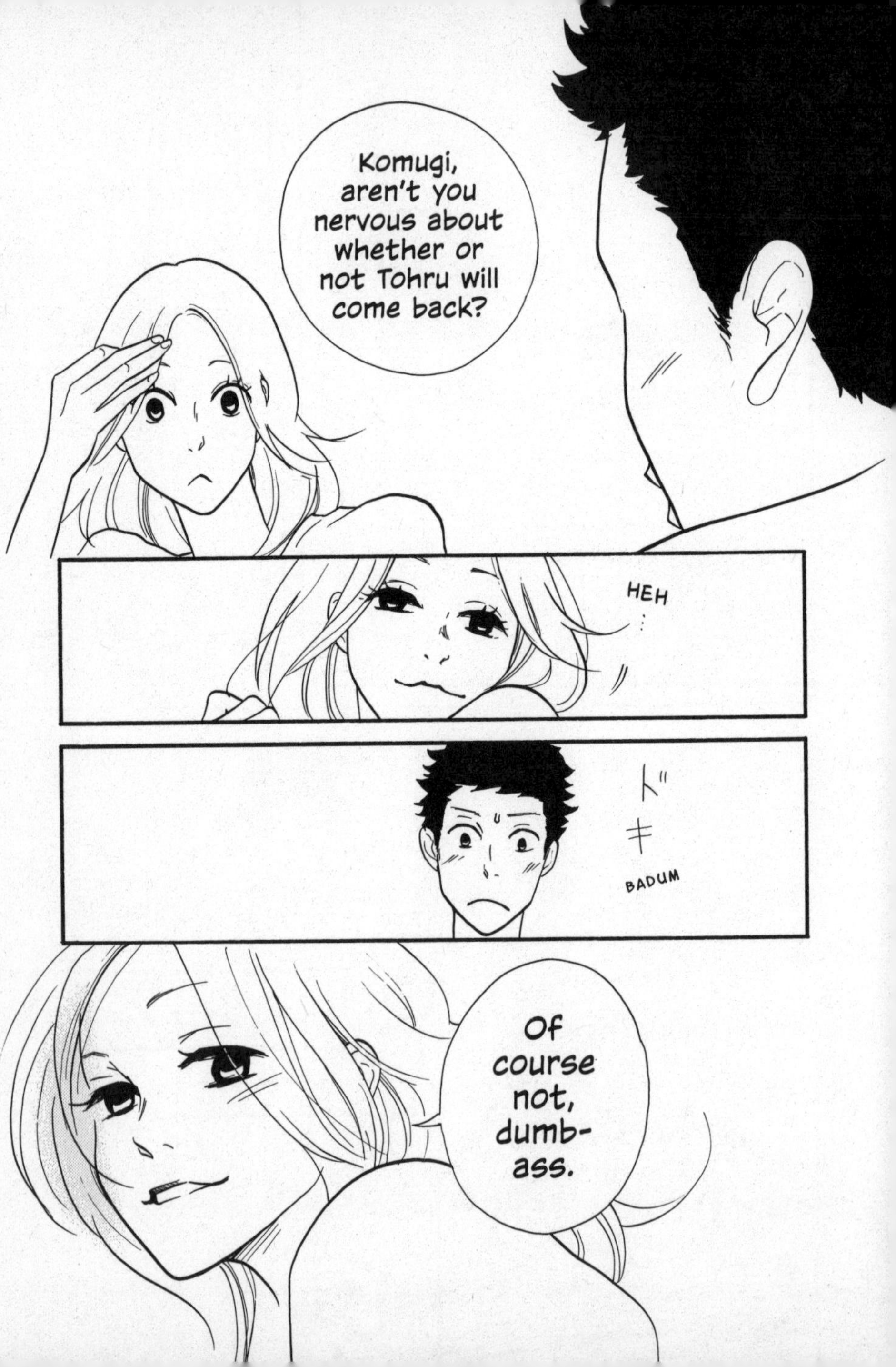
Komugi, aren't you nervous about whether or not Tohru will come back?
HEH...
ドキ
BADUM
Of course not, dumb-ass.

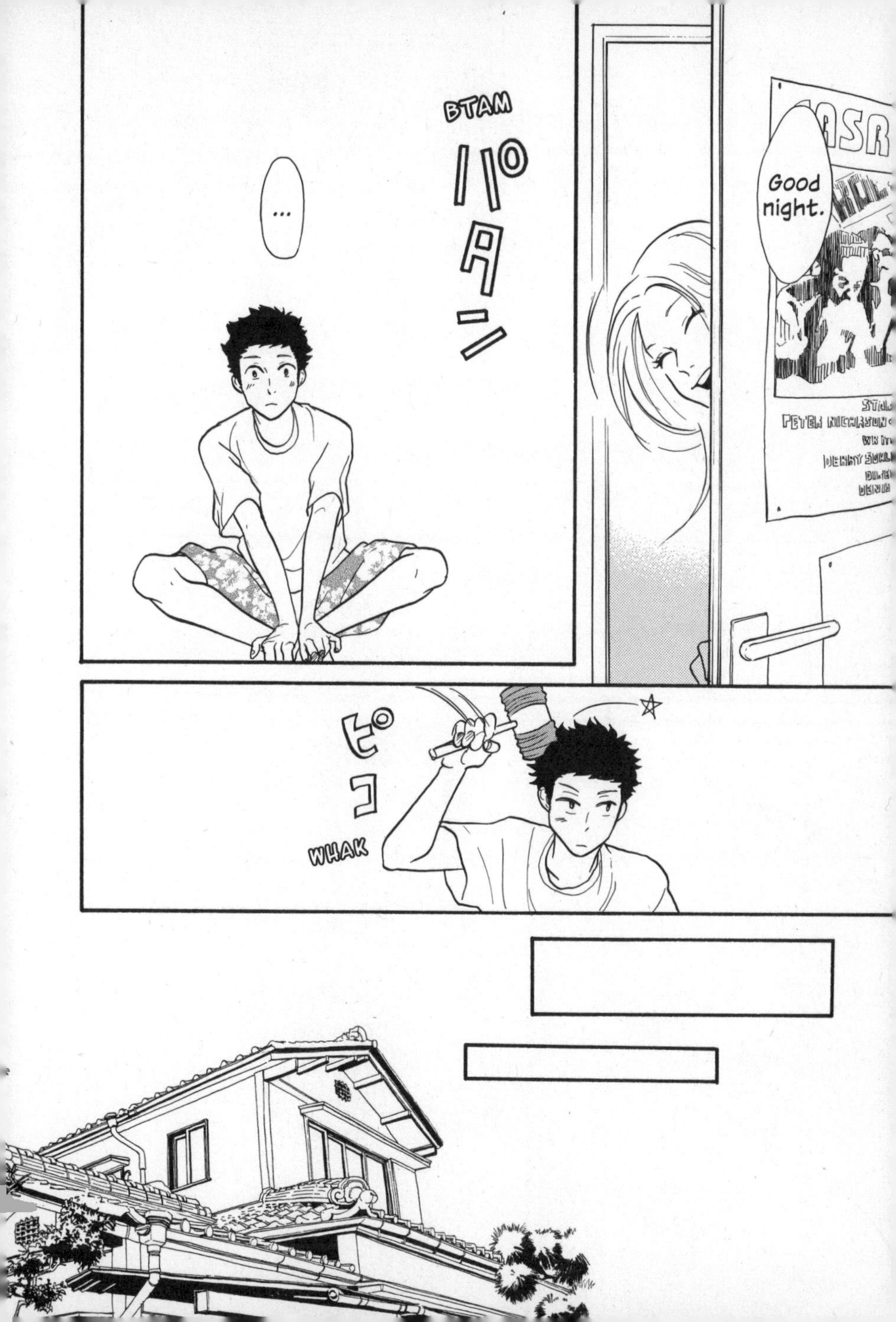
Good night.
...
BTAM
パタン
ピコ
WHAK

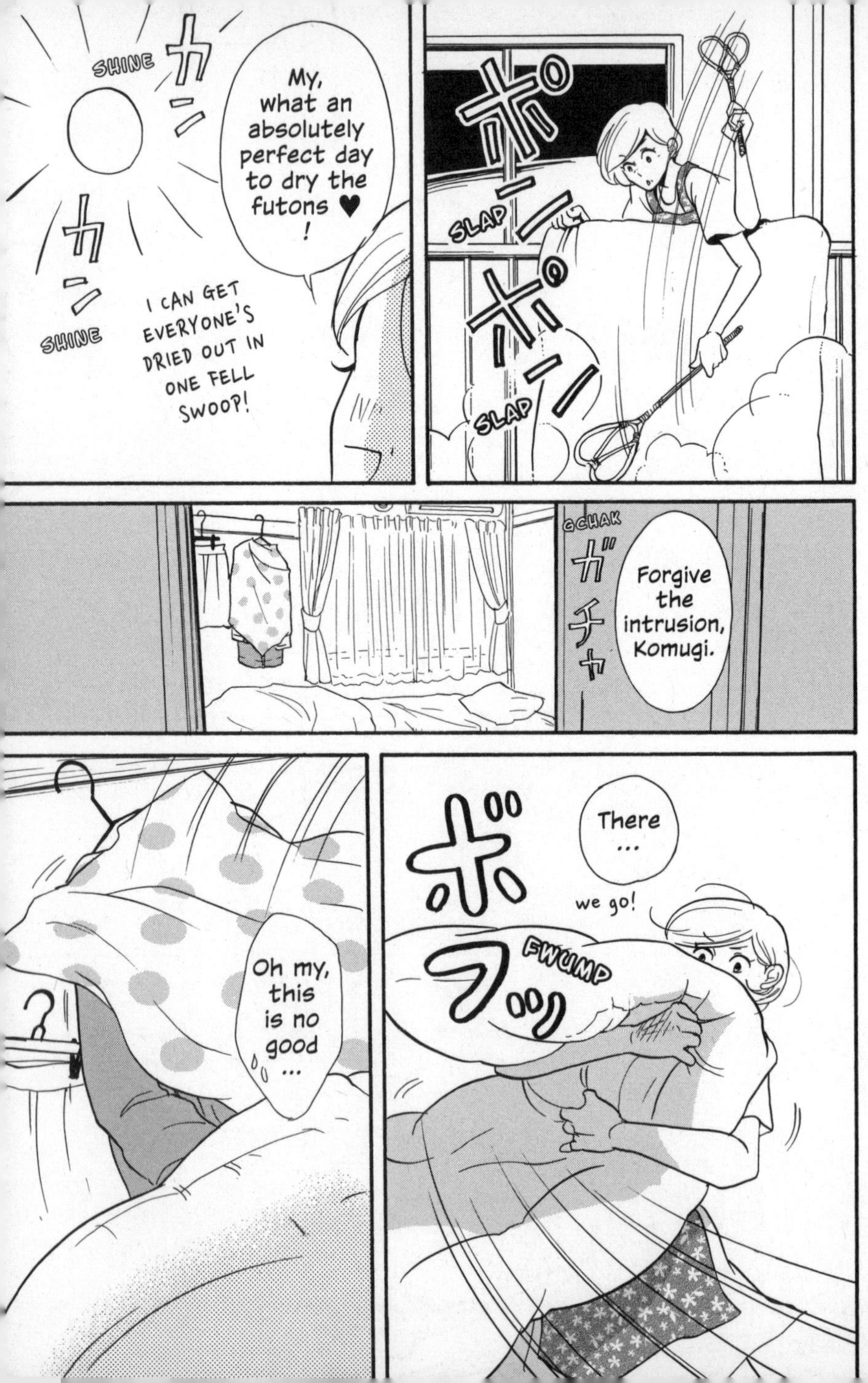
ポーン
SLAP
ポーン
SLAP
SHINE
カン
カン
SHINE
My, what an absolutely perfect day to dry the futons ♥ !
I CAN GET EVERYONE'S DRIED OUT IN ONE FELL SWOOP!
GCHAK
ガチャ
Forgive the intrusion, Komugi.
There ...
we go!
ボ
FWUMP
フッ
Oh my, this is no good ...

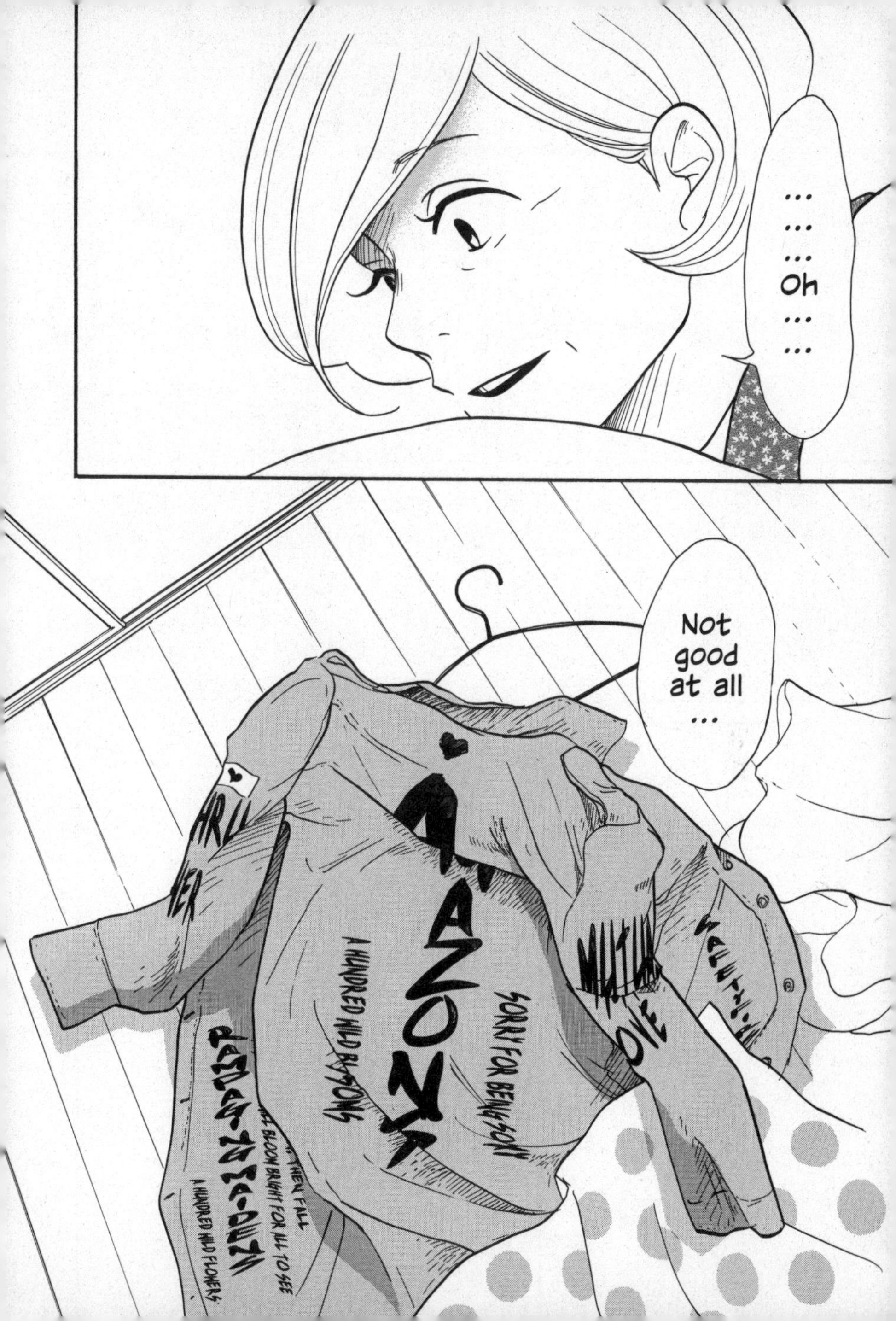
… … … Oh … …
Not good at all …
SORRY FOR BEING SORRY
A HUNDRED WILD BLOSSOMS
A HUNDRED WILD FLOWERS

to be continued!

Hello!

This is Nemu Yoko.

Thank you very much for picking up The Delinquent Housewife!

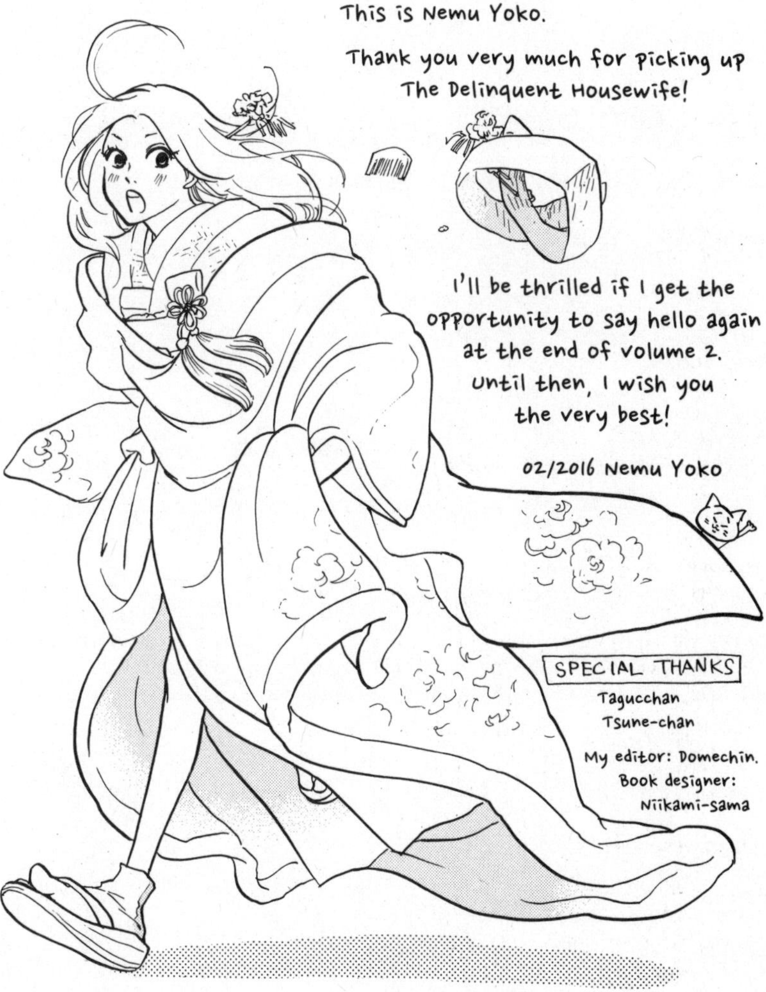

I'll be thrilled if I get the opportunity to say hello again at the end of volume 2. Until then, I wish you the very best!

02/2016 Nemu Yoko

SPECIAL THANKS

Tagucchan

Tsune-chan

My editor: Domechin.

Book designer: Niikami-sama

The Delinquent Housewife! 1

Translation: David Musto
Production: Risa Cho
         Eve Grandt

FUTSUTSUKA NA YOME DESUGA! Vol. 1
by Nemu Yoko

Translation provided by Vertical Comics, 2018
Published by Vertical Comics, an imprint of Vertical, Inc., New York

Originally published in Japanese as *Futsutsuka Na Yome Desuga!* 1 by Shogakukan, 2016
Futsutsuka Na Yome Desuga! serialized in *Shuukan Biggu Komikku Supirittsu*,
Shogakukan, 2016

This is a work of fiction.

ISBN: 978-1-947194-17-5

Manufactured in the United States of America

First Edition

Vertical, Inc.
451 Park Avenue South
7th Floor
New York, NY 10016
www.vertical-comics.com

Vertical books are distributed through Penguin-Random House Publisher Services.

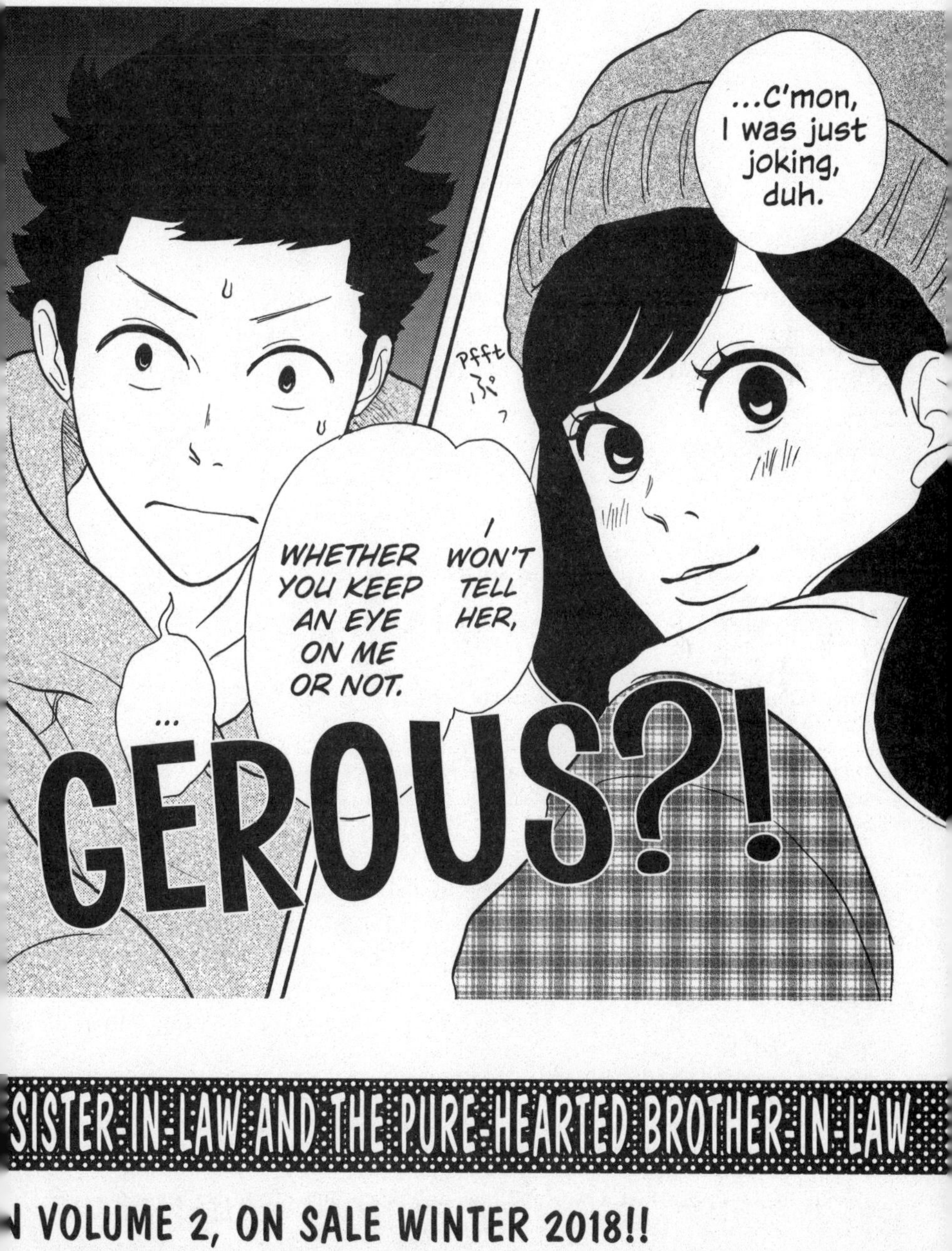
...C'mon, I was just joking, duh.
Pffft
ぷっ
I WON'T TELL HER, WHETHER YOU KEEP AN EYE ON ME OR NOT.
...
GEROUS?!

SISTER-IN-LAW AND THE PURE-HEARTED BROTHER-IN-LAW

N VOLUME 2, ON SALE WINTER 2018!!

Next volume:

Yoshino, a girl in Dai's class who has a crush on him, learns Komugi's secret...

ISN'T THIS GIRL

KINDA DAN

THE DOMESTIC COMEDY FEATURING THE TROUBLEMAKER

LOVE'S COURSE GROWS EVEN MORE COMPLICATED